Presidential Succession

Ford, Rockefeller
& the 25th Amendment

Presidential Succession

Ford, Rockefeller & the 25th Amendment

Edited by Lester A. Sobel

Contributing editors: Joseph Fickes, Mary Elizabeth Clifford,
Stephen Orlofsky, Gerry Satterwhite

FACTS ON FILE, INC.   NEW YORK, N.Y.

Presidential Succession

Ford, Rockefeller
& the 25th Amendment

© Copyright, 1975, by Facts on File, Inc.

Published by Facts on File, Inc.,
119 West 57th Street, New York, N.Y. 10019.

Library of Congress Catalog Card Number 75-20840
ISBN 0-87196-264-0

9 8 7 6 5 4 3 2 1
PRINTED IN
THE UNITED STATES OF AMERICA

Contents

Presidential Succession 1787-1972

RICHARD M. NIXON WAS REELECTED PRESIDENT of the United States and Spiro T. Agnew was reelected Vice President Nov. 7, 1972 by record electoral and popular votes. Yet within two years both had resigned in disgrace. Nixon was the first man to resign from the Presidency and Agnew only the second man to give up the Vice Presidency in the nearly two-hundred-year history of the nation.

Agnew, the first to go, was succeeded by Gerald R. Ford, who became the first person to be Vice President of the United States without being elected to the office. When Nixon also departed, he too was replaced by Ford, who thus achieved the additional distinction of being the first American President who had not been elected either President or Vice President. And Ford's choice for Vice President, Nelson A. Rockefeller, became the second man to serve in the post without being elected to it.

The succession of an unelected President and the appearance of two unelected Vice Presidents came about through the operation of the Twenty-Fifth Amendment, which had become part of the U.S. Constitution in 1967. But it is necessary to go back much further in time to explain how peaceful and lawful Presidential succession had become so traditional in the United States that the American government could change hands under these remarkable conditions without a hint of violence or threat of military intervention.

As Arthur M. Schlesinger, Jr. suggested (in *The Imperial Presidency*), "The place to begin is Philadelphia in the summer of 1787."

1

The Constitution & the Presidency

When the Founding Fathers met in a closed session in Philadelphia May 25, 1787 to write a Constitution, perhaps the hardest problem they had to solve was the creation of a national executive. Initially, as James Madison reported to Thomas Jefferson, the delegates held long discussions on whether to entrust the role of executive to "a single person, or a plurality of coordinate members," as well as "on the mode of appointment, on the duration in office," on eligibility for reelection and on similar issues. After a week, however, a majority had agreed to support a single "Executive Magistracy," but this was the only major decision on the matter that endured. Other early majority formulations, such as that the executive should be elected by the national legislature (later called Congress), that he should serve for a seven-year term and that he should be ineligible for reelection, were ultimately dropped. While a fairly small minority, including Madison and Gouverneur Morris of Pennsylvania, favored popular election of the chief executive, most delegates strongly opposed any such idea. George Mason of Virginia appeared to speak for a majority when he argued July 17 that "it would be as unnatural to refer the choice of a proper character for chief Magistrate to the people, as it would, to refer a trial of colors to a blind man."

By August 24, with the problem of the executive still undecided, the Constitutional Convention agreed to refer the matter to a committee made up of a delegate from each state. The committee's proposals, introduced Sept. 4, were ultimately accepted Sept. 7 with little significant change. The method of election, as proposed by more than one delegate previously, would be by electors chosen in each state in a manner determined by the state legislature. Electors would vote for two persons, "of whom one at least shall not be an Inhabitant of the same State with themselves." A candidate receiving a majority of the votes would be declared President. The candidate with the second largest number of votes would become Vice President and would serve as president of the Senate. The office of Vice President had not even been mentioned during the convention before this, yet the committee's proposal was soon accepted by the delegates despite the criticism of many of them that the post would serve no important purpose.

Throughout the convention, delegates frequently expressed misgivings over the thought of puting great executive powers into the hands of a single individual. Yet, since it was considered almost certain that the first President would be George Washington, if he could be persuaded to accept the role, most delegates seemed prepared to confer these powers on the first President. It was pointed out with some frequency and dismay, however, that Washington would be followed by successors who, perhaps, should not be entrusted with so much power.

Some delegates unquestionably were persuaded to agree to the Presidential powers by the thought that Congress retained the right to dismiss a President who grossly misbehaved. This right of dismissal was conferred on Congress by the Constitutional provision for impeachment. Benjamin Franklin held in the debate July 20 that impeachment "would be the best way for the regular punishment of the Executive, where his misconduct should deserve it, and for his honorable acquittal, where he should be unjustly accused." Madison called it "indispensable that some provision should be made for defending the community against the 'incapacity, negligence, or perfidy of the Chief Magistrate.' "

As finally adopted by the Constitutional Convention Sept. 17, 1787, the U.S. Constitution contained the following provisions applying to the President and Vice President:

ARTICLE I . . .
Section 2 . . . .
The House of Representatives . . . shall have the sole Power of Impeachment.
Section 3 . . . .
The Vice President of the United States shall be President of the Senate, but shall have no Vote, unless they be equally divided.

The Senate shall chuse . . . a President pro tempore, in the Absence of the Vice President, or when he shall exercise the Office of President of the United States.

The Senate shall have the sole Power to try all Impeachments. When sitting for that Purpose, they shall be on Oath or Affirmation. When the President of the United States is tried, the Chief Justice shall preside: And no Person shall be convicted without the Concurrence of two thirds of the Members present.

Judgment in Cases of Impeachment shall not extend further than to removal from Office, and disqualification to hold and enjoy any Office of honor, Trust or Profit under the United States: but the Party convicted shall nevertheless be liable and subject to Indictment, Trial, Judgment and Punishment, according to law. . . .
Section 7 . . . .
Every Bill which shall have passed the House of Representatives and the Senate, shall, before it become a Law, be presented to the President of the United States; If he approve he shall sign it, but if not he shall return it, with his Objections to that House in which it shall have originated, who shall enter the Objections at large on their Journal, and proceed to reconsider it. If after such Reconsideration two thirds of that House shall agree to pass the Bill, it shall be sent, together with the Objections, to the other House, by which it shall likewise be reconsidered, and if approved by two thirds of that House, it shall become a Law. . . . If any Bill shall not be returned by the President within ten Days (Sundays excepted) after it shall have been presented to him, the Same shall be

a Law, in like Manner as if he had signed it, unless the Congress by their Adjournment prevent its Return, in which Case it shall not be a Law.

Every Order, Resolution, or Vote to which the Concurrence of the Senate and House of Representatives may be necessary (except on a question of Adjournment) shall be presented to the President of the United States; and before the Same shall take Effect, shall be approved by him, or being disapproved by him, shall be repassed by two thirds of the Senate and House of Representatives, according to the Rules and Limitations prescribed in the Case of a Bill. . . .

ARTICLE II

Section 1. The executive Power shall be vested in a President of the United States of America. He shall hold his Office during the Term of four Years, and, together with the Vice President, chosen for the same term, be elected, as follows

Each State shall appoint, in such Manner as the Legislature thereof may direct, a Number of Electors, equal to the whole Number of Senators and Representatives to which the State may be entitled in the Congress: but no Senator or Representative, or Person holding an Office of Trust or Profit under the United States, shall be appointed an Elector.

The Electors shall meet in their respective States, and vote by Ballot for two Persons, of whom one at least shall not be an Inhabitant of the same State with themselves. And they shall make a List of all the Persons voted for, and of the Number of Votes for each; which List they shall sign and certify, and transmit sealed to the Seat of the Government of the United States, directed to the President of the Senate. The President of the Senate shall, in the Presence of the Senate and House of Representatives, open all the Certificates, and the Votes shall then be counted. The Person having the greatest Number of Votes shall be the President, if such Number be a Majority of the whole Number of Electors appointed; and if there be more than one who have such Majority, and have an equal Number of Votes, then the House of Representatives shall immediately chuse by Ballot one of them for President: and if no Person have a Majority, then from the five highest on the List the said House shall in like Manner chuse the President. But in chusing the President, the Votes shall be taken by States, the Representation from each State having one Vote; A quorum for this Purpose shall consist of a Member or Members from two thirds of the States, and a Majority of all the States shall be necessary to a Choice. In every Case, after the Choice of the President, the Person having the greatest Number of Votes of the Electors shall be the Vice President. But if there should remain two or more who have equal Votes, the Senate shall chuse from them by Ballot the Vice President.

The Congress may determine the Time of chusing the Electors, and the Day on which they shall give their Votes; which Day shall be the same throughout the United States.

No Person except a natural born Citizen, or a Citizen of the United States, at the time of the Adoption of this Constitution, shall be eligible to the Office of President; neither shall any Person be eligible to that Office who shall not have attained to the Age of thirty five Years, and been fourteen Years a Resident within the United States.

In Case of the Removal of the President from Office, or of his Death, Resignation, or Inability to discharge the Powers and Duties of the said Office, the Same shall devolve on the Vice President, and the Congress may by Law provide for the Case of Removal, Death, Resignation or Inability, both of the President and Vice President, declaring what Officer shall then act as President, and such Officer shall act accordingly, until the Disability be removed, or a President shall be elected.

The President shall, at stated Times, receive for his Services, a Compensation, which shall neither be encreased nor diminished during the Period for which he shall have been elected, and he shall not receive within that Period any other Emolument from the United States, or any of them.

Before he enter on the Execution of his Office, he shall take the following Oath or Affirmation:—''I do solemnly swear (or affirm) that I will faithfully execute the Office of President of the United States, and will to the best of my Ability, preserve, protect and defend the Constitution of the United States.''

Section 2. The President shall be Commander in Chief of the Army and Navy of the United States, and of the Militia of the several States, when called into the actual Service of the United States; he may require the Opinion, in writing, of the principal Officer in each of the executive Departments, upon any Subject relating to the Duties of their respective Offices, and he shall have Power to grant Reprieves and Pardons for Offences against the United States, except in Cases of Impeachment.

He shall have Power, by and with the Advice and Consent of the Senate, to make Treaties, provided two thirds of the Senators present concur; and he shall nominate, and by and with the Advice and Consent of the Senate, shall appoint Ambassadors, other public Ministers and Consuls, Judges of the supreme Court, and all other Officers of the United States, whose Appointments are not herein otherwise provided for, and which shall be established by Law: but the Congress may by Law vest the Appointment of such inferior Officers, as they think proper, in the President alone, in the Courts of Law, or in the Heads of Departments.

The President shall have Power to fill up all Vacancies that may happen during the recess of the Senate, by granting Commissions which shall expire at the End of their next Session.

Section 3. He shall from time to time give to the Congress Information of the State of the Union, and recommend to their Consideration such Measures as he shall judge necessary and expedient; he may, on extraordinary Occasions, convene both Houses, or either of them, and in Case of Disagreement between them, with Respect to the Time of Adjournment, he may adjourn them to such Time as he shall think proper; he shall receive Ambassadors and other public Ministers; he shall take Care that the Laws be faithfully executed, and shall Commission all the Officers of the United States.

Section 4. The President, Vice President and all civil Officers of the United States, shall be removed from Office on Impeachment for, and Conviction of, Treason, Bribery, or other High Crimes and Misdemeanors.

ARTICLE III . . .

Section 2. . . .

The Trial of all Crimes, except in Cases of Impeachment, shall be by Jury. . . .

Section 3. Treason against the United States, shall consist only in levying War against them, or in adhering to their Enemies, giving them Aid and Comfort. . . .

The Congress shall have Power to declare the Punishment of Treason. . . .

ARTICLE VI . . .

The Senators and Representatives before mentioned, and the Members of the several State Legislatures, and all executive and judicial Officers, both of the

United States and of the several States, shall be bound by Oath or Affirmation, to support this Constitution; but no religious Test shall ever be required as a Qualification to any Office or public Trust under the United States. . . .

Legislation regularizing the Presidential succession was enacted by Congress in 1792. The act provided that following the President and Vice President, the chief legislative officers (the president pro tempore of the Senate and then the Speaker of the House) would be in line of succession. The new law directed the Presidential electors to meet in their respective states on the first Wednesday in December of the election year. They were to have been chosen during the preceding month. They were each to vote for two candidates, and they were not to indicate that either of the two was preferred for President or Vice President. Each state was to send a certificate recording the vote to the presiding officer of the Senate before the first Wednesday of the following January. The votes were to be counted in the Senate on the second Wednesday in February.

Washington & His Successors

With no possible candidate of sufficient stature to even think of contesting George Washington for election as the nation's first President, Washington had reluctantly accepted the call to office. The election of 1789, however, was an agonizingly slow affair. The Presidential electors, duly chosen, met on the first Wednesday of February, but their votes could not be counted until a quorum of both houses of Congress had assembled. March 4, the scheduled day for the inauguration of the first President, passed without a quorum being present. It took another full month, until April 5, before the final Congress member required for a quorum arrived in New York.

In the meantime, the Federalists, with no competition facing their Presidential candidate, narrowed down their Vice Presidential choices until John Adams was agreed on. Since the electors were each to cast two votes, with no indication that one vote might be for President and the other for Vice President, Alexander Hamilton instructed at least two Federalist electors not to vote for their party's Vice Presidential choice lest "the man intended for Vice President may in fact turn up President."

When the electoral votes were opened in Congress April 6, Washington had received 69 votes, the highest number possible, and Adams was elected Vice President with a vote of 34.

Washington, who had hoped to leave office before completing even a first term, was persuaded in 1792 to accept a second term for the good of the troubled young nation. As in the first election, Washington received a unanimous vote, which by then meant 132 electoral votes, and Adams was reelected with 77 votes.

During much of Washington's second term the nation was rent by factionalism. Supporters of Thomas Jefferson, mainly centered in the South and based on a plantation-type agrarian life-style, opposed the largely New England-rooted backers of Alexander Hamilton with their urban interests in industry and finance and preference for centralized government. The Jeffersonians, known sometimes as Democrats or Republicans but often assailed by Hamilton's Federalists as "Jacobins," were strong partisans of Republican France in its war with Great Britain, whereas the commerce-oriented Federalists were more interested in trade with the British. The antagonism was exacerbated by Washington's assignment of Chief Justice John Jay to negotiate a U.S.-British treaty intended to keep America neutral. Benjamin Franklin Bache, grandson of Benjamin Franklin and editor of the *Aurora*, charged editorially that Washington sought to be a dictator. "If ever a nation was debauched by a man, the American Nation has been debauched by Washington," Bache wrote. ". . . Let the history of the Federal Government instruct mankind, that the masque of patriots may be worn to conceal the foulest designs against the liberties of a people."

Despite this political rancor, from which, as is seen, Washington did not escape, it was assumed by many that the esteem in which Washington was generally held had much to do with keeping the nation from being torn apart. It was feared, therefore, that the departure of Washington from government might cause unbearable strains. Many Americans were unsure that a legally elected successor to Washington would be allowed to assume office without violent opposition. There were warnings that the nation might not be able to survive a transfer of power. But John Adams, who himself had given vent to such fears, finally concluded in February 1796 that there would be "no more danger in the change than there would be in changing a member of the Senate." He held also that Washington's self-effacing behavior as President had allowed the character of the Presidency to emerge too clearly to allow for major change by his successors.

It seemed obvious, from the moment that Washington, in his Farewell Address Sept. 17, declined a third term, that the election of 1796 would be one of the most important (and some thought possibly the last) in American history. The results of this election proved all the forebodings false.

John Adams, by no means a popular man, was elected Presi-

dent by a bare 71 electoral votes, and his rival Thomas Jefferson
became Vice President with 68. Yet Jefferson almost immediately
called on Adams to promise his support, and similar pledges of
support were showered on the President-elect from all sides.

Taking the oath of office March 4, 1797, Adams warned in his
Inaugural Address that "we should be unfaithful to ourselves if
we should ever lose sight of the danger to our liberties if anything partial or extraneous should infect the purity of our free,
fair, virtuous, and independent elections. If an election is to be
determined by a majority of a single vote, and that can be pro-
cured by a party through artifice or corruption, the Government
may be the choice of a party for its own ends, not of the nation
for the national good. . . ."

Thomas Jefferson, author of the Declaration of Independence
and Washington's first Secretary of State, served simultaneously
as Adams' Vice President and as leader of the opposition Republicans, whose chief aim was to supplant Adams and his
Federalists at the head of the American government.

In the hard-fought election campaign of 1800, the Republicans
achieved their goal. A President was defeated for reelection for
the first time as Adams emerged with only 65 electoral votes.
Much more surprisingly, however, there was a tie at 73 votes
each for Jefferson and his Republican co-candidate, Aaron Burr,
who had been chosen by the party as Vice Presidential nominee.

Thus, for the first of only two times in the nation's history, the
election was forced into the House of Representatives. The decision, moreover, was made not by the new, Republican-controlled
House but by the outgoing Federalist-controlled body. Balloting
began Feb. 11, 1801, and it took 36 separate ballots—or until
Feb. 17—for enough Federalists to abstain so that Jefferson could
claim the Presidency and Burr become Vice President. The new
administration took office March 4, and one party handed over
power to another for the first time.

Largely because of his equivocal role in 1800, Burr was dropped
from the Republican ticket in 1804 and was replaced by
George Clinton as Vice Presidential candidate. Jefferson, running
for reelection, and his new running-mate received 162 electoral
votes each under the provisions of the recently ratified 12th
Amendment. They won a landslide victory over the Federalist
candidates, Charles Cotesworth Pinckney and Rufus King, who
received a scant 14 electoral votes each.

12th Amendment

The tie vote for Jefferson and Burr in 1800 had disclosed a

Constitutional deficiency. To avoid future impasses such as the one the 1800 results had produced, Congress adopted a Constitutional amendment, the 12th Amendment, providing for the electors to cast separate ballots for President and Vice President. The amendment was ratified by the requisite three-quarters of the states by July 27, 1804, and it took effect in September.

Text of the 12th Amendment:

The Electors shall meet in their respective states and vote by ballot for President and Vice-President, one of whom, at least, shall not be an inhabitant of the same state with themselves; they shall name in their ballots the person voted for as President, and in distinct ballots the person voted for as Vice-President, and they shall make distinct lists of all persons voted for as President, and of all persons voted for as Vice-President, and of the number of votes for each, which lists they shall sign and certify, and transmit sealed to the seat of the government of the United States, directed to the President of the Senate;—The President of the Senate shall, in the presence of the Senate and House of Representatives, open all the certificates and the votes shall then be counted;—The person having the greatest number of votes for President, shall be the President, if such number be a majority of the whole number of Electors appointed; and if no person have such majority, then from the persons having the highest numbers not exceeding three on the list of those voted for as President, the House of Representatives shall choose immediately, by ballot, the President. But in choosing the President, the votes shall be taken by states, the representation from each state having one vote; a quorum for this purpose shall consist of a member or members from two-thirds of the states, and a majority of all the states shall be necessary to a choice. And if the House of Representatives shall not choose a President whenever the right of choice shall devolve upon them, before the fourth day of March next following, then the Vice-President shall act as President, as in the case of the death or other constitutional disability of the President.—The person having the greatest number of votes as Vice-President, shall be the Vice-President, if such number be a majority of the whole number of Electors appointed, and if no person have a majority, then from the two highest numbers on the list, the Senate shall choose the Vice-President; a quorum for the purpose shall consist of two-thirds of the whole number of Senators, and a majority of the whole number shall be necessary to a choice. But no person constitutionally ineligible to the office of President shall be eligible to that of Vice-President of the United States.

Other Early Presidents & Vice Presidents

James Madison, Jefferson's Republican Secretary of State, won the 1808 Presidential election with 122 electoral votes to the 47 received by Charles Cotesworth Pinckney, Federalist. Jefferson's Vice President, George Clinton, was reelected with 113 electoral votes, and he also received 6 votes for President. Clinton died April 20, 1812 and became the first Vice President to die in office.

The election of 1812 took place barely five months after the outbreak of the War of 1812. The unpopularity of the war in many areas undoubtedly deprived Madison of some support he otherwise could have expected. Madison, reelected President, received 128 electoral votes to the 89 of his opponent, fusion candidate DeWitt Clinton, nephew of the late Vice President. Madison's running mate, Elbridge Gerry, was elected Vice President with 131 votes, and he died in office Nov. 23, 1814. His death left the country without a Vice President for the second time in two successive terms.

James Monroe, who had served as Madison's Secretary of State, was elected President in 1816 by an electoral vote of 183 against 34 votes for Sen. Rufus King. Gov. Daniel D. Tompkins of New York was chosen Vice President by a similar vote. With virtually no organized opposition, the Republican ticket was reelected in 1820, with Monroe receiving 231 of the 232 electoral votes cast (John Quincy Adams, Monroe's Secretary of State, received the 232nd) and Tompkins collecting 218 votes.

Following the 1824 election, for the first (and only) time, the son of a former President was chosen as America's chief executive. John Quincy Adams, son of the nation's second President and Secretary of State in the Monroe Cabinet, received only 84 electoral votes, in 1824, against 99 won by Andrew Jackson (the leader in the balloting), 41 received by William H. Crawford and 37 by Henry Clay. Since no candidate had won a majority of the vote, the election was forced into the House of Representatives for the second time in U.S. history. With Clay finally asking his supporters to back Adams, the latter was chosen President by the House Feb. 9, 1825 by a vote of 13 states for Adams, seven for Jackson and four for Crawford. Despite a hotly denied charge that Adams had bought Clay's support by an offer of appointment as Secretary of State, Adams shortly thereafter did name Clay to head the Department of State. John C. Calhoun, meanwhile, had been elected Vice President with 182 electoral votes.

By 1824, electors were chosen by popular vote in 18 states and by appointment of state legislatures in only six states. The *History of American Presidential Elections* (Volume I, 1789-1844), noting that this was the first Presidential election in which the popular vote data was preserved, lists the following totals (but warns that "no great reliance can be given to these figures"): Jackson, 152,901; Adams, 114,023; Crawford, 46,979, and Clay, 47,217.

Jackson initially took his defeat in the House of Representatives in good grace. But the nomination of Clay to the post of Secretary of State, already a traditional stepping-stone to the Presidency, convinced him that he had been cheated of Presidential election by a "corrupt bargain." The exploitation of this issue in

ning as candidate of the new Free Soil party. Millard Fillmore, Whig, was elected Vice President.

Following Taylor's death of typhus July 8, 1850, Fillmore July 10 became the second Vice President to succeed a dead President.

Franklin Pierce of New Hampshire, nominated by the Democrats, was elected President in 1852 by an electoral vote of 254 against 42 votes for Gen. Winfield Scott, the Whig candidate. Sen. William R. King, Pierce's running mate, was elected Vice President (and he died in office April 18, 1853).

In 1856, Democratic nominee James Buchanan was elected President by an electoral vote of 174 against 114 for Republican nominee John Charles Fremont and 8 for ex-President Millard Fillmore, a Whig running with the American (Know Nothing) party's nomination. John C. Breckinridge, Buchanan's running mate, was elected Vice President. Buchanan's popular vote (South Carolina excluded) was 1,838,169, against 1,341,264 for Fremont and 874,534 for Fillmore.

Buchanan had served as Polk's second Secretary of State. The seventeenth man to head the Department of State, Buchanan was the sixth former Secretary of State to be elected President. Thereafter, nobody who had been Secretary of State (a post once considered a stepping stone to the Presidency) became President.

Lincoln & the Preservation of the Union

By 1860 the differences between the North and South were forcing the nation quite literally to the breaking point. The issue was slavery—and the economic, social and political conditions that slavery evoked.

Abraham Lincoln, a Republican who had described slavery as "a moral, social, and political evil" and who had said he "looks hopefully to the time when as a wrong it may come to an end," was elected President in 1860 by a minority of the popular votes in a contest against two Democrats and a Constitutional Union nominee.

One of the Democratic candidates was Sen. Stephen A. Douglas, who had received the party nomination over Southern opposition by a vote of 181½ to 7½ for Vice President John C. Breckenridge. The other Democratic nominee was Breckenridge, who was chosen by the defeated Southern delegates.

In the 1860 election, Lincoln received 180 electoral votes against 72 for Breckenridge, 12 for Douglas and 39 for John Bell of the Constitutional Union party. In the popular vote, the total opposition outpolled Lincoln by 949,165 votes, the Democrats outpolled him by 360,286. The popular vote (South Carolina excluded) was 1,866,452 for Lincoln, 1,376,957 for Douglas, 849,781 for Breckenridge and 588,879 for Bell. Hannibal Hamlin, Lincoln's running mate, was elected Vice President.

After Lincoln's election, South Carolina seceeded from the Union Dec. 20, 1860. It was followed out of the Union by Mississippi Jan. 9, 1861, Florida Jan. 10, Alabama Jan. 11, Georgia Jan. 19, Louisiana Jan. 26 and Texas Feb. 1. Four border states joined them later. Delegates of the seceding states agreed to a provisional constitution of the "Confederate States" Feb. 8. Jefferson Davis was inaugurated as provisional Confederate president Feb. 18, and A. H. Stevens became vice president. A "permanent" Confederate constitution was adopted March 11. The first military actions between seceding states and Union forces consisted of the expulsion by the Confederacy of Union detachments then in the South. Fort Sumter was attacked and forced to surrender April 13-14, 1861, and the four-year-long Civil War was on. Lincoln, who had called preservation of the Union more important than ending slavery, issued the Emancipation Proclamation Sept. 22, 1862 as a wartime measure designed to strengthen the Union hand.

In 1864, although the nation was divided and at war, the Presidential election took place as scheduled. Lincoln was reelected President by an electoral vote of 212 to 21 for Gen. George B. McClellan, the Democratic nominee, in a contest in which there were no votes from the seceded states. The popular vote from the 25 states then in the Union was 2,213,665 for Lincoln, 1,802,237 for McClellan. In a separately counted soldiers' poll (in which the votes from Kansas and Minnesota came too late to be recorded), Lincoln received 116,887 votes, McClellan 33,748. Lincoln's running mate, Andrew Johnson, was elected Vice President.

Lincoln was shot April 14, 1865 by John Wilkes Booth, and he died April 15, just three days before the last major Confederate force surrendered. Vice President Johnson, a Democrat who had run with Lincoln on the National Union ticket, succeeded to the Presidency.

The Impeachment of Johnson

Johnson took office at a time when the first priority for the administration was the restoration of the Union. In general conformity with the Lincoln policy, Johnson's treatment of the South was relatively lenient. He thus clashed with Congress, which was dominated by Radical Republicans who favored harsh treatment for the former rebels.

In an effort to curb Johnson's power, Congress March 2, 1867, passed over his veto a Tenure of Office Act that prohibited the President from dismissing, without prior Senate agreement, any government officer who had been appointed by and with Senate consent. Johnson soon tested the new law by acting against Secretary of War Edwin M. Stanton, with whom he had been feuding.

Seeking a Supreme Court verdict on the constitutionality of the tenure act, Johnson dismissed Stanton Feb. 21, 1868 despite Senate refusal to give its consent.

The House of Representatives, however, forestalled a Supreme Court test by bringing impeachment charges against Johnson. The Senate, equally antagonistic toward the President, voted to convict Johnson by 35 to 19 May 26, 1868. Since a two-thirds vote was necessary to convict, he escaped conviction by a single vote.

Johnson was the only U.S. President ever impeached. His case, however, failed to provide a workable definition of an offense warranting removal of a President from office. The attempt to impeach Johnson had begun as early as the fall of 1867 but initially failed because several important Congress members insisted that impeachment required at least some evidence that Johnson had broken the law. Other members disagreed.

By dismissing Stanton, Johnson enabled his enemies to persuade the Congressional hold-outs that he had violated a law and thus was impeachable. Many of those involved in the case, however, insisted that a President could be properly impeached without violating the law. Benjamin Butler, one of the House's impeachment managers, insisted that the President could be impeached if he merely abused his "discretionary powers from improper motives or for any improper purpose." He held that an impeachable offense was one that "in its nature of consequences [was] subversive of some fundamental or essential principle of government or highly prejudicial to the public interest." Contradicting this opinion, one of Johnson's attorneys told the Senate that a President could be impeached only for "high criminal offenses against the United States, made so by some law of the United States existing when the acts complained of were done."

Post-Civil War Presidents & Vice Presidents

The Civil War hero Ulysses Simpson Grant, nominated

unanimously by the National Union Republican convention on the first ballot May 30, 1868, was elected President by an electoral vote of 214 against 80 for Horatio Seymour, the Democratic candidate. The popular vote (excluding Florida, whose electors were appointed by the state legislature in 1868, and the "unreconstructed" states of Mississippi, Texas and Virginia) was 3,012,833 for Grant, 2,703,249 for Seymour. Schuyler Colfax, Grant's running mate, was elected Vice President.

Grant was reelected in 1872 with an electoral vote of 286. The competing Liberal Republican candidate, the New York *Tribune* editor Horace Greeley, died Nov. 29, before the electoral college vote, and Greeley's electoral vote was distributed among four other men. Henry Wilson, elected Vice President as Grant's running mate, died in office Nov. 22, 1875.

The election of 1876 was close and its outcome disputed. According to the count of both parties, the Democratic candidate, Samuel J. Tilden, had received a plurality of more than 250,000 popular votes over the Republican, Rutherford B. Hayes. The dispute centered on which of the two candidates had won South Carolina, Florida, Louisiana and Oregon. To settle the issue, Congress created a 15-member electoral commission consisting of five members each from the House of Representatives, the Senate and the Supreme Court. The disputed votes ultimately were awarded to Hayes, who was declared winner of the Presidential election by an electoral vote of 185 to 184. His running mate, William A. Wheeler, was declared elected Vice President.

In 1880 the Republican candidate, James Abram Garfield, defeated Gen. Winfield Scott Hancock by 214 electoral votes to 155 although the popular vote was much narrower—4,454,416 to 4,444,952. Within months of his inauguration as President, Garfield was shot July 2, 1881 by Charles J. Guiteau, a mentally unstable office-seeker, and Garfield died Sept. 19. Chester Alan Arthur, elected Vice President as Garfield's 1880 running mate, then became President. But for most of the 80-day period that Garfield lay dying, there was no Constitutionally chosen official to perform the President's duties or exercise his powers.

In a close election in 1884, Democratic candidate Grover Cleveland was elected President by an electoral vote of 219 against 182 for James G. Blaine, Republican. The popular vote was 4,874,986 for Cleveland, 4,851,981 for Blaine and some 325,739 for two other candidates. Thomas A. Hendricks, elected Vice President, died in office Nov. 25, 1885.

Cleveland lost the contest for reelection in 1888 when Republican candidate Benjamin Harrison defeated him by 233 electoral votes to 168. Cleveland lost after narrowly outpolling Harrison by 5,540,329 to 5,439,853 in the popular vote. Levi P. Morton was elected Vice President.

In 1892 Cleveland defeated Harrison by 277 votes to 145 to become the only President to serve two non-consecutive terms. (Cleveland was the 22nd person to be President, but, according to Department of State reckoning, he was both the 22nd President and the 24th.)

William McKinley, Republican, was elected President in 1896 by an electoral vote of 271 against 176 for William Jennings Bryan. Garrett A. Hobart, elected Vice President, died in office Nov. 21, 1899.

Twentieth Century Chief Executives

McKinley defeated Bryan again in the 1900 election by an electoral vote of 292 to 155. His new running mate, Theodore Roosevelt, was elected Vice President.

McKinley was shot Sept. 6, 1901 by Leon Czolgosz, an anarchist, and he died Sept. 14. Roosevelt succeeded him as President.

Roosevelt was reelected in 1904 by an electoral vote of 336 to 140 for Alton B. Parker, Democrat, and Charles W. Fairbanks was elected Vice President.

William Howard Taft, chosen by Roosevelt as the latter's successor, was elected President on the Republican ticket in 1908 by an electoral vote of 321 against 162 for William Jennings Bryan. James S. Sherman, elected Vice President, died in office Oct. 30, 1912.

As the election of 1912 approached, Roosevelt, finding Taft too conservative, organized a new party, the Progressives, in a bid for Presidential election. His action weakened the Republican Party, and the Democratic candidate, Woodrow Wilson, was elected President by an electoral vote of 435 against 88 for Roosevelt and 8 for Taft. Thomas Riley Marshall was elected Vice President.

Wilson was reelected in 1916 by an electoral vote of 277 against 254 for Justice Charles Evans Hughes, Republican. Marshall was reelected Vice President. Wilson suffered a paralyzing stroke in October 1919 and was said to have been incapable of performing his Presidential duties for much of the rest of his term. His wife, Edith Wilson, led a group of White House personnel in handling the Presidential functions.

In 1920 Warren Gamaliel Harding, Republican, was elected

President with an electoral vote of 404 against 127 for James M. Cox, Democrat. Calvin Coolidge was elected Vice President, and Franklin Delano Roosevelt was defeated for the office.

Harding died Aug. 2, 1923 and was succeeded by Coolidge as President.

Coolidge was reelected in 1924 with 382 electoral votes against 136 for Democratic candidate John W. Davis and 13 for Robert M. La Follette, Progressive. Charles G. Dawes was elected Vice President.

Herbert Clark Hoover, Republican, defeated Democratic candidate Alfred E. Smith by 444 electoral votes to 87 in the 1928 Presidential election, and Charles Curtis was elected Vice President.

Franklin D. Roosevelt, Democrat, the only President ever elected for four terms, won his first term in 1932 by defeating Hoover by 472 electoral votes to 59. Roosevelt won his second term in 1936, by 523 electoral votes to 8, with a victory over Alfred M. Landon. John Nance Garner was elected Vice President for both of Roosevelt's first two terms.

Roosevelt broke the two-term tradition during the wartime election of 1940, when he defeated Wendell Willkie by 449 votes to 82. Henry A. Wallace was elected Vice President. In the 1944 election, Roosevelt won with 432 electoral votes against 99 for Thomas E. Dewey.

Roosevelt died in office April 12, 1945 and was succeeded by Harry S. Truman, who had been elected Vice President on the Roosevelt ticket in 1944.

Truman was reelected in 1948 by an electoral vote of 303 against 189 for Thomas E. Dewey and 39 for J. Strom Thurmond, States Rights candidate. Alben W. Barkley was elected Vice President.

Gen. Dwight D. Eisenhower, the World War II hero, accepted the Republican nomination in 1952 and was elected President with an electoral vote of 442 against 89 for Adlai E. Stevenson, Democrat. Eisenhower defeated Stevenson again, 457 electoral votes to 73, in the 1956 election. Richard Milhous Nixon was elected Vice President for both of Eisenhower's terms.

John F. Kennedy, Democrat, the first Roman Catholic to be elected President, defeated Richard M. Nixon by 303 electoral votes to 219 in the 1960 election.

Kennedy was shot to death in Dallas, Tex. Nov. 22, 1963, and was succeeded as President by Lyndon Baines Johnson, who had been elected Vice President in 1960.

Johnson was reelected in 1964 with an electoral vote of 486

against 52 for Sen. Barry M. Goldwater, Republican, and Sen. Hubert H. Humphrey was elected Vice President.

Richard M. Nixon won the Presidency in the 1968 election with 301 electoral votes against 191 for Hubert Humphrey and 46 for third-party candidate George C. Wallace. Nixon was reelected in 1972 with a 520-17 electoral vote triumph over Sen. George S. McGovern, Democrat. Spiro T. Agnew won the Vice Presidential election in each of Nixon's two victorious Presidential campaigns.

The 20th & 22nd Amendments

Two more amendments relating to Presidential succession were added to Constitution before the 25th Amendment.

The 20th Amendment, ratified Jan. 23, 1933, moved up the day of succession from March 4 to Jan. 20 and provided rules for succession should a President-elect die before inauguration day. Text of the 20th Amendment:

Section 1. The terms of the President and Vice President shall end at noon on the 20th day of January, and the terms of Senators and Representatives at noon on the 3d day of January, of the years in which such terms would have ended if this article had not been ratified; and the terms of their successors shall then begin.

Section 2. The Congress shall assemble at least once in every year, and such meeting shall begin at noon on the 3d day of January, unless they shall by law appoint a different day.

Section 3. If, at the time fixed for the beginning of the term of the President, the President elect shall have died, the Vice President elect shall become President. If a President shall not have been chosen before the time fixed for the beginning of his term, or if the President elect shall have failed to qualify, then the Vice President elect shall act as President until a President shall have qualified; and the Congress may by law provide for the case wherein neither a President elect nor a Vice President elect shall have qualified, declaring who shall then act as President, or the manner in which one who is to act shall be selected, and such person shall act accordingly until a President or Vice President shall have qualified.

Section 4. The Congress may by law provide for the case of the death of any of the persons from whom the House of Representatives may choose a President whenever the right of choice shall have devolved upon them, and for the case of the death of any of the persons from whom the Senate may choose a Vice President whenever the right of choice shall have devolved upon them.

Section 5. Sections 1 and 2 shall take effect on the 15th day of October following the ratification of this article.

Section 6. This article shall be inoperative unless it shall have been ratified as an amendment to the Constitution by the legislatures of three-fourths of the several States within seven years from the date of its submission.

The 22nd Amendment, drafted in reaction to Franklin D. Roosevelt's election for four terms, limited Presidents to two terms. It was ratified Feb. 27, 1951. Text of the 22nd Amendment:

Section 1. No person shall be elected to the office of the President more than twice, and no person who has held the office of President, or acted as President, for more than two years of a term to which some other person was elected President shall be elected to the office of the President more than once. But this Article shall not apply to any person holding the office of President when this Article was proposed by the Congress, and shall not prevent any person who may be holding the office of President, or acting as President, during the term within which this Article becomes operative from holding the office of President or acting as President during the remainder of such term.

Section 2. This article shall be inoperative unless it shall have been ratified as an amendment to the Constitution by the legislatures of three-fourths of the several States within seven years from the date of its submission to the States by the Congress.

Succession Revision & Agreements on Inability

The line of Presidential succession had been revised Jan. 19, 1886 by the Presidential Succession Act, which put the chief Cabinet officers next in line should there be no Vice President. The order of Cabinet succession would start with the Secretary of State and the Secretary of the Treasury and continue on in the order of rank or in which the Cabinet departments had been created. On July 18, 1947, however, a new law restored the House Speaker, followed by the Senate president pro tempore, to the line of succession ahead of the Cabinet officers. In requesting such legislation, President Harry S. Truman had said in 1945 that ''it now lies within my power to nominate the person who would be my immediate successor. . . . I do not believe that in a democracy this power should rest with the chief executive.''

Prompted by a heart attack suffered by President Dwight D. Eisenhower Sept. 24, 1955, Congress considered various legislative proposals to provide for the handling of the President's powers and responsibilities should the President become disabled. Since no legislation resulted from this Congressional consideration, Eisenhower and Vice President Richard M. Nixon drafted a limited, written agreement under which Nixon was to take over the President's duties temporarily as Acting President should Eisenhower become disabled.

The Eisenhower-Nixon agreement, made public by the White House March 3, 1958, provided that: ''(1) In the event of inability the President would—if possible—so inform the Vice President, and the Vice President would serve as Acting President, exercising the powers and duties of the Office until the inability had ended. (2) In the event of an inability which would prevent the President from communicating with the Vice President, the Vice President, after such consultation as seems to him appropriate . . . would decide upon the devolution of the powers and duties of the Office and would serve as Acting President until the inability had ended. (3) The President, in either event, would determine when the inability had ended and at that time would resume the full exercise of the powers and duties of the Office." The statement said Eisenhower and Nixon intended the agreement "to apply to themselves only" and felt it would "implement" the "clear intent" of the Constitution's "purposes and provisions" on Presidential inability. House Speaker Sam Rayburn called the plan Constitutionally defective. "I don't see how the Vice President can exercise the powers and duties of the Presidency without taking the oath as President," Rayburn said. "After he once takes it, I don't see how the President can reclaim the office." But Attorney General William P. Rogers, explaining the Administration's view, said that a Vice President would not have to take the oath of office when assuming the duties of a disabled President yet that while acting as President, he would have full Presidential powers, including those of signing or vetoing legislation. Since he would not have taken the oath, there would be no question about the Vice President's returning the powers to a President who had recuperated, Rogers indicated. He said that when the Constitution's provisions were compared with the draft approved by the Constitutional Convention, it became clear that a Vice President's own office gave him the duty of exercising Presidential powers during a President's inability. He held further that the Constitution required a Vice President to act as President when a President died but did not vest him with the office of President. Rogers agreed, however, that historical precedent had legalized a Vice President's assumption of the Presidency in such cases.

In 1961, President John F. Kennedy and Vice President Lyndon B. Johnson made an agreement almost identical to the Eisenhower-Nixon agreement. Following Kennedy's death and Johnson's succession to the Presidency in 1963, Johnson and then-Speaker of the House John W. McCormack agreed verbally to "follow the example" set by the Eisenhower-Nixon and Kennedy-Johnson inability agreements. After his reelection and just prior to his inauguration Jan. 20, 1965, Johnson signed a similar agreement with Vice President-elect Hubert H. Humphrey.

THIS BOOK IS A RECORD OF the events that led to the succession of the nation's first unelected President and to the appointment of its first two unelected Vice Presidents. The major developments include the adoption of the Twenty-Fifth Amendment, the downfall of Vice President Spiro T. Agnew and then of President Richard M. Nixon, the appointment of Gerald R. Ford as Vice President, his elevation to the Presidency and the appointment of Nelson A. Rockefeller to be Vice President. The material presented consists largely of the record compiled by FACTS ON FILE in its weekly reports on world events. As in all FACTS ON FILE works, a sincere effort was made to keep this volume free of bias and to produce an accurate and balanced reference book.

LESTER A. SOBEL

New York, N.Y.
September, 1975

The 25th Amendment

President Authorized
to Appoint Vice President

The 25th Amendment, authorizing a President to appoint a new Vice President whenever the latter office became vacant, became part of the U.S. Constitution Feb. 10, 1967 on ratification by Nevada, the 38th ratifying state. (Ratification by three-quarters of the states was required for the amendment's adoption.)

The new amendment also specified procedure for the performance of a President's duties should he become disabled, and this provision was probably the one considered most vital by those who drafted the amendment and who worked for its ratification.

The 25th Amendment became law after more than four years of Congressional and state consideration of similar proposals on Presidential and Vice Presidential inability, succession and vacancy.

1963 inability action. Three major resolutions on Presidential inability had been introduced in the Senate in 1963, but all died after subcommittee action. All three would have amended the Constitution to enable the Vice President to take over the President's "powers and duties" (but not succeed to his "office") at such times as the President was unable to discharge the powers and duties of his office.

The first of the three resolutions (SJ Res. 28), introduced by Sen. Estes Kefauver (D, Tenn.) Jan. 23, would have provided that, should the President be unable to declare his inability to handle his powers and duties, a majority of the heads of the executive agencies could give written approval for the Vice President to become Acting President. Should the President later declare his inability ended and the Vice President disagree, the latter would continue as Acting President if a majority of the heads of the executive agencies and two-thirds of Congress agreed that the President's inability had not ended.

The second of the 1963 inability resolutions (SJ Res. 35), introduced by Kefauver Feb. 5, would have enabled Congress to specify by law when the President's inability had started and ended.

The third of the resolutions (SJ Res. 84), introduced by Sen. Roman Hruska (R, Neb.) May 28, proposed that Presidential inability be determined by Congress and that such a determination must be compatible with the maintenance of the distinction among the branches of Congress and must preserve the governmental system of checks and balances.

Provisions of the 25th Amendment

Section 1. In case of the removal of the President from office or of his death or resignation, the Vice President shall become President.

Section 2. Whenever there is a vacancy in the office of the Vice President, the President shall nominate a Vice President who shall take office upon confirmation by a majority vote of both Houses of Congress.

Section 3. Whenever the President transmits to the President pro tempore of the Senate and the Speaker of the House of Representatives his written declaration that he is unable to discharge the powers and duties of his office, and until he transmits to them a written declaration to the contrary, such powers and duties shall be discharged by the Vice President as Acting President.

Section 4. Whenever the Vice President and a majority of either the principal officers of the executive departments or of such other body as Congress may by law provide, transmit to the President pro tempore of the Senate and the Speaker of the House of Representatives their written declaration that the President is unable to discharge the powers and duties of his office, the Vice President shall immediately assume the powers and duties of the office as Acting President.

Thereafter, when the President transmits to the President pro tempore of the Senate and the Speaker of the House of Representatives his written declaration that no inability exists, he shall resume the powers and duties of his office unless the Vice President and a majority of either the principal officers of the executive department or of such other body as Congress may by law provide, transmit within four days to the President pro tempore of the Senate and the Speaker of the House of Representatives their written declaration that the President is unable to discharge the powers and duties of his office. Thereupon Congress shall decide the issue, assembling within forty-eight hours for that purpose if not in session. If the Congress, within twenty-one days after receipt of the latter written declaration, or, if Congress is not in session, within twenty-one days after Congress is required to assemble, determines by two-thirds vote of both Houses that the President is unable to discharge the powers and duties of his office, the Vice President shall continue to discharge the same as Acting President; otherwise, the President shall resume the powers and duties of his office.

The Senate Judiciary Committee's Constitutional Amendments Subcommittee held hearings on the three resolutions June 11 and 18. Deputy Attorney General Nicholas deB. Katzenbach, representing the Department of Justice, told the subcommittee that SJ Res. 35 would provide the best assurance that the Presidential powers would be placed in authorized hands. The subcommittee approved the latter resolution and reported it unanimously June 25 to the full committee, where no further action was taken.

Senate passes inability proposal in 1964. A new Presidential inability resolution (SJ Res. 139) was introduced in the Senate in 1964 by Chairman Birch Bayh (D, Ind.) of the Judiciary Committee's Constitutional Amendments Subcommittee and was passed by 65-0 vote Sept. 29. But the measure died in the House.

The 1964 Bayh amendment, as accepted by the Senate, would have provided that: (a) Should a President be removed from office by death or resignation, "the Vice President shall become President." (b) If the Vice President's office should become vacant, the President would nominate a new Vice President, who would require confirmation by majority vote in both houses of Congress. (c) Should the President declare in writing that he was unable to discharge his office's powers and duties, the Vice President would become Acting President and discharge the duties and powers (but not succeed to the office). (d) Should the President fail to make such a declaration, a majority of the Cabinet or of any other body specified by Congress could make the declaration, and the Vice President would become acting President. (e) The President would resume his powers and duties on informing Congress in writing that his disability no longer existed; but he could be blocked from doing so, and the Vice President would remain Acting President, if, within two days, the Vice President, with the written agreement of a majority of the Cabinet or of any other body specified by Congress, informed Congress in writing that the President's inability continued.

The Senate Constitutional Amendments Subcommittee had held hearings on SJ Res. 139 and various other Presidential and Vice Presidential inability, succession and vacancy proposals Jan. 22-23, Feb. 24-25 and 28 and March 5. Sen. Sam J. Ervin Jr. (D, N.C.), who had submitted a resolution (SJ Res. 147) to fill Vice Presidential and Presidential vacancies, testified Jan. 22. He said that under SJ Res. 147, whenever a vacancy occurred in the Vice Presidential office, a joint session of Congress would convene within ten days to select a new Vice President by majority vote. Should the Presidential and Vice Presidential office become vacant simultaneously, Congress would convene within ten days and elect both a President and a Vice President by majority vote, and in the meantime, the Speaker of the House would serve as President.

Representatives of the American Bar Association, testifying Jan. 22 and 24, favored adoption of SJ Res. 139 as closest to the recommendations of an ABA Special Conference on Presidential Inability & Succession, held Jan. 20-21.

The Bayh amendment was approved by the Constitutional Amendments Subcommittee May 27 and by the Judiciary Committee, with minor amendments, Aug. 13. Before the roll-call passage of the bill by the Senate Sept. 29, the measure received voice vote passage in the Senate Sept. 28 with only nine members on the floor.

CED proposal. Efforts to solve the Presidential and Vice Presidential inability, succession and vacancy problems continued on into 1965.

The Committee for Economic Development (CED) Jan. 7 proposed another Constitutional amendment establishing procedures for continuing Presidential leadership in case of Presidential disability and for filling a vacancy in the office of Vice President. Warning that a President's death or disability "creates the risk of national disaster," the CED recommended that: (a) The President nominate a Vice President whenever there was a vacancy in that office and that nomination be confirmed by a joint session of Congress. (b) The responsibility for making a decision concerning Presidential disability be vested primarily with the Cabinet with the concurrence of the Vice President; decision on the termination of such disability be made by the Cabinet with the concurrence of the President. (c) The Presidential line of succession, which was changed in 1947, revert back to the status under an 1886 statute providing that the Secretaries of State and

Treasury and other Cabinet members be the successors of the President and Vice President. The CED said that the 1947 change, inserting the Speaker of the House and the president pro tempore of the Senate into the line of succession before the Cabinet, would give the House "a possible series of succession choices during a single 4-year term [in the event that a Speaker, who was elected from the House, succeeded to the Presidency]." The committee held that the Speaker's preparation for "sudden elevation to the Presidency could not approach that of a Vice President, nor that of a leading cabinet member."

Johnson & Bayh-Celler proposals. President Lyndon B. Johnson sent to Congress Jan. 28, 1965 a special message requesting that Congress amend the Constitution (a) to provide for the execution of the President's duties during Presidential disability and for the filling of a vacancy in the office of Vice President and (b) to reform the electoral system.

Johnson endorsed a Presidential disability amendment introduced in the House Jan. 4 by Chairman Emanuel Celler (D, N.Y.) of the House Judiciary Committee (as HJ Res. 1) and in the Senate Jan. 6 by Sen. Birch Bayh (as SJ Res 1). (The Bayh-Celler resolutions, with some modification ultimately became the ratified 25th Amendment.)

Provisions of the Bayh-Celler plan: (a) If the President decided he was unable to perform his duties, he would inform the Vice President, who would become acting President. (b) If the President did not declare his disability and the Vice President believed him disabled, the Vice President, with written approval of a majority of the cabinet, could declare the President disabled in a letter to Congress and become acting President. (c) If the President declared his disability ended and the Vice President did not respond, the President could resume his duties; if the Vice President disagreed, he could, with written approval of a majority of the cabinet, submit to Congress the question of disability, to be decided by a two-thirds majority vote of both houses. (d) If a vacancy occurred in the office of Vice President, the President could name a new Vice President subject to the approval of a majority vote of both houses of Congress (the naming of a Vice President was not mandatory, and Congress

could reject the President's choice).

Johnson's electoral proposal provided that the entire electoral vote of a state would go to the candidate getting a simple plurality of the votes in that state, and that all electoral votes would be sent to Congress, within 45 days of the election, by the states' official electoral custodians. The proposal would eliminate the Electoral College but retain the electoral system. It also provided that the Vice President-elect would become President if the President-elect died before inauguration; if both died before inauguration, "Congress should be made responsible for providing the method of selecting officials for both positions."

Bayh's resolution was passed by 72-0 Senate vote Feb. 19 and sent to the House.

Recommending SJ Res. 1 to the full Senate Judiciary Committee Feb. 1, the Constitutional Amendments Subcommittee had reported: "This amendment seeks to remove a vexatious Constitutional problem from the realm of national concern. It seeks to concisely clarify the ambiguities of the present provision in the Constitution. . . . In so doing, it recognizes . . . the necessity to maintain continuity of the Executive power of the United States. We must not gamble with the constitutional legitimacy or our nation's Executive Branch. . . . Only a Constitutional amendment can supply the necessary air of legitimacy."

Bayh added in Senate debate Feb. 19 that the proposed amendment "is an effort to guarantee continuity within the Executive Branch of government. It is designed to provide that we shall always have a President physically and mentally alert. Second, and of equal importance, it is to assure that whoever the man be, there will be no question as to the legality of his authority to carry out the powers and duties of the office."

Prior to the approval of SJ Res. 1, the Senate Feb. 19 defeated by 60-12 vote a more general substitute proposal by minority leader Everett Dirksen (Ill.) that would have authorized Congress to legislate on Presidential inability and succession. Dirksen had announced Feb. 11 his opposition to the Administration-backed proposal on the grounds that the method for determining Presidential disability and recovery should not be frozen into Constitutional form.

The Senate Feb. 19 also rejected proposals by Sens. John O. Pastore (D, R.I.) and Ross Bass (D, Tenn.) for a guarantee against Congressional delay in the event the President and Vice President disagreed about a President's recovery and resumption of duties.

The House Apr. 13 passed and sent to conference with the Senate by 368-29 vote the similar Cellar resolution (HJ Res. 1).

Before House passage of HJ Res. 1, an effort was made to eliminate the provision under which the President would fill a vacancy in the Vice Presidency by nomination subject to majority-vote confirmation by both houses of Congress. The attempt to kill this provision was rejected by 44-140 vote.

Other variations from the Senate version of the bill had been made before HJ Res. 1 was reported Mar. 24 by the House Judiciary Committee. These changes provided that: (a) A dispute between a deposed President and an Acting President must be resolved within 10 days (no time limit had been set by Senate); (b) the Vice President and cabinet had only 2 days in which to challenge an attempt of a disabled President to resume office (the Senate would have permitted 7 days); (c) a President who voluntarily relinquished his office could automatically resume it on application (a challenge to such resumption of office was possible under the Senate bill). Explaining the latter provision, the committee said in its report: "To permit the Vice President and the Cabinet to challenge such an assertion of recovery might discourage a President from voluntarily relinquishing his powers in case of illnesses."

Congress approves amendment. The bill (SJ Res. 1) that ultimately became the 25th Amendment was passed by House voice vote June 30, 1965 and by 68-5 Senate vote July 6. The measure, not requiring the President's signature, was submitted to the states for ratification.

Final Congressional action on the bill had been delayed about 10 weeks because of a dispute among House-Senate conferees over the provision (in the House version) limiting to 10 days the period during which Congress was required to act in the event of a disagreement between the President and Vice President as to the termination of any specific case of a Presidential disability. The Senate version's lack of a time limitation was opposed by House conferees

because of concern over the possibility that a filibuster could delay final resolution of such a disagreement. A 21-day limitation was eventually inserted into the final version.

Another dispute arose in Senate consideration of the conference report June 30 when Sens. Robert F. Kennedy (D, N.Y.), Albert Gore (D, Tenn.) and Eugene J. McCarthy (D, Minn.) questioned a provision permitting the Vice President "and a majority of either the principal officers of the executive departments [the Cabinet] or such other body as Congress may by law provide" to declare the President disabled. Kennedy said a "disruptive situation" could arise under the provision whereby 2 Cabinets could be contesting for power claimed both by the President and Vice President. Gore contended that the provision would permit the Vice President to choose to act either with the Cabinet or with the other body designated by Congress. The principal author of the provision, Sen. Birch Bayh, said the "either/or" language was intended to vest exclusivity in one or other of the bodies, that the Cabinet would act with the Vice President in such a situation unless Congress designated another body, in which case "the Cabinet loses the responsibility and it rests solely in the other body."

The debate was deferred until July 6, when Gore reaffirmed his opposition to the ambiguity of the text's language, which, he said, could lead to "the potentially disastrous spectacle of competing claims to the power of the Presidency." He voted against SJ Res. 1 in the final vote and was joined by McCarthy and Sens. Frank J. Lausche (D, O.), Walter F. Mondale (D, Minn.) and John G. Tower (R, Tex.).

25th Amendment ratified. The 25th Amendment became part of the U.S. Constitution Feb. 10, 1967 when it was ratified by the 38th state. The amendment, specifying the procedure for the performance of a President's duties should he become disabled, was formally proclaimed at a White House ceremony Feb. 23.

(Several states were involved in a race to be the 38th state to ratify the amendment. Nevada had ratified it Feb. 8 but nullified its ratification on learning that it was only 37th. North Dakota did the same thing Feb. 9, but at first the validity of its nullification attempt was uncertain. The next ratifications were Minnesota's at 11:31 a.m. [CST] Feb. 10 and Nevada's at 10:44 a.m. [PST], one hour and 13 minutes later because of the 2-hour time differential. When the withdrawal action by North Dakota was verified, Nevada thus became the 38th and deciding state.)

The dates of ratification by the states:

1. Nebraska . . . . .July 12, 1965
2. Wisconsin . . . . .July 13, 1965
3. Oklahoma . . . . .July 16, 1965
4. Massachusetts . . . . .August 9, 1965
5. Pennsylvania . . . . .August 18, 1965
6. Kentucky . . . . . . .September 15, 1965
7. Arizona . . . . .September 22, 1965
8. Michigan . . . . .October 5, 1965
9. Indiana . . . . .October 20, 1965
10. California . . . . .October 21, 1965
11. Arkansas . . . . .November 4, 1965
12. New Jersey . . . . .November 29, 1965
13. Delaware . . . . .December 7, 1965
14. Utah . . . . .January 7, 1966
15. West Virginia . . . . .January 20, 1966
16. Maine . . . . .January 24, 1966
17. Rhode Island . . . . . .January 28, 1966
18. Colorado . . . . .February 3, 1966
19. New Mexico . . . . . .February 3, 1966
20. Kansas . . . . .February 8, 1966
21. Vermont . . . . .February 10, 1966
22. Alaska . . . . .February 18, 1966
23. Idaho . . . . .March 2, 1966
24. Hawaii . . . . .March 3, 1966
25. Virginia . . . . .March 8, 1966
26. Mississippi . . . . .March 10, 1966
27. New York . . . . .March 14, 1966
28. Maryland . . . . .March 23, 1966
29. Missouri . . . . .March 30, 1966
30. New Hampshire . . . . . .June 13, 1966
31. Louisiana . . . . .July 5, 1966
32. Tennessee . . . . .January 14, 1967
33. Wyoming . . . . .January 25, 1967
34. Washington . . . . .January 26, 1967
35. Iowa . . . . .January 26, 1967
36. Oregon . . . . .February 3, 1967
37. Minnesota . . . . .February 10, 1967
38. Nevada . . . . .February 10, 1967

Agnew's Downfall

Agnew Accused of Bribery, Resigns as Vice President

The Nixon Administration, politically battered by the Watergate charges, suffered a further blow in 1973 when Vice President Spiro T. Agnew was accused of bribery, conspiracy and tax evasion. Faced with an apparently airtight case against him, Agnew resigned the Vice Presidency and pleaded no contest to a tax count in satisfaction of all the charges against him.

Agnew's plea & resignation. Spiro T. Agnew resigned as Vice President of the U.S. Oct. 10, 1973 and pleaded no contest (nolo contendere) to one count of income tax evasion. In return, the Justice Department agreed to drop all pending charges against Agnew and request leniency on the tax evasion charge.

In a dramatic courtroom hearing in Baltimore shortly after he submitted his letter of resignation, Agnew avoided imprisonment by pleading no contest to a federal charge that he had failed to report $29,500 of income he received in 1967, when he was governor of Maryland. Such a plea, while not an admission of guilt, was tantamount to a plea of guilty on the charge. Agnew had faced federal indictment for violation of bribery, conspiracy and tax laws.

As required by law, Agnew's formal instrument of resignation was a statement transmitted to Secretary of State Henry A. Kissinger. The statement, delivered at 2:05 p.m., said in its entirety: "I hereby resign the Office of Vice President of the United States, effective immediately."

Agnew also formally notified President Nixon by letter, saying "the accusations against me cannot be resolved without a long, divisive and debilitating struggle in the Congress and in the courts." Agnew had concluded that it was "in the best interest of the nation" that he relinquish the office.

Nixon said in his letter of acceptance that Agnew's resignation "leaves me with a great sense of personal loss." He praised Agnew's "strong patriotism" and "all that you have contributed to the nation by your years of service as vice president."

Almost simultaneously with the delivery of his resignation letter to Kissinger, Agnew appeared before U.S. District Court Judge Walter E. Hoffman in Baltimore to plead no contest to the charge of filing a "false and fraudulent" income tax return for the year 1967 and attempting to evade payment of $13,551.47 in federal taxes. According to the charge, Agnew had understated his and Mrs. Agnew's joint income by $29,500.

Hoffman asked Agnew if he understood the implications of waiving indictment and entering a plea of no contest, which

Hoffman noted, was "the full equivalent of a plea of guilty" and would protect Agnew only in that it could not be used in a civil suit as evidence that Agnew had actually committed the offense. As Hoffman pointed out in a formal statement, a no contest plea used in tax evasion cases "merely permits the parties to further litigate the amount due without regard to the conviction following such a plea."

Hoffman cited the provisions of Agnew's agreement with the Justice Department: that Agnew resign; that the department would not prosecute on other charges while reserving the right to use Agnew's name in proceedings against others; and that Agnew might still be subject to action by the State of Maryland "or some private organization."

"Do you understand and ratify the agreement as I have stated it?" Hoffman asked.

"I do so understand it," Agnew said.

Agnew was sentenced to a fine of $10,-000 and three years' unsupervised probation. Hoffman said that without the recommendation for leniency by Attorney General Elliot L. Richardson, he would have been inclined to follow his usual procedure in tax evasion cases of imposing a fine and prison sentence of two to five months. But, Hoffman added, "I am persuaded that the national interests in the present case are so great and so compelling . . . that the ends of justice would be better served by making an exception to the general rule."

In a statement read to the court, Richardson said no agreement could have been reached without a provision that he appeal for leniency. Mindful of the "historic magnitude of the penalties inherent in the vice president's resignation from his high office and his acceptance of a judgment of conviction of a felony," Richardson said that a prison sentence was more than he could "recommend or wish."

Richardson emphasized that a central element of the agreement was that the department be allowed to present the details of its other evidence against Agnew while agreeing to waive prosecution based on it.

Richardson said that for the people to "fairly judge the outcome" of the Agnew case, he would offer "for the permanent record" an "exposition of evidence" which "establishes a pattern of substantial cash payments to the defendant during the period when he served as governor of Maryland in return for engineering contracts with the State of Maryland." Richardson added that none of the government's major witnesses had been promised immunity from prosecution and that each who would have testified to making direct payments to Agnew had signed a sworn statement "subject to the penalties of perjury."

According to the "exposition of evidence," Agnew—shortly after becoming governor in 1967—established a system of taking payments from engineering firms. I.H. Hammerman 2d, a Baltimore investment banker, acted as "collector" from companies designated by Jerome B. Wolff, then chairman of the Maryland State Roads Commission. After initial disagreements about division of the payments, the three agreed—on Agnew's order—that the payments would be divided 50% for Agnew and 25% each for Hammerman and Wolff. The three would then discuss which firms should be awarded contracts, but "the governor always exercised the final decision-making authority."

The evidence also detailed the relationship between Agnew and the presidents of two engineering firms who made direct cash payments. Agnew allegedly complained to Allen Green of Green Associates, Inc. about the "financial burdens" of the office of governor, and Green began making payments which continued until the beginning of the Maryland grand jury investigation in January 1973.

A similar relationship existed with Lester Matz of Matz, Childs and Associates who also continued making "corrupt payments" to Agnew after he became vice president. In addition to payments "still owed" for contracts awarded to Matz while Agnew was Maryland governor, Matz allegedly paid $2,500 in April 1971 in return for the awarding of a federal contract to a Matz company.

According to the evidence, Agnew received payments totaling about $100,-000.

Green and Hammerman had agreed to plead guilty to single tax charges and to cooperate with the prosecution. Matz and Wolff had agreed to cooperate with the prosecution with assurances that their testimony before the grand jury would not be used against them in subsequent criminal trials.

In acknowledging to the court that he had received taxable payments in 1967, Agnew conceded that such payments had been made by companies receiving state contract awards in 1967 "and other years," but he denied that the payments had "in any way" influenced his official actions.

Settlement voids other issues—Agnew's plea of no contest to the tax evasion charge and the Justice Department's agreement not to pursue prosecution rendered moot the litigation on two constitutional issues which had become central to the Agnew case: whether a vice president could be indicted while in office and the confidentiality of newsmen's sources. At the end of the Agnew hearing Oct. 10, Judge Hoffman said the questions had no further legal standing in the Agnew case.

Summary of criminal charges. U.S. Attorney George Beall s statement of the criminal information returned by the grand jury contained the following summary:

I. The relationship of Mr. Agnew, I. H. Hammerman 2d and Jerome B. Wolff.

In the spring of 1967, shortly after Mr. Agnew had taken office as governor of Maryland, he advised Hammerman that it was customary for engineers to make substantial cash payments in return for engineering contracts with the State of Maryland. Mr. Agnew instructed Hammerman to contact Wolff, then the new chairman-director of the Maryland State Roads Commission, to arrange for the establishment of an understanding pursuant to which Wolff would notify Hammerman as to which engineering firms were in line for state contracts so that Hammerman could solicit and obtain from those engineering firms cash payments in consideration therefore.

Hammerman, as instructed, discussed the matter with Wolff, who was receptive but who requested that the cash payments be elicited from the engineers be split in three equal shares among Agnew, Hammerman and Wolff. Hammerman informed Mr. Agnew of Wolff's attitude; Mr. Agnew informed Hammerman that the split of the cash monies would be 50 per cent for Mr. Agnew; 25 per cent for Hammerman and 25 per cent for Wolff. Hammerman carried that message to Wolff, who agreed to that split.

The scheme outlined above was then put into operation. Over the course of the approximately 18 months of Mr. Agnew's remaining tenure as governor of Maryland, Hammerman made contact with approximately eight engineering firms. Informed periodically by Wolff as to which engineering firms were in line to receive state contracts, Hammerman successfully elicited from seven engineering firms substantial cash payments pursuant to understandings between Hammerman and the various engineers to whom he was talking that the substantial cash payments were in return for the state work being awarded to those engineering firms. The monies collected in that manner by Hammerman were split in accordance with the understanding earlier reached: 50 per cent to Mr. Agnew, 25 per cent to Hammerman and 25 per cent to Wolff. An eighth engineer contacted by Hammerman flatly refused to make payments and, instead, complained—first to his attorney and later to Governor Agnew himself—about Hammerman's solicitation. Wolff, informed of the complaint, reduced the share of work being awarded to the complaining engineer, but decided not to cut that engineering firm off completely from state work for fear of further exacerbating the situation.

Wolff, as chairman-director of the Maryland State Roads Commission, made initial tentative decisions with regard to which engineering firms should be awarded which state contracts. These tentative decisions would then be discussed by Wolff with Governor Agnew. Although Governor Agnew accorded Wolff's tentative decisions great weight, the governor always exercised the final decision-making authority. Often Wolff would present the governor with a list of engineering firms competent in Wolff's judgment for a state job, and the governor would make the final selection of which particular firm would be awarded that job.

Hammerman also successfully solicited, at Governor Agnew's instruction, a substantial cash payment from a financial institution in return for that institution's being awarded a major role in the financing of a large issue of state bonds.

II. The relationship between Mr. Agnew and Allen Green.

Shortly after Mr. Agnew's election in November, 1966, as governor of Maryland, he complained to Allen Green, principal of a large engineering firm, about the financial burdens to be imposed upon Mr. Agnew by his role as governor. Green responded by saying that his company had benefited from state work and had been able to generate some cash funds from which he would be willing to provide Mr. Agnew with some financial assistance. Mr. Agnew indicated that he would be grateful for such assistance.

Beginning shortly thereafter, Green delivered to Mr. Agnew six to nine times a year an envelope containing between $2,000 and $3,000 in cash. Green's purpose was to elicit from the Agnew administration as much state work for his engineering firm as possible. That purpose was clearly understood by Governor Agnew both because Green occasionally expressed his appreciation to the governor for state work being received by his company and because Green frequently asked for and often received from the governor assurances that his company would get further state work, including specific jobs.

Between Mr. Agnew's election and inauguration as vice president, Wolff contacted Green, at Mr. Agnew's instruction, for the purpose of preparing for Mr. Agnew a detailed written computation of the work and fees which had been awarded to Green's company by Governor Agnew's administration. After assisting Wolff in the preparation of such a compilation, Green subsequently met with Mr. Agnew, who noted that Green's company had received a lot of work from Governor Agnew's administration and stated that he was glad that things had worked out that way. Mr. Agnew then went on to complain about the continuing financial burden which would be imposed upon him by his position as vice president and to express the hope that Green would not stop his financial assistance to Mr. Agnew. To Green's surprise, Mr. Agnew went on to state expressly that he hoped to be able to be helpful to Green with respect to the awarding of federal engineering contracts to Green's company.

As a result of that conversation, Green continued to make cash payments to Vice President Agnew three or four times a year up to and including December, 1972. These payments were usually about $2,000 each. The payments were made both in Mr. Agnew's vice presidential office and at his residence in the Sheraton Park Hotel, Washington, D.C. The payments were not discontinued until after the initiation of the Baltimore County investigation by the United States attorney for the District of Maryland in January 1973.

III. The relationship between Mr. Agnew and Lester Matz.

Lester Matz, a principal in another large engineering firm, began making corrupt payments while Mr. Agnew was county executive of Baltimore County in the early nineteen-sixties. In those days, Matz paid 5 per cent of his fees from Baltimore County contracts in cash to Mr. Agnew through one of Mr. Agnew's close associates.

After Mr. Agnew became governor of Maryland, Matz decided to make his payments directly to Governor Agnew. He made no payments until that summer of 1968 when he and his partner calculated that they owed Mr. Agnew approximately $20,000 in consideration for the work which their firm had already received from the governor's administration. The $20,000 in cash was generated in an illegal manner and was given by Matz to Governor Agnew in a manila envelope in Governor Agnew's office on or about July 16, 1968. In handing the envelope to Governor Agnew, Matz expressed his appreciation for the substantial amounts of state work his company had been receiving and told the governor that the envelope contained the money that Matz owed to the governor in connection with that work.

Matz made no further corrupt payments to Mr. Agnew until shortly after Mr. Agnew became vice president, at which time Matz calculated that he owed Mr. Agnew approximately $10,000 more from jobs and fees which the Matz firm had received from Governor Agnew's administration since July 1968. After generating $10,000 in cash in an illegal manner, Matz met with Mr. Agnew in the vice president's office and gave him approximately $10,000 in cash in an envelope. Matz informed the vice president at that meeting that the envelope contained money still owed to Mr. Agnew in connection with work awarded to Matz's firm by Governor Agnew's administration and that more such monies would be owed and paid in the future. Matz did make several subsequent payments to the vice president; he believes that he paid an additional $5,000 to Mr. Agnew in cash.

In or around April 1971, Matz made a cash payment to Vice President Agnew of $2,500 in return for the awarding by the General Services Adminis-

tration of a contract to a small engineering firm in which Matz had a financial ownership interest. An intermediary was instrumental in the arrangement for that particular corrupt payment.

(Maryland Gov. Marvin Mandel [D] said Oct. 31 that he had returned $53,950 in contributions for his 1974 re-election campaign from consulting engineers and architects eligible for nonbid contracts from the state. Federal prosecutors in the Agnew case had described such contributions as a "long-standing system of kickbacks.")

Agnew office urged GSA contract awards.

Arthur F. Sampson, administrator of the General Services Administration (GSA), said Oct. 10 that Vice President Agnew's office had urged the GSA on numerous occasions to select certain companies for government contracts.

Among the three companies cited by Sampson was the Baltimore architectural firm of Gaudreau, Inc., which had been named in a federal indictment returned against Baltimore County Executive N. Dale Anderson Aug. 23. Neither the firm, which allegedly paid $24,000 to Anderson in connection with a contract award, nor the firm's head Paul L. Gaudreau, who was granted immunity from prosecution in return for his testimony, was named a defendant.

Sampson's disclosure came at a press conference he had called to announce the termination of Gaudreau, Inc.'s services for the second phase of a design project concerning the nearly $200 million expansion of the Social Security Administration's headquarters in suburban Baltimore. Dropped because of the adverse publicity stemming from the Anderson case, Gaudreau, Inc. had received $318,000 of an estimated $5.1 million total fee for initial design work. The fee was to be split with two other companies.

According to Sampson, a member of Agnew's staff had telephoned his agency in 1969 or 1970 on behalf of Gaudreau in connection with a contract for modernization plans for the Justice Department. The GSA awarded Gaudreau the contract in December 1971 and paid a $16,000 fee for renovation plans that were never used because of high cost estimates. Sampson said a check of GSA records had failed to reveal the identity of the Agnew staff member or the GSA employe who received the call.

The Social Security Administration contract had been awarded to Gaudreau by Sampson over the recommendations of the Social Security Administration and a GSA advisory panel of architects and engineers in private practice, the New York Times reported Oct. 10.

The other two firms that Sampson said had been recommended to the GSA by Agnew's office were Greiner Environmental Systems, Inc., a Baltimore engineering consulting firm, and Planner, Inc., a Washington urban planning firm. Both had been linked to the federal investigation of Agnew.

Richardson defends agreement. Urging "consideration and compassion" for Agnew, Attorney General Elliot L. Richardson Oct. 11 called the agreement culminating in Agnew's resignation "just and honorable" to the parties involved, "but above all to the American people."

Speaking at a joint news conference with Maryland U.S. Attorney George Beall, Richardson reiterated his feeling that leniency for Agnew had been justified. While commending Beall and his assistants for their "tenacious pursuit of justice and wise counsel" in the case, Richardson acknowledged that "they did not always agree with me, particularly with regard to the painful issue of sentencing."

Asked whether acceptance of a plea to a single count of tax evasion might have been too lenient in view of the weight of the evidence accumulated against Agnew, Richardson replied that "the very essence of a negotiated plea" was the yielding by both sides to achieve agreement.

Richardson added that the Justice Department had not initiated the plea bargaining. He said the first period of negotiations—which had failed—had begun in early September after a call from "the President's counsel" asking if Richardson would be willing to meet with Agnew's attorneys. Responding to a later question, Richardson said the call had come from White House counsel J. Fred Buzhardt Jr., who, Richardson said, "did not indicate

that he was acting at the President's behest." Richardson said Buzhardt had "at various stages" of the negotiations served in a capacity of "facilitating communications."

Referring to Nixon's personal role in the negotiations, Richardson said the President had been kept "fully informed at all times" and had "fully approved each of the major steps." But, Richardson added, Nixon had not participated "in the negotiations as such," nor had he suggested any of the elements of the agreement. According to Richardson, the President also felt "it was not appropriate for him to be informed of the details of the case."

Richardson said he had first discussed the case with Nixon in early August after informing White House chief of staff Alexander M. Haig Jr. in July. He had "no reason" to believe that Nixon knew of Agnew's misconduct before then.

Richardson rejected a suggestion that the agreement with Agnew had reflected "permissiveness" on the part of the Justice Department and was a political rather than a prosecutorial judgment. He said, however, that "in the fundamental sense" of the word, the agreement was indeed seriously "political" since a lengthy and divisive prosecution of the person second in line to the presidency would not have been in the national interest.

Buzhardt role detailed—Contrary to Richardson's assertion that the role in the Agnew case of presidential counsel J. Fred Buzhardt Jr. had been one of "facilitating communications" during the negotiations, Agnew's attorneys and Administration sources portrayed a more important role.

Judah Best, one of Agnew's lawyers, said Oct. 11 that the key meeting to work out the final details of the agreement was between him and Buzhardt in a Miami hotel Oct. 5-6. According to the Agnew defense team, the core of the Best-Buzhardt accord was that Agnew would be free to deny in court the charges in the criminal information submitted by the Justice Department and would retain the right to review the summary of the government's evidence against him.

According to the New York Times Oct. 12, a "source close to Agnew's lawyers" said the document detailing the Agnew payoff system was about "10%" of the evidence developed by the prosecution.

The Times also cited Administration sources as saying that Buzhardt had assumed the role of middleman at Nixon's behest. According to one official, Buzhardt "couldn't do that without the full cognizance, support and direction of the President."

Sources "close to Agnew" told the Times that Agnew had been prepared to resign in exchange for a halt to the prosecution as early as Sept. 13, the occasion of the first negotiating session with the Justice Department. The most troublesome point in the talks was the extent to which the department would be allowed to reveal evidence against Agnew. According to the sources, the talks dragged on without agreement because Agnew felt that his bargaining position was worsening because of the news leaks on the evidence.

Probe in Maryland

Prior to the action against Agnew, related investigations into questionable Maryland GOP activities had been started in June 1973.

Funds manipulated for Agnew. Federal and Maryland officials began investigations June 7 into the Maryland Republican party's failure to report a $50,000 cash loan from the Nixon re-election committee. The funds were used to inflate the proceeds of a May 19, 1972 testimonial dinner for Agnew.

Former Nixon finance committee treasurer Hugh W. Sloan Jr. had testified June 6 that he had given the money in $100 bills to Alexander M. Lankler Jr., Maryland GOP chairman, after April 7, 1972 and that the transaction had been authorized by finance committee chairman Maurice H. Stans.

Official state financial records originally had listed 31 individuals who were reported to have contributed the. money. But the Maryland records were amended June 1 to show that the actual source of funds had been the Finance Committee to Re-elect the President.

The finance committee had filed its quarterly statement with the General Accounting Office (GAO), which released the figures June 11. According to the report, Lankler had delivered a $150,000 contribution from an unidentified Maryland resident to the finance committee in March 1972 and "had exacted a commitment . . . that $50,000 of these funds would be transferred" back to Maryland for use in the presidential campaign.

The $50,000 loan was returned to Stans' committee July 26, 1972 with an additional $25,000 raised at the Agnew testimonial. The money was reported to the GAO at that time, although the initial $150,000 and subsequent loan were never reported because, the committee claimed, the money was collected and its disbursement was pledged before the April 7, 1972 reporting deadline occurred.

Lankler admitted June 6 that efforts at concealing the money were "stupid," but he defended the political strategy behind the decision: "It was political puffery to make it [the Agnew event] look as good as possible . . . We hadn't sold the house out. We knew the press would look at the success of the affair. Don't forget, Agnew was not yet on the ticket. We were anxious to make Agnew look as good as possible."

A county judge Nov. 19 fined the "Salute to Ted Agnew Committee" $2,000 after the committee entered guilty pleas to four counts of violating state election laws by reporting the Nixon re-election committee loan as individual contributions to the Agnew testimonial.

The GAO had accused the Maryland GOP organization July 5 of eight election law violations.

The Maryland Republicans were also accused of failing to report to the GAO $47,000 in corporate contributions received by the Agnew committee.

Vice President Agnew said July 5 that he "took no part, direct or indirect, in the solicitation, collection or reporting of the funds used by the state committee." He added that he had "no knowledge" of the fund transfer "until the matter was reported in the press."

Agnew Named as Probe's Target

The fact that Agnew himself was charged with exacting "kickbacks" was not confirmed until August.

Agnew accused. Agnew announced Aug. 6, 1973 that he had been informed that he was under investigation for possible violations of criminal law. The investigation, being conducted by George Beall, U.S. attorney for Maryland, involved the allegations of kickbacks by contractors, architects and engineers to officials of Baltimore County.

Another target of the Baltimore probe, William E. Fornoff, administrative officer of Baltimore County under four executives (including Agnew and his Democratic successor, incumbent Dale Anderson), was reported to have pleaded guilty to a minor tax charge in exchange for testimony against other targets—politicians and businessmen.

Agnew's statement was issued late Aug. 6 after the Aug. 7 issue of the Wall Street Journal went to press with a story of the investigation of Agnew concerning allegations of bribery, extortion and tax fraud. The Journal had advised Agnew's office of its story. After Agnew's statement of innocence was published, Knight Newspapers carried a report that the government was investigating allegations that Agnew received $1,000 a week from contractors while county executive and governor and a lump sum payment of $50,000 after he became vice president.

Agnew held a televised press conference Aug. 8 to deny wrongdoing. He called reports that he took kickbacks "damned lies."

Agnew said reports that he received payoffs from contractors were "false, scurrilous and malicious."

Asked if ever had "a political slush fund financed by Baltimore County contractors," Agnew said "never." Had he ever received money from contractors or businessmen for his personal use? "Absolutely not." Had anyone "threatened to drag you into this unless you helped to kill the Baltimore County investigation?" "I'm not going to foreclose the possibility that such things may have happened," he said. "Neither am I going to assert at this moment that they did." But no one had directly asked him to kill the probe, Agnew said.

"Defamatory" statements were "being leaked to the news media," he said, and he could not "remain silent." Whatever their source, he asserted, "I have no intention to be skewered in this fashion."

Agnew suggested that the allegations against him be "looked at as accusations that are coming from those who have found themselves in very deep trouble and are looking to extricate themselves from this trouble and are flirting with the idea that they can obtain immunity or reduced charges, perhaps, by doing so."

Agnew said he first heard rumors of the Baltimore probe in February. He said he had retained Washington attorney Judah Best in April to assure U.S. attorney Beall "I would in no way attempt to impede the investigation."

He said he believed he discussed the matter in April with Nixon's chief of staff, Gen. Alexander Haig. He had not discussed the matter directly with Nixon until Aug. 7, he said, when he had a "far-reaching" conversation of an hour and three-quarters, during which Nixon had "unequivocally" expressed his support.

Agnew fails in effort to get House to investigate. Agnew met Sept. 25 with Speaker Carl Albert and other House leaders of both parties to transmit a letter asking that the House, because of its "sole power of impeachment," investigate the charges against him.

Citing what he believed to be his constitutional immunity to ordinary court proceedings, Agnew said he "cannot acquiesce in any criminal proceeding being lodged against me in Maryland or elsewhere."

As a precedent for his request, Agnew relied on the 1826–27 case of Vice President John C. Calhoun, who had asked the House to inquire into newspaper allegations of profiteering on military contracts while Calhoun was secretary of war. A report by a select House committee had exonerated Calhoun.*

Noting that he had been the subject of "public attacks" that might "assume the character of impeachable offenses," Agnew called on the House to "discharge its constitutional obligation" and follow the Calhoun precedent.

After conferring with House Democratic leaders Sept. 26, Albert—without further comment—issued a statement which said in its entirety: "The vice president's letter relates to matters before the courts. In view of that fact, I, as speaker, will not take any action on the letter at this time."

House Republican Leader Gerald R. Ford Jr. (Mich.) called Albert's decision "unfortunate" and political but conceded that there would be little chance of a vote overturning it. Nevertheless, two Republican-sponsored resolutions were introduced Sept. 26 seeking some form of House inquiry. The first, by Rep. Paul Findley (Ill.), called for a select committee to determine whether the House should begin impeachment proceedings. The second, by John B. Anderson (Ill.) and William S. Cohen (Me.), called on Albert to appoint an "appropriate committee" to investigate whether any of Agnew's alleged improper activities occurred after he became vice president. (Anderson had said after Albert's statement that the speaker should have asked the Justice Department for such information before making his decision.)**

Fourteen Republican members of the

Judiciary Committee Sept. 27 introduced a resolution directing the committee to investigate the charges and report to the House within three months.

Majority Whip John J. McFall (D, Calif.) said Sept. 26 that part of the reasoning behind a quick decision on the Agnew request was the fear that Agnew's lawyers might attempt to block the grand jury not only on broad constitutional grounds but with the procedural argument that an inquiry was pending in the House. But the basic reasoning, according to Judiciary Committee Chairman Peter W. Rodino Jr. (D, N.J.), was that the question of the validity of Agnew's "broad claim of immunity from criminal prosecution" while holding office could not be resolved by Congress "but must be dealt with by the courts."

Effort to halt probe. Agnew's lawyers filed suit in federal district court in Baltimore Sept. 28 in an attempt to halt the grand jury investigation of the criminal charges against Agnew.

In a formal motion and accompanying affidavit, Agnew's lawyers launched a two-pronged attack on the investigation, citing constitutional restraints on the prosecution of a vice president in office, and charging the Justice Department with conducting "a deliberate campaign" of news leaks "calculated and intended to deprive [Agnew] of his basic rights to due process and fair hearing."

The suit asked the court to prohibit the

---

*The Calhoun case did not supply a complete parallel to the Agnew situation, since Calhoun was not the subject of a criminal investigation by a judicial body.

Calhoun had requested a House probe immediately after the Alexandria (Va.) Gazette, on Dec. 28, 1826, published—with editorial comment—a letter alleging that Calhoun had profited from an 1818 contract for a military fort.

The contract had been investigated in 1822 by a House committee, which had found no "facts which clearly stamp the transaction with a fraudulent character." The committee, however, expressed its "disapprobation of the conduct" of the War Department's engineering section.

As requested by Calhoun, the speaker appointed a seven-man committee to re-investigate the charges, and Calhoun temporarily relinquished his duties as presiding officer of the Senate. The committee issued its report Feb. 13, 1827, stating that Calhoun was innocent of the charge of having participated in War Department contracts. Calhoun resumed his duties the next day.

**Lawyers for Agnew and House leaders concerned with impeachment precedents were reportedly studying the 1872–73 case of Vice President Schuyler Colfax, who had been charged with illegal activities, all of which took place before he became vice president in 1869.

A House committee began hearings in December 1872 into charges that Colfax, while speaker of the House, had been given shares in Credit Mobilier, the company formed to build, with government subsidies, the Union Pacific railroad. During its probe, the committee discovered other incidents of possible bribery. Despite the evidence of misconduct, the committee concluded that impeachment was intended to remove a person from an office he had abused while occupying it. The committee decided not to impeach.

On the question of whether a vice president could be indicted while in office, some legal historians cited the 1804 indictment of Vice President Aaron Burr on state charges of murder in connection with the slaying of Alexander Hamilton in a duel in New Jersey. Both the crime and the indictment occurred while Burr was vice president. Burr was never arrested or prosecuted on the charge.

grand jury "from conducting any investigation looking to possible indictment" of Agnew and from "issuing any indictment, presentment or other charge or statement" pertaining to the vice president. The suit also petitioned the court "to enjoin the attorney general of the United States, the United States attorney for the District of Maryland and all officials of the United States Department of Justice from presenting to the grand jury any testimony, documents or other materials" that might be used to indict Agnew.

Citing the "awesome responsibility" of Agnew's office, the suit said the nation should "not be deprived of his services while he defends himself against an indictment voted by perhaps 12 of 23 grand jurors, or an information filed at the whim of a prosecutor."

The Justice Department filed its first reply Oct. 5 to Agnew's suit to stop the probe, arguing that a vice president could be indicted and tried on criminal charges while in office, but offering to submit the evidence to the House for possible impeachment proceedings before trial if Agnew were indicted.

Text of Agnew's Sept. 25 Letter to House

The Honorable Carl Albert
Speaker of the House of Representatives
Washington, D.C. 20515

Dear Mr. Speaker:

I respectfully request that the House of Representatives undertake a full inquiry into the charges which have apparently been made against me in the course of an investigation by the United States attorney for the District of Maryland.

This request is made in the dual interests of preserving the constitutional stature of my office and accomplishing my personal vindication.

After the most careful study, my counsel have advised me that the Constitution bars a criminal proceeding of any kind—federal or state, county or town—against a president or vice president while he holds office.

Accordingly, I cannot acquiesce in any criminal proceeding being lodged against me in Maryland or elsewhere. And I cannot look to any such proceeding for vindication.

In these circumstances, I believe, it is the right and duty of the vice president to turn to the House. A closely parallel precedent so suggests.

Almost a century and a half ago, Vice President [John C.] Calhoun was beset with charges of improper participation in the profits of an Army contract made while he had been secretary of war. On Dec. 29, 1826, he addressed to your body a communication whose eloquent language I can better quote than rival.

"An imperious sense of duty, and a sacred regard to the honor of the station which I occupy, compel me to approach your body in its high character of grand inquest of the nation.

"Charges have been made against me of the most serious nature, and which, if true ought to degrade me from the high station in which I have been placed by the choice of my fellow-citizens, and to consign my name to perpetual infamy.

"In claiming the investigation of the House, I am sensible that, under our free and happy institutions, the conduct of public servants is a fair subject of the closest scrutiny and the freest remarks, and that a firm and faithful discharge of duty affords, ordinarily, ample protection against political attacks; but, when such attacks assume the character of impeachable offences and become, in some degree, official, by being placed among the public records, an officer thus assailed, however base the instrument used, if conscious of innocence, can look for refuge only to the hall of the immediate representatives of the people."

Vice President Calhoun concluded his communication with a "challenge" to "the freest investigation of the House, as the only means effectually to repel this premeditated attack." Your body responded at once by establishing a select committee, which subpoenaed witnesses and documents, held exhaustive hearings, and submitted a report on Feb. 13, 1827. The report, exonerating the vice president of any wrongdoing, was laid on the table (together with minority views even more strongly in his favor) and the accusations were thereby put to rest.

Like my predecessor Calhoun, I am the subject of public attacks that may "assume the character of impeachable offences," and thus require urgent investigation by the House as the repository of "the sole power of impeachment" and the "grand inquest of the nation." No investigation in any other forum could either substitute for the investigation by the House contemplated by Article I, Section 2, Clause 5 of the Constitution or lay to rest in a timely and definitive manner the unfounded charges whose currency unavoidably jeopardizes the functions of my office.

The wisdom of the framers of the Constitution in making the House the only proper agency to investigate the conduct of a president or vice president has been borne out by recent events. Since the Maryland investigation became a matter of public knowledge some seven weeks ago, there has been a constant and ever-broadening stream of rumors, accusations and speculations aimed at me. I regret to say that the source, in many instances, can have been only the prosecutors themselves.

The result has been so to foul the atmosphere that no grand or petit jury could fairly consider this matter on the merits.

I therefore respectfully call upon the House to discharge its constitutional obligation.

I shall, of course, cooperate fully. As I have said before, I have nothing to hide. I have directed my counsel to deliver forthwith to the clerk of the House all of my original records of which copies have previously been furnished to the United States attorney. If there is any other way in which I can be of aid, I am wholly at the disposal of the House.

I am confident that, like Vice President Calhoun, I shall be vindicated by the House.

Respectfully yours,
Spiro T. Agnew.

In its memorandum to the court, the department contended that a president should not be made to answer criminal charges while in office, since such an action would "incapacitate" the government. In contrast, the department said, the office of vice president—while a "high one"—was not "indispensible to the orderly operation of government."

Pressure to Resign

Agnew giving up fight. By mid-September there appeared to be growing evidence that Agnew was becoming more and more convinced that he would have to resign.

David S. Broder reported in the Washington Post Sept. 18 that Agnew had held discussions recently on the "advisability of resigning voluntarily."

Agnew was intent on such a course, according to the report, first because of the pressure on his family from his current position, facing, as he was, grand jury investigation of possible criminal wrongdoing, and secondly because of "the plain indication that the White House—and apparently the President himself—wants Agnew out."

The Broder report stressed that Agnew staff members and his political supporters "expressed strong and uniform skepticism" that Agnew would, in fact, resign.

Reports identifying Sen. Barry Goldwater (R, Ariz.), a friend of Agnew, as the source of the Broder article were denied by Goldwater. "I don't think he's going to quit," Goldwater told reporters Sept. 18. "My hunch is that he's going to stay. I would advise him to fight it out."

At a news conference in New York Sept. 19, Goldwater expressed belief Agnew would consider resigning if he were indicted rather than have the country and himself go through the ordeal of a long impeachment process.

According to a report published by the New York Times Sept. 19, some high White House officials had been saying privately that it might be best for Agnew to resign and allow President Nixon to choose a new vice president.

According to a Washington Post report Sept. 20, a principal White House official had predicted Agnew's resignation in the

"next few weeks." That report was said to have come from an "Eastern Republican" who was told by the official that Agnew's resignation "would give the President an opportunity to set a whole new tone for the Administration."

However, Gerald L. Warren, deputy White House press secretary, denied the Post report Sept. 20 and said Nixon was not seeking to apply any pressure on Agnew to leave office.

House Dems would seek caretaker— The New York Times reported Sept. 21 that House Democratic leaders assured a group of freshmen Democratic congressmen Sept. 19 that a caretaker vice president would be sought by them if Agnew were to resign.

"The will of the [House Democratic] leadership . . . was to strive for a stand-in vice president who would be committed to bypass the 1976 [presidential] election," the Times quoted one of the meeting's participants.

Democratic National Chairman Robert Strauss Sept. 20 echoed the concern of the House Democrats when he commented that President Nixon should avoid a "tricky, treacherous situation" by choosing a "nonpresidential person."

Nixon comments. Publicly, however, Agnew still said he would not resign even if indicted, and President Nixon asserted at a press conference Oct. 3 that this attitude was "altogether proper."

Nixon said he had never requested Agnew's resignation and that Agnew's decision to remain in office "should be respected." The President drew a distinction between Agnew, who was "elected by all the people," and Nixon's appointed aides, who he had said would be suspended if indicted in relation to the Watergate case.

As for the charges against Agnew, Nixon noted they had been denied publicly and "to me privately on three occasions."

Responding to another question, Nixon said there had "certainly not" been any "contingency planning" for a possible replacement for Agnew should he leave office. Nixon again urged that Agnew be presumed innocent until his case was heard, adding that this presumption of innocence "should be underlined in view of his years of distinguished service as vice president; having in mind, too, the fact that the charges that have been made against him do not relate in any way to his activities as vice president of the United States."

Agnew's Departure

Agnew denies enriching himself. Following his resignation, Agnew delivered a nationally televised farewell address Oct. 15 to correct "misconceptions" relating to his resignation and acceptance of conviction for income tax evasion.

Agnew denied he had ever "enriched" himself in betrayal of public trust. He said he had resigned "to still the raging storm" of controversy swirling around his family and nation. He attacked the news media for "scurrilous and inaccurate reports" of leaks from a grand jury investigation and denounced his accusers as "self-confessed bribe-brokers, extortionists and conspirators."

And Agnew suggested reform of the system in which he became enmeshed:

■ Campaign financing, where "the opportunity for evil or the appearance of evil" should be removed by public funding, and state and local governments should "close the loopholes in their laws which invite abuse or suspicion of abuse in letting lucrative contracts to private business."

■ Grants of immunity, where control should be exercised over prosecutors trying "to coax from frightened defendants accusations against higher targets."

"As things now stand," Agnew said, "immunity is an open invitation to perjury. In the hands of an ambitious prosecutor it can amount to legalized extortion and bribery."

"If these beneficial changes do flow from our current national trauma," he said, "then the suffering and sacrifice that I've had to undergo in the course of all this will be worthwhile."

Agnew did not offer a point-by-point rebuttal of the charges in the Justice Department's case against him submitted to the court in Baltimore. Excepting his "decision not to contest the 1967 tax charge," he repeated his denial of wrongdoing. His plea to the court, he said, was "not an admission of guilt but a plea of no contest,

done to still the raging storm, delivering myself for conviction in one court on one count, the filing of a false income tax return for 1967." The "prosecution's assertion that I was the initiator and the gray eminence in an unprecedented and complex scheme of extortion is just not realistic," he said.

"For trained prosecution's witnesses," he continued, "who have long been experienced and aggressive in Maryland politics to masquerade as innocent victims of illegal enticements from me is enough to provoke incredulous laughter from any experienced political observer. All knowledgeable politicians and contractors know better than that. They know where the questionable propositions originate. They know how many shoddy schemes a political man must reject in the course of carrying out his office."

Agnew said "at every level of government in this country, local, state and national, public officials in high executive positions must make choices in the course of carrying out engineering and architectural projects undertaken for the public good."

He continued: "Public officials who do not possess large personal fortunes face the unpleasant but unavoidable necessity of raising substantial sums of money to pay their campaign and election expenses. In the forefront of those eager to contribute always have been the contractors seeking non-bid state awards.

"Beyond the insinuation that I pocketed large sums of money, which has never been proven, and which I emphatically deny, the intricate tangle of criminal charges leveled at me which you've been reading and hearing about during these past months boils down to the accusation that I permitted my fund-raising activities and my contract-dispensing activities to overlap in an unethical and unlawful manner. Perhaps, judged by the new post-Watergate political morality, I did."

His current net worth, Agnew declared, "less than $200,000, is modest for a person of my age and position. Every penny of it can be accounted for from lawful sources."

He spoke of "this technological age," where "image becomes dominant, appearance supersedes reality," where an appearance of wrongdoing whether true or false in fact is damaging to any man" and "fatal to a man who must be ready at any moment to step into the presidency."

"The American people," he said, "deserve to have a vice president who commands their unimpaired confidence and implicit trust. For more than two months now you have not had such a vice president. Had I remained in office and fought to vindicate myself through the courts and the Congress, it would have meant subjecting the country to a further agonizing period of months without an unclouded successor for the presidency. This I could not do. ... To put his country through the ordeal of division and uncertainty that that entailed would be a selfish and unpatriotic action for any man in the best of times. But at this especially critical time, with a dangerous war raging in the Mideast and with the nation still torn by the wrenching experiences of the past year, it would have been intolerable."

By taking the course of action he did, Agnew said, he spared his family "great anguish" and gave the President and Congress the opportunity to select a new vice president "who can fill that office unencumbered by controversy."

Agnew claims 'highest level' pressure. The Nashville (Tenn.) Banner reported Oct. 14, on the basis of an interview with Agnew, that Agnew did not wish to resign and that "terrific pressure" from the highest levels of the Nixon Administration forced him to take that course.

The report coincided with other press reports that the White House was not only the initiator of the plea-bargaining negotiations in the case but that it also had been instrumental in resumption of plea-bargaining sessions where the final settlement was reached.

During the suspension in the negotiations, Agnew, in Los Angeles had made a speech in which he had vowed not to resign if indicted. He also began diversionary actions against indictment of a sitting vice president and prejudicial news stories. A protracted legal battle involving constitutional issues loomed on these points before resolution of the criminal case.

Newsweek magazine, in its Oct. 22 issue, reported that the White House "evidently got the message" on the prospect of protracted preoccupation with the Agnew problem and "quickly reopened private contacts." With this development, and apparently bereft of White House support, Agnew was said to have forsaken his position and signaled approval for his attorney to reopen plea bargaining. The attorney was said to have contacted presidential counsel J. Fred Buzhardt, and it was arranged.

One last sticking point was the insistence of the prosecutors that Agnew be jailed, according to Newsweek, and "the persuader in the end was the President himself. Mr. Nixon, according to one high Administration source, cleared that one last concession to his veep" and Attorney General Elliot L. Richardson, emphasizing the trauma of an arduous trial or impeachment, finally prevailed upon the prosecutors to relent on the jailing.

One of the attorneys brought in by the department to defend its officials on the press leaks issue—James Thompson Jr., U.S. attorney for Northern Illinois—was widely quoted after his return to Chicago Oct. 10 as saying that he had "never seen a stronger extortion case," that "the man [Agnew] is a crook" and the country "well rid of him."

Ford Becomes Vice President

Search for Successor to Agnew

Following Agnew's resignation, the search for a new vice president quickly became the dominant issue at the White House and in Congress. Within two days, however, Nixon had announced his choice—Gerald R. Ford, Republican leader in the House of Representatives.

Nixon seeks advice. President Nixon consulted widely before deciding on his choice of a replacement for Agnew.

Nixon met Oct. 10, 1973 with Republican Congressional leaders. He talked with GOP National Chairman George Bush and Sen. James O. Eastland (D, Miss.), chairman of the Senate Judiciary Committee. Later he consulted with House Speaker Carl Albert (D, Okla.) and Senate Democratic Leader Mike Mansfield (Mont.).

The President asked for suggestions—up to three names each—from the Republican members of the House and Senate, the 19 Republican governors, members of the Republican National Committee and the GOP state chairmen. The suggested nominations were to be received in sealed letters, signed or unsigned.

Mansfield, who along with Albert also had been invited to present recommendations, offered his choices at a news conference Oct. 10: Former Secretary of

State William P. Rogers and former Sen. John Sherman Cooper (R, Ky.).

Other speculation on possible choices centered on former Treasury Secretary John B. Connally Jr., who became a Republican in 1973, Chief Justice Warren E. Burger, White House counselor Melvin R. Laird, New York Gov. Nelson Rockefeller (R), former Gov. William W. Scranton (R, Pa.) and Gov. Ronald Reagan (R, Calif.).

Senate GOP Leader Hugh Scott (Pa.) stressed after meeting with Nixon that the President was keeping an "open mind" on the selection. He also reported a qualification the President was applying to the selection, that the nominee should share his foreign policy views. House GOP Leader Gerald R. Ford (Mich.) revealed two other Nixon criteria Oct. 11: the nominee should have the ability to be president and stand a reasonable chance to gain confirmation. Ford was mentioned as another possible choice.

In the meantime, plans for an Oct. 12–29 Senate recess was canceled, and Congressional leaders began discussing procedures to handle confirmation of a vice presidential nominee, a situation unprecedented in the nation's history.

Ford Chosen

Ford replaces Agnew. Rep. Gerald R. Ford (Mich.), Republican leader in the House of Representatives, was named by

President Nixon Oct. 12, 1973 as his choice to replace Agnew as Vice President. The nomination, submitted to the Senate Oct. 13, was confirmed by 92–3 Senate vote Nov. 27.

Initial reaction to the nomination was overwhelmingly favorable in Congress, where a majority vote of approval in both houses was required for confirmation. Ford, 60, had been a member of the House for 25 years and House Republican leader since 1965.

The President's choice was a well-kept secret until he announced it at a nationally televised ceremony in the East Room of the White House attended by Cabinet members, Congressional leaders and other federal officials.

Nixon asked Congress "to act as expeditiously as possible" on the nomination "because of the great challenges we face at home and abroad." It was a time of "great dangers but also a time of very great opportunity," he said in his remarks announcing the nomination.

Nixon said the nation could be thankful that for the first time in 12 years it was "at peace with every nation of the world," and the economy was undergoing "a rising expansion." But "on the other side" the peace was threatened because of the outbreak of war in the Mideast and "the prosperity that we seek is plagued by an inflation."

Strong and effective leadership was required, Nixon said, and "it is vital that we turn away from the obsessions of the past and turn to the great challenges of the future. This is a time for a new beginning for America, a new beginning in which we all dedicate ourselves to the tasks of meeting the challenges we face, seizing the opportunities for greatness and meeting the dangers wherever they are at home or abroad."

Nixon expressed confidence that the dangers would be met and the opportunities seized if the public supported the effort, there was bipartisan support in Congress and "strong effective leadership in the executive branch."

He cited his criteria in selecting the vice presidential nominee: the person "must be qualified to be president," "one who shares the views of the President on the critical issues of foreign policy and national defense," and one "who can work with members of both parties in the Congress in getting approval for those programs of the Administration which we consider are vital for the national interest."

In his preliminary comments, Nixon described his yet-unidentified choice as a man who had served for 25 years in the House "with great distinction," a hint that evoked a standing ovation from the assembled guests.

After twitting the group that it should not "be premature, there's several here who have served 25 years in the House," the President further described his nominee as one who had "earned the respect of both Democrats and Republicans," a man "who has been unwavering in his support of the policies that brought peace with honor for America in Vietnam and in support of the policies for a strong national defense." He then identified Ford as his choice.

In his remarks following the President, Ford said: "Mr. President, I'm deeply honored and I'm extremely grateful and I'm terribly humble." He pledged to the President, to his colleagues in Congress and to the American people that, if confirmed, "I will do my utmost to the best of my ability to serve this country well and to perform those duties that will be my new assignment as effectively and as efficiently and with as much accomplishment as possible."

"I hope I have some assets," he said, "that might be helpful in working with the Congress in doing what I can throughout our country to make America a united America."

White House domestic adviser Melvin R. Laird said Oct. 16 that he had been unofficial campaign manager for Ford's nomination to the vice presidency and had told Nixon of the "broad support" in Congress for such a move. He said he had also told the President after soundings that any of the four potential nominees reportedly on the President's final list would have been confirmed—Ford, Gov. Nelson A. Rockefeller (N.Y.), Gov. Ronald Reagan (Calif.) and former Treasury Secretary John B. Connally Jr. Attorney General Richardson was said to have also been on the list but withdrew because of the impropriety of replacing Agnew after prosecuting him.

Ford bars '76 candidacy—Meeting with reporters in the House press gallery Oct. 13, Ford stated "as emphatically and as strongly as I can, I have no intention of being a candidate for any office—president, vice president or anything else—in 1976."

He also promised to make a full disclosure of his financial assets to Congress and to make available his income tax returns if requested.

Praise from both sides—The choice of Ford drew immediate praise from Congressional leaders of both parties. "I think I was the first in Congress," House Speaker Carl Albert (D, Okla.) said Oct. 12, "to tell the President that Jerry would be the easiest candidate to sell to the House. He's a very fine man to work with. I think he earned this."

The Senate party leaders, Mike Mansfield (D, Mont.) and Hugh Scott (R, Pa.), used the same adjective—"excellent"—in hailing the choice of Ford, although Mansfield added that the Senate would conduct "in-depth" hearings on the nomination. Scott observed that Nixon's choice "resolves many differences." A confirmation fight had been threatened by Democrats if the nominee had been a figure more prominently associated with presidential ambitions.

Congress Questions Ford

Ford hearings open. The nation's first Congressional confirmation hearings on the selection of a Vice President began Nov. 1 when President Nixon's choice for the post, House Republican leader Gerald R. Ford (Mich.), appeared before the Senate Rules Committee.

Committee Chairman Howard W. Cannon (D, Nev.) had opened the hearing saying the committee should not challenge Ford because of "a virtually unbroken record of favoring big business during his 25 years in the House," or because of a voting record "indicating an indifference to the needs of the disadvantaged." Such a challenge, Cannon said, would deny Nixon the right to "choose whom he wishes," someone "whose philosophy and politics are virtually identical to his own."

Under questioning by Cannon, Ford described himself as "moderate on domestic affairs, conservative on fiscal affairs, but a very dyed-in-the-wool internationalist in foreign policy."

Some committee members asserted that in view of the current clamor for the impeachment of Nixon, the committee's deliberations would go beyond Ford's qualifications to be Vice President. Sen. Claiborne Pell (D, R.I.) told Ford "you could be President next year if history continues to unravel itself along its current sad path."

Under questioning, Ford defended Nixon, but said the House Judiciary Committee's inquiry into impeachment proceedings "will be very helpful in clearing the air." "I don't think there are grounds," he said, "but that's a personal judgment."

Citing Ford's leading role in the 1970 attempt to impeach Supreme Court Justice William O. Douglas and his assertion that an impeachable offense was anything the House deemed it to be, Pell asked whether Ford's position had changed. Ford replied he was still of the opinion that "impeachment is, to a substantial degree if not entirely, a political decision."

In a prepared opening statement, Ford portrayed himself as a possible "conciliator and calm communicator between the White House and Capitol Hill." He said he was "very much mindful" of the fact that the "very same Americans" who gave Nixon an overwhelming margin in the 1972 election chose Democratic majorities in both houses of Congress.

Ford said he had made available all his political and personal financial records—"even our children's savings accounts." "I am not a saint," he added, "and I'm sure I have done things I might have done better or differently or not at all. . . . But I believe and hope that I have been honest with myself and with others, that I have been faithful to my friends and fair to my opponents. . . ."

In response to questions, Ford made clear that he differed with Nixon on some of the issues which had arisen from the Watergate scandal. On the question of executive privilege, Ford said he did not think a President had "unlimited authority" in the area of privilege. But, he added, "I don't think the Congress or the public generally have unlimited right to the personal confidential conversations between a President and his advisers" or to related documents. Pressed by Sen. Robert C. Byrd (D, W. Va.), Ford said "where you have allegations—serious allegations—of criminality, where those documents have a material impact on the guilt or innocence of an individual, it seems to me . . . they should be made available." He agreed with Byrd that "in the normal context" any concealment of information relating to commission of crimes would constitute obstruction of justice.

Ford was questioned closely on possible irregularities in campaign finances. He denied that he had "laundered" $11,500 in 1970 campaign funds, which he said had been turned over to the Republican Congressional Campaign Committee for the use of others. He conceded that the committee had then sent about $13,000 to his Michigan re-election campaign, but he said no attempt had been made to "evade the law."

Ford was also confronted with charges on his health and finances made by Robert Winter-Berger, a former lobbyist, in an affidavit to the committee and in the book "The Washington Payoff." Ford denied Winter-Berger's assertion that he had once undergone treatment by a New York psychotherapist, calling himself "disgustingly sane." He also denied that he had borrowed $15,000 from Winter-Berger.

Winter-Berger appeared before the committee at a closed session Nov. 7. Afterward, he told newsmen he stood by his allegations that he loaned Ford a total of $15,000.

Dr. Arnold Hutschnecker, the psychotherapist, testified Nov. 7 that he had not treated Ford, despite Winter-Berger's claim, and that during a 15-minute visit by Ford to his office, they had talked politics.

Ford completes testimony. Ford ended his testimony before the Senate committee Nov. 5.

Ford told the panel he believed President Nixon was "completely innocent" of any wrongdoing in the Watergate affair but said the "public wants the President to prove that, through documents and so forth." "Whatever doubts there are must be cleared up," Ford said.

"Can Richard Nixon save his presidency?" asked Sen. Mark Hatfield (R, Ore.). "I think so," Ford replied. "It's going to take a lot of help from a lot of people. And I intend to devote myself to that."

Ford also praised the news media as one of the "most significant contributors to exposure of the Watergate" scandal and said he did not share in the Administration's condemnation of the media. "You get a more equitable understanding by being open and frank with the news media," he told the committee.

Saying "there has to be a two-way street" between Congress and the executive branch, Ford advocated a bigger role for Congress in formulation of foreign policy. He would not restrict himself, if president, to consultation with White House advisers but would seek advice on difficult problems from members of Congress and department heads.

On other matters, Ford opposed forced busing of school children to attain racial balance but favored "compensatory education" for the disadvantaged. He advocated full disclosure of financial assets by presidents, vice presidents and the federal judiciary.

Opponents of Ford testify. Witnesses opposed to Ford's nomination began testimony before the Senate Rules Committee Nov. 14.

Joseph L. Rauh Jr., a vice chairman of Americans for Democratic Action, contended that a long and consistent record of opposition by Ford to civil rights and social welfare legislation was sufficient to disqualify him for the office. Rauh said Ford, currently House Republican leader, had usually tried first to cripple legislation, "and after he fails he then votes for the final version."

Rauh also charged Ford with "extreme partisanship and reckless disregard of constitutional principles" and a leading role in the attempted impeachment of Supreme Court Justice William O. Douglas in 1970.

Clarence Mitchell of the National Association for the Advancement of Colored People, who noted he neither opposed nor favored Ford's nomination, criticized Ford's voting record and "narrow-gauge approach" on civil rights issues. In reply to Rauh and Mitchell, committee member Robert P. Griffin (R, Mich.) read letters of endorsement from United Auto Workers President Leonard Woodcock and the black mayor of Ford's home town, Grand Rapids.

Rep. Bella S. Abzug (D, N.Y.) urged that confirmation be deferred until the House acted on the impeachment of President Nixon and until Congress decided whether to enact legislation for a special election if Nixon were to leave office.

John F. Banzhaf 3rd, a law professor at George Washington University, accused Nixon of "official misconduct" in the events leading to the resignation of former vice president Spiro T. Agnew, and argued that Ford's confirmation be delayed until the issue could be investigated.

House holds hearings. House hearings on the nomination began Nov. 15 before the Judiciary Committee. Several members urged that consideration be delayed because of the pending impeachment issue, and Ford was again questioned on his role in the Douglas case. Most questioning concentrated on issues arising from the Watergate scandal.

Describing his views as "similar to those of the President but not necessarily identical," Ford said Nixon should have released the White House tapes earlier and that he [Ford] had played a part in persuading Nixon to finally submit the tapes to the court. He added that he opposed the taping of conversations without the knowledge of everyone involved.

Ford admitted that Nixon had developed a "credibility image" problem because of Watergate and indicated he had urged Nixon to be more forthright on the issue with Congress and the public.

Questioned about Watergate and related matters, Ford said Nov. 16 that he had no prior knowledge of or involvement in campaign "dirty tricks" or other irregularities attributed to Administration aides. Ford insisted that his own campaigns had been completely honest, adding that he had planned to run for Congress "just one more time, and I'd just about decided I wouldn't spend a cent next time."

Ford's leadership qualities were questioned in testimony Nov. 19 by Rep. Michael J. Harrington (D, Mass.), who, while conceding Ford's "honesty and decency," said these qualities were "not enough." Committee member John F. Seiberling Jr. (D, Ohio) said Ford struck him as "more a messenger for the White House than a man coming to grips with big issues." Other members from both parties defended Ford's competence and intelligence and contended he had the capacity to rise to the leadership requirements of the presidency if the occasion demanded.

Ford submits financial data. Ford Nov. 15 submitted a statement to both Congressional committees showing a net worth of $256,378; assets were $261,078 and liabilities $4,700.

The assets included $162,000 in real estate; furnishings valued at $19,600; $1,282 in bank accounts; $13,570 in securities; insurance cash value of $8,487; contributed cost to Congressional retirement fund, $49,414; and "automobiles and other vehicles" valued at $6,752.

Liabilities included two items: $3,200 in short-term notes and $1,500 in "general bills outstanding."

Ford also disclosed to the House Judiciary Committee Nov. 15 his income and taxation figures for the years 1967–72. Total income was $454,667; net taxable income was $375,402; and taxes were $150,250.

Committees OK Ford. The nine members of the Senate Rules Committee Nov. 20 unanimously approved the nomination of Rep. Gerald R. Ford as vice president, after what Chairman Howard W. Cannon (D, Nev.) called "the most exhaustive examination of a nominee ever undertaken by a Senate committee."

In the House, the Judiciary Committee, after completing six days of hearings Nov. 26, voted by a 29–8 margin Nov. 29 to report Ford's nomination to the floor for action.

Opposition to Ford in the Judiciary Committee was centered among liberal Democrats. Rep. Elizabeth J. Holtzman (D, N.Y.) criticized Ford for a letter to a friend in Michigan, in which he called the citizen's lobby group, Common Cause, "a means of promoting the liberal Democratic viewpoint and . . . therefore dangerous to our way of life and our political philosophy."

Rep. John Conyers (D, Mich.) expressed apprehension about Ford's civil rights record in Congress, which Conyers termed an effort to cripple the legislation.

Rep. Jerome Waldie (D, Calif.) charged that Ford's effort to impeach Supreme Court Justice William O. Douglas in 1970 had been part of a plan drawn up by President Nixon after the Senate rejected the Supreme Court nomination of Clement F. Haynsworth Jr. Ford countered that the investigation of Douglas had been his own doing and that he had never discussed the matter with Nixon. However, Ford conceded, he had approached Attorney General John N. Mitchell concerning Douglas, but denied that the Justice Department's assistance had been of ultimate value.

Ford Confirmed, Takes Office

Congress confirms Ford. Gerald R. Ford was confirmed as vice president by 92–3 vote of the Senate Nov. 27 and by 387–35 vote of the House Dec. 6.

The senators opposed to Ford's nomination were Thomas Eagleton (D, Mo.), William Hathaway (D, Me.) and Gaylord Nelson (D, Wis.). Eagleton and Nelson indicated they questioned Ford's leadership ability, and Hathaway wanted to defer the nomination until the matter of President Nixon's role in Watergate had been resolved.

In his speech opposing Ford's confirmation, Nelson pointed out that "we are selecting a potential President. . . . On this appointment we are acting in a unique capacity as electors in behalf of 200 million American people." "On the most important issues of the past decade, including human and civil rights and the war in Vietnam, our [Ford's and Nelson's] respective positions have been fundamentally and irreconcilably at odds," Nelson said. "Our differences are of such significance that I cannot support his nomination just as in other circumstances he would not be able to support mine." But Nelson added that "I intend nothing I have said to be interpreted as a reflection upon Mr. Ford's character or his leadership qualifications within the Congressional environment. He is properly

respected as an honest and honorable member of Congress."

Sen. Charles H. Percy (R, Ill.), supporting Ford's nomination, also noted that "we are substituting our judgment, as 535 members of Congress, for months of campaigning, the convention process, and the votes of 70 million people." He added that those voting would realize "the insight in the words of the first Vice President of the United States, John Adams, who philosophized about his job, saying: 'In this job, I am nothing, but I may become everything.' . . ."

In the five hours of debate prior to the House vote, Ford drew bipartisan support on his personal merit and some opposition from Democratic liberals on public issues, such as his undeviating support for the Administration's war policy in Indochina and his voting record against civil rights legislation, Medicare, food stamps, federal aid to education and housing for the poor. The vote against confirmation included an almost solid black bloc; only one black present, Rep. Andrew Young (D, Ga.), supported Ford. He expressed reservation on Ford's civil rights record but hoped that he would act differently as vice president.

Rep. Peter W. Rodino Jr. (D, N.Y.), chairman of the House Judiciary Committee which conducted the hearings on the Ford nomination, voted against confirmation. While he respected Ford's character and integrity, Rodino told the chamber, his home district of Newark "typifies the plight which the cities of our nation face today," a plight of the poor and disadvantaged he said was unmet by the Nixon Administration. "I vote, not against Gerald Ford's worth as a man of great integrity," Rodino said, "but in dissent with the present Administration's indifference to the plight of so many Americans."

The debate was also marked by frequent reference to the possibility that Ford might succeed to the presidency should Nixon not serve out his term. Rep. Jerome H. Waldie (D, Calif.) said the situation was proceeding "to its inevitable result" of either impeachment or resignation. Rep. John B. Anderson (Ill.), chairman of the House Republican Conference, quoted the nation's first vice president, John Adams, that "'I am nothing, but I may be everything.'"

Ford takes oath of office. Gerald R. Ford was sworn in as the 40th vice president of the U.S. Dec. 6. Upon taking office, he pledged loyalty to President Nixon and dedication to the rule of law, cited the "living unity" of the occasion and promised "to do the very best" he could for America.

Ford became the first non-elected vice president to take office through the 25th Amendment to the Constitution. The office, vacant 17 times in the country's history, had been vacant since Oct. 10 when Spiro T. Agnew resigned before pleading no contest to a charge of income tax evasion.

Ford took the oath of office in the chamber of the House of Representatives before a joint session of Congress and in the presence of Nixon, who had accompanied him to the Capitol for the ceremony. With his wife holding the bible, Ford was sworn in by Chief Justice Warren E. Burger.

In attendance were other members of the Supreme Court, the Cabinet, ambassadors and other foreign dignitaries and visitors totaling 1,500 persons.

Prior to the swearing in, House Speaker Carl Albert (D, Okla.), who was next in succession to the presidency until Ford was sworn, announced confirmation by Congress and Ford's resignation as a Representative of the 5th District of Michigan.

In a brief speech upon assuming office, Ford pointed to the successful completion of the demands imposed by the 25th Amendment. "In exactly eight weeks we have demonstrated to the world that our great republic stands solid, stands strong upon the bedrock of the Constitution."

"I'm a Ford, not a Lincoln," he said. "My addresses will never be as eloquent as Mr. Lincoln's. But I will do my very best to equal his brevity and his plain speaking."

Ford said he would "try to set a high example of respect for the crushing and lonely burdens which the nation lays upon the President of the United States." "Mr. President," he declared, "you have my support and my loyalty."

Ford expressed "heartfelt thanks" to Congress and reaffirmed his conviction "that the collective wisdom of our two great legislative bodies, while not infallible, will in the end serve the people faithfully and very, very well."

Noting the attendance of members of the Supreme Court, he pledged to them, "as I did the day I was first admitted to the bar, my dedication to the rule of law and equal justice for all Americans."

He expressed the deep meaning to him of the presence of his wife and children. Noting the presence of members of the legislative, executive and judicial branches of government, Republicans and Democrats, he said:

"At this moment of visible and living unity, I see only Americans. I see Americans who love their country. Americans who work and sacrifice for their country and their children. I see Americans who pray without ceasing for peace among all nations and for harmony at home."

He promised his fellow citizens "only this: to uphold the Constitution, to do what is right as God gives me to see the right and within the limited powers and duties of the vice-presidency to do the very best that I can for America. I will do these things with all the strength and good sense that I have and with your help and through your prayers."

Watergate & Related Scandals

The Watergate Break-In

Richard M. Nixon resigned as President in August 1974 as a result of revelations of White House involvement in political chicanery during the 1972 Presidential election campaign. The disclosures began after the arrest of five men who had broken into the Democratic headquarters in the Watergate building in Washington in an obvious attempt at political spying. Nixon himself appeared to be increasingly implicated in the activities of White House personnel accused of involvement in this and other political crimes. The revelations took place at a time of—and added to—increasing estrangement between Nixon and Congress. They provoked growing demands for Nixon's resignation or impeachment. The whole "Watergate atmosphere," perhaps as much as the specific charges, ultimately made Nixon's abrupt departure from the White House inevitable.

Watergate break-in crew seized. Five men were seized at gunpoint at 2 a.m. June 17, 1972 in the headquarters of the Democratic National Committee in the Watergate office-and-hotel complex in Washington. Alerted by a security guard, police apprehended five men, along with cameras and electronic surveillance equipment in their possession, after file drawers in the headquarters had been opened and ceiling panels removed

near the office of Democratic National Chairman Lawrence F. O'Brien.

Those arrested and charged with second-degree burglary were: Bernard L. Barker, alias Frank Carter; James W. McCord, alias Edward Martin; Frank Angelo Fiorini, alias Edward Hamilton; Eugenio L. Martinez, alias Frank A. Sturgis, originally listed as Gene Valdes; Virgilio R. Gonzales, alias Raul Godoy. All but McCord were from Miami.

McCord, who had retired from the CIA in 1970 after 19 years with the agency, currently was employed as a security agent by both the Republican National Committee and the Committee for the Re-Election of the President.

Barker, apparently the leader of the raid, reportedly played some role for the CIA in the abortive invasion of Cuba in 1961 and had met in Miami in early June with E. Howard Hunt Jr., CIA official in charge of the invasion. Hunt recently was a consultant to Charles W. Colson, special counsel to President Nixon and other high White House officials. The White House confirmed this June 19 and said Hunt had ended his consulting work March 29.

Nixon's campaign manager, John N. Mitchell, said June 18 that none of those involved in the raid were "operating either on our behalf or with our consent."

49

Hunt, the five men seized in the Watergate and G. Gordon Liddy, a former presidential assistant and currently counsel to the Finance Committee of the Committee to Re-elect the President, were indicted by a federal grand jury Sept. 15.

According to the indictment: Liddy had been in telephone communication with Barker before the raid, and Barker with Hunt; McCord had rented a room at a motor lodge across from the Watergate from about May 5 through June 17, had bought a device to intercept wire and oral communications, had met with Liddy and Hunt May 26 and on May 27 had inspected with them the headquarters of Sen. George McGovern, then seeking the presidential nomination; Liddy gave McCord $1,600 in cash June 11–15; Liddy, Hunt, McCord and the four men from Miami, having in their possession a device to intercept oral communication and another to intercept wire communication, broke into the Democratic headquarters June 17 to steal property, tap phones and intercept telephone calls.

The indictment also accused Liddy, Hunt and McCord of intercepting phone calls from about May 25 up to or about June 16 in the Democratic offices, primarily the telephone of Robert Spence Oliver, executive director of the Associations of State Chairmen.

In announcing the indictment, Attorney General Richard G. Kleindienst said the investigation was "one of the most intensive, objective and thorough . . . in many years, reaching out to cities all across the United States as well as into foreign countries." John W. Hushen, director of public information for the Justice Department, said "we have absolutely no evidence to indicate that any others should be charged."

The seven men charged in the case pleaded not guilty Sept. 19 and were released on bonds ranging from $10,000 to $50,000.

McGovern commented Sept. 15 that "the indictments do point up the seriousness in the matter and what now needs to be pursued is how it was funded and whether there are violations there, which there seem to be." He called for "an impartial investigation conducted by somebody entirely outside the Department of Justice."

In a statement Sept. 16, McGovern accused Nixon of ordering a "whitewash," deplored the "questions left unanswered" by the grand jury and linked the affair to "the moral standards of this nation." "There has been a growing pattern of immorality," McGovern said, "associated with the Russian wheat deal, with the ITT case, with the handling of campaign funds, and now the latest revelation with regard to the invasion of the Democratic headquarters."

McGovern said the "unanswered questions" in the case were: "Who ordered this act of political espionage? Who paid for it? Who contributed the $114,000 that went from the Nixon campaign committee to the bank account of one of the men arrested, and that paid off the spies for their work? Who received the memoranda of the tapped telephone conversation?"

McGovern indicated disbelief that the seven men indicted "dreamed up and carried out this shabby scheme to spy on the Democratic party all on their own, with no authority from above."

Watergate tied to Nixon committee. A report by the General Accounting Office (GAO), Congress' auditing agency, cited a connection between one of the Watergate conspirators and funds from the Finance Committee to Re-Elect the President. The GAO reported Aug. 26, 1972 that it had found "apparent and possible" violations of the Federal Election Campaign Act by the Nixon committee involving amounts of up to $350,000.

The GAO cited failure to keep adequate records concerning (a) a $25,000 contribution made to the Republicans by Minnesota businessman Dwayne O. Andreas through Kenneth H. Dahlberg, chairman of the Minnesota re-election committee for Nixon, (b) $89,000 from four checks drawn on a Mexican bank and (c) the balance of some $350,000 in cash deposited May 25 to a media affiliate of the Nixon committee.

Funds from the Dahlberg check and the Mexican checks had turned up in possession of Bernard L. Barker.

At the time of his arrest, Barker was found to be in possession of bills traced to part of $114,000 he had withdrawn in cash from a Miami bank after having deposited the Mexican bank drafts and the Dahlberg check. Both instances apparently involved contributions from normally Democratic backers who desired anonymity. The Mexican bank checks were said to have come from GOP campaign funds collected in Texas.

The $25,000 contribution from Andreas, who had donated $75,000 to the Democratic presidential primary campaign of Sen. Hubert H. Humphrey (Minn.), was collected in cash near April 7. Andreas had put the cash in the custody of a third party in a Miami area hotel April 5. Dahlberg arrived April 7, when the hotel vault was closed, so he collected the money April 9 and, for security, converted it to a cashier's check to himself April 10, endorsed it and handed it to President Nixon's campaign finance chairman, Maurice Stans, April 11. Stans reportedly turned the check over without delay to Hugh W. Sloan Jr., treasurer of a separate GOP committee, the Committee to Re-elect the President (who resigned July 14), who turned it over to G. Gordon Liddy, lawyer for the Finance Committee to Re-elect the President (who was later dismissed).

Rep. Wright Patman (D, Tex.), whose Banking and Currency Committee was investigating the case, expressed concern Aug. 26 about news reports that Andreas was one of the investors granted a federal bank charter Aug. 23 in a Minneapolis suburb. Dahlberg was another of the five applicants for the charter.

The Washington Post June 3, 1973 provided this chronological account of the movement of the money that was "laundered" by routing through Mexico and then allegedly used to finance the Watergate break-in:

Gulf Resources & Chemical Corp. allegedly contributed $100,000 to the Nixon campaign April 3, 1972 in violation of federal campaign laws prohibiting political donations from corporations.

The money was routed from a Mexican subsidiary of Gulf Resources to the personal bank account of Mexico City lawyer Manuel Ogarrio, 82.

Ogarrio converted the money to four bank drafts totaling $89,000, and $11,000

in cash and passed the funds to Houston, where they were transported in an oil executive's suitcase to Washington April 6, 1972.

According to Maurice Stans, chairman of the Finance Committee to Re-elect the President, and committee treasurer Hugh W. Sloan Jr., the checks, which were received one day before the new federal reporting law for campaign funds took effect, were given to G. Gordon Liddy.

Liddy gave the checks to Bernard L. Barker. Barker returned the cash to Washington, but the checks were traced by the FBI in a routine investigation to Barker's Miami bank account.

Watergate prosecutor Earl Silbert received word from the FBI June 22, 1972 that Barker's account contained Nixon re-election committee checks.

■ E. Edward Hunt's wife, Dorothy, was killed Dec. 8 in a jetliner crash in Chicago. She was found with $10,000 in cash in her purse in $100 bills.

The Washington Post carried a report Dec. 8, based on an interview with a former White House personal secretary, that Hunt was one of a team of officials, known as the "plumbers," assigned by the White House to investigate leaks to the news media. A private, non-government telephone installed for use in the effort was apparently used almost exclusively for conversations between Hunt and Bernard L. Barker,according to the secretary. She said the bills for the phone service were submitted for payment to an aide in the office of John Ehrlichman, President Nixon's chief domestic affairs aide.

White House Press Secretary Ronald L. Ziegler confirmed the "plumbers" operation Dec. 12 and said the work was supervised by Ehrlichman, but he said he did not believe Hunt had worked on the project.

Secret Funds, Political Espionage & Sabotage

While Watergate was the 1972 campaign's most sensational scandal, the contest produced many other charges that political funds had been used for campaign espionage and sabotage.

Watergate & other spy operations. A former FBI agent disclosed Oct. 5, 1972 that he had delivered information obtained by espionage from the Democratic headquarters at the Watergate building in Washington to an official at the Nixon campaign office. In an interview published in the Los Angeles Times, the ex-FBI agent, Alfred C. Baldwin 3rd, said he had monitored telephone and other conversations at Watergate for three weeks while employed by the Committee to Re-elect the President, working from a room in a motor lodge across from Watergate.

The Washington Post reported Oct. 6 that Baldwin had informed the FBI that memorandums describing the intercepted Democratic conversations were sent to members of the White House staff and Nixon campaign staff.

The Post reported Oct. 10 that the Watergate raid was but part of a larger espionage and sabotage effort against the Democrats on behalf of the Nixon re-election effort. The newspaper quoted federal investigators as describing the intelligence operation by the Nixon campaign organization as "unprecedented in scope and intensity." The story reported attempts to disrupt campaigns of Democratic candidates for president. One such effort, according to the story, involved a letter used in the New Hampshire primary against Sen. Edmund S. Muskie (Me.). He was accused in it of having condoned use of the epithet "Canucks" in reference to Americans with French-Canadian background. Post reporter Marilyn Berger reported that White House aide Ken W. Clawson, deputy director of communications for the executive branch, had told her Sept. 25 that it was he who had written the letter. The Post reported that Clawson later denied authorship of the letter.

The Post article also related an account from three attorneys that they had been offered, and rejected, proposals to work as agents provocateurs on behalf of the Nixon campaign. The Post report said the FBI had information that at least 50 undercover Nixon operatives were at work throughout the country in an attempt to disrupt and spy on Democratic campaigns.

Milk funds, Watergate figures linked. Evidence revealed Oct. 28 in a suit, which charged that contributions made by dairy associations were actually political payoffs for an Administration-approved increase in the price of milk supports, linked those campaign contributions to Republicans implicated in the Watergate raid.

Testimony showed that E. Howard Hunt Jr., his wife, Dorothy, and Douglas Caddy served as chairmen of dummy committees used to secretly funnel the dairymen's contributions to the Nixon re-election effort. (Caddy, a lawyer, was contacted immediately after their arrest by those indicted for the Watergate break-in.)

Mitchell linked to secret GOP fund. The Washington Post reported Sept. 29 that former Attorney General John N. Mitchell controlled a secret Republican fund utilized for gathering information about the Democrats. The fund was said to have fluctuated between $350,000 and $700,000, and Mitchell was said to have approved withdrawals for almost a year before he left the Cabinet to become President's Nixon's campaign manager.

The Post said former Commerce Secretary Maurice H. Stans later was among four persons in addition to Mitchell permitted to approve payments from the secret fund.

A spokesman for the Committee to Re-elect the President said there was "no truth" to the charges.

The Administration Oct. 25 denied a new report linking H. R. Haldeman, President Nixon's White House chief of staff, with the secret fund, which was allegedly used in part to finance intelligence gathering and political espionage. The report, published by the Washington Post Oct. 25, said Haldeman was one of five persons authorized to approve payments from the GOP fund. The other four authorized to approve payments were said to be Mitchell, former Commerce Secretary Maurice C. Stans, Jeb Stuart Magruder, a former White House assistant to Haldeman and currently deputy director of the President's re-election campaign, and Herbert W. Kalmbach, the President's personal lawyer.

The secret fund was reported to have been used in part to pay for an undercover effort to discredit or hinder Democratic campaigns. Funds involved in financing the break-in at Democratic national headquarters in the Watergate building in Washington also reportedly derived from the secret fund, whose only record reportedly had been destroyed by a Nixon campaign official after the Watergate arrests. The General Accounting Office previously had reported the existence of a $350,000 fund in cash kept in a safe in Stans' office.

The Washington Post story Oct. 25 cited sources as federal investigators and accounts of sworn grand jury testimony taken in the Watergate case.

The report carried Haldeman's denial of the story as "untrue."

The story also was denied Oct. 25 by White House Press Secretary Ronald L. Ziegler and Nixon campaign director Clark MacGregor. Ziegler said Haldeman never had access to such a fund and, in fact, such a fund never existed.

GOP spying linked to White House. A report in the Oct. 23 issue of Time Magazine (made available Oct. 15) linked a Republican political sabotage effort against the Democrats directly to the White House. It said Los Angeles attorney Donald H. Segretti, previously identified as a recruiter for an undercover spy operation against Democratic campaigns, had been hired in September 1971 by Dwight Chapin, a deputy assistant to President Nixon, and Gordon Strachan, a White House staff assistant. Time said the information came from Justice Department files.

The report said Segretti was paid more than $35,000 for his services by Herbert Kalmbach, Nixon's personal attorney, provided by the Committee to Re-elect the President out of funds kept in the safe of Maurice Stans, chief political fund-raiser for Nixon.

According to the Washington Post Oct. 15, California attorney Lawrence Young, in a sworn statement, said Segretti had told him "Dwight Chapin was a person I reported to in Washington" and he received political sabotage and spying assignments from E. Howard Hunt Jr.

The New York Times Oct. 18 linked Segretti to a number of telephone calls made in the spring to the White House and to Chapin's home and to Hunt's home and office.

The Administration Oct. 16 rebutted the charges that a political sabotage and spying effort involved high Nixon aides. White House Press Secretary Ronald L. Ziegler called the charges "hearsay, innuendo and guilt by association" and said he refused to "dignify" them by discussing them. Clark MacGregor, chairman of the Nixon re-election effort, attacked the Post for using "unsubstantiated charges" to "maliciously" link the White House to Watergate.

Time magazine carried a report Nov. 6 that federal investigators had been told by Chapin that he had hired Segretti to engage in disruptive tactics against the Democrats and by Kalmbach that he had paid Segretti from cash kept in Stans' office.

Special GOP fund conceded. President Nixon's campaign manager Clark MacGregor confirmed Oct. 26 the existence of a special Republican campaign fund controlled by top Nixon aides. He said the fund, which he acknowledged could have amounted to as much as $350,000, had been disbursed for preliminary planning of Nixon's campaign and, in one instance, to gather information on possible organized disruption at GOP rallies in New Hampshire.

MacGregor, appearing on a (taped) television interview with Elizabeth Drew of the National Public Affairs Center for Television, denied that the fund had been used to finance a sabotage effort against the Democrats or that White House aide H. R. Haldeman had any tie whatever to the funds.

MacGregor identified Maurice Stans, Nixon's chief fund raiser, and G. Gordon Liddy, counsel for the Finance Committee to Re-elect the President, as two of the top Nixon aides having control over the special fund. The others he named were former Nixon campaign manager John N. Mitchell, Jeb Stuart Magruder, a deputy Nixon campaign manager, and Herbert L. Porter, an advance man for Nixon's re-election campaign.

Carpet industry gift charges. Sen. Warren G. Magnuson (D, Wash.) charged Oct. 6 that Maurice Stans, who headed the Republican fund raising operations, arranged to postpone federal flammability regulations for carpet manufacturers at a meeting held in Washington July 27 in order to obtain $94,850 in campaign gifts from Martin B. Seretean, chairman of Coronet Industries, Inc. of Dalton, Ga.

Magnuson alleged that Seretean acted "on behalf of the industry." Coronet, one of many carpet companies in the Dalton area, was a subsidiary of RCA Corp., of which Seretean was one of the three largest stockholders. Contributions from him in the form of 30 separate checks were received by the Finance Committee to Re-elect the President, which Stans headed, between Aug. 11 and Aug. 16.

Magnuson had been one of the principal sponsors of the Flammable Fabric Amendment of 1967, according to the Washington Post Oct. 6.

Implementation of testing and enforcement standards was being delayed by the Nixon Administration, Magnuson charged. He claimed Stans called the meeting to "appease the fears" of carpet manufacturers regarding enactment of more stringent federal regulations.

Stans said Oct. 6 that the meeting was limited to "technical industry matters that had no political purpose." Seretean was not among the industry representatives who attended. Stans, Charles W. Colson, a White House aide who had been linked with Stans to the Watergate break-in, and an Office of Consumer Affairs spokesman represented the Administration at the gathering.

GOP sabotage plot charged. Based on a preliminary examination of grand jury evidence, federal investigators believed that former top Nixon aide H. R. Haldeman had planned and coordinated an extensive, well-financed operation of political sabotage and espionage, beginning in early 1971 and continuing throughout the 1972 presidential campaign, in an effort to insure the nomination of Sen. George McGovern (D, S.D.) as the Democratic contender for the presidency.

The New York Times, reporting May 2, 1973 on this alleged Administration strategy, said White House and campaign committee officials had considered McGovern the weakest candidate President Nixon could face in the 1972 race and every effort was made to influence McGovern's selection as the Democratic party's nominee.

The government's case focused on Haldeman, who, working with the Committee to Re-elect the President, allegedly controlled three networks of intelligence agents. The Watergate bugging operation was only a small part of the overall campaign effort, investigators emphasized.

The GOP plot had a double aim—to deny the Democratic presidential nomination to Sen. Edmund S. Muskie (D, Me.) and to enhance the nomination prospects of McGovern. According to the government, Administration aides considered Muskie to be the President's strongest rival.

Government evidence showed that a Nixon agent had infiltrated Muskie headquarters in early 1972 and was able to steal, photograph and leak to the press confidential campaign documents.

Federal investigators were unable to assess the full impact of the sabotage effort on the 1972 campaign but Democrats had made numerous prior allegations that Republicans were responsible for inexplicable disruptions in the Muskie campaign and were guilty of smear tactics, causing embarrassment to Muskie, and the campaigns of Sens. Hubert H. Humphrey (D, Minn.) and Henry M. Jackson (D, Wash.).

The government case traced Haldeman's initial authorization of the sabotage operations to a substratum of Administration aides and minor re-election committee functionaries, all reporting ultimately to Haldeman:

■ President Nixon's personal lawyer, Herbert P. Kalmbach, was reported to have begun secret fund-raising efforts during early 1971 with the aim of financing Haldeman's sabotage activities.

■ In June 1971, a group of White House assistants called the "plumbers" were organized to discover the source of Pentagon Papers leaks to the press and to stop other leaks of confidential Administration information.

■ Haldeman's chief aide and the President's appointments secretary, Dwight Chapin, recruited Donald H. Segretti in mid-1971 to direct the espionage activities. Segretti made at least 20 contacts throughout 1971 and succeeded in establishing a network of an estimated 10 persons. These operatives were paid either directly by Kalmbach or with money routed to them through Segretti.

Kalmbach had been named previously as the "paymaster" of a $500,000 secret fund used for Segretti's operations.

■ Two Watergate case defendants, G. Gordon Liddy and E. Howard Hunt Jr., reassigned from the White House "plumbers" in early 1972 to the re-election committee, also recruited informers, especially in the Miami area.

■ During February 1972, Hunt and Liddy conferred in Miami with Segretti at a meeting arranged by Haldeman's aide, Gordon Strachan. According to the government, Hunt and Liddy began to assume increasingly important roles coordinating Segretti's operations, a function formerly performed by Strachan. Federal investigators cited the merging of White House and re-election committee personnel in the espionage activities as a key strategy move in the sabotage effort.

■ By March 1972, 30-40 paid informers were assigned by the GOP to the offices of Democratic candidates for the nomination and party officials. Muskie was no longer the chief target of attack, federal investigators said, charging that the sabotage operation had widened to include all principal Democratic contenders. According to the Times sources, the Administration considered that their most important victory in the plot to influence the Democratic nomination was the Florida primary in March 1972, won by Alabama Gov. George C. Wallace, in a campaign notable for its smear tactics and embarrassing incidents for Democrats.

Trials & Inquiries Disclose Abuses

Trial opens; Hunt pleads guilty. E. Howard Hunt Jr., a former White House consultant, pleaded guilty Jan. 11, 1973 to all six charges against him in the conspiracy trial of the seven defendants indicted in connection with the June 1972 break-in and alleged bugging of Democratic party national headquarters at the Watergate complex in Washington.

Hunt had offered the preceding day to plead guilty on three charges, but Chief Judge John J. Sirica of U.S. District Court in Washington said Jan. 11 he would refuse the offer, because of "the apparent strength of the government's case" against Hunt, and because the public must be assured "not only the substance of justice but also the appearance of justice."

The six counts, which carried a maximum sentence of 35 years, were conspiracy to obtain information illegally from the Democrats, breaking into and entering the Watergate headquarters, knowingly intercepting wire communications, attempting to intercept wire communications, attempting to intercept oral communications, and an additional breaking and entering charge.

The chief prosecutor at the trial was Assistant U.S. Attorney Earl J. Silbert.

Silbert's two-hour opening statement Jan. 10 depicted the Watergate incident as part of a well-financed espionage program against the Democratic party and Democratic presidential candidates. According to Silbert, G. Gordon Liddy, one of the defendants and at that time counsel to the Committee to Re-elect the President, had been given $235,000 by other committee officials, Jeb Stuart Magruder and Herbert L. Porter, to uncover plans for demonstrations against Republicans campaigning for Nixon or against the Republican National Convention, and for other "special intelligence assignments," including a probe of certain campaign contributions made to a Democratic presidential candidate.

4 more plead guilty. Four more defendants in the Watergate case pleaded guilty Jan. 15 to all counts of a federal indictment charging them with conspiracy, second-degree burglary and wiretapping. The four were Bernard L. Barker, Frank A. Sturgis, Eugenio Rolando Martinez and Virgilio R. Gonzalez.

The four pleading guilty Jan. 15 all denied that pressure had been put on them by "higher-ups," as Sirica phrased it in questioning them, or money offered them to plead guilty. Gonzalez and Sturgis, in response to further questioning, indicated, as Barker previously had in interviews, that their participation in the Watergate affair was based on a belief they were furthering the cause of Cuban liberation from Communist control.

A report that "great pressure" was being exerted upon Sturgis, Gonzalez, Barker and Martinez to plead guilty was carried by the New York Times Jan. 15 in an article by Seymour M. Hersh. Another report in Time magazine Jan. 22 said the Watergate defendants had been promised a cash settlement as high as $1,000 a month if they pleaded guilty, with additional funds to come after release from prison. Hersh had reported in the Times Jan. 14, that, according "to sources close to the case," at least four of those arrested in the Watergate raid were still being paid, by unnamed sources.

Liddy, McCord convicted. G. Gordon Liddy and James W. McCord Jr. were convicted by a jury in U.S. district court in the District of Columbia Jan. 30, 1973 of attempting to spy on Democratic headquarters in the Watergate.

The jury, which deliberated less than 90 minutes, found Liddy and McCord, former officials of President Nixon's political organization, guilty of conspiracy, second-degree burglary, attempted wiretapping, attempted bugging and wiretapping. McCord was also found guilty of possessing wiretapping and bugging equipment.

Liddy's defense contended that he thought the other defendants, five of whom were arrested during the break-in, had been engaged in a legitimate intelligence operation and he, like other officials at Nixon headquarters, was "on the safe side of the line of innocence."

McCord's defense was that he had not participated in the raid with "criminal intent" and was therefore not guilty as charged. The prosecution had charged that McCord was in the operation for financial gain and more power within the re-election committee.

A proposed defense argument that McCord had acted at Watergate out of "duress" to prevent harm to officials,

including President Nixon, was disallowed Jan. 24 by Chief Judge John J. Sirica, who dismissed it as "ridiculous."

Several times during the trial Sirica had interrupted examination of witnesses by both the defense and prosecution to conduct the questioning himself. In doing so Jan. 22, he said neither side was developing "all the facts." It was under probing by Sirica that Hugh W. Sloan Jr., former treasurer of the Nixon re-election finance committee, disclosed Jan. 23 that $199,000 in campaign funds had been paid to Liddy after verification from former Attorney General John N. Mitchell, also former Nixon campaign manager, and former Commerce Secretary Maurice H. Stans, Nixon's chief fundraiser.

Magruder testified Jan. 23 that about $235,000 had been budgeted by the Nixon organization for an intelligence operation, assigned to Liddy, to (1) learn plans of radical groups that might disrupt political rallies or inflict "possibly bodily harm" on presidential surrogates, and to (2) discover the intentions of demonstrators at the Republican National Convention.

One such assignment, he related, was to investigate reports that a Democratic presidential candidate known for his anti-pollution stand, presumably Sen. Edmund S. Muskie (Me.), had received money from a major polluter.

Senate authorizes probe. The Senate, by a 70–0 vote Feb. 7, 1973, resolved to establish a seven-member select committee—four Democrats and three Republicans—to probe all aspects of the Watergate bugging case and other reported attempts of political espionage against the Democrats in the 1972 presidential election campaign.

Sen. Sam J. Ervin Jr. (D, N.C.) was named chairman of the special panel Feb. 8. The other members were Democrats Joseph M. Montoya (N.M.), Herman E. Talmadge (Ga.) and Daniel K. Inouye (Hawaii) and Republicans Howard H. Baker (Tenn.), Edward J. Gurney (Fla.) and Lowell P. Weicker Jr. (Conn.).

A preliminary report on the same subject by a Senate panel Feb. 1 stated that the federal government had failed to conduct a substantial investigation. Sen. Edward M. Kennedy (D, Mass.), chairman of a Judiciary Committee subcommittee that had conducted the study, said his panel had found evidence that "strongly indicates that a wide range of espionage and sabotage activities did occur" during the recent campaign and "neither the federal criminal investigation nor the White House administrative inquiry included any substantial investigation of the alleged sabotage and espionage operations apart from those surrounding the Watergate episode itself."

Executive privilege. President Nixon issued a policy statement March 12 saying that members and former members of his personal staff normally would refuse to testify formally before a committee of Congress if so requested.

"The manner in which the President personally exercises his assigned executive powers is not subject to questioning by another branch of government," he argued. "If the President is not subject to such questioning, it is equally inappropriate [sic] that members of his staff not be so questioned, for their roles are in effect an extension of the presidency."

At the same time, Nixon said, it would "continue" to be his policy, "to provide all necessary and relevant information through informal contacts between my present staff and committees of the Congress in ways which preserve intact the constitutional separation of the branches."

Nixon pledged not to use executive privilege "as a shield to prevent embarrassing information from being made available."

At one point, he split the issue in half. His four Cabinet members who also held presidential titles, he said, would testify in their Cabinet role but not in their White House role.

The President had indicated at his news conference Jan. 31 a policy statement on executive privilege would be forthcoming. He wanted "a precise statement" of policy prepared so "you will know exactly what it is," he said. His "general attitude" was "to be as liberal as possible in terms of making people available to testify" before Congress and not to use executive privi-

lege "as a shield for conversations that might be just embarrassing to us but that really don't deserve executive privilege." He added that such cases as arose would be handled "on a case by case basis." "We are not going to be in a position," he said, "where an individual, when he gets under heat from a Congressional committee, can say, 'Look, I am going to assert executive privilege.' He will call down here and Mr. Dean, the White House counsel, will then advise him as to whether or not we approve it."

Senate challenge—A direct challenge to the policy was approved by the Senate Judiciary Committee March 13. It voted unanimously (9 Democrats & 7 Republicans) to "invite" the President's chief legal counsel, John W. Dean 3rd, to testify at its hearings on the nomination of L. Patrick Gray 3rd to become director of the Federal Bureau of Investigation (FBI).

Sen. John V. Tunney (D, Calif.), who proposed the invitation, said afterwards he thought it "quite improbable" that the committee would vote to confirm Gray unless Dean testified on matters related to him during the hearings.

Gray had supplied the committee March 12 with a requested list of contacts he had with Dean between June and September of 1972—33 of them, 28 by telephone, five in Gray's office. Gray previously had testified he supplied Dean with 82 FBI investigative reports on the Watergate break-in at Democratic national headquarters in 1972. Dean had conducted the White House investigation that cleared then-employed White House personnel of complicity in the raid.

Gray also had testified previously that FBI interviews of White House personnel concerning Watergate had been conducted in Dean's presence and that he had received from the FBI accounts of the agency's confidential interviews of employees of the Committee to Re-elect the President conducted without the presence of a committee lawyer. Several committee employees had requested the private sessions after committee lawyers had sat in on the first FBI interview.

Tunney told the Judiciary Committee March 8 one of the convicted Watergate defendants, G. Gordon Liddy, a former counsel to the Nixon committee, had been recommended for that post by Dean.

Nixon aide declines to appear—Presidential counsel Dean informed the Judiciary Committee by letter March 14 he would not appear before it for testimony. He offered to accept and reply to written questions from the panel that were directly related to the Gray nomination. He based his action on Nixon's March 12 statement that all members of his personal staff would decline such appearances.

White House Press Secretary Ziegler said later he did not consider Dean's refusal utilization of executive privilege but rather adherence to the constitutional separation of the branches of government.

Nixon reaffirms stand—The President reaffirmed his stand against a Congressional appearance by Dean at an impromptu news conference March 15.

Excerpts From March 12 Statement on Executive Privilege

The doctrine of executive privilege is well established. It was first invoked by President Washington, and it has been recognized and utilized by our Presidents for almost 200 years since that time.

The doctrine is rooted in the Constitution, which vests "the executive power" solely in the President, and it is designed to protect communications within the executive branch in a variety of circumstances in time of both war and peace.

Without such protection, our military security, our relations with other countries, our law enforcement procedures and many other aspects of the national interest could be significantly damaged and the decision-making process of the executive branch could be impaired.

The general policy of this Administration regarding the use of executive privilege during the next four years will be the same as the one we have followed during the past four years: Executive privilege will not be used as a shield to prevent embarrassing information from being made available but will be exercised only in those particular instances in which disclosure would harm the public interest.

During the first four years of my Presidency, hundreds of Administration officials spent thousands of hours testifying before committees of the Congress. Secretary of Defense [Melvin] Laird, for instance, made 86 separate appearances before Congressional committees, engaging in over 327 hours of testimony.

By contrast, there were only three occasions during the first term of my Administration when executive privilege was invoked anywhere in the executive branch in response to a Congressional request for information. These facts speak not of a closed Administration but of one that is pledged to openness and is proud to stand on its record.

Requests for Congressional appearances by members of the President's personal staff present a different situation and raise different considerations. Such requests have been relatively infrequent through the years, and in past Administrations they have been routinely declined.

I have followed that same tradition in my Administration, and I intend to continue it during the remainder of my term.

Under the doctrine of separation of powers, the manner in which the President personally exercises his assigned executive powers is not subject to questioning by another branch of government. If the President is not subject to such questioning, it is equally inappropriate [sic] that members of his staff not be so questioned, for their roles are in effect an extension of the Presidency.

This tradition rests on more than constitutional doctrine: It is also a practical necessity. To insure the effective discharge of the executive responsibility, a President must be able to place absolute confidence in the advice and assistance offered by the members of his staff. And in the performance of their duties for the President, those staff members must not be inhibited by the possibility that their advice and assistance will ever become a matter of public debate, either during their tenure in government or at a later date. Otherwise, the candor with which advice is rendered and the quality of such assistance will inevitably be compromised and weakened.

What is at stake, therefore, is not simply a question of confidentiality but the integrity of the decision-making process at the very highest levels of our government.

As I stated in my press conference on Jan. 31, the question of whether circumstances warrant the exercise of executive privilege should be determined on a case-by-case basis.

In making such decisions, I shall rely on the following guidelines:

1. In the case of a department or agency, every official shall comply with a reasonable request for an appearance before the Congress, provided that the performance before the Congress, provided that the performance of the duties of his office will not be seriously impaired thereby. If the official believes that a Congressional request for a particular document or for testimony on a particular point raises a substantial question as to the need for invoking executive privilege, he shall comply with the procedures set forth in my memorandum of March 24, 1969. Thus, executive privilege will not be invoked until the compelling need for its exercise has been clearly demonstrated and the request has been approved first by the attorney general and then by the President.

2. A Cabinet officer or any other governmental official who also holds a position as a member of the President's personal staff shall comply with any reasonable request to testify in his non-White House capacity, provided that the performance of his duties will not be seriously impaired thereby. If the official believes that the request raises a substantial question as to the need for invoking executive privilege, he shall comply with the procedures set forth in my memorandum of March 24, 1969.

3. A member or former member of the President's personal staff normally shall follow the well-established precedent and decline a request for a formal appearance before a committee of the Congress. At the same time, it will continue to be my policy to provide all necessary and relevant information through informal contacts between my present staff and committees of the Congress in ways which preserve intact the constitutional separation of the branches.

Nixon said he felt it was his duty to defend the principle of separation of powers. If the Senate "feels that they want a court test" on the issue "we would welcome it," he said. "Perhaps this is the time to have the highest court of the land make a definitive decision with regard to this matter."

The President added that he felt the court "will uphold, as it always usually has, the great constitutional principle of separation of powers rather than to uphold the Senate."

Noting "some speculation to the effect that the Senate might hold Mr. Gray as hostage to a decision on Mr. Dean," Nixon said he could not believe that "such responsible members" of the Senate would do that. Dean had what the President called a "double privilege," a lawyer-client relationship as well as a presidential privilege because he had served as counsel to a number of people on the White House staff.

Dean would furnish "pertinent information" to Congress when it was requested, Nixon said, but he was "not going to have the counsel to the President" testify in a formal session before Congress.

The President said his Administration had "not drawn a curtain down and said that there could be no information furnished by members of the White House staff because of their special relationship to the President."

"All we have said," he continued, "is that it must be under certain circumstances, certain guidelines, that do not infringe upon or impair the separation of powers."

Within these bounds, he said, Dean would "be completely forthcoming. Something that other Administrations have totally refused to do until we got here, and I am very proud of the fact that we are forthcoming. . . .'"

To a question about whether the executive privilege extended to personnel in the re-election committee, Nixon said "none of them have the privilege" and none would refuse testimony when asked.

Executive privilege 'a myth'—At a two-day Capitol Hill conference on the conflict between the President and Congress, University of Washington Professor Arthur Bester advised members of Congress attending the symposium March 8 that the theory of "executive privilege" was "a myth" and that White House aides could be held in contempt of Congress and put in jail for refusing witness.

The first use of executive privilege was attributed to President Washington in 1796 when he refused the House's request for documents on the Jay Treaty with Great Britain. Noting the absence of constitutional authority for the House to pass on treaties, Washington contended "a just regard to the Constitution and to the duty of my office" forbade compliance.

Nixon sets new probe, yields on executive privilege. Nixon announced April 17, 1973 that there had been "major developments" from a new probe he had initiated into the Watergate case.

The President also announced he had agreed to permit testimony under certain conditions by his aides before a Senate investigating committee. "I believe," he said, an agreement had been reached with the committee on ground rules for the testimony which would "preserve," he said, "the separation of powers without suppressing the fact."

In his statement, Nixon said he had begun "intensive new inquiries into this whole matter" March 21 "as a result of serious charges which came to my attention, some of which were publicly reported." He said he had met Sunday, April 15 in the Executive Office Building adjoining the White House with Attorney General Richard G. Kleindienst and Assistant Attorney General Henry Peterson "to review the facts which had come to me in my investigation and also to review the progress" of a separate investigation by the Justice Department.

He stated "that there have been major developments in the case" but said "it would be improper to be more specific now except to say that real progress has been made in finding the truth."

Nixon also said:

For several weeks, Senator Ervin and Senator Baker and their counsel have been in contact with White House representatives John Ehrlichman and Leonard Garment. They have been talking about ground rules which would preserve the separation of powers without suppressing the fact.

I believe now an agreement has been reached which is satisfactory to both sides. The committee ground rules as adopted totally preserve the doctrine of separation of powers. They provide that the appearance by a witness may, in the first instance, be in executive session, if appropriate.

Second, executive privilege is expressly reserved and may be asserted during the course of the questioning as to any questions. . . .

All members of the White House staff will appear voluntarily when requested by the committee. They will testify under oath and they will answer fully all proper questions.

I should point out that this arrangement is one that covers this hearing only in which wrongdoing has been charged. This kind of arrangement, of course, would not apply to other hearings. Each of them will be considered on its merits. . . .

If any person in the executive branch or in the government is indicted by the grand jury, my policy will be to immediately suspend him. If he is convicted, he will, of course, be automatically discharged.

I have expressed to the appropriate authorities my view that no individual holding, in the past or at present, a position of major importance in the Administration should be given immunity from prosecution.

The judicial process is moving ahead as it should; and I shall aid it in all appropriate ways and have so informed the appropriate authorities.

As I have said before and I have said throughout this entire matter, all government employes and especially White House staff employes are expected fully to cooperate in this matter. I condemn any attempts to cover up in this case, no matter who is involved.

After Nixon's statement, White House Press Secretary Ronald L. Ziegler said the President's previous statements denying Watergate involvement by White House staff members were now "inoperative" since they were based on "investigations prior to the developments announced today."

Payoffs to defendants alleged. James W. McCord Jr. was reported April 9 to have told a federal grand jury investigating the Watergate case that cash payments had been paid to defendants in the criminal case for their silence and pressure applied for guilty pleas.

He was also reported to have named, on a hearsay basis, Kenneth W. Parkinson, then attorney for the Committee to Re-elect the President, as the person he believed responsible for applying the pressure and channeling the payments. The New York Times confirmed the testimony, originally leaked from "sources close to the case," in a telephone interview with McCord.

The reports noted that McCord's testimony concerning Parkinson's alleged role was based on talks with Mrs. Dorothy Hunt, who was named by McCord as the conduit for the cash payments.

Parkinson, currently a member of a Washington law firm, was also contacted by the Times and said the allegations against him were "absolutely false."

The amount of the cash payments was said to be $1,000 per month for each of the four defendants arrested with McCord at the Watergate building June 17, 1972 during the bugging operation inside the Democratic national headquarters, and, according to the Washington Post April 10, $3,000 a month for McCord.

Mitchell involvement alleged—According to a Post report April 12, also confirmed by McCord, of his further testimony before the grand jury, McCord claimed that convicted co-conspirator G. Gordon Liddy had told him transcripts of wire-tapped conversations of Democratic officials had been hand-carried to former Attorney General John N. Mitchell. Liddy also told him, according to the report, that Mitchell had ordered a priority list of electronic eavesdropping operations against the Democrats—first the Watergate headquarters, then the campaign headquarters of Sen. George S. McGovern, then the Miami hotel rooms to be occupied by presidential candidates and party officials attending the national convention.

Mitchell's denial of both charges was relayed through the Committee to Re-elect the President.

McCord's lawyer, Bernard W. Fensterwald, told reporters April 9 that McCord had no first-hand knowledge that anybody "higher up" than Liddy knew of the Watergate operation.

The Washington Post reported April 19 that Jeb Stuart Magruder, Mitchell's former aide in the Nixon re-election campaign, had told federal prosecutors April 14 that he, Mitchell, Liddy and presidential counsel John W. Dean 3rd had planned and approved the Watergate wiretapping at a meeting in the attorney general's office in February 1972.

Magruder was said to have told the prosecutors that Mitchell and Dean later arranged to buy the silence of the seven convicted Watergate conspirators.

A New York Times report April 20 said Mitchell had disclosed in private conversations with friends that he had participated in three meetings on the proposed wiretapping plan—on Jan. 24 and Feb. 4, 1972 while he was attorney general and in March 1972, when he was manager of the Nixon re-election campaign. Mitchell was said to have confirmed that Liddy and Magruder had discussed spying on the Democrats at these meetings, but Mitchell reportedly said he had rejected the plans on each occasion. Dean was said to have been present at one or more of the sessions. Mitchell appeared before the Watergate grand jury April 20 and confirmed the substance of the report in the Times.

Mitchell told reporters later April 20 that he had "heard discussions" of plans to spy on the Democrats during the 1972 presidential campaign but he had "never approved any bugging plans during any period during the campaign."

The April 20 Times report said that Dean allegedly had supervised cash payments of more than $175,000 in GOP funds to the Watergate defendants and their lawyers. The allegation was denied later April 20 as "absolutely untrue" by Dean's lawyer, Robert C. McCandless of Washington.

Clemency offer to McCord reported. Following a May 13 Los Angeles Times report that he had offered executive clemency to James W. McCord, Treasury official John J. (Jack) Caulfield May 13 asked for and was granted "administrative leave" from his post as assistant director for criminal enforcement of the alcohol, tobacco, and firearms division.

Caulfield, 44, an ex-White House aide, reportedly met with McCord twice in January, while McCord was on trial for the Watergate burglary. Caulfield allegedly told McCord if he kept silent during the trial and accepted imprisonment, he could expect executive clemency in 10 or 11 months, the Times reported.

Dean's disclosures. Reports that John W. Dean 3rd had gone to the federal Watergate prosecutors April 6 with information about the break-in and about later developments were published by the Washington Post April 27 and in the April 30 edition of Time magazine. Time said the information had provided the first corroboration of the largely hearsay testimony of James W. McCord Jr.

The Post report said Dean had divulged everything he knew about the bugging and subsequent White House coverup of the involvement of Presidential aides.

The Post account, attributed to Dean's associates, said he had told President Nixon March 20 that to "save the presidency" Dean, Nixon chief of staff H. R. Haldeman and Ehrlichman would have to reveal all they knew about the case and might have to face jail terms. The story said there was no suggestion that Haldeman or Ehrlichman had approved the Watergate operation. It said their role lay in a possible cover-up of White House aides' involvement in the bugging and in authorization of Dean's role in the cover-up.

According to the Post sources, Dean told Nixon March 20 that Haldeman and Ehrlichman had instructed him after June 17, 1972 never to discuss the bugging with the President and they would transmit any messages that Dean cared to convey.

Sloan charges proposals of perjury. Sworn testimony by Hugh W. Sloan Jr. cited an attempt to persuade him to perjure himself concerning the amount of money he paid G. Gordon Liddy.

The information was contained in Sloan's deposition in Watergate civil litigation. A transcript was made public May 10.

Sloan had testified previously that he paid $199,000 in campaign cash to Liddy. In his deposition, he said suggestions to testify to a much smaller payment—$70,-000 or $80,000 was suggested first, later a $40,000 figure—came from Jeb Stuart Magruder, then deputy director of the Committee to Re-elect the President. Sloan told of meeting with GOP campaign aide Frederick C. LaRue and emerging with the impression the committee was moving in that direction, to get him to "tell an untrue story."

Sloan said he attempted to apprise several Administration officials of the apparent problem concerning the funds. He said he suggested to Nixon aide John D. Ehrlichman that there was a problem about the funds and their use, possibly for the break-in, but Ehrlichman had told him "to go no further, that he didn't want any of the details" and "his position was that he would have to take executive privilege until after the election in any case."

Sloan said he approached GOP fundraiser Maurice H. Stans prior to the break-in with a complaint the funds being paid "were mounting up without any knowledge on our part of what, in fact, had happened to the money." Stans "indicated to me at that point," Sloan said, "in response to any inquiry along those lines that 'I don't want to know and you don't want to know.'"

Watergate: Low point in tactics. The Fair Campaign Practices Committee's report on the 1972 presidential campaign, released May 26, termed the Watergate scandal and related charges of political sabotage and espionage conducted by the Nixon re-election committee "a conscious conspiracy to violate laws, to manipulate voters and to make a mockery of the democratic system of self-government."

"Theft, spying, sabotage and subversion are not the tactics of the political profession. In nearly 20 years of studying the political processes, the Fair Campaign Committee has uncovered no campaign tactics comparable in extent or in potential damage to a free, self-governing society."

Nixon Aides Lose Posts

The disclosure of evidence increasingly connecting Nixon Administration personnel to the Watergate scandal forced many of the President's close associates out of their government jobs.

Gray resigns FBI post. L. Patrick Gray 3rd announced his resignation as acting director of the Federal Bureau of Investigation April 27, 1973.

Gray said he was resigning, effective immediately, "as a consequence" of reports he had burned files removed from the office safe of E. Howard Hunt Jr.

The reports of Gray's connection with the Watergate case originated with the New York Daily News late April 26 and were confirmed by the New York Times and other newspapers the next morning.

According to the Times, the Hunt files were handed to Gray at a White House meeting June 28, 1972 with John D. Ehrlichman, assistant to the President for domestic affairs, and John W. Dean 3rd, counsel to the President. The story, at-

tributed to Sen. Lowell P. Weicker Jr. (R, Conn.), a close friend of Gray, reported that Dean had cautioned the files "should never see the light of day."

While he could not swear that either Dean or Ehrlichman "ordered" destruction of the papers, Gray was said to have remembered Dean describing the files as "political dynamite" but not dealing with the Watergate bugging. Gray accepted receipt of the files according to the account and then, after Dean left, had a discussion with Ehrlichman about Watergate probe news leaks, the original purpose of his White House appointment. Gray reportedly took the Hunt files home, where they remained until July 3 when he took them to FBI headquarters, tore them up without looking at them and put them in his FBI "burn bag,' a container whose contents were destroyed at the end of each day.

Gray, serving as acting FBI director since May 1972, had been nominated by Nixon Feb. 17, 1973 as permanent director, but the nomination had been opposed by several Democratic members of the Senate Judiciary Committee on the ground that Gray had been "openly partisan" during the 1972 presidential election.

Sen. Robert C. Byrd (D, W. Va.), Gray's most vocal oponent, also objected to Gray because of charges that the FBI had supplied the White House and the Nixon campaign committee with information gathered in its investigation of the Watergate break-in.

Gray acknowledged Feb. 28 that extensive records of the FBI probe had been made available to the White House and claimed that the late FBI director, J. Edgar Hoover, had provided other Administrations with progress reports of important investigations.

Gray said he based his decision on advice from his legal staff after John W. Dean 3rd, a presidential counsel conducting a separate White House inquiry into the Watergate breakin, "asked us to give him what we had to date." The request was made in August 1972, according to Gray.

Gray said he had provided Attorney General Richard G. Kleindienst with the report and added, "I have every reason to believe that it then went to the White House."

Haldeman, Ehrlichman, Kleindienst & Dean resign.

The resignations of four top Nixon Administration officials were announced April 30, 1973 as a consequence of the widening Watergate affair.

Those who resigned were H. R. Haldeman, President Nixon's chief of staff; John D. Ehrlichman, Nixon's assistant for domestic affairs; Attorney General Richard G. Kleindienst and John W. Dean 3rd, Nixon's counsel.

In their letters of resignation, Haldeman and Ehrlichman said their ability to carry out their daily duties had been undermined by the Watergate disclosures and the time required to deal with them.

Kleindienst said he had resigned because of the apparent implication in "Watergate and related cases" of persons "with whom he has had a close personal and professional association."

The President said without amplification that he had "requested and accepted" the resignation of his counsel, Dean.

Kleindienst was replaced as attorney general by Secretary of Defense Elliot L. Richardson.

Nixon takes responsibility.

President Nixon, in a nationally televised broadcast April 30, accepted responsibility for the Watergate affair and told the American people that he was not personally involved in the political espionage or the attempt at coverup.

The President reiterated this determination throughout his speech. "There can be no whitewash at the White House," he said, and he would do "everything in my power" to insure that the guilty were "brought to justice" and that such abuses as occurred at Watergate were "purged from the political processes." When he had assumed control March 21 over "intensive new inquiries" into the Watergate affair, Nixon said, he was determined to "get to the bottom of the matter" and have the truth "fully brought out."

Nixon said the new probe was begun after he received new information which persuaded him "there was a real possibility" of involvement by members of his Administration and indicated "there had been an effort to conceal the facts both from the public . . . and from me."

When he first learned from news reports of the Watergate break-in June 17, 1972, Nixon said, "I was appalled at this senseless, illegal action and I was shocked to learn that employes of the re-election committee were apparently among those guilty." He said he had immediately ordered an investigation "by appropriate government authorities," and had repeatedly asked those conducting it "whether there was any reason to believe that members of my Administration were in any way involved."

"I received repeated assurances that there were not," Nixon said. Because of that and because he believed the "continuing reassurances" and had faith in the persons giving them, he had "discounted" press reports that "appeared to implicate" members of his Administration or GOP campaign officials.

The President said he had remained convinced that the denials were true until March, and "the comments I made during this period, the comments made by my press secretary in my behalf, were based on the information provided to us at the time we made those comments."

The President said those who committed criminal acts must "bear the liability and pay the penalty." "For the fact that alleged improper actions took place within the White House or within my campaign organization," he continued, "the easiest course would be for me to blame those to whom I delegated the responsibility to run the campaign. But that would be a cowardly thing to do."

"I will not place the blame on subordinates," Nixon declared, "on people whose zeal exceeded their judgment and who may have done wrong in a cause they deeply believed to be right. In any organization the man at the top must bear the responsibility. That responsibility, therefore, belongs here in this office. I accept it."

"I know," Nixon said, "that it can be very easy under the intensive pressures of a campaign for even well-intentioned people to fall into shady tactics, to rationalize this on the grounds that what is at stake is of such importance to the nation that the end justifies the means. And both of our great parties have been guilty of such tactics."

Moss broaches impeachment question —Rep. John E. Moss (D, Calif.) brought up the possibility April 30 of an impeachment inquiry, reportedly discussing the matter with House Democratic leaders. "I'm not saying we should do it, but we should prepare ourselves to have all the facts," Moss argued.

Nixon rejects resignation bids—White House Press Secretary Ronald L. Ziegler told reporters May 18 that President Nixon had no intention of resigning despite speeches delivered May 17 by two prominent Democrats, Sargent Shriver, the Democratic candidate for vice president in 1972, and Joseph A. Califano Jr., a former key aide to President Johnson, calling for Nixon's resignation because of the widening Watergate scandal.

Ziegler repeated a denial issued May 7 regarding Nixon's involvement in a Watergate cover-up, saying "the President did not participate in any way, or have any knowledge regarding the cover-up and at no time authorized anyone to represent him in offering executive clemency."

The denial followed shortly after convicted Watergate defendant James W. McCord Jr. charged he had been offered executive clemency with the full knowledge of the President.

CIA involvement was sought. High Administration officials sought to involve the Central Intelligence Agency (CIA) in the Watergate affair, according to testimony presented to the Senate Armed Services Committee. The committee was inquiring into the CIA's involvement in domestic undercover work, which was barred under the 1947 National Security Act.

The hearings were closed, but Sen. Stuart Symington (D, Mo.), the committee's acting chairman, reported May 14, 1973, after the first session, on some of the disclosures produced.

On the basis of testimony by Lt. Gen. Vernon A. Walters, deputy director of the CIA, Symington reported that the White House aides involved in the apparent attempt to compromise the CIA were ex-White House aides H.R. Haldeman, John D. Ehrlichman and John W. Dean 3rd.

"Ehrlichman, and Haldeman—particularly Haldeman," Symington said, "were up to their ears in this, along with Dean, in trying to involve the CIA in this whole Watergate mess."

In releasing a summary of Walters testimony May 15, Symington said "it is very clear to me that there was an attempt to unload major responsibility for the Watergate bugging and cover-up on the CIA." According to the summary:

■ Dean asked Walters 10 days after the Watergate break-in (in June 1972) if the CIA could provide bail or pay the salaries for the men apprehended there. Walters refused and declared he would rather resign than implicate the agency in such a scheme.

■ Haldeman and Ehrlichman intervened in an attempt to have the CIA press the FBI to call off its probe in 1972 into Nixon campaign funds that had been routed—or "laundered" to prevent tracing—through a Mexican bank and, at one point, through several of the Watergate defendants. The CIA's approach to the FBI would be made on the ground that national security was involved and pursuit of the probe would compromise certain CIA activities and resources in Mexico. Walters met with Acting FBI Director L. Patrick Gray 3rd several times. The first time he related to Gray that senior White House aides had told him pursuit of the FBI probe would uncover some CIA activities in Mexico. After Gray later said he would need a written statement to that effect—that CIA assets would be endangered—before the FBI inquiry could be ended Walters, apparently on word from then CIA Director Richard M. Helms, informed Gray the CIA activity actually was not in jeopardy by the FBI probe.

Helms, currently ambassador to Iran, testified May 16 before a Senate Appropriations subcommittee, which was examining the same issue. Chairman John L. McClellan (D, Ark.) said afterward that Helms had expressed concern about the White House overtures to the CIA for domestic activity, which he considered improper, but said he had never conveyed his concern to President Nixon.

More testimony was released May 17, as Helms and Walters returned before the Armed Services panel. Walters said he told Gray in their meeting in early July 1972 he considered the attempts "to cover this up or to implicate the CIA or FBI would be detrimental to their integrity" and he was "quite prepared to resign on this issue."

Gray "shared my views" and "he, too, was prepared to resign on this issue," Walters said.

Symington disclosed May 21 that Haldeman had told Walters that "it is the President's wish" that Walters ask Gray to halt the FBI investigation into the laundering of campaign funds through a bank in Mexico City. This information was contained in one of 11 memoranda written by Walters and given to the Senate Foreign Relations Committee.

Another Walters memorandum revealed that Gray told Nixon during a telephone conversation that the Watergate case could not be covered up and that the President should get rid of those who were involved.

Cox named special prosecutor. Attorney General-designate Elliot L. Richardson May 18 appointed Harvard Law School professor Archibald Cox special prosecutor for the Watergate case.

Richardson said he would have no control over the investigation "for all practical day-to-day purposes." He would make no effort to keep tabs on the special prosecutor, he said, and Cox "will determine to what extent he will keep me informed" and the "occasions on which to consult me."

Secret funds & Watergate payoffs linked. The General Accounting Office May 19, 1973 charged former Commerce Secretary Maurice H. Stans, President Nixon's chief fund raiser and chairman of the Finance Committee to Re-elect the President, with an "obvious attempt to evade the disclosure requirements" of the new federal campaign spending law

According to the GAO, at least $1.7 million in cash and a "larger total" in checks and securities were not reported to the Office of Federal Elections, the watchdog agency within the government's auditing office. Of the $1.7 million, at least $460,000 was used to pay cover-up money to the Watergate defendants or their attorneys.

Results of the GAO investigation, based on testimony from former finance committee treasurer Hugh W. Sloan Jr. and Herbert W. Kalmbach, one of the major fund raisers for the Nixon re-election campaign during 1971, were referred to the Justice Department for possible prosecution.

Among the disclosures:

■ Kalmbach collected at least $210,000 during the summer of 1972 for payment to "the Watergate defendants or their attorneys." The money was raised from three sources: Stans, giving $75,100 on June 29, 1972; Frederick C. LaRue, a re-election campaign official, giving $30,000–$40,000 in early July and the same amount again in late August; Thomas V. Jones, chairman of the Northrop Corp., a Defense Department contractor, giving $75,000 on July 31, 1972.

The Washington Post reported May 20 that Jones claimed he donated only $50,-000 and intended it as a contribution that would have been reported to the GAO.

According to Newsweek magazine May 21, Kalmbach was ordered to make the Watergate payoffs by then White House counsel John W. Dean 3rd and John D. Ehrlichman, at that time assistant to the President for domestic affairs, with the knowledge of campaign director John N. Mitchell and his committee aide LaRue.

Kalmbach refused to carry out a second fund-raising venture for the Watergate defendants in September 1972 when requested to do so by then presidential chief of staff H. R. Haldeman, the magazine said.

■ A $350,000 cash payment was made "immediately prior to April 7, 1972" by Sloan to Kalmbach under orders from Stans and campaign director Mitchell. The money was picked up by Gordon Strachan, an aide to Haldeman.

Sources told the Post that LaRue eventually received the money and that all but $100,000 of it was paid to the Watergate conspirators.

Other sums of cash were distributed before April 7, 1972 to several re-election committee officials and Administration aides: Liddy, at that time a re-election committee lawyer, received $199,000; Jeb Stuart Magruder, deputy campaign director, received $20,000; Herbert L. Porter of the re-election committee received $100,000; Ron Walker of the White House staff received $2,000; Robert C. Hitt, an aide to Interior Secretary Rogers C. B. Morton, received $25,000 for a secret cash contribution to the campaign of Rep. William O. Mills (R, Md.).

A total of $900,000 was paid in cash to the various officials; the balance of the unreported $1.7 million went to small campaign finance committees before April 7, 1972.

Ervin Committee Starts Hearings

Senate hearings begin. The Senate Select Committee on Presidential Campaign Activities began hearings May 17, 1973 in Washington into the Watergate scandal and related charges of wrongdoing during the 1972 presidential campaign.

Chairman Sam J. Ervin Jr. (D, N.C.) declared in an opening statement delivered before a crowded Senate Caucus Room in the Old Senate Office Building: "A clear mandate of the unanimous Senate resolution provides for a bipartisan investigation of every phase of political espionage."

In his opening remarks, Ervin declared that an "atmosphere of the utmost gravity" demanded a "probe into assertions that the very [political] system itself has been subverted and its foundations shaken. Our citizens do not know whom to believe, and many of them have concluded that all the processes of government have become so compromised that honest government has been rendered impossible."

He said:

"The questions that have been raised in the wake of the June 17 break-in strike at the very undergirding of our democracy. If the many allegations made to this date are true, then the burglars who broke into the headquarters of the Democratic National Committee at the Watergate were in effect breaking into the home of every citizen of the United States. And if these allegations prove to be true, what they were seeking to steal was not the jewels, money or other property of American citizens, but something much more valuable—their most precious heritage, the right to vote in a free election."

Ervin said the hearing's purpose was not "prosecutorial or judicial but rather investigative and informative. The aim of the committee is to provide full and open public testimony in order that the nation can proceed toward healing of the wounds that now afflict the body politic."

The hearings, which were broadcast nationally on television and radio, began on a low-key note.

The committee appeared to be seeking evidence in three areas: the Watergate burglary itself; alleged attempts at a cover-up by White House officials; and charges of a widespread plot of political espionage and sabotage initiated and operated by the White House and officials of the Committee to Re-Elect the President.

Robert C. Odle Jr. and Bruce A. Kehrli were the first witnesses to be questioned by the panel members. They were also questioned by Samuel Dash, chief counsel and staff director, and Fred D. Thompson, chief minority counsel.

Odle testified that deputy campaign director Jeb Stuart Magruder had ordered a "strategy file" and an "advertising" file to be removed from his desk at committee headquarters only hours after the Watergate burglary.

Odle testified that convicted Watergate conspirator G. Gordon Liddy, then a lawyer with the re-election committee, asked to use a paper shredding machine during the afternoon of June 17, 1972.

Odle's testimony provided the Senate committee with an explanation of the staffing of the Nixon re-election committee and its working relationship with the White House during the campaign.

According to Odle, John N. Mitchell was involved in "major campaign decisions" in 1971 while still attorney general. Mitchell had testified in March 1972 before a Senate committee investigating Administration links to the International Telephone & Telegraph Corp. that he "did not have any [party] responsibilities" before his resignation from the Cabinet

March 1, 1972. Mitchell quit the committee post July 1, 1972, soon after the Watergate break-in.

Bruce Kehrli, a White House staff member, indicated that little distinction was made within the Administration between service in the executive branch of government and political duties for the Nixon re-election campaign. The White House retained overall direction of the 1972 campaign, despite existence of the Committee to Re-elect the President, Kehrli said.

James W. McCord Jr., a convicted Watergate conspirator, testified May 18 that, before his trial, he had been offered executive clemency to keep silent about Watergate. The offer, he said, was made at three secret meetings with John J. Caulfield, former White House aide and Nixon re-election committee employe.

McCord said he had been told that the offer came from "the very highest levels of the White House." He was told President Nixon had been informed of their meeting and would be told its results.

"The President's ability to govern is at stake," he was told, and he was "not following the game plan." One remark— warning that "if the Administration gets its back to the wall it will have to take steps to defend itself"—McCord took as a threat.

McCord testified that Caulfield had assured him "that if I had to go off to jail ...the Administration would help with the bail premiums." McCord continued:

"I advised him that it was not a bail premium, but $100,000 straight cash and that that was a problem I would have to worry about, through family and friends. On the night before sentencing, Jack called me and said that the Administration would provide the $100,000 in cash if I could tell him how to get it funded through an intermediary. I said that if we ever needed it I would let him know. I never contacted him thereafter; neither have I heard from him."

He also disclosed he had received since his arrest June 17, 1972, $46,000 in cash, $25,000 of which was used for legal fees. He said Mrs. Hunt provided the fees, which he presumed came from the Nixon campaign committee.

McCord revealed to the committee he had access in his security role for the Nixon re-election committee to confidential memorandums from the Justice Department's Internal Security Division.

McCord testified about a scheme that he believed was never consummated. McCord told of a fellow Watergate conspirator's plans to burglarize a Las Vegas newspaper for information damaging to a Democratic presidential candidate. Part of the scheme involved escape to Central America by the burglary team on a plane owned by industrialist Howard R. Hughes.

Caulfield corroborated much of McCord's testimony about the clemency offer, except for the remark about Nixon being informed of their meeting. Caulfield May 22 explained the threat differently saying it was "a small piece of friendly advice," to the effect that the people he worked with were "as tough-minded as you and I" and not to "underestimate them."

Caulfield testified that the order for the offer of executive clemency came from ex-presidential counsel John W. Dean 3rd. Caulfield said he had no personal knowledge that Nixon had approved the offer.

Caulfield arranged to have the message relayed to McCord by Anthony Ulasewicz, a retired New York City detective who was working with Caulfield on "investigative functions" and reporting "to the White House through me," Caulfield said.

Ulasewicz called McCord with Dean's message, Caulfield continued, and reported that "McCord's attitude had been one of satisfaction."

Dean was informed, Caulfield said, and called again the next day to say "McCord wanted to see me" and persuaded Caulfield, who said he was reluctant, to relay in person the same message to McCord.

At that first meeting, Caulfield said, "I stated that I was only delivering a message" but considered "it was a 'sincere offer.'"

"He asked me who I was speaking with at the White House, and I said I could not reveal any names but that they were from the 'highest level of the White House.' "

At their second meeting, Caulfield related, he affirmed his belief the clemency offer was sincere.

"At no time on this occasion or on any other occasion," Caulfield insisted, "do I recall telling Mr. McCord to keep silent if called before the grand jury or any Congressional committees."

Responding to questioning by Sen. Lowell P. Weicker Jr. (R, Conn.), Caulfield said May 23 that he "knew that the offer of executive clemency in this matter was wrong" but that he "felt very strongly about the President" and was "very loyal to his people that I worked for."

Ulasewicz testified May 23 that he had been a contact for Caulfield with McCord. He confirmed that he had been paid by Kalmbach's law firm.

Bernard Barker told the committee May 24 he broke into the Democratic National Committee headquarters in search of evidence that the Democrats were receiving financial support from the Castro regime in Cuba. (No proof was found.)

Barker, steadfastly denying that any pressure had been brought against him to enter a plea of guilty, said his "prime motivation" in participating in the break-in had been his belief that he later would obtain help from E. Howard Hunt Jr. and "others in high places" in speeding the liberation of Cuba.

At the Watergate, he said, the documents he was seeking—he was the document-finder, another the photographer—were those "that would prove that the Democratic party and Sen. [George] McGovern [D, S.D.] were receiving contributions nationally and national and foreign contributions from organizations that were leftist organizations and inclined to violence in the United States and also from the Castro government."

Barker testified that almost $50,000 had been given him by Hunt's late wife, for bail, expenses and legal fees for him and his comrades.

Under close questioning, he denied that executive clemency had been offered.

Haldeman ordered files destroyed. H. R. Haldeman, President Nixon's former chief of staff, ordered aide Gordon C. Strachan to destroy documents that showed he knew of "actual data" obtained from the wiretap of the Democratic National Committee headquarters in the Watergate complex.

The information was contained in a report submitted to the Senate committee investigating Watergate by member Sen. Lowell P. Weicker (R, Conn.) after he interviewed former White House Counsel John W. Dean 3rd May 3, the New York Times reported June 10.

According to the report, about June 18, 1972, "Strachan told Dean that he had been ordered by Haldeman to destroy documents which indicated that Haldeman had awareness of actual data received from the wiretap at the Democratic National Committee."

Dean told Weicker that Strachan admitted to him he had destroyed the documents in his office June 17 or 18, 1972.

Administration Involvement

Nixon explains White House role. In a statement released May 22, President Nixon conceded the probable involvement of some of his closest aides in concealing some aspects of the Watergate affair and acknowledged that he had ordered limitations on the investigation because of national security considerations "of crucial importance" unrelated to Watergate.

He reiterated, however, his own lack of prior knowledge of the burglary and the attempted cover-up while acknowledging that aides might have "gone beyond" his directives to protect "national security operations in order to cover up any involvement they or certain others might have had in Watergate."

In his detailed statement, Nixon sought to separate secret investigations begun earlier in his term from the Watergate case.

The President said that in 1970 he was concerned about increasing political disruption connected with antiwar protests and decided a better intelligence operation was needed. He appointed the late J. Edgar Hoover, director of the Federal Bureau of Investigation (FBI), as head of a committee to prepare suggestions. On June 25 1970, Nixon said, the committee recommended resumption of "certain intelligence operations that had been suspended in 1966," among them the "authorization for surreptitious entry—breaking and entering, in effect"—in specific situations related to national security.

He said Hoover opposed the plan and it was never put into effect. "It was this unused plan and related documents that [his former counsel] John Dean removed from the White House and placed in a safe deposit box," Nixon added.

After the New York Times began publishing the Pentagon Papers in June 1971, Nixon said, he approved the formation of a special investigations unit in the White House to "stop security leaks." The unit, known as the "plumbers," was directed by Egil Krogh Jr. and included convicted Watergate conspirators E. Howard Hunt and G. Gordon Liddy. Nixon recalled that he had impressed upon Krogh the importance of protecting the national security and said this might explain how "highly motivated individuals could have felt justified in engaging in specific activities" he would have disapproved had he known of them.

Nixon said he had "wanted justice done in regard to Watergate" but he had not wanted the investigation to "impinge adversely upon the national security area." He noted that, shortly after the break-in, he was informed that the CIA might have been involved and that he instructed H. R. Haldeman and John Ehrlichman to "insure that the investigation of the break-in not expose either an unrelated covert operation of the CIA or the activities of the White House investigations unit." He said he gave similar instructions to Assistant Attorney General Henry E. Petersen April 18.

The President reiterated that in the months following the Watergate incident, he was given repeated assurances that the White House staff had been cleared of involvement. But with hindsight, Nixon conceded, it was apparent that "I should have given more heed to the warning signals I received along the way . . . and less to the reassurances." Nixon continued:

With respect to campaign practices, and also with respect to campaign finances, it should now be obvious that no campaign in history has ever been subjected to the kind of intensive and searching inquiry that has been focused on the campaign waged in my behalf in 1972.

It is clear that unethical, as well as illegal, activities took place in the course of that campaign.

None of these took place with my specific approval or knowledge. To the extent that I may in any way have contributed to the climate in which they took place, I did not intend to; to the extent that I failed to prevent them, I should have been more vigilant.

It was to help insure against any repetition of this in the future that last week I proposed the establishment of a top-level, bipartisan, independent commission to recommend a comprehensive reform of campaign laws and practices.

Nixon concluded by retreating on the issue of executive privilege, saying that it would not be invoked "as to any testimony concerning possible criminal conduct or discussions of possible criminal conduct, in the matters presently under investigation, including the Watergate affair and the alleged cover-up."

In a summary accompanying the statement, Nixon made the following replies to specific allegations against White House activities:

"1) I had no prior knowledge of the Watergate operation.

2) I took no part in, nor was I aware of, any subsequent efforts that may have been made to cover up Watergate.

3) At no time did I authorize any offer of executive clemency of the Watergate defendants, nor did I know of any such offer.

4) I did not know, until the time of my own investigation, of any effort to provide the Watergate defendants with funds.

5) At no time did I attempt, or did I authorize others to attempt, to implicate the CIA in the Watergate matter.

6) It was not until the time of my own investigation that I learned of the break-in at the office of [Pentagon Papers case defendant Daniel] Ellsberg's psychiatrist, and I specifically authorized the furnishing of this information to Judge [William M.] Byrne.

7) I neither authorized nor encouraged subordinates to engage in illegal or improper campaign tactics."

Nixon bars own testimony. President Nixon would not give oral or written testimony to the grand jury or the Senate select committee investigating the Watergate case, White House Press Secretary Ronald L. Ziegler said May 29. "It would be Constitutionally inappropriate," he said. "It would do violence to the separation of powers."

The statement was issued after a report by the Washington Post May 29 that the Watergate prosecutors had informed the Justice Department there was justification for calling Nixon to answer questions before the grand jury. The report, by Carl Bernstein and Bob Woodward, said the President's role in the Watergate affair was the one key element remaining to be clarified in the investigation and questioning was justified about how top Nixon aides could pursue such massive obstruction of justice without the President's knowledge.

According to the Post, a "department source" said "there is no bombshell tucked away" about the President's role but "there is an evidentiary pattern" that raised questions about it.

There was a strong White House reaction to the story. In a statement issued May 28 and carried by the Post alongside its story, Ziegler said the story reflected "a shocking and irresponsible abuse of authority on the part of the federal prosecutors, if in fact, they made the statements attributed to them." Communicating information and allegations relating to grand jury proceedings "in this fashion," he said, was a violation of law.

Reaffirming this position to reporters May 29, Ziegler said the White House's "very, very severe concern" about the Post's report had to do with the secrecy of the grand jury process and the anonymous and indirect charges against the President.

Ziegler said the White House had protested the matter to Attorney General Elliot L. Richardson and Archibald Cox, the special Watergate prosecutor.

Cox also issued a statement May 29 saying all decisions about the conduct of the investigation "will be made by me" and that he had as yet "made no such decisions and authorized none." He said the prosecutors and Justice Department officials "have been instructed to refrain from any kind of statement, comment or speculation about any aspect of the investigation."

Ehrlichman ties Mitchell to bugging. Former Attorney General John N. Mitchell personally chose three sites for electronic bugging in the 1972 presidential campaign, John D. Ehrlichman, former

presidential domestic affairs adviser, said in a deposition in the $6.4 million civil suit filed by the Democratic party against the Committee to Re-elect the President.

The deposition, given in private May 22–24, 1973, was released June 5.

The information given by Ehrlichman was obtained for the most part from Jeb Stuart Magruder, Mitchell's assistant at the Nixon re-election committee, and former presidential counsel John W. Dean 3rd. As such the testimony was hearsay. Ehrlichman said the President had asked him to conduct an investigation March 30 after Dean had failed to provide a written report of his own investigation into Watergate.

In his deposition, Ehrlichman spoke of three meetings, held January–March 1972, during which proposals for an intelligence and information facility were discussed. Attending the meetings were Mitchell, Dean, Magruder, and G. Gordon Liddy.

Ehrlichman said Magruder told him that at the first two meetings Liddy presented plans that were rejected as too grandiose and extreme. A third plan was finally accepted, with Mitchell giving oral approval to the bugging operation.

Ehrlichman reported Dean as saying Mitchell had approved the plans in writing "by circling or checking" three targets for bugging from a list.

The three sites were the Democratic national headquarters in the Watergate complex, the Fontainebleau Hotel in Miami Beach during the Democratic convention, and the Washington headquarters of Sen. George McGovern.

Ehrlichman testified that the second Watergate break-in resulted from Liddy's initiative rather than on orders from anyone high in the Nixon re-election committee. Ehrlichman said Mitchell had been furious that a bug placed on Democratic National Chairman Lawrence F. O'Brien had failed to produce satisfactory results.

In response to Mitchell's criticism, Liddy initiated a second entry into Watergate, at which time the burglars were caught.

Nixon's concern over Watergate. Before and after his re-election, President Nixon expressed concern about the Watergate affair, his former chief of staff, H. R. Haldeman, testified May 22, 24 and 25. Prior to the election, Nixon feared the effect Watergate might have on his campaign; afterward, he wanted the matter cleared up so that it would not "be hanging over into the second term," Haldeman said.

The information came from a deposition given by Haldeman in the $6.4 million suit filed by the Democratic party against the Committee to Re-elect the President. The testimony was released June 6.

Haldeman's testimony generally complemented the deposition given by Ehrlichman.

Haldeman revealed a March 28 meeting he held with Mitchell at the White House. Mitchell told of a conversation he had with Jeb Stuart Magruder, deputy Nixon campaign director, in which the latter related that pressure on him had been applied by Special Counsel to the President Charles W. Colson for the gathering of intelligence on the Democrats.

Colson called Magruder while Watergate conspirators G. Gordon Liddy and E. Howard Hunt Jr. sat in his office. Colson told Magruder the two had an intelligence gathering plan that merited study. (Haldeman noted Colson later said he was not aware the Liddy-Hunt plan involved anything illegal. They had come at the end of the day, at a time when Colson had felt rushed.)

In response to the pressure by Colson, Magruder launched the Liddy-Hunt plan. Mitchell told Haldeman the Watergate bugging was conducted with the full knowledge and approval of Magruder.

'73 Nixon talks with Dean admitted. The White House acknowledged June 4 that President Nixon had conferred a number of times early in 1973 with his then-counsel John W. Dean 3rd about the Watergate investigation. The acknowledgment was made in response to reports in the Washington Post and the New York Times June 3 that Dean had told federal and Senate Watergate investigators of the meetings.

The Times report, attributing "sources close to Mr. Dean," said Dean had told Samuel Dash, chief counsel for the Senate select committee investigating the Watergate case, that he met alone and in small groups with Nixon more than 40 times between late January and early April and that Nixon showed a "great interest" in ascertaining "things were handled right—taken care of"—with respect to the Watergate investigation. Dean also contended, according to the report, that he could provide first-hand information indicating the President had a "substantial knowledge" of the activities of high White House officials regarding the Watergate investigation.

The Post report, from "reliable sources," said Dean told Senate and federal investigators he had discussed aspects of the Watergate cover-up with Nixon or in Nixon's presence on at least 35 occasions between January and April. Former top Nixon aides H. R. Haldeman and John D. Ehrlichman were said to have been present at many of the meetings.

The immediate White House reaction to the Times and Post reports was a denial, carried by both papers the same day.

The Post article said Dean told the investigators of a conversation he had with Nixon just prior to the sentencing of the Watergate defendants in March 1972. According to the report: Nixon asked the cost of buying their continued silence, Dean said about $1 million and Nixon said that would be no problem. In an Easter call a little later in March, when Nixon told Dean "You're still my counsel," the story continued, Dean said Nixon also told him that at that time he had been "kidding" when he asked about the cost of buying silence of the conspirators.

(In an interview in the June 4 Time magazine, Dean called Nixon's May 22 statement a "public relations" document and said "some of it was not quite accurate" and "some of it was not accurate at all.")

In acknowledging the Nixon-Dean talks in early 1973, Deputy White House Press Secretary Gerald L. Warren said June 4 "obviously there were topics of interest this year that would have involved the office of counsel."

Warren specified, however, that White House logs recording the time and place of the Nixon-Dean conferences would not be released either to the federal or Senate Watergate investigators. "That would be

Constitutionally inappropriate," he said. In answer to reporters' questions, he said the proscription was based on "the basic doctrine of separation of powers."

This conflicted with statements from Attorney General Elliot L. Richardson and special prosecutor Archibald Cox June 4. Cox said he had been assured of access to all White House papers relating to Watergate and "if there is any waffling on it, I intend to make the waffling plain."

Richardson said at a news conference if Cox considered the logs necessary he should subpoena them.

The White House position was revised June 5 in a "speech of contrition" by Warren, who said he had only been authorized to say "that Presidential logs of visitors and phone calls are considered to be presidential papers and▾ as such their production cannot be required under subpoena." He "did not intend to state" what information "would or would not be made available," Warren said. That was a question for the President's counsel, he said.

CIA memos dispute security issue. Central Intelligence Agency (CIA) memoranda released by the Senate Appropriations Committee's Subcommittee on Intelligence Operations June 3 showed that key White House officials were not worried about danger to national security by Federal Bureau of Investigation (FBI) probes of the Watergate break-in. Rather, they were concerned over the massive political implications of a public airing of the scandal.

The memos, written for the most part by Deputy CIA Director Vernon A. Walters, recollected a series of meetings in June–July 1972 that he held with former presidential aides H. R. Haldeman, John D. Ehrlichman, and John W. Dean 3rd as well as former Acting FBI Director L. Patrick Gray 3rd, in which the ramifications of Watergate were discussed.

In a memo dated June 28, 1972, Walters described a White House meeting held five days before, attended by Walters, Haldeman, Ehrlichman, and then CIA Director Richard Helms.

At the meeting Walters was asked by Haldeman to talk to Gray and suggest that, since five suspects had already been arrested, the FBI not push its inquiries into Watergate, especially in Mexico. This was done over Helms' assurances that the CIA was not implicated in the affair.

Haldeman's reasoning was that the FBI investigation could lead to a "lot of important people" and that "the whole affair was getting embarrassing and it was the President's wish that Walters call on Gray." (In a cover note submitted by Walters along with the documents, the Haldeman statement, "it is the President's wish," was disclaimed. Walters said the "thought was implicit in my mind. I did not, however, correct the memo since it was for my use only.")

In another memorandum dated June 28, 1972, Walters detailed the Haldeman-instigated meeting with Gray. As per Haldeman's request, Walters warned Gray that continued FBI investigation into Mexican aspects of Watergate "could trespass" on covert CIA operations and that it would be best if it tapered off. Gray, noting "this was a most awkward matter to come up during an election year," said he would see what could be done.

Other Walters memoranda dealt with private meetings he had with Dean June 26 and 28, 1972. At the first meeting, Walters rejected a request by Dean that the CIA provide bail and salaries for the Watergate conspirators, warning that such news would be quickly leaked and "the scandal would be 10 times greater."

The second meeting was similar, with Walters again warning Dean that CIA involvement in Watergate was too risky.

Further Walters memoranda told of a July 6, 1972 meeting with Gray following a phone conversation between the men the previous evening, in which Gray said he would need written authorization to curb the FBI investigation.

"He [Gray] did not see why he or I should jeopardize the integrity of our organizations to protect some mid-level White House figures who had acted imprudently. . . . He felt it important that the President should be protected from his would-be-protectors."

Testimony on Administration involvement. Further testimony linking Nixon Administration officials to Watergate espionage was heard by the Senate Select

Committee on Presidential Campaign Activities as televised hearings were resumed June 5-7, 1973.

The major witnesses were Robert Reisner, administrative assistant during the 1972 Nixon campaign to Jeb Stuart Magruder, who was deputy director of the Nixon re-election committee; Hugh W. Sloan Jr., the committee's treasurer; and Herbert L. Porter, campaign scheduling director.

Reisner disclosed he had never been approached by FBI personnel or federal prosecutors prior to receiving a subpoena from the Ervin committee. Sloan, who said his testimony was essentially the same he gave to the grand jury in 1972, said the prosecutors at the trial had never asked him anything about Magruder's role he portrayed as suborning him. Porter indicated that the government lawyers had not attempted to corroborate his account—which he acknowledged was perjured—with Sloan's account.

Reisner testified June 5 that former Attorney General John N. Mitchell regularly received reports based on the illegal espionage material obtained from the clandestine listening post tapped into telephones at the Democratic national headquarters. He said duplicate copies of memoranda sent to Mitchell were sent to the White House. He spoke of the destruction, after the Watergate break-in, of the politically "sensitive" material in the files of the Nixon committee. And he told of a meeting in early 1972 attended by Mitchell, Magruder, John W. Dean 3rd, then White House counsel, and G. Gordon Liddy, later convicted in the Watergate case. Reisner's testimony was the first given publicly and under oath linking Mitchell to data from the illegal wiretaps at Democratic headquarters at the Watergate.

Reisner testified he had seen, a week or two prior to the aborted break-in, reports marked "Gemstone," the code word for material obtained from the wiretaps and other political spying activity of the committee. He said Magruder one time handed him a Gemstone document "in such a way that it was indicated to me very clearly that it was not for me to observe." He was instructed to put the document in files Magruder maintained

for his daily meetings with Mitchell, Reisner said. And he testified that as each document was sent to Mitchell through him, a duplicate copy of that document was sent to the office of John D. Ehrlichman, then chief Nixon domestic adviser.

The day of the Watergate break-in, Reisner testified, Magruder, who was in California, ordered him by telephone to remove the Gemstone file, which Magruder termed "sensitive" material, from the office over that weekend.

Much or all of the "sensitive" material in the files was destroyed after the break-in, Reisner testified.

This apparently would have included material marked "Sedan Chair 2," which Reisner identified as that dealing with information from the Democratic presidential campaign of Sen. Hubert H. Humphrey.

Sally J. Harmony, Liddy's former secretary, testified June 5 that she had typed memoranda, mostly dictated by Liddy, for Gemstone. On several occasions she transcribed directly from logs of conversations delivered to her directly from the secret listening post by James W. McCord Jr.

She also recalled making a fake entry pass to the headquarters of Democratic presidential contender George McGovern and shredding her shorthand notebooks, at Liddy's request, after the break-in.

Sloan testified the next day that Magruder and others made persistent efforts to have him perjure himself or "take the Fifth Amendment" in his scheduled testimony about the large amount of cash he disbursed from campaign funds to Liddy for his operations.

Sloan June 6 also testified that John Mitchell was making decisions about campaign spending while he was attorney general months before he left to head the Nixon campaign on March 1, 1972.

Liddy was a special problem. Sloan said he gave Liddy $199,000 in cash in the spring of 1972. Liddy presented him with a budget of $250,000, Sloan said, with an initial request for $83,000 in cash. He checked the request with Nixon campaign finance chairman Maurice Stans, Sloan said, who told him, "I do not want to know and you do not want to know" what the money was for.

After the Watergate break-in, Sloan testified: About June 21 or 22, 1972, he spoke with Magruder about the funds Magruder had authorized for Liddy. "He indicated to me that we are going to have to [disclose to investigators] or suggested to me a figure of what I had given to Mr. Liddy in the range of, somewhere, $75,000 to $80,000." Sloan said he "did not know the precise amount of money that I had given to Mr. Liddy at that point. However, I did know that the sum was considerably larger than that because Mr. Magruder himself had authorized a payment for $83,000 in one single installment.

"I must have indicated to him, well, that just is not the right figure, I did not have the right figure, but that is too low. He indicated to me at that time that I said to him, he must have been insistent because I remember making to him on that occasion a statement I have no intention of perjuring myself."

Committee counsel Samuel Dash asked Sloan: "What did he say to you when you said that?"

Sloan responded: "He said you may have to."

That night, Sloan attended a party along with several White House aides and arranged with them to meet the next day with Nixon's appointments aide Dwight C. Chapin and Ehrlichman.

With Chapin, Sloan said, "I believe probably the tone of the conversation was that there is a tremendous problem there, something has to be done. Mr. Chapin evaluated my condition at that point as being somewhat overwrought and suggested a vacation, which in fact, I was planning to leave on the next week. It had been planned for a long time. He suggested that the important thing is that the President be protected.

"In the Ehrlichman meeting, . . . I believe I expressed my concern, my personal concern with regard to the money. I believe he interpreted my being there as personal fear and he indicated to me that I had a special relationship with the White House, if I needed help getting a lawyer, he would be glad to do that, but 'do not tell me any details; I do not want to know. My position would have to be until after

the election that I would have to take executive privilege.' "

After his vacation, Sloan met July 5, 1972 with Magruder, who told him " 'we have to resolve this Liddy matter. We have to agree on a figure.' " "This time," Sloan testified, "the figure was even less than the time before. It was $40,000 or $45,000."

Sloan told him "if I am asked point blank, did Mr. Liddy ever receive $45,000, of course, I will say yes. But, I said, I will not stop there. If I am asked more than that, I will also say yes. If he asks what the total figure is, I will tell him to the best of my knowledge."

Porter testified June 7 that he had committed perjury, upon the motivation of Magruder, at the grand jury investigation in 1972 and at the Watergate trial in January. His reported false evidence concerned the funds paid Liddy. He said he lied about it because of "a deep sense of loyalty" to President Nixon and because of "the fear of group pressure that would ensue from not being a team player."

He told the committee this story:

On June 28 or 29, 1972, he met with McGruder, who told him it was "apparent" that "Mr. Liddy and others had on their own illegally participated in the break-in of the Watergate Democratic National Committee, and Mr. Magruder swore to me that neither he nor anybody higher than Mr. Liddy in the campaign organization or at the White House had any involvement . . . in Watergate. . . ."

McGruder informed Porter, however, that "'there is a problem with some of the money.' He said, 'Now, Gordon was authorized money for some dirty tricks, nothing illegal,' he said, but nonetheless, 'things that could be very embarrassing to Mr. Mitchell and Mr. Haldeman and others. Now, your name was brought up as someone who we can count on to help in this situation.' And I asked what is it you are asking me to do, and he said, 'Would you corroborate a story that the money was authorized for something a little bit more legitimate-sounding than dirty tricks. Even though the dirty tricks were legal, it still would be very embarrassing.'

". . . You were in charge of the surrogate campaign, you were very concerned about radical elements disrupting rallies and so forth, and I said yes, and he said suppose that we had authorized Liddy, instead of the dirty tricks, we had authorized him to infiltrate some of these radical groups?

"He said, how could such a program have cost a hundred thousand? And I thought very quickly of a conversation I had with a young man in California in December, as a matter of fact, and I said, Jeb, that is very easy. You could get 10 college-age students or 24- or 25-year-old students, people, over a period of 10 months. Mr. Magruder had prefaced his remark by saying from December on. And I said, you can pay them $1,000 a month, which they would take their expenses out of that, and I said that is $100,-000. I said that is not very much for a $45 million campaign. And he said, now that is right.

"He said, would you be willing, if I made that statement to the FBI, would you be willing to corroborate that when I came to you in December and asked you how much it would cost, and that is what you said? That was the net effect, the net of his question. I thought for a moment and I said, yes, I probably would do that. I don't remember saying yes, but I am sure I gave Mr. Magruder the impression I would probably do that and that was the end of the conversation."

Q. Later, did you tell the FBI what Mr. Magruder asked you to tell them?

A. Yes, sir, I did.

Q. What did you tell the federal grand jury?

A. The same thing.

Q. Were you a witness at the trial of the seven defendants who were indicted in the Watergate case?

A. Yes, sir.

Q. And did you give the same account?

A. Yes sir, I did.

Q. Did Mr. Magruder ask you to make any other statements which you knew to be false?

A. Yes, sir, he did. Shortly after that, he asked me to, if I would increase the amount of money that I was going to say that I gave to Mr. Liddy, and I said, no, I would not do that. He said, why not?

I said, because I just absolutely, I did not give him that amount of money and I will not say I gave him that amount of money.

I said, the conversation that you are asking me to relate, I can conceive of it happening because I would have told you that in December if you had asked me. And that is a strange answer, but that is the answer I gave him. And I would not increase the amount of money. He wanted me to say that I gave Mr. Liddy $75,000, when in fact, I had given him some $30,000 to $35,000—$32,000.

On April 11, Porter continued, Magruder advised him to contact a lawyer and tell the federal prosecutor "what you know." In a chance encounter three days later, Porter said, Magruder told him, "He had just come from a meeting at the White House and that it is all over, he said, and I said, what do you mean, it is all over? He said, it is all over, the President has directed everybody to tell the truth. Those were his exact words. He said I had a meeting with Mr. Ehrlichman and I told him the whole story and, boy, was he really shocked, words to that effect."

Magruder told him then that Mitchell "was going to deny complicity until the end," Porter said.

Colson reiterates Nixon's innocence. Charles W. Colson, former special counsel to the President, told the New York Times June 9 he would stake his life on President Nixon's disclaimer of any knowledge of a cover-up of the Watergate affair.

Colson said that as late as March 21 the President did not believe Mitchell or any of his senior aides were guilty nor would he consent to making a scapegoat of Mitchell, an innocent man.

Colson said he told federal prosecutors that in early February he informed Chief of Staff H. R. Haldeman of his concern over possible perjury and obstruction of justice in the first Watergate trial in January. Payments by Nixon associates to the Watergate defendants could be construed as criminal "hush money." Haldeman's response, Colson said, was that he knew about the money and he was not concerned.

Colson claimed he first expressed his suspicions of Mitchell's involvement to the President shortly after his inauguration in January. The President told him "Get me evidence and I'll act on it," Colson said.

Impeachment study urged in House. In a sparsely-attended evening session June 12, Rep. Bella S. Abzug (N.Y.) led a group of liberal Democrats in urging the House to open an inquiry into whether there were grounds for impeaching President Nixon because of the Watergate affair.

The speeches, generally low-key, avoided a direct call for impeachment. Abzug said some form of House action was necessary, since "no other body is conducting a direct investigation into the conduct of the President, because no other body has the authority to do so." Rep. Ronald V. Dellums (Calif.) called on the House to begin to "draw the line" on what would be considered impeachable offenses.

While cautioning against immediate impeachment proceedings, Rep. Fortney H. Stark (Calif.) suggested that government investigators be required to give the House "all information necessary to make a responsible decision" on impeachment grounds.

Rep. Paul N. McCloskey Jr. (R, Calif.) had attempted to lead a similar discussion June 6. After McCloskey had read two of the 11 pages of a speech suggesting that Nixon might have violated federal criminal laws, Administration supporter Rep. Earl F. Landgrebe (R, Ind.) called for a quorum. With only about 60 House members on the floor, the Landgrebe motion halted debate. After procedural wrangling amid signs that the Democratic leadership might be willing to wait hours to gather a quorum, McCloskey decided that the length of the session was "unreasonable" and called for adjournment.

Impeachment resolution proposed—An impeachment resolution against Nixon for "high crimes and misdemeanors" was presented in the House July 31 by Rep. Robert F. Drinan (D, Mass.). Drinan, a Jesuit priest, said the House should inquire not only into the Watergate scandal but also the secret bombing of Cambodia in 1969–70, Nixon's taping of White House conversations, impoundment of legislated funds and establishment of "a super-secret security force within the White House." Before going to the floor for consideration, the resolution would have to be considered either by the House Judiciary Committee or a specially-appointed House panel.

Stans denies involvement. The Senate committee investigating Watergate and other illegal campaign practices held its third week of nationally televised hearings June 12–14, 1973.

Finance Committee Chairman Maurice H. Stans testified June 12–13. Under pointed questioning from committee chairman Sam J. Ervin Jr. and other senators, Stans denied any knowledge of or involvement in the Watergate break-in attempt or subsequent cover-up.

Stans first delivered a 23-minute statement declaring he had no knowledge of the Watergate break-in or "of the efforts to cover up after the event," of any political "sabotage program" against the Democrats or any "intentional violations" of the campaign finance laws.

Stans was questioned by committee deputy counsel Rufus Edmisten.

Edmisten asked Stans about $83,000 cash given to convicted Watergate conspirator G. Gordon Liddy.

Stans recalled that committee treasurer Hugh W. Sloan Jr. had questioned him, near April 6, 1972, about Liddy's request for "a very substantial amount of money" and whether he should give it to him. Stans continued:

"And I said, 'I don't know. I will find out from John Mitchell.' I will quote my conversation with John Mitchell as best I can paraphrase it. It is not precise. But I saw John Mitchell a relatively short time after and said, 'Sloan tells me that Gordon Liddy wants a substantial amount of money. What is it all about?'

"And John Mitchell's reply was, 'I don't know. He will have to ask Magruder because Magruder is in charge of the campaign and he directs the spending.'

"I said, 'Do you mean, John, that if Magruder tells Sloan to pay these amounts or any amounts to Gordon Liddy that he should do so, and he said, 'That is right.' . . .

"Apparently Mr. Liddy showed Mr. Sloan a budget of $250,000 against which he intended to draw. To the best of my knowledge, Mr. Sloan did not tell me about that budget and I did not know that Mr. Liddy had authority to draw an amount of money of that size."

In reply to a question, Stans told the committee he received on June 29, 1972 (12 days after the Watergate break-in), "an urgent call" from Herbert W. Kalmbach, President Nixon's former personal attorney, for a meeting, at which Kalmbach said, "I am here on a special mission on a White House project and I need all the cash I can get." Kalmbach insisted on cash, Stans said, and told him "this has nothing to do with the campaign, but I am asking for it on high authority" and "you will have to trust me that I have cleared it properly."

Stans testified that he gave Kalmbach $75,000 in "two parcels outside the committee"—$45,000 in a safe deposit box for "unusual expenses," which had been left behind by Kalmbach during his tenure as fund raiser for Nixon preceding Stans, and $30,000 from three Philippine nationals.

Stans said Kalmbach told him about six weeks ago that the request for the funds had come from presidential counsel John W. Dean 3rd, that Dean had assured him the purpose was legal and that Kalmbach had checked with Nixon aide John D. Ehrlichman, who corroborated Dean.

In a closing statement, Stans expressed confidence that no one in the finance committee, except Liddy, "had any knowledge of or participation in the Watergate affair or any other espionage or sabotage activities."

Sen. Daniel K. Inouye (D, Hawaii) recalled testimony from Sloan that on being questioned about the large sums paid to Liddy, Stans had remarked to him, "'I do not want to know and you do not want to know.'" Stans responded that it was made in the context "of total frustration that I had with the spending program of the campaign committee." "The remark I made," he said, was "something to the effect that 'I don't know what's going on in this campaign and I don't think you ought to try to know.' We were the cashiers, we received the money, and we paid the bills. They [the campaign committee] had responsibility for everything they did."

Magruder implicates Mitchell. Jeb Stuart Magruder, former deputy director of the Committee to Re-elect the President, told the Watergate committee June 14 that he, campaign director John N. Mitchell and other high White House and campaign officials had authorized the wiretapping of the Democratic National Committee headquarters at the Watergate building as part of a "broad intelligence-gathering" scheme.

When their agents were arrested at the Watergate, Magruder said, the same Nixon aides decided immediately and without debate to fabricate a cover-up story in order to protect Nixon's re-election chances. Magruder admitted he had perjured himself numerous times by denying involvement in the break-in attempt and provided the committee with its only first-hand account linking former Attorney General Mitchell to the plot. Magruder also named former White House chief of staff H. R. Haldeman and former Nixon counsel John W. Dean 3rd as parties to the cover-up conspiracy.

Magruder also claimed that Stans had been told of the cover-up about the funds.

Magruder told this story:

At a meeting of Mitchell, Magruder, Presidential counsel John W. Dean and G. Gordon Liddy in Mitchell's office Jan. 27, 1971, Liddy presented a spy plan he budgeted at $1 million. The proposed projects included wiretapping, electronic surveillance and photography. One proposal was to abduct radical leaders and detain them in Mexico to prevent them from disrupting the Republican National Convention.

Another project "would have used women as agents to work with members of the Democratic National Committee at their convention and here in Washington and, hopefully, through their efforts, they would obtain information from them." The project included rental of a yacht at Miami, "set up for sound and photographs," for "call girls" to "work with" prominent Democrats.

The reaction to the plan, Magruder continued, was that "all three of us were appalled" because of "the scope and size of the project." Mitchell indicated "that this was not an acceptable project" and that Liddy should "go back to the drawing board and come up with a more realistic plan."

Magruder made a telephoned report on the meeting to Gordon Strachan, then assistant to Nixon chief of staff H. R. Haldeman. "Everything that I did at the committee," Magruder told the committee, "everything that we did was staffed to Mr. Strachan so that he could alert other officials at the White House as to our activities."

A second meeting on the Liddy plan was held Feb. 4, 1972 at the Justice Department with the same participants. The topic was "the potential target" of the Democratic National Committee headquarters and "the possibility of using electronic surveillance" at the Democratic convention headquarters and at the presidential contender's headquarters. Either Mitchell or Dean also brought up the point that information relating to Sen. Edmund S. Muskie (Me.), then a Democratic presidential aspirant, possibly could be obtained in a newspaper office in Las Vegas and Liddy "was asked to review the situation in Las Vegas to see if there would be potential for any entry."

In general, he said, information also was being sought to offset the effectiveness of then Democratic National Chairman Lawrence F. O'Brien.

The reaction to this Liddy plan, which had been scaled down to a $500,000 cost, was "that it would not be approved at that time but we would take it up later."

Another development at this time was word to Magruder from the White House to get the Liddy plan approved. According to Magruder, Charles Colson, then a counsel to the President, "called me one evening and asked me in a sense would we get off the stick and get the budget approved for Mr. Liddy's plans, that we needed information, particularly on Mr. O'Brien. He did not mention, I want to make clear, anything relating to wiretapping or espionage at that time."

A third and final meeting on the Liddy plan was held on or about March 30, 1972. It was at Key Biscayne, where Mitchell was on vacation. The participants were Mitchell, Magruder, Liddy and Frederick C. LaRue, former White House aide and chief deputy to Mitchell at the campaign committee. This plan, scaled down to a $250,000 cost, involved entry into the Democratic National Committee headquarters (in the Watergate building in Washington) and possible later entry into the Democratic presidential contenders' headquarters and

the Democratic convention headquarters. The plan included electronic surveillance and photography of documents.

"No one was particularly overwhelmed with the project," Magruder said. "But I think we felt that the information could be useful and Mr. Mitchell agreed to approve the project and I then notified the parties of Mr. Mitchell's approval."

Magruder recalled being questioned by Hugh W. Sloan Jr., treasurer of the campaign committee's finance arm, about the initial large sum of money requested by Liddy, $83,000, for the operation.

"I indicated that Mr. Liddy did have that approval. Mr. Sloan evidently then went to Mr. Stans. Mr. Stans went to Mr. Mitchell. Mr. Mitchell came back to me and said why did Gordon need this much money and I explained to him this was in effect front end money that he needed for the equipment, and the early costs of getting his kind of an operation together. Mr. Mitchell understood, evidently told Mr. Stans it had been approved and the approval was complete."

The first break-in at the Watergate occurred May 27, 1972. Liddy indicated to Magruder afterward "he had made a successful entry and had placed wiretapping equipment in the Democratic National Committee." About a week and a half later, Magruder received "the first reports" from the bugging in the form of recapitulated telephone conversations and pictures of documents. He "brought . the materials into Mr. Mitchell," who "reviewed the documents" and "indicated that there was really no substance" to them.

Liddy was called in and "Mitchell indicated his dissatisfaction with the results of his work." Magruder said Mitchell "did not ask for anything more." Liddy indicated "there was a problem with one wiretap" (the one on O'Brien's phone was not working) and "he would correct these matters and hopefully get the information that was requested."

Magruder called Strachan, who came to his office "and look[ed] over the documents and indicate[d] to me the lack of substance to the documents."

Magruder testified that the morning after the break-in of June 17, 1972, in which five participants were arrested, Liddy had called him with the news. Magruder, in California, talked to LaRue, who talked to Mitchell. The three discussed it, then Mitchell ordered Robert C. Mardian, a campaign committee official, to call Liddy to ask him to see Attorney General Richard G. Kleindienst "and see if there was any possibility" that James W. McCord Jr., one of those arrested at the Watergate and an employe of the campaign committee, "could be released from jail."

Magruder also called Strachan and told him of the problem. He also received a call from Haldeman, who "asked me what had happened" and, after being told, "indicated that I should get back to Washington immediately" to take care of the problem.

Back in Washington, Magruder met June 19 with Mitchell, LaRue, Mardian and Dean. "One solution was recommended in which I was to, of course, destroy the Gemstone [Liddy plan] file." "As I recall," Magruder said, "we all indicated that we should remove any documents that could be damaging, whether they related at all to the Watergate or not."

Magruder related discussions with Sloan, who had testified that Magruder asked him to perjure himself concerning the amount of money given Liddy. Magruder said he thought Sloan would be personally liable for the cash funds provided Liddy, since they were not reported funds. So he indicated to Sloan, he said, "that I thought he had a problem and might have to do something about it. He said, you mean commit perjury? I said, you might have to do something like that to solve your problem and very honestly, was doing that in good faith to Mr. Sloan to assist him at that time."

He met later with Sloan three times on the subject of the Liddy money, the exact amount of which Sloan did not know. "I think the real problem was that he knew it was $199,000 and I was aghast at that figure because there was no way Mr. Liddy should have received that much...."

There were a "series of meetings," mainly held in Mitchell's office, attended by Mitchell, LaRue, Mardian, Dean and Magruder. At one point, "there was some discussion about me and I volunteered at one point that maybe I was the guy who

ought to take the heat, because it was going to get to me, and we knew that. And I think it was, there were some takers on that, but basically, the decision was that because I was in a position where they knew that I had no authority to either authorize funds or make policy in that committee, that if it got to me, it would go higher, whereas Mr. Liddy, because of his past background, it was felt that would be believable that Mr. Liddy was truly the one who did originate it."

Q. When you testified to the grand jury that time, did you testify to the false story?

A. Yes, I did.

Q. What role did Mr. Dean play in preparing you for your grand jury appearance?

A. I was briefed by our lawyers and Mr. Mardian. Also, I was interrogated for approximately two hours by Mr. Dean and approximately a half hour in a general way by Mr. Mitchell.

Q. Now, after you appeared before the grand jury for the second time, did Mr. Dean give you any report?

A. Yes, the day after Mr. Dean indicated that I would not be indicted.

Q. During your appearances before the grand jury or preceding it what, if anything, was told to you concerning the question of executive clemency for yourself or for those who were going to accept the blame in the story?

A. They made assurances about income and being taken care of from the standpoint of my family and a job afterwards and also that there would be good opportunity for executive clemency. But having worked at the White House and being aware of our structure there, I did not take that as meaning that had a direct relationship to the President at all.

Magruder told of a meeting with Haldeman in January before the Nixon inauguration. It was held to discuss future employment for Magruder and Nixon campaign aide Herbert L. Porter. "Also," Magruder said, "I thought I had better see Mr. Haldeman and tell him what had actually happened. I thought probably that this maybe was becoming scapegoat time and maybe I was going to be the scapegoat, and so I went to Mr. Haldeman and I said I just want you to know that this whole Watergate situation and the other activities was a concerted effort by a number of people, and so I went through a literally monologue on what had occurred. That was my first discussion with Mr. Haldeman where I laid out the true facts."

He and Mitchell met with Haldeman in late March, Magruder said, and were urged to meet with Dean to agree on a story. The three met but could not agree. "The election was now over and the reason for the cover-up [Nixon's re-election] was no longer valid," Magruder said. Then Dean was indicating "some reluctance" to abide by the story Magruder had told the grand jury, and Magruder felt "the story would not hold up" under further investigation by the Senate committee as well as the grand jury, which was reviving its probe.

So he told the "true" story to the federal prosecutors April 12.

Sen. Lowell P. Weicker Jr. (R, Conn.), referring to Magruder's January meeting with Haldeman, which had occurred before Magruder testified at the criminal trial, asked if Haldeman "knew that perjury was going to be committed" at the trial. Magruder said Haldeman did.

Magruder told Baker, "I do not think there was ever any discussion that there would not be a cover-up." The planning for it, he said, began the day they "realized there was a break-in." Magruder said he felt that if the story had "gotten out that people like Mr. Mitchell and others had been involved," that Nixon's re-election "would be probably negated." "I think it was felt," he continued, "that if it ever reached Mr. Mitchell before the election, the President would lose the election."

Hunt blackmail reported. Convicted Watergate conspirator E. Howard Hunt Jr. "effectively blackmailed" the White House with threats he would expose involvement of high Nixon Administration officials in secret illegal activities unless he received large sums of money and a guarantee of executive clemency, the Washington Post reported June 15, 1973.

According to Post sources, Hunt received, along with promises of clemency, amounts totaling more than $200,000. In late March, Hunt allegedly asked for an additional $130,000, which was never paid.

Reportedly, acquiescence by key White House officials was in part the result of fears that Hunt would reveal the Administration's secret plans against radicals, political opponents, and the press.

Post sources said Hunt's demands clearly established a case of obstruction of justice against White House officials. "Hunt was being paid to keep quiet. It demolishes the argument that the money was just for lawyers' fees and care for the families of the defendants," Post sources were quoted as saying.

Hunt allegedly relayed his first demand to the White House only a few days after the Watergate break-in by warning, "The writer has a manuscript or play to sell," government investigators told the Post. Hunt was the prolific author of more than 40 novels.

In the beginning, payments were made to Hunt by Nixon campaign aide Frederick C. LaRue, who delivered the cash to either Hunt directly or Hunt's attorney William O. Bittman. Bittman, sources said, admitted receiving three or four sealed envelopes, which he passed to Hunt, but Bittman denied knowledge of their contents.

Hunt, meanwhile, had received through Nixon re-election committee members assurances of executive clemency, Post sources said.

"Hunt viewed it as similar to a Central Intelligence Agency operation," another Post source observed. "If a deal blows up, everybody's taken care of."

By the fall of 1972 Hunt was reported to have become dissatisfied with his channels to the White House and fearful about promises of clemency, facts he had relayed to the White House in a three-page memo. Hunt reportedly upped his demands for money and for better White House channels.

Hunt sent at least five messages to the White House, the last on March 16, one week before he was given a provisional prison sentence of 35 years and after his wife, Dorothy, had been killed in a plane crash. Hunt, worried that no one would take care of his children, made a final demand for $130,000—$70,000 for personal expenses and $60,000 for legal fees, Post sources said.

White House Counsel John W. Dean

3rd, recipient of the demand, "hit the ceiling" and refused to accede to Hunt's demands, the Post reported.

LaRue pleads guilty to cover-up attempt.
Frederick C. LaRue, former campaign strategist for President Nixon, pleaded guilty June 27 to one count of conspiracy to obstruct justice in the Watergate affair.

In return for the reduction of the charges, LaRue agreed to testify as a government witness against others implicated in the scandal.

LaRue, a wealthy Mississippian who worked closely with Nixon's campaign director, former Attorney General John N. Mitchell, admitted taking part in a scheme to destroy incriminating documents and to mislead the FBI and the Watergate grand jury in 1972 with false testimony. He also acknowledged funneling more than $300,000 to the seven men arrested in the Watergate break-in, in an effort to buy their silence.

In entering his plea, LaRue admitted the following "overt acts of conspiracy":

At a meeting June 19, two days after the Watergate burglary, LaRue met with "others unnamed" and they agreed to destroy "certain incriminating records" relating to the break-in. James F. Neal of the special prosecutor's office identified these as wiretapping logs and summary sheets.

On July 19, he delivered "a sum of money" to Herbert M. Kalmbach at the Old Executive Office Building. Kalmbach was then President Nixon's personal lawyer and one of his chief fund-raisers.

LaRue delivered another unspecified sum of money to Kalmbach July 26.

Prior to Aug. 16, 1972, he met with "others unnamed" at the re-election headquarters, "where Jeb S. Magruder's false, misleading and deceptive statement, previously made to the Federal Bureau of Investigation, was further discussed."

On Aug. 16, Magruder falsely testified, as planned, before the grand jury investigating the case.

On Sept. 19, 1972, LaRue received $20,000 in cash.

On Dec. 1, he received $280,000, again in currency.

Dean testimony to panel leaked.
Dean met June 16 with the Senate Watergate committee's staff members and lawyers in a preparatory session for his public testimony. The panel's chief counsel, Samuel Dash, and its Republican counsel, Fred D. Thompson, prepared separate summaries of Dean's testimony at the session and these summaries were distributed to the seven senators on the committee. Leaked accounts of Dean's testimony began appearing in the press soon after-

wards and continued through the following week, the week Dean's public appearance had been canceled.

By midweek, excerpts from a summary prepared by the committee staff were being published. Also being published at the same time were excerpts from a White House account of conversations between President Nixon and Dean that had been sent to the committee. The New York Times published both sets of excerpts June 21, 1973.

Dean's story—The Times reported June 17, from various sources, one of them "a Dean associate," that Dean had informed government investigators about being told by White House aide Egil Krogh Jr. in early January that the orders for the burglary of files belonging to Pentagon Papers defendant Daniel Ellsberg's former psychiatrist came "from the oval office" (President Nixon's office). The account pictured Dean as having become convinced of Nixon's knowledge of the Watergate cover-up and feeling that his frequent meetings with Nixon early in 1973, when the President was concerned over executive privilege and national security, were related to the cover-up. The account said Dean attempted to tell Nixon on at least two occasions in mid-March about the scope of the scandal and, after arranging for his own personal defense and setting up a meeting with federal prosecutors, told the President the whole account of Watergate.

In the news accounts based on leaks after Dean's session with the Senate panel, Dean reportedly told the investigators:

■ Nixon asked Dean to see that Internal Revenue Service tax audits "be turned off on friends" of the President.

■ Dean promised to provide the committee with documents showing that he and top Nixon aides H. R. Haldeman and John D. Ehrlichman began immediately after the Watergate break-in to devise a cover-up story.

The summary of Dean's testimony before the Senate panel revealed further allegations by Dean. Among them:

■ In September 1972 Nixon directed that an effort be made to muffle a Watergate investigation by a House committee.

■ There was an attempt to persuade former Attorney General John N. Mitchell to "take the heat" off other officials by assuming the blame for the Watergate break-in.

■ Ehrlichman had instructed Dean to throw wiretapping equipment "in [the] river" after it had been found in the White House safe of E. Howard Hunt Jr.

■ Mitchell at first ignored a request to obtain money for the Watergate defendants, but Hunt sent word, through Dean to Ehrlichman and Mitchell, he wanted $72,000 for living expenses and $50,000 for lawyers' fees or, as the summary phrased it, "Hunt would have things to say about the seamy things Hunt did for Ehrlichman while Hunt was at the White House." On March 21 or 22, the account continued, "Ehrlichman asked Mitchell if Hunt's problem had been taken care of and Mitchell said 'Yes.'" The next sentence in the summary was: "Hunt's asking for money came to the attention of the President."

Dean then was said to have discussed the question of executive clemency for the defendants with Nixon in the spring.

■ Intelligence data on Democrats was coming into the White House in early 1970 and reports by a private intelligence gathering unit in the White House were sent to Nixon through Haldeman and Ehrlichman.

■ On Ehrlichman's instructions, an attempt was made to extend White House influence into the Republican side of the Senate Watergate committee. A call was made to Sen. Howard H. Baker Jr. (R, Tenn.), but Baker's response was "he did not want any White House input" on the decision of choosing a minority counsel.

(Baker disclosed the incident on the ABC "Issues and Answers" broadcast June 17. He said he rejected the overture and that it was the only contact the panel had with the White House since its probe began except for a request for an organizational chart.)

White House summary—The White House summary of Nixon's discussions with Dean portrayed Dean as deflecting persistent questioning by Nixon about White House involvement in the Watergate burglary and cover-up until March 21. The two met almost daily during the first three weeks of March, according to the account, with Dean insisting there was no White House involvement.

The report said on March 13 Dean told Nixon that Haldeman aide Gordon C. Strachan "could be involved" and on March 21 Dean "gave the President his theory of what happened"—revealing "that [Jeb Stuart] Magruder probably knew, that Mitchell possibly knew, that Strachan probably knew, that Haldeman had possibly seen the fruits of the wiretaps through Strachan, that Ehrlichman was vulnerable because of his approval of [Herbert W.] Kalmbach's fund-raising efforts."

According to the summary, Nixon was told March 21 that Hunt "was trying to blackmail Ehrlichman about Hunt's prior plumber [plugging news 'leaks' such as Pentagon Papers' publication] activities unless he was paid what ultimately might amount to $1 million. The President said how could it possibly be paid. 'What makes you think he would be satisfied with that?' Stated it was blackmail, that it was wrong, that it would not work, that the truth would come out anyway. Dean had said that a Cuban group could possibly be used to transfer the payments. Dean said [Charles W.] Colson [special counsel to the President] had talked to Hunt about executive clemency."

Dean's testimony. Former presidential counsel John W. Dean 3rd testified for five consecutive days before the Senate Watergate committee June 25–29, 1973.

Dean's reading of a statement—245 triple spaced legal-size pages—occupied the full June 25 session and lasted more than six hours. In addition, Dean submitted 47 documents to the committee to accompany his statement.

Dean admitted to the committee his own involvement in the effort to cover up the Watergate conspiracy and related how that effort spread among the White House staff, the Committee to Re-elect the President, the Justice Department and President Nixon.

While Dean's account was the first before the committee to directly accuse Nixon of involvement in the Watergate cover-up, Dean asserted that Nixon did not "realize or appreciate at any time the implications of his involvement." Dean said, however, that Nixon had permitted the cover-up to continue even after Dean had told him about some of the cover-up plans. Dean added that Nixon had discussed with him the possibility of executive clemency for some of the Watergate conspirators and "hush money" payments to maintain the cover-up.

Dean's statement detailed the "excessive concern" in the White House for data on antiwar activists and other political opponents of the Administration. Dean suggested that this concern, along with the "do-it-yourself White House staff, regardless of the law," created the climate for the Watergate affair.

Dean described his superiors in the White House—former presidential aides H. R. Haldeman and John D. Ehrlichman—as the principals in the efforts to conceal the ramifications of the Watergate break-in. But he also implicated, among others, former Attorney General John N. Mitchell, former special counsel to the President Charles W. Colson, U.S. District Court Judge Charles R. Richey, Assistant Attorney General Henry E. Petersen, former Acting FBI Director L. Patrick Gray 3rd, White House Press Secretary Ronald L. Ziegler, presidential aide Richard Moore and former presidential aides Frederick C. LaRue and Gordon C. Strachan.

In summary, his statement said: "The Watergate matter was an inevitable outgrowth of a climate of excessive concern over the political impact of demonstrators, excessive concern over leaks, an insatiable appetite for political intelligence, all coupled with a do-it-yourself White House staff, regardless of the law. However, the fact that many of the elements of this climate culminated with the creation of a covert intelligence operation as part of the President's re-election committee was not by conscious design, rather an accident of fate."

"The White House was continually seeking intelligence information about demonstration leaders and their supporters that would either discredit them personally or indicate that the demonstration was in fact sponsored by some foreign enemy. There were also White House requests for information regarding ties between major political figures [specifically members of the U.S. Senate]

who opposed the President's war policies and the demonstration leaders."

There was a lack of information showing such ties between the demonstrators and either foreign governments or major political figures, and this "was often reported to a disbelieving and complaining White House staff that felt the entire system for gathering such intelligence was worthless."

Soon after joining the White House staff in July of 1970, Dean learned about "the project to restructure the government's intelligence gathering capacities vis-a-vis demonstrators and domestic radicals." He was "told of the presidentially-approved plan that called for bugging, burglarizing, mail covers and the like." White House Chief of Staff H. R. Haldeman instructed him "to see what I could do to get the plan implemented."

Dean considered the plan "totally uncalled for and unjustified." He talked about it with Attorney General John N. Mitchell, who opposed it.

In early March, "as a part of the planned counteroffensive for dealing with the Senate Watergate investigation," Nixon "wanted to show that his opponents had employed demonstrators against him during his re-election campaign." But, he said, "We never found a scintilla of viable evidence indicating that these demonstrators were part of a master plan; nor that they were funded by the Democratic political funds; nor that they had any direct connection with the McGovern campaign. This was explained to Mr. Haldeman, but the President believed that the opposite was, in fact, true."

There was also considerable concern at the White House about news leaks. This concern "took a quantum jump" when the Pentagon Papers were published in June 1971.

Another concern at the White House was obtaining "politically embarrassing" information on leading Democrats.

In the spring of 1971, Haldeman discussed with Dean "what my office should do" during the coming campaign year. "He told me that we should take maximum advantage of the President's incumbency and the focus of everyone in the White House should be on the re-election of the President."

Part of Dean's task, in addition to "keeping the White House in compliance with the election laws," was "improving our intelligence regarding demonstrators," he said.

This brought him in touch with G. Gordon Liddy, who was being considered for a post as general counsel for the Nixon campaign committee. Dean interviewed Liddy and told him one of his responsibilities "would be keeping abreast of the potential demonstrations that might affect the campaign."

The next time Dean met Liddy was at a meeting Jan. 27, 1972 in Mitchell's office, with Magruder also there, when Liddy presented a "mind-boggling" plan for "mugging squads, kidnapping teams, prostitutes to compromise the opposition and electronic surveillance."

Liddy explained: The mugging squad could "rough up demonstrators that were causing problems. The kidnapping teams could remove demonstration leaders and take them below the Mexican border. The prostitutes could be used at the Democratic convention to get information as well as compromise the person involved."

Mitchell told Liddy the plan "was not quite what he had in mind and the cost was out of the question." He suggested that Liddy "go back and revise" it, "keeping in mind that he was not interested in the demonstration problem."

At a second meeting of the same four men Feb. 4, 1972, Dean ended the meeting by interjecting that such discussions could not be held in the attorney general's office. He said he did not know "to this day who kept pushing for these plans." He told Liddy he "would never again discuss this matter with him" and "if any such plan were approved," he "did not want to know."

Dean then informed Haldeman of "what had been presented by Liddy" and "that I felt it was incredible, unnecessary and unwise. I told him that no one at the White House should have anything to do with this. . . . Haldeman agreed and told me I should have no further dealings on the matter."

Dean returned from a Far East trip June 18, 1972 when he was told of the Watergate break-in. Liddy June 19 told him that "Magruder had pushed him

into doing it." That afternoon, Ehrlichman instructed Dean "to call Liddy to have him tell Hunt to get out of the country." He did this without thinking, then "realized that no one in the White House should give such an instruction." He checked with special presidential counsel Charles W. Colson and Ehrlichman, who agreed. Liddy was recalled but said he had already passed the message.

Also on June 19, Gordon Strachan told Dean he had been instructed by his superior, Haldeman, to go through the files and "remove and destroy damaging materials." Strachan said the "material included such matters as memoranda from the re-election committee, documents relating to wiretap information from the D.N.C. [Democratic National Committee], notes of meetings with Haldeman, and a document which reflected that Haldeman had instructed Magruder to transfer his intelligence gathering from Senator Muskie to Senator McGovern." Strachan told Dean "his files were completely clean."

One or two days later, Dean was given $15,200 to hold. The money, from Haldeman's office, was said to have been from an unexpended portion of funds authorized for Colson. Dean kept the cash in his safe, telling his assistant about it, until Oct. 12, 1972 when he removed $4,850, replacing it with his personal check, after he had "failed to make arrangements" to pay for the expenses of his wedding and honeymoon.

On June 20, 1972, Dean investigated the contents of Hunt's safe, including a briefcase with electronic equipment.

"Among the papers were numerous memoranda to Chuck Colson regarding Hunt's assessment of the plumbers unit, a number of materials relating to Mr. Daniel Ellsberg, a bogus cable, that is other cables spliced together into one cable, regarding the involvement of persons in the Kennedy Administration in the fall of the Diem regime in Vietnam, a memorandum regarding some discussion about the bogus cable with Colson and [writer] William Lambert, some materials relating to an investigation Hunt had conducted for Colson at Chappaquiddick, some materials relating to the Pentagon papers."

Ehrlichman told Dean "to shred the documents and...toss the briefcase into the river."

Then acting FBI director L. Patrick Gray told Dean on or about June 21, 1972 that the FBI had checked banking transactions of one of those arrested at the Watergate and had traced checks for $114,000 to a Mexico bank. "The fact that the FBI was investigating these matters was of utmost concern to Mr. [Maurice] Stans when he learned of it."

Mitchell, Ehrlichman and Haldeman thought Dean "should see the FBI reports," and in early July 1972 Dean broached the matter with Gray. Gray wanted assurance that the information would be reported to the President.

Dean assured him, "Even though I was not directly reporting to the President at that time, I was aware of the fact that Ehrlichman or Haldeman had daily discussions with the President, and I felt certain, because Haldeman often made notes, about the information I was bringing to their attention, that this information was being given to the President."

A summary report of the investigation to that stage was sent to Dean sometime after July 21, 1972. Former Assistant Attorney General Robert C. Mardian, who served as a top Nixon campaign official, "clearly thought that Gray was being too vigorous" and he "demanded that I tell Gray to slow down, but I never did so."

Several days later, Mardian proposed "that the CIA could take care of this entire matter if they wished." "Mitchell suggested I explore with Ehrlichman and Haldeman having the White House contact the CIA for assistance. Ehrlichman thought it was a good idea. He told me to call General [Vernon A.] Walters because he was a good friend of the White House and the White House had put him in the [CIA] deputy director position so they could have some influence over the agency."

"When Gen. Walters came to my office I asked him if there was any possible way the CIA could be of assistance in providing support for the individuals involved. Gen. Walters told me that while it could, of course, be done, he told me that he knew the director's feelings about such a

matter and the director would only do it on a direct order from the President. He then went on to say that to do anything to compound the situation would be most unwise and that to involve the CIA would only compound the problem because it would require that the President become directly involved. When I reported this to Ehrlichman, he very cynically said that Gen. Walters seems to have forgotten how he got where he is today."

There was a discussion in Mitchell's office June 28, 1972 "of the need for support money in exchange for the silence for the men in jail." But only $70,000 or $80,000 was on hand and "more would be needed." Mitchell asked Dean to get approval from Haldeman and Ehrlichman for Herbert Kalmbach to raise the necessary money. This was done. Mitchell told Dean that the White House, in particular Ehrlichman, should be "anxious to accommodate the needs of these men. He was referring to activities that they had conducted in the past that related to the White House, such as the Ellsberg break-in."

Dean learned from Haldeman and Colson Sept. 9 or 10, 1972 that Nixon felt the best defense against the Democrats and the lawsuits being filed by the Democrats was a "counteroffensive with our own series of lawsuits against the Democrats." About that time, Dean learned during a meeting in Mitchell's office that the White House exerted influence on the judge—Charles R. Richey—hearing the Democratic civil suit to have the case delayed until after the election.

On the day the Watergate indictments were handed down, Sept. 15, 1972, Dean went to Nixon's office, where "the President told me that Bob [Haldeman] had kept him posted on my handling of the Watergate case, told me I had done a good job and he appreciated how difficult a task it had been and the President was pleased that the case had stopped with Liddy."

Nixon expressed hope that the criminal case would not come to trial before the election, and Dean told him "the Justice Department had held off as long as possible the return of the indictments" and that "the lawyers at the re-election committee were very hopeful of slowing down the civil suit ... because they had been making ex-parte contacts with the judge . . . and the judge was very understanding and trying to accommodate their problems."

Dean also recalled "the President telling me to keep a good list of the press people giving us trouble, because we will make life difficult for them after the election."

"The conversation then turned to the use of the Internal Revenue Service to attack our enemies." Dean said not much use had been made because the White House "didn't have the clout," the IRS was "a rather Democratically oriented bureaucracy and it would be very dangerous to try any such activities. The President seeemed somewhat annoyed and said that the Democratic Administrations had used this tool well and after the election we would get people in these agencies who would be responsive to the White House requirements."

Dean called Assistant Attorney General Henry E. Petersen in the summer of 1971 at the time that Donald Segretti was being called before the grand jury about alleged political sabotage during the campaign. Dean told him to the best of his knowledge Segretti was not involved in the Watergate incident but was being paid by Kalmbach and had been recruited by Chapin and Strachan. "I said that these facts, if revealed, would be obviously quite embarrassing and could cause political problems during the waning weeks of the election. Mr. Petersen said that he understood the problem," Dean said.

"I later learned from Segretti that the names [Kalmbach, Chapin and Strachan] had come out during the grand jury appearance and I had a discussion later with Petersen also on the subject in which he told me that Mr. [prosecutor Earl J.] Silbert had tried to avoid getting into this area and in fact did not ask him the question which resulted in his giving names, rather that a grand juror had asked the question despite the fact that the prosecutors had tried to gloss over it.

"I had by this time learned the full story, that in fact Haldeman, in a meeting with Kalmbach, had approved Segretti's activities and authorized Kalmbach to make the payments to Segretti."

In about late November 1972, after the election was over, Mitchell called and said part of a $350,000 White House fund under Haldeman's aegis would have to be used "to take care of the demands that were being made by Hunt and the others [defendants] for money." Neither Dean nor Haldeman liked the idea of using White House money for that purpose, but no other answer was found and, under the assurance the amount would be returned, some funds were turned over to the campaign committee. Dean thought the amount was "either $40,000 or $70,000."

But the demands "reached the crescendo point once again" shortly before the trial, Mitchell made another request for funds and "Haldeman said send the entire damn bundle to them but make sure that we get a receipt for $350,000." The actual transfer of money was made by Strachan, who later told Dean the receiver, Frederick C. LaRue, Mitchell's deputy at the committee, refused to give him a receipt.

An attorney for the campaign committee, Paul L. O'Brien, informed Dean "that Hunt was quite upset and wished to plead guilty but before he did so he wanted some assurances from the White House that he would receive executive clemency."

Colson met with Ehrlichman in Dean's presence. He said "he felt it was imperative that Hunt be given some assurances of executive clemency . . . Ehrlichman said that he would have to speak with the President. Ehrlichman told Colson that he should not talk with the President about this. On Jan. 4th, I learned from Ehrlichman that he had given Colson an affirmative regarding clemency for Hunt."

Colson later told Dean he thought the matter so important he had discussed it with Nixon himself.

Dean said the President raised the subject with him on two occasions—March 13 and April 15.

At a Feb. 27 meeting, "the President directed that I report directly to him regarding all Watergate matters. He told me that this matter was taking too much time from Haldeman's and Ehrlichman's normal duties, and he also told me that they were principals in the matter, and I, therefore, could be more objective than they."

At a March 1 meeting, Nixon told Dean that "there should be no problem with the fact that I had received the FBI reports [on its Watergate probe]. He said that I was conducting an investigation for him and that it would be perfectly proper for the counsel to the President to have looked at these reports. I did not tell the President that I had not conducted an investigation for him because I assumed he was well aware of this fact and that the so-called Dean investigation was a public relations matter, and that frequently the President made reference in press conferences to things that never had, in fact occurred. I was also aware that often in answering Watergate questions that he had made reference to my report and I did not feel that I could tell the President that he could not use my name."

When Dean and Nixon met March 13, Dean told Nixon about the money demands by the defendants and, after Haldeman came in, that there was no money to pay the demands. Nixon asked Dean "how much it would cost. I told him that I could only make an estimate that it might be as high as a million dollars or more. He told me that that was no problem."

"He then asked me who was demanding this money and I told him it was principally coming from Hunt through his attorney. The President then referred to the fact that Hunt had been promised executive clemency. He said that he had discussed this matter with Ehrlichman and . . . expressed some annoyance at the fact that Colson had also discussed this matter with him."

In reply to a question, Dean told Nixon the payment money "was laundered so it could not be traced" and the deliveries were secret.

Dean told the President March 15 that he had received a new demand for support money from Hunt, through O'Brien, "that he wanted $72,000 for living expenses and $50,000 for attorney's fees and if he did not receive it that week, he would reconsider his options and have a lot to say about the seamy things he had done for Ehrlichman while at the White House." Dean felt he "had about reached the end of the line and was now in a position to deal with the President to end the cover-up."

Dean met with Nixon March 21 and warned him that "a cancer . . . on the Presidency" was "growing more deadly every day" and must be "removed" or "the President himself would be killed by it "

Dean said he told the President that he had been told Mitchell had received wiretap information; Haldeman had received such information through Strachan; Kalmbach had been used to raise funds to pay the defendants for their silence on orders from Ehrlichman, Haldeman and Mitchell; Dean had relayed the orders and assisted Magruder in preparing his false story for the grand jury; cash at the White House had been used to pay the defendants; more funds would be required for the cover-up to continue; and Dean "didn't know how to deal" with the blackmail problem.

Dean concluded "by saying that it was going to take continued perjury and continued support of these individuals to perpetuate the cover-up and that I did not believe it was possible to continue it; rather I thought it was time for surgery on the cancer itself and that all those involved must stand up and account for themselves and that the President himself get out in front of this matter. I told the President that I did not believe that all of the seven defendants would maintain their silence forever. In fact, I thought that one or more would very likely break rank.

"After I finished, I realized that I had not really made the President understand because after he asked a few questions, he suggested that it would be an excellent idea if I gave some sort of briefing to the Cabinet and that he was very impressed with my knowledge of the circumstances but he did not seem particularly concerned with their implications."

Dean, Haldeman and Ehrlichman met with Nixon again later March 21, and it then became "quite clear that the cover-up as far as the White House was going to continue."

"I for the first time said in front of the President that I thought that Haldeman, Ehrlichman and Dean were all indictable for obstruction of justice and that was the reason I disagreed with all that was being discussed at that point in time."

Dean told Ehrlichman aide Egil Krogh Jr. March 28 or March 29 that it was very likely the Ervin committee "could stumble into the Ellsberg burglary" because documents at the Justice Department contained pictures left in a camera, of Liddy standing in front of the break-in site. He said Ehrlichman wanted him to retrieve the documents and return them to the Central Intelligence Agency (CIA) "where they might be withheld" from Congressional committees probing the CIA but the CIA was "unwilling."

Krogh made a statement that startled Dean into asking him to repeat it. Dean had asked Krogh "if he had received his authorization to proceed with the burglary from Ehrlichman. Krogh responded that no, he did not believe that Ehrlichman had been aware of the incident until shortly after it had occurred: Rather, he had received his orders right out of the 'Oval Office'."

Dean's attorneys informed the prosecutors April 2 that "I was willing to come forward with everything I knew about the case." Dean felt he should tell Haldeman he was going to meet the prosecutors. Haldeman told him he should not.

Dean said he told Mitchell April 9 if he were called he would testify honestly. Mitchell understood "and did not suggest that I do otherwise." But he told Dean he should avoid testifying if at all possible because his testimony "would be very harmful to the President."

Haldeman and Ehrlichman at that time still "talked about pinning the entire matter on Mitchell."

Dean had a meeting with Nixon April 15. As the meeting progressed, Dean realized Nixon was asking him "a number of leading questions, which made me think that the conversation was being taped and that a record was being made to protect himself."

Nixon recalled a previous discussion in which he said there was no problem raising a million dollars to keep the defendants silent. "He said that he had of course, only been joking when he made that comment." Dean became more convinced "that the President was seeking to elicit testimony from me and put his perspective on the record and get me to agree to it."

Nixon had Dean come to his office April 16 and asked him to sign a letter of resignation or an alternative letter of indefinite leave of absence, which had been prepared. Nixon said "he would not do anything with them at this time but thought it would be good if he had them." Dean read the letters, then "looked the President squarely in the eyes and told him that I could not sign the letters. He was annoyed with me, and somewhat at a loss for words. . . . I told him that the letters that he had asked me to sign were virtual confessions of anything regarding the Watergate. I also asked him if Ehrlichman and Haldeman had signed letters of resignations. I recall that he was somewhat surprised at my asking this and he said no they had not but they had given him a verbal assurance to the same effect. I then told him that he had my verbal assurance to the same effect.

"It was a tense conversation. . . . The President said that he would like me to draft my own letter and would also like a suggested draft letter for Haldeman and Ehrlichman or maybe a form letter that everyone could sign."

Nixon sent for Dean later April 16 to see his draft letter. Dean told him "I would not resign unless Haldeman and Ehrlichman resigned. I told him that I was not willing to be the White House scapegoat for the Watergate. He said that he understood my position and he wasn't asking me to be a scapegoat."

"On April 30th, while out of the city, I had a call from my secretary in which she informed me that . . . my resignation had been requested and accepted and that Haldeman and Ehrlichman were also resigning."

Dean cross-examined — Committee members and counsel began to cross-examine Dean June 26. Dean then disputed the President's public statements on Watergate as "broad," misleading, unfounded or simply untruthful.

He said an "enemies list" of persons considered unfriendly to the Nixon Administration was maintained and kept updated. And he told of incidents of harassment against some individuals considered unfriendly, incidents utilizing federal services such as the Internal Revenue Service, the Secret Service and the FBI.

The committee's Democratic chief counsel Samuel Dash opened the cross-examination.

Is it not true, Dash asked, that you played a role in the cover-up activities? "That is correct," Dean said. Was it on his own initiative or under orders from someone? "I inherited a situation," Dean said. "The cover-up was in operation when I returned to my office" two days after the Watergate break-in "and it just became the instant way of life at that point in time."

He was "a conveyor of messages" between the White House and the Mitchell committee, Dean testified, and his reporting relationship was directly to Haldeman and to Ehrlichman.

When Nixon complimented him on Sept. 15, 1972 about the good job he had done, did he have any doubt what the President was talking about? "No, I did not," Dean replied. Whatever doubts he may have had prior to Sept. 15, 1972 about the President's involvement in the cover-up, did he have any doubts about this after Sept. 15? "No, I did not."

Dean was confronted June 27–28 with a White House response to his charges in the form of a memorandum and questions submitted to the committee by special presidential counsel J. Fred Buzhardt Jr. The memo, read by Sen. Daniel K. Inouye (D, Hawaii), portrayed Dean as the "mastermind" of the cover-up and Mitchell as his "patron." Buzhardt's charges failed to shake Dean's insistence that he fell into an existing cover-up situation as a conduit between Haldeman and Ehrlichman and the campaign committee.

In a statement released June 28, Buzhardt insisted that the memo "does not represent a White House position" and had not been reviewed by the President. Its sole purpose, the statement said, was "to facilitate the examination" of Dean by the committee.

The White House statement charged:

It is a matter of record that John Dean knew of and participated in the planning that went into the break-in at Watergate, though the extent of his knowledge of that specific operation or of his approval of the plan ultimately adopted have not yet been established. There is no reason to doubt, however, that John Dean was the principal actor in the Watergate cover-up, and that while other motivations may have played a part, he had a great interest in covering up for himself, pre-June 17th.

... It must have been clear to Dean as a lawyer when he heard on June 17 of Watergate that he was in personal difficulty. The Watergate affair was so clearly the outgrowth of the discussion and plans he had been in on that he might well be regarded as a conspirator with regard to them. He must immediately have realized that his patron, Mitchell, would also be involved.

Dean and Mitchell were Magruder's principal contacts on the cover-up. Dean was not merely one of the architects of the cover-up plan. He was also its most active participant. Magruder correctly concluded that Dean 'was involved in all aspects of this cover-up,' and this is from the Magruder testimony.

Dean was perfectly situated to mastermind and to carry out a cover-up since, as counsel to the President and the man in charge for the White House, he had full access to what was happening in the investigation. He sat in on FBI interviews with White House witnesses and received investigative reports.

Dean's activity in the cover-up also made him, perhaps unwittingly, the principal author of the political and constitutional crisis that Watergate now epitomizes. It would have been embarrassing for the President if the true facts had become known shortly after June 17th, but it is the kind of embarrassment that an immensely popular president could easily have weathered. The political problem has been magnified one thousand-fold because the truth is coming to light so belatedly, because of insinuations that the White House was a party to the cover-up, and above all, because the White House was led to say things about Watergate that have since been found untrue. These added consequences were John Dean's doing.

Dean responded to the White House statement frequently, often basing his defense on previously stated testimony that his role within the Administration during the period preceding and following the Watergate break-in was an exponent of reason and caution. While continuing to admit his active role as a participant in the cover-up, Dean repeated his assertions that he served principally as a point of contact for top level White House personnel and re-election committee officials with lesser Nixon aides who actually carried out the cover-up.

Weicker charges intimidation effort. Senate Watergate Committee member Sen. Lowell P. Weicker (R, Conn.) charged that high Nixon Administration officials tried to intimidate him after he became a member of the committee.

Weicker, who leveled the charges on national television June 28 as he prepared to question committee witness John W. Dean 3rd, said later he had reported these attempts to special Watergate prosecutor Archibald Cox.

Weicker specifically charged former White House Counsel Charles W. Colson with trying to plant a story during the past week with a newsman that Weicker had accepted improper contributions during his 1970 campaign for the Senate. Weicker said he had been told by Dean May 3 that the White House was attempting to "embarrass" him.

Weicker also read from the transcript of a March 28 phone conversation between John D. Ehrlichman, then presidential domestic affairs adviser, and Richard Kleindienst, then Attorney General. Weicker quoted Ehrlichman as saying to Kleindienst: "The President's feeling is that it wouldn't be too bad for you in your press conferences in the next couple of days to take a swing" at Weicker's announcement that he had information about White House involvement in Watergate.

Kleindienst questioned the advisability of that tactic and assured Ehrlichman that Weicker was "essentially with us."

Mitchell feared exposure of 'horror stories.' After a holiday recess, the hearings of the Senate committee investigating Watergate resumed June 10–12, 1973 with ex-Attorney General John N. Mitchell testifying.

Mitchell's testimony began amid indications of a serious conflict between the committee and President Nixon over the question of a possible presidential appearance before the committee and access to White House documents. In a letter to committee chairman Sam J. Ervin Jr. (D, N.C.) July 7, Nixon said that, because of his "constitutional obligation to preserve intact the powers and prerogatives of the presidency," he would not testify or allow access to White House files.

In three days of testimony, Mitchell maintained that Nixon had not been involved in the Watergate break-in scheme or the subsequent cover-up. Mitchell said July 10 that he had withheld information from Nixon to prevent damage to the re-election campaign and the presidency.

He said he was concerned not so much about Nixon's ability to withstand exposure of the Watergate case as the fact that an inquiry might lead to the exposure of other "White House horror stories," such as the break-in at the office of Daniel Ellsberg's psychiatrist, the proposed firebombing of the Brookings Institution and the falsification of cables relating to the

1963 death of South Vietnamese President Ngo Dinh Diem.

Mitchell told committee chief counsel Samuel Dash that he was aware of the 1970 White House plan for a secret intelligence operation, some of it illegal. He and J. Edgar Hoover opposed "its implementation," Mitchell said. He had talked to President Nixon and his aide H. R. Haldeman about it, and the plan was reconsidered and dropped.

Regarding his relationship with the Nixon campaign committee while he was still attorney general, Mitchell said he "played a role" because Nixon had asked him "to keep my eye on their activities over there to make sure they did not get out of line."

Mitchell told the committee that the plan presented in his office Jan. 27, 1972 by G. Gordon Liddy was "a complete horror story that involved a mishmash of code names and lines of authority, electronic surveillance, the ability to intercept aircraft communications, the call girl bit and all the rest of it." It was "just beyond the pale." His reaction: "I told him to go burn the charts and that this was not what we were interested in. What we were interested in was a matter of information gathering and protection against the demonstrators."

Mitchell contended there were "faulty recollections" about the discussion during the second meeting Feb. 4, 1972 on the Liddy operation. "I violently disagree with Mr. [Jeb Stuart] Magruder's testimony to the point that the Democratic National Committee was discussed as a target for electronic surveillance for the reasons that he gave, number one with respect to the Democratic kickback story. . . . These targets were not discussed."

What was the reaction to this plan? "Dean, just like myself, was again aghast" and "was quite strong to the point that these things could not be discussed in the attorney general's office. I have a clear recollection of that and that was one of the bases upon which the meeting was broken up." Mitchell's observation at the meeting was "that this was not going to be accepted. It was entirely out of the concept of what we needed."

What about previous testimony by Maurice H. Stans that he asked Mitchell about Liddy's request for "a substantial amount of money" and whether Magruder had authority to approve payments to Liddy?

A. Well, I would respectfully disagree with Mr. Stans on the fact of substantial amounts or that the discussions had to do with respect to the authorization by Magruder in.the continuity of the way he had been acting.

Mitchell testified that he had been unaware at the time of the early break-in at the Democratic offices at Watergate in May 1972. He said he did not know of the "Gemstone" file of wiretap information generated from it "until a great deal later," "much after" June 17, 1972, the second break-in date.

Did he recall Magruder testifying that he had shown these documents to him.

A. I recall it very vividly because it happens to be a palpable, damnable lie.

Among other things, he had a White House appointment at the time period he was said to have been shown the files. And he never saw or talked to Liddy from Feb. 4, 1972 until June 15, 1972 so he could not have berated Liddy about the inadequate results of the first break-in, as Magruder also testified.

Mitchell told the committee that following the break-in, Liddy was debriefed and Mitchell learned for the first time of what he repeatedly referred afterwards to as "the White House horrors"— the surveillance of McGovern headquarters, the "plumbers" group and Liddy's extensive activity while at the White House in connection with "the Ellsberg matter, in the Dita Beard matter and a few of the other little gems."

Other items cited by Mitchell as "horror stories" were a false cable purporting to link President Kennedy to the death of South Vietnamese President Ngo Dinh Diem, the proposal to firebomb the Brookings Institution and what he termed other "extracurricular" eavesdropping.

Did he become aware during that June and July of Magruder's involvement in the break-in? He was aware that Magruder had provided the money, and the focus seemed to be at that time on how much money had been given Liddy.

Mitchell said Magruder was shifting his story and, facing grand jury testimony, was asked to put his statement in writing. "It got to the point where I had a very, very strong suspicion as to what the involvement was," Mitchell said, but he did not know at the time Magruder's story was not a true one.

Mitchell said he "had no specific knowledge" that Haldeman and Ehrlichman were being kept informed about Magruder's testimony. He had never discussed the subject with them, to the best of his recollection. But he had discussions with Haldeman or Ehrlichman, prior to Magruder's grand jury appearance, about "the so-called White House horror stories," or the actions revealed in Liddy's debriefing.

Prior to Magruder's third appearance before the grand jury, Magruder, Dean and Mitchell met, not primarily to discuss the question of how to handle Magruder's testimony, but to discuss "what the recollection was" of the planning meeting and "what could be said about it to limit the impact."

Q. And you were aware, then, in December that he would testify not completely, if not falsely, concerning the meetings on Jan. 27 and Feb. 4?

A. Well, that is generally correct. As I say again, this is something that Dean and I were listening to, as to his story as to how he was going to present it.

Q. Well, wasn't it the result of your effort or program to keep the lid on? You were interested in the grand jury not getting the full story. Isn't that true?

A. Maybe we can get the record straight so you won't have to ask me after each of these questions: Yes, we wanted to keep the lid on. We were not volunteering anything.

Mitchell said he became aware "in the fall sometime" that payments were being made to the defendants. He also learned of the involvement in the payoffs of Nixon's personal lawyer, Herbert W. Kalmbach, and Mitchell's aide Frederick C. LaRue.

Dash explored Mitchell's opinion about Nixon's awareness of the Watergate events and aftermath.

Did he believe the President was aware of the events prior to or after the break-in, the actual bugging or the cover-up?

A. I am not aware of it and I have every

reason to believe, because of my discussions and encounters with him up through the 22nd of March, I have very strong opinions that he was not.

Asked to explain, Mitchell said of Nixon, "I think I know the individual, I know his reactions to things, and I have a very strong feeling that during the period of time in which I was in association with him . . . that I just do not believe that he had that information or had that knowledge; otherwise, I think the type of conversations we had would have brought it out."

Had he told Nixon what he discovered from Liddy's debriefing? "No, sir. I did not." Why not?

A. Because I did not believe that it was appropriate for him to have that type of knowledge, because I knew the actions that he would take and it would be most detrimental to his political campaign.

Mitchell said that sometime in the fall of 1972 one of the Watergate defendants, E. Howard Hunt Jr., called White House aide Charles W. Colson to demand money. Mitchell heard in March about oral communications from Hunt or his attorney "relating to requests for legal fees and so forth, which were communicated to the White House." Mitchell said his informant was probably LaRue, who told him "in this context: I have got this request, I have talked to John Dean over at the White House, they are not in the money business any more, what would you do if you were in my shoes and knowing that he had made prior payments? I said, if I were you, I would continue and I would make the payment."

Eventually, the source of the funds being paid to the defendants ran out, and Mitchell suggested seeing if the $350,000 fund "sitting" in the White House since April "was available for the purpose."

What about Dean's testimony that he had assured Ehrlichman "Hunt had been taken care of" in the payoff matter? It was "absolutely false," he had never discussed such payments with Ehrlichman.

When Mitchell talked with Nixon June 20, 1972, shortly after the break-in, "I apologized to him for not knowing what the hell had happened and I should have kept a stronger hand on what the people in the committee were doing."

Later there were political meetings and discussions about appointing a special investigating commission and prosecutors "and things like that."

Mitchell had "never promised" executive clemency to anybody. "Obviously, there is no basis upon which I could." When Magruder came to see him in March, he told him "I thought he was a very outstanding young man and I liked and I worked with him and to the extent that I could help him in any conceivable way, I would be delighted to do so."

"And this was exactly the same conversation that we had the next day down at Haldeman's office," Mitchell added. Haldeman made no promises to Magruder "other than the fact to help him as a friend."

Sen. Herman Talmadge asked Mitchell about his political role while attorney general. Mitchell insisted it was a "consulting" role. Talmadge asked if he had not testified to the contrary before the Senate Judiciary Committee March 14, 1972, when he stated he had no "party responsibilities" while at the Justice Department. He drew a distinction between "party" activities and activities for the re-election campaign committee, Mitchell said.

Mitchell told Talmadge that he had not gone to Nixon with the "horrors" story because "I was sure" that Nixon "would just lower the boom on all of this, and it would come back to hurt him, and it would affect him in his reelection."

Q. Am I to understand from your response that you placed the expediency of the next election above your responsibilities as an intimate to advise the President of the peril that surrounded him? Here was the deputy campaign director involved, here were his two closest associates in his office involved, all around him were people involved in crime, perjury, accessory after the fact, and you deliberately refused to tell him that. Would you state that the expediency of the election was more important than that?

A. Senator, I think you have put it exactly correct. In my mind, the re-election of Richard Nixon, compared with what was available on the other side, was so much more important that I put it in just that context.

At the July 11 session, Mitchell conceded that he had failed in his obligations to Nixon by not informing him of the ramifications of the Watergate affair, but he also implicated former presidential advisers John D. Ehrlichman and H.R. Haldeman in participating in a "design not to have the stories come out." Mitchell insisted that Nixon had not asked him for a complete account of Watergate.

Sens. Daniel K. Inouye (D, Hawaii) and Howard H. Baker Jr. (R, Tenn.) sought to attack Mitchell's credibility before the committee, pressing him on how far he might go to shield Nixon. Mitchell maintained that he had never needed to fabricate stories about Watergate; he simply withheld information.

Under intense questioning July 12 by the committee's chief counsel, Samuel Dash, Mitchell conceded that some of his testimony during the hearings differed from earlier statements. Mitchell attributed this to memory lapses and the fact that he was not "volunteering" information to earlier Watergate investigators—including the FBI—in the months following the break-in.

Moore disputes Dean. Richard A. Moore, 59, a special counsel to the President since 1971, began testifying July 12.

Called at the request of Leonard Garment, counsel to the President, Moore read a 20-page statement centering on his "deep conviction that the critical facts about Watergate did not reach the President" until White House counsel John W. Dean 3rd supplied them March 21.

Moore gave his version of the California meetings Feb. 10–11 attended by H. R. Haldeman, then White House chief of staff, John D. Ehrlichman, former domestic affairs adviser to the President, Dean and himself.

According to Moore, Dean said casually Feb. 11 that "he had been told by the lawyers [for the Watergate defendants] that they may be needing some more money and did we have any ideas?" When Mitchell's name was mentioned, Moore, a former aide to Mitchell, was asked to enlist his help. Moore said that Mitchell turned him down Feb. 15; "I believe he said something like, 'Tell them to get lost.'"

Moore said, "Mr. Dean has testified we left the meeting together and that . . . he cautioned me against conveying this fund-raising request when I saw Mr. Mitchell. I have absolutely no recollection of any such conversation and I am convinced it never took place."

A series of meetings, attended only by Nixon, Dean and Moore, were held March 15, 19 and 20 to discuss executive privilege, Moore said. Another meeting had occurred March 14, with presidential press secretary Ronald L. Ziegler present. "At no time during this meeting [March 14] or during succeeding meetings . . . did anyone say anything in my presence which related to or suggested the existence of any cover-up or any knowledge of involvement by anyone in the White House, then or now, in the Watergate affair," Moore stated.

In the interval between the March 19–20 meetings, Moore said Dean told him that convicted Watergate conspirator E. Howard Hunt Jr. was threatening to "say things that would be very serious for the White House" if he were not given a large sum of money. Moore said this was blackmail and he urged Dean to have nothing to do with it.

"This," Moore said, "brings me to the afternoon of March 20, when Mr. Dean and I met with the President in the Oval Office. . . . As I sat through the meeting . . . I came to the conclusion in my own mind that the President could not be aware of the things that Dean was worried about or had been hinting at to me, let alone [Watergate defendant] Howard Hunt's blackmail demand. Indeed, as the President talked about getting the whole story out—as he had done repeatedly in the recent meetings—it seemed crystal clear to me that he knew of nothing that was inconsistent with the previously stated conclusion that the White House was uninvolved in the Watergate affair, before or after the event.

"As we closed the door of the Oval Office and turned into the hall, I decided to raise the issue directly with Mr. Dean. I said that I had the feeling that the President had no knowledge of the things that were worrying Dean. I asked Dean whether he had ever told the President about them. Dean replied that he had not, and I asked whether anyone else had. Dean said he didn't think so."

That evening Moore received a call from Dean, who said he had arranged a private meeting the next day with the President. Meeting Moore after seeing the President, Dean said he had told Nixon "everything." "I asked if the President had been surprised and he said yes," Moore testified.

Moore said July 13 that the President April 17 had related to him his reaction to Dean's March 21 revelation of Hunt's blackmail and clemency demands. When told by Dean that the cost would be $1 million and that the demands would go on, Nixon said he had replied: " 'That isn't the point. Money isn't the point. You could raise money, money is not the point. It's wrong, we could not, shouldn't consider it and it's stupid because the truth comes out anyway.' "

At one point a question asked Moore by Sen. Edward J. Gurney (R, Fla.) provoked an angry objection from the committee chairman, Sen. Sam J. Ervin Jr. (D, N.C.). Gurney had asked whether, if Dean had discussed blackmail money and clemency with Nixon March 13, would he not have told Moore about it because he had confided in Moore about other aspects of the cover-up. Ervin objected but finally consented to the question.

Moore replied, "I kind of go along with the notion."

(In his testimony to the committee June 20, Dean said he "did not discuss with Moore the fact that I had discussed money and clemency with the President earlier, but I told him I really didn't think the President understood all the facts involved in the Watergate and the implication of the facts.")

Hearings uncover 'bugging' system. The existence of a recording system installed to secretly tape President Nixon's White House conversations was revealed July 16 at the continued Watergate hearings of the Senate Select Committee on Presidential Campaign Activities.

The existence of the secret White House recording system was revealed at the committee's televised hearings by Alexander P. Butterfield, a former presidential aide

then serving as administrator of the Federal Aviation Administration. Butterfield said that the system automatically recorded the President's meetings and telephone conversations in his offices in the White House and the adjacent Executive Office Building for "historical purposes." He said that the President's conversations with dismissed White House counsel John W. Dean 3rd and other persons involved in the Watergate case would have been recorded by the system routinely.

According to committee sources July 16, staff members uncovered the story of the secret recordings almost by accident July 13 while privately questioning Butterfield. Donald G. Sanders, the assistant minority counsel, said that Butterfield was asked, "out of the blue," about Dean's testimony June 25 that he suspected Nixon was recording one of their meetings. Butterfield then described the recording system, which he and Secret Service agents had maintained.

Kalmbach discusses funds. Herbert W. Kalmbach, Nixon's former personal attorney and political fund raiser, testified before the committee July 16–17. Kalmbach detailed how he had raised and channeled $220,000 to the original seven defendants in the Watergate break-in. He said he had been acting on orders from John Dean and John D. Ehrlichman, then a top Nixon adviser. But Kalmbach insisted he had thought the funds were "humanitarian" and only for the defendants' legal fees and family support.

Kalmbach also described how in 1970 he passed $400,000 to unknown persons on orders of an aide to former Nixon adviser H. R. Haldeman. Kalmbach said he suspected the money was used in an attempt to sabotage George C. Wallace's 1970 campaign for governor of Alabama.

Kalmbach told the committee July 16 that from January 1969 until February 1972 he had served at the request of Maurice Stans, Nixon's chief fund raiser during the 1968 and 1972 elections, as the "trustee" for "certain surplus funds" accruing from the 1968 presidential primary elections. He disbursed these funds "only" at the direction of Haldeman "or others clearly having the authority," Kalmbach said.

In his statement, Kalmbach denied having any prior knowledge of the Watergate break-in or of participating in a conspiracy to cover-up the burglary or other acts of campaign sabotage.

Throughout the questioning by Dash and minority counsel Thompson, Kalmbach maintained that by collecting payoff money for the Watergate defendants, he was discharging a "moral obligation" to raise funds for their legal defense and family support. "The fact that I had been directed to undertake these actions by the Number 2 and Number 3 men on the White House staff [Ehrlichman and Dean] made it absolutely incomprehensible to me that my actions in this regard could have been regarded in any way as improper or unethical," he said.

Kalmbach testified that on June 28, 1972 Dean made an urgent request for a meeting in Washington to discuss raising $50,000–$100,000 "for the legal defense of these [Watergate] defendants and for the support of their families." Kalmbach said he and Dean met June 29, 1972 in Lafayette Park, across from the White House. According to Kalmbach, he urged Dean to establish a public committee for the purpose of raising the funds.

Dean rejected the idea, Kalmbach said, because a "public committee might be misinterpreted." According to Dean, the project required "absolute secrecy" in order not to jeopardize Nixon's re-election chances. Anthony J. Ulasewicz, identified in previous testimony as the White House contact with convicted Watergate conspirator James W. McCord Jr., should distribute the money Kalmbach collected, Dean told him.

Kalmbach testified that his meetings and conversations with Ulasewicz were secretive, utilizing codewords and clandestine meetings in hotel rooms and cars to exchange money. According to Kalmbach, Mrs. E. Howard Hunt Jr., wife of one of the convicted Watergate conspirators, received the money from Ulasewicz. A total of $220,000 was collected for pay-off purposes. Stans and ex-Nixon campaign official Frederick C. LaRue contributed funds they held.

Kalmbach said his doubts about the project prompted him to request a meeting with Ehrlichman. Kalmbach re-called the meeting July 26, 1972 in Ehrlichman's office:

"I said, John, I want you to tell me, and you know, I can remember it very vividly because I looked at him, and I said, John, I am looking right into your eyes. I said, I know that my family and my reputation mean everything to me, and it is just absolutely necessary, John, that you tell me, first, that John Dean has the authority to direct me in this assignment, that it is a proper assignment and that I am to go forward on it.

"He said, Herb, John Dean does have the authority. It is proper, and you are to go forward.

"Now, he said, in commenting on the secrecy, ... this ... could get into the press and be misinterpreted. And then I remember he used the figure of speech, he said, they would have our heads in their laps, which again would indicate to me that it would jeopardize the campaign."

In mid-August 1972, Kalmbach was asked to collect more money for the Watergate defendants but he refused to comply with the request because "this whole degree of concern had come back to me to the level that I knew that I did not want to participate any longer in this assignment." The fund raising request was repeated at a meeting Jan. 19, 1973 in Mitchell's Washington office, with Mitchell, Dean and LaRue present. Kalmbach said he again rejected the bid.

Kalmbach conceded in testimony July 17 that he now realized his fund raising efforts for Watergate defendants represented an "improper, illegal act."

In retrospect, Kalmbach told the committee, he felt "used" by Nixon's chief aides: Haldeman, Ehrlichman, Mitchell and Dean.

Kalmbach cited his "implicit trust" in Dean and Ehrlichman as justification for his actions. "It is incomprehensible to me, and was at that time, I just didn't think about it that these men would ask me to do an illegal act," he said.

Sen. Talmadge tried to establish that Kalmbach undertook the assignment because "the President himself might have approved it," but Kalmbach rejected that explanation.

What was there about the "nature of the White House or the presidency or the aura that surrounds it" that would cause Kalmbach to have such enormous faith and trust in the propriety of the cover-up requests, Sen. Baker inquired.

Kalmbach replied, "It was a composite of all those factors"—reverence for the institution of the presidency, personal friendship for Nixon and long acquaintanceship with Dean. It never occurred to him to talk to Nixon about his doubts, Kalmbach testified, because he knew that Ehrlichman, and Dean "had the absolute trust" of Nixon.

Kalmbach also testified that in 1970 he had delivered a total of $400,000 in cash to persons not known to him under instructions from Lawrence Higby, Haldeman's aide. Kalmbach said that at the time he was unaware of the money's purpose but acknowledged that he now knew the money was used—unsuccessfully—in an effort to defeat Gov. George C. Wallace (D, Ala.).

The three deliveries were made secretly: twice in New York City hotels and once in a Los Angeles bank lobby. The cash was surplus money from the 1968 presidential campaign.

Kalmbach confirmed previous reports that his orders to provide funds to Donald Segretti, identified by other Administration officials as responsible for the Nixon re-election campaign's "dirty tricks," came from Dwight Chapin, "one of Haldeman's senior deputies." Kalmbach emphasized that Chapin was "standing, clearly standing in the shoes of Haldeman" and issuing directives on Haldeman's behalf.

Anthony T. Ulasewicz, who had testified May 23, returned July 18 to detail the secretive methods he used to deliver money to the Watergate defendants for Kalmbach.

Ulasewicz told how he had secretly disbursed $219,000—sometimes unsuccessfully—to Watergate conspirator G. Gordon Liddy; Dorothy Hunt, the late wife of conspirator E. Howard Hunt Jr.; Hunt himself; lawyers for the conspirators; and Frederick C. LaRue, former campaign strategist for Nixon.

Under examination by the committee's assistant majority counsel, Terry Lenzner, Ulasewicz related the details of a June 30, 1972 meeting he had with Kalmbach in a Washington hotel room. Ulasewicz, as-

sured by Kalmbach on the question of legality, agreed to provide funds to the lawyers of the Watergate defendants and "payment to assist their families during some troublesome period."

The first payment through Ulasewicz was a $25,000 advance fee to William O. Bittman, Hunt's lawyer.

Another recipient of funds from Ulasewicz was Dorothy Hunt, killed in a plane crash Dec. 8, 1972. On three separate occasions—the last Sept. 19, 1972—Mrs. Hunt picked up a locker key taped to the underside of a phone in Washington's National Airport, allowing her to collect a total of $136,500; in a like manner her husband accepted another $18,000.

Ulasewicz testified that Mrs. Hunt was his main contact to channel funds to the Watergate defendants. He said that each time he talked to her, she increased her demands. In the end, Ulasewicz calculated she wanted $450,000.

Ulasewicz testified that he made two other payments. In July 1972 he left $8,000 in a National Airport locker for Liddy. Two months later he gave LaRue an envelope containing $29,900.

Ulasewicz said Mrs. Hunt's demands caused him concern over the role he was playing and eventually led to his resignation. He said he had told Kalmbach, at a California meeting in August 1972, that "something here is not kosher" and then informed Kalmbach of his plans to quit.

Frederick C. LaRue, testifying July 18, offered a third version of the March 30, 1972 meeting at which former Attorney General John Mitchell was alleged to have approved a $250,000 intelligence plan against the Democrats.

According to LaRue, Mitchell neither approved the bugging plan, as former deputy campaign director Jeb Stuart Magruder had testified June 14, nor flatly rejected the project, as Mitchell himself had claimed July 10. LaRue recollected that Mitchell said of the plan, "Well, this is not something that will have to be decided at this meeting."

The bulk of LaRue's testimony, which extended to July 19, related to $230,000 he had distributed. LaRue indicated that he had funneled $210,000 to Bittman.

LaRue said he also sent $20,000 to Peter Maroulis, Liddy's attorney.

LaRue said he had obtained the funds from a secret $350,000 kitty of surplus 1968 campaign funds kept in the White House.

In other testimony, LaRue said that before he made the final payment of $75,000 to Bittman, he became concerned over his own criminal liability. He said he had voiced his apprehension to Mitchell and asked if he should make the payment. Informed by LaRue the money was for legal fees, Mitchell counseled him to make the payment, LaRue said.

LaRue further testified that Mitchell advised Magruder to burn documents relating to the Watergate bugging scheme.

Mardian denies any role in cover-up. Robert C. Mardian, a former assistant attorney general and official of the Committee to Re-Elect the President, testified July 19. Mardian disputed earlier witnesses, denying he played an illegal role in trying to conceal the events surrounding the Watergate case.

In his opening statement, Mardian said that immediately after the Watergate burglars' arrests June 17, 1972, in the Democratic National Committee's headquarters, he was relieved of his political duties at the re-election committee and was named the committee's attorney on matters related to the Watergate case. He cited this role at several points as his justification—under the canon of attorney-client confidentiality—for not revealing the information he gained as the scandal unfolded.

Questioned by James Hamilton, an assistant committee counsel, Mardian related how, after the arrests, he was asked by Jeb Stuart Magruder, then the re-election committee's deputy director, to help with the "slight problem" of the arrested burglars.

Hamilton asked if Magruder had described events leading to the break-in:

Q. Did Mr. Magruder inform you who had approved the budget for dirty tricks . . .?

A. Yes.

Q. Whom did he say?

A. He told me that the budget had been approved by Mitchell.

Q. Did Mr. Mitchell later that afternoon confirm that he had approved such a budget?

A. I would like to put it this way: It is my best recollection that I think the subject was discussed and he didn't deny it. And again, it may have come up when Mr. Mitchell wasn't in the room. I want to be fair on that point.

Mardian disputed the testimony of Magruder and Frederick C. LaRue, another campaign aide, that Mardian had been present at a June 19, 1972 meeting when Mitchell suggested that Magruder destroy documents on the Watergate plans. Mardian said "no such discussion took place in my presence."

Hamilton pressed Mardian on the meetings held in the few days after the break-in. Mardian replied, describing a June 21, 1972 interview of conspirator G. Gordon Liddy at LaRue's apartment.

Liddy, who had been portrayed to Mardian as "some kind of nut," entered the apartment, turned on a radio and asked LaRue and Mardian to sit beside it—so that "this conversation can't be recorded," as Mardian quoted Liddy. Liddy then told of the break-in and assured LaRue and Mardian there was no need to worry because the job had been done by "real pros" who would divulge nothing.

According to Mardian, Liddy told the details of his involvement in other operations by the White House "plumbers" unit—the burglary of the office of Daniel Ellsberg's psychiatrist and the removal of Dita Beard, a lobbyist for International Telephone & Telegraph Corp., to a Denver hospital to keep her away from Congressional investigators.

Mardian said he asked Liddy on whose authority he carried out the burglary of Ellsberg's psychiatrist, and, Mardian said, ". . . I don't know that he used the name of the President, but the words he did use were clearly meant to imply that he was acting on the express authority of the President of the United States, with the assistance of the Central Intelligence Agency."

Mardian testified that former presidential counsel John Dean had been "dead wrong" in telling the Ervin committee that Mardian had access to confidential FBI files on the Watergate investigation and had tried to involve the CIA in the cover-up.

Mardian also denied participating in discussions of Magruder's plans to maintain the cover-up by giving perjured testimony to the Watergate grand jury.

Questioned July 20 by Sen. Lowell P. Weicker Jr. (R, Conn.), Mardian testified that in 1971 Nixon had personally asked him to transfer from FBI files to John D. Ehrlichman the logs of wiretaps authorized by the White House on National Security Council employes and newsmen.

Gordon C. Strachan, an aide to White House chief of staff H. R. Haldeman, testified under a grant of immunity from the committee July 20. In his opening statement, Strachan said he was told little about the Watergate break-in by the people "at the White House . . . who have confessed to criminal wrongdoing."

Strachan, who served as liaison between the White House and the Committee to Re-elect the President, said he had told Haldeman two months before the Watergate break-in about a "sophisticated political intelligence gathering system" set up by the re-election committee. Strachan said he had destroyed documents that might link the burglars to the White House. Strachan also said he was the courier who transmitted $350,000 in White House "polling" funds to others who used the money to pay off the Watergate defendants.

Strachan testified that after the March 30, 1972 meeting at Key Biscayne, Magruder had called him and reported on "about 30 major campaign decisions" that included "a sophisticated political intelligence gathering system [that] has been approved with a budget of 300 [$300,000]." Strachan said that soon after the conversation, he wrote a "political matters" memo for Haldeman that included the matter along with a sample of a political intelligence report, entitled "Sedan Chair II," dealing with the Pennsylvania campaign organization of Sen. Hubert Humphrey (D, Minn.).

Strachan's statement placed major responsibility for the Watergate operation on Jeb Magruder. Strachan disputed Magruder's testimony that Strachan had been informed of the three meetings in early 1972 at which the intelligence

schemes were discussed. Strachan also said that John Dean, and not he, had been responsible for keeping Haldeman informed of political intelligence matters.

Describing his role in turning over $350,-000 in White House funds to Fred LaRue after the election, money subsequently paid to the Watergate defendants, Strachan said that he "was not told by anyone, nor did I know what use was being made of this money." He said that he "became more than a little suspicious" when he delivered about $10,000 to LaRue who "donned a pair of gloves" before touching the money, "and then said, 'I never saw you'."

Strachan asserted in testimony July 23 that Haldeman had told him three days after the Watergate break-in to "make sure our files are clean."

In response to a question by majority counsel Samuel Dash, Strachan said "I believe I was following his orders" in destroying the papers. Strachan testified that he had no doubt that the papers showed Haldeman had knowledge of the intelligence plan. Among the papers shredded were the memo Strachan had sent to Haldeman describing the Liddy plan and its budget and a "talking paper" Haldeman had used in an April 1972 meeting with John Mitchell that mentioned the plan.

Strachan said he believed Haldeman was aware of Liddy's intelligence activities before the break-in because Haldeman had told him in April 1972 "to contact Mr. Liddy and tell him to transfer whatever capability he had from Muskie to McGovern with particular interest in discovering what the connection between McGovern and Sen. [Edward] Kennedy was." Strachan told the committee that Haldeman had held a series of meetings with John Mitchell in 1971-72 to discuss intelligence gathering. He testified that Haldeman had proposed putting a "24-hour tail" on Sen. Kennedy because he was "particularly interested in the area of political intelligence and information" on the Senator.

In response to interrogation, Strachan said that Magruder did not report to him about the Feb. 4 meeting, as he had testified. Strachan denied that Magruder had showed him the Gemstone papers—transcripts of the wiretap at the Democratic National Committee headquarters. Strachan also testified that Magruder had unsuccessfully attempted to persuade him to commit perjury before the Watergate grand jury.

Ehrlichman testifies, defends actions. One of the two men closest to President Nixon, John D. Ehrlichman, until April 30 Nixon's assistant for domestic affairs, appeared before the committee July 24.

In his testimony he defended every aspect of his and the President's actions before, during and after the Watergate break-in and wiretapping. He singled out former White House counsel John Dean as the principal source of information implicating him and the President in the case, and he rejected it as false.

He challenged Dean's contention that the Watergate issue was a major preoccupation of the Nixon Administration during the three months following the June 17 break-in. Under questioning, Ehrlichman explained his role in the Labor Day 1971 burglary of the office of Daniel Ellsberg's psychiatrist and in the events surrounding it. Despite the committee's disbelief, Ehrlichman insisted that the President had statutory authority to order the break-in in the name of national security.

Ehrlichman said that events of 1969 and 1970—described as bombings of public buildings, radicals' harassment of political candidates, violent street demonstrations that endangered life and property—had to be taken as "more than a garden variety exercise of the 1st Amendment." The President felt that these events affected his ability to conduct foreign policy, and he gave them "balanced attention along with other events and factors."

Countering Dean's statement that the White House was engaged by the events of the campaign, Ehrlichman said, "in 1972 with the foreign situation as it was, the President decided quite early that he simply could not and would not involve himself in the day-to-day details of the presidential primaries, the convention and the campaign. He made a very deliberate effort to detach himself from the day-to-day strategic and tactical problems."

"In 1972, the President had to delegate most of his political role and it went to people not otherwise burdened with governmental duties. As a result, I personally saw very little of the campaign activity during the spring and early summer of 1972."

Ehrlichman rejected Dean's contention that he and Haldeman blocked access to the President. Dean, like others, had only to submit a memorandum to get the President's attention, Ehrlichman testified.

Ehrlichman admitted discussing the Watergate affair with Dean, but he said this was only to keep posted on campaign issues. He said he devoted only half of 1% of his time to the campaign and Watergate.

Ehrlichman's interrogation began with questioning by Samuel Dash on the 1971 break-in at the office of Ellsberg's psychiatrist.

After being assured by Ehrlichman that he played no role in the stillborn 1970 interagency intelligence plan, Dash asked if he had been requested to develop a White House capability for intelligence gathering. In reply, Ehrlichman said that Egil Krogh Jr., a White House aide, had been ordered to form a special unit, and he was designated as the person Krogh should see in connection with the unit.

Ehrlichman recalled how the special unit became operational in 1971. A copy of the Pentagon Papers had been turned over to the Soviet Embassy in Washington.

Soon afterward, Krogh came to him, Ehrlichman said, with the complaint that the FBI was not pressing its investigation into the matter. Ehrlichman said a call to Attorney General Mitchell revealed that FBI Director J. Edgar Hoover was blocking the investigation because of friendship with Ellsberg's father-in-law, Louis Marx.

"So it was this set of facts, and the real strong feeling of the President that there was a legitimate and vital national security aspect to this, that it was decided, first on Mr. Krogh's recommendation, with my concurrence, that the two men in this special unit who had had considerable investigative experience, be assigned to follow up on the then leads." (The two men were E. Howard Hunt Jr. and G.

Gordon Liddy; the special unit was the group later known as the White House "plumbers.")

Ehrlichman said the break-in at the psychiatrist's office "was totally unanticipated. Unauthorized by me."

Dash then read part of an August 11, 1971 memorandum from Krogh and David R. Young Jr., his associate in the unit, to Ehrlichman which referred to a planned meeting with a CIA psychiatrist who was doing a personality profile of Ellsberg: "In this connection," the memo said, "we would recommend that a covert operation be undertaken to examine all the medical files still held by Ellsberg's psychoanalyst covering the two-year period in which he was undergoing analysis." At the bottom, Dash pointed out, was Ehrlichman's approval and a short note in his handwriting, "If done under your assurance that it is not traceable."

Under probing by Dash, Ehrlichman argued that "covert" as used in the memo meant a "covered operation" in which the investigators were not to identify themselves as being from the White House. Ehrlichman denied he had agreed to a break-in.

Ehrlichman strongly disagreed with John Mitchell's view, as cited by Dash, that revelation to the President of the Ellsberg break-in and other "White House horrors" would have forced Nixon to pursue publicly the matters and that this might have cost him the presidency in 1972. Ehrlichman replied, with reference to the Ellsberg break-in, that the President had been protected by the fact that it involved national security.

"I think if it is clearly understood that the President has the constitutional power to prevent the betrayal of national security secrets, as I understood he does, and that is well understood by the American people, and an episode like that is seen in that context, there shouldn't be any problem."

"In point of fact, on the first occasion when I did discuss this with the President, which was in March of this year, he expressed essentially the view that I have just stated, that this was an important, a vital national security inquiry, and that he considered it to be well within the constitutional, both obligation and function of the presidency."

Under questioning by minority counsel Fred Thompson, Ehrlichman partially contradicted testimony given by Herbert W. Kalmbach. Ehrlichman denied he had told Kalmbach July 26, 1972 that payments to the Watergate defendants were legal and proper. Ehrlichman also said he did not recollect telling Kalmbach the payments were being kept secret to avoid embarrassment to the President.

Ehrlichman reiterated his denial that he had sought CIA aid for E. Howard Hunt Jr. He disclaimed any part in asking the CIA to formulate an excuse to block FBI investigation of financial links between the Watergate conspirators and the Committee to Re-elect the President.

Talmadge elicited from Ehrlichman that the President had not "in express terms" authorized the break-in at Ellsberg's psychiatrist's office. The President had told Egil Krogh, at the time he chartered the special unit, that he wanted Krogh to take whatever steps were necessary to perform his assignment, Ehrlichman testified.

Sen. Gurney quizzed Ehrlichman July 25 about the allegation that the Watergate defendants had been offered executive clemency to secure their silence about others connected with the case. Gurney asked: had Ehrlichman, as John Dean testified, told Charles Colson Jan. 3 that he had checked with the President and he could assure attorney William O. Bittman that his client, E. Howard Hunt Jr., would receive clemency?

Ehrlichman denied the allegation. He said he had been told by the President in July 1972 that it was a closed subject "and we must never get near it, and that it would be the surest way of having the actions of these [Watergate] burglars imputed to the President."

Under further questioning by Gurney, Ehrlichman challenged Dean's testimony that Ehrlichman ordered him to throw into the Potomac River politically sensitive documents found in Hunt's White House safe. Ehrlichman noted that he had helped arrange the opening of Hunt's safe in the presence of witnesses and it "would have been folly for me at some time later ... to suggest that the briefcase be thrown into the flood tide of the Potomac."

Ehrlichman similarly took issue with statement made by former Acting FBI Director L. Patrick Gray 3rd. Gray had told government investigators that at a June 28, 1972 meeting with Ehrlichman and Dean, Ehrlichman had told him the Hunt documents should "never see the light of day." Consequently he burned them, Gray said.

Ehrlichman contended that before the meeting Dean had suggested splitting the Hunt documents into two parcels: one for the FBI's Washington field office, the other, containing politically sensitive papers, for Gray. (Ehrlichman and Dean feared news leaks from the FBI field office.) At the June 28, 1972 meeting, Dean handed Gray the parcel, and Ehrlichman warned it was to be kept secret, Ehrlichman testified.

Not only had he not ordered Gray to destroy the documents, Ehrlichman testified, but he was "nonplussed" when informed of their destruction.

In a phone conversation April 15, Gray told Ehrlichman of his intention to deny that Dean had given him the documents, Ehrlichman claimed. Ehrlichman said he called Gray back to make clear that if asked he would have no choice but to say that he had been present when Dean gave Gray the documents.

Sen. Daniel Inouye's (D, Hawaii) interrogation dealt mainly with the propriety of the offer of appointment as FBI director made by Ehrlichman April 5 to the judge presiding at Ellsberg's trial, William M. Byrne Jr. Ehrlichman told Inouye that he had been willing to delay their discussion, but Byrne had failed to see why the Ellsberg case was an obstacle to it. Ehrlichman said he met Byrne twice and nothing improper was said. The second meeting had come at the request of Byrne, Ehrlichman said. Ehrlichman denied the offer was an effort to compromise Byrne. It was an effort to find the best man for the FBI job, he argued.

In another exchange with Inouye, Ehrlichman flatly denied that he or H.R. Haldeman had been fired. The President had been "content" to give them a leave of absence until Watergate was resolved, but they had insisted on a clean break, Ehrlichman said.

In other testimony before the committee, Ehrlichman said that contrary to John

Mitchell's testimony, he had briefed the former attorney general in 1971 on the activities of the plumbers.

Ehrlichman maintained that the intervention of the plumbers in the Ellsberg matter was justified because the FBI investigation was marked by "lassitude."

Ehrlichman reiterated he had been ordered by the President, through Haldeman, to seek assurances from the CIA that an FBI investigation of Nixon campaign funds found in the possession of the Watergate burglars would not impinge on CIA operations in Mexico. Ehrlichman insisted Nixon had given Acting FBI Director Gray authority to determine the scope of the Bureau's investigation.

Ervin expressed skepticism that the President had in the summer of 1972 sought a vigorous inquiry into the Watergate scandal. Ehrlichman replied that Dean and Kleindienst told the President that the "most vigorous" FBI investigation since the assassination of John F. Kennedy had shown that the break-in had been perpetrated only by the seven men already implicated.

In later questioning by Sen. Gurney, Ehrlichman stated he had felt in August 1972 that the President could "take the shock" of the disclosure that campaign officials had been involved in the bugging. However, his proposal to "lay out the whole story" was rejected at a meeting that month, attended by John Mitchell, Charles Colson, then-campaign director Clark MacGregor, and former White House official Bryce N. Harlow. Thus, on the basis of information given him, Nixon made his Aug. 29, 1972 statement that no one at the White House was involved in Watergate, Ehrlichman stated.

At another point, Weicker drew from the witness the fact that the President abandoned L. Patrick Gray 3rd when his nomination as FBI director ran into trouble in the Senate. Ehrlichman admitted saying that the White House "ought to let him [Gray] hang there, let him twist slowly, slowly in the wind."

In his fourth day of testimony July 27, Ehrlichman challenged Dean's version of a March 21 meeting with Nixon during which, according to Dean, Nixon had been given a thorough accounting of the case. Ehrlichman said Nixon did not get a detailed version until Ehrlichman reported on his own investigation April 14. During that two-week investigation, Ehrlichman contended, he first learned the details of the campaign intelligence plan which culminated in the Watergate break-in and the cover-up.

Ehrlichman's testimony also conflicted with Dean concerning a Feb. 27 meeting Dean had with the President, in which Nixon ordered Dean to assume full responsibility for matters relating to Watergate.

According to Ehrlichman, who was being interrogated by Sen. Gurney, the President at the Feb. 27 meeting told him and H. R. Haldeman, former White House chief of staff, that they were to divorce themselves from Watergate. Nixon, Ehrlichman testified, wanted them to "press on" entirely different projects. In their stead Nixon ordered Dean to concentrate on executive privilege, the Senate Watergate committee, the Watergate grand jury and collateral questions.

Under further questioning by Gurney, Ehrlichman said he was brought into the Watergate matter by the President March 30, when Nixon concluded that Dean was so heavily involved that he could no longer have anything to do with it.

In an April 5 interview with Paul O'Brien, an attorney for the Committee to Re-elect the President, Ehrlichman said he first learned of Watergate conspirator G. Gordon Liddy's plans against the Democrats. Among the information Ehrlichman claimed to have gleaned in the O'Brien interview:

■ Deputy Nixon campaign director Jeb Stuart Magruder named Mitchell as the person who approved plans to bug the Democratic National Committee headquarters.

■ Watergate conspirator E. Howard Hunt Jr. supervised undercover agents planted in the headquarters of Democratic Presidential contenders.

■ A Magruder statement to O'Brien that "the President wants this project [the bugging] to go on" was based on a statement White House aide Gordon C. Strachan allegedly made to Haldeman, his superior.

■ The President's former personal lawyer Herbert W. Kalmbach arranged a $70,000 blackmail payment to Hunt through Hunt's attorney, William O. Bittman.

When he had finished his own investigation, Ehrlichman said, he brought what he had learned to the President April 14–15. The President immediately instructed him to contact the attorney general, which Ehrlichman said he did.

In other testimony, Ehrlichman alluded to an April 8 meeting he and Haldeman had with Dean. While Dean said neither was indictable, each would have an awkward time explaining his connection with money that ended in the hands of the Watergate defendants, Ehrlichman testified.

Ehrlichman also suggested that the Watergate cover-up was intended to mask the role played by Mitchell in the intelligence plan that culminated in the Watergate burglary. He said Haldeman had asked if it were possible "we are taking all this anguish just to protect John Mitchell?"

Haldeman defends Nixon & himself.
H. R. Haldeman, Nixon's other former chief aide, began his testimony July 30 with a vigorous defense of the President and a general denial of guilt in the Watergate affair.

Haldeman's statement contained an admission that on two occasions, at Nixon's request, Haldeman had listened to tapes of two controversial meetings between the President and John Dean. Haldeman had been present during all of one meeting and part of another. Dean had based his testimony that the President was involved in the Watergate cover-up on recollections of those meetings held Sept. 15, 1972 and March 21, 1973.

A refutation of Dean's charges was at the heart of Haldeman's defense. He denied that he or the President had "knowledge of or involvement in" either the Watergate break-in or the subsequent cover-up.

He declared they were unaware of the cover-up attempt until March 1973, when the President "intensified his personal investigation into the facts of the Watergate."

Dean "apparently did not keep us [Ehrlichman and Haldeman] fully posted and it now appears he did not keep us accurately posted," Haldeman declared.

"As it now appears, we were badly misled by one or more of the principals and even more so by our own man [Dean], for reasons which are still not completely clear."

Haldeman's version of the post-break-in events closely resembled Ehrlichman's. Both insisted that they and the President had been too busy with other matters to investigate the Watergate affair.

"The view of all three of us through the whole period was that the truth must be told, and quickly; although we did not know what the truth was. Every time we pushed for action in this direction we were told by Dean that it could not be done," he testified.

Haldeman denied he had ordered Dean "to cover up anything," although he admitted it was "obvious that some people at the [re-election] committee were involved." Not knowing who to believe, Haldeman said he remained uncertain as to which campaign officials were involved.

He admitted there had been a White House effort during the 1972 election year "to contain the Watergate case in several perfectly legal and proper aspects."

One effort was made "to avoid the Watergate investigation possibly going beyond the facts of the Watergate affair itself and into national security activities totally unrelated to Watergate." Haldeman cited discussions with Central Intelligence Agency officials June 23, 1972 as part of this effort to limit the Watergate probe.

We discussed the White House concern regarding possible disclosure of non-Watergate-related covert CIA operations or other nonrelated national security activities that had been undertaken previously by some of the Watergate participants, and we requested Deputy Director [Vernon A.] Walters to meet with Director Gray of the FBI to express these concerns and to coordinate with the FBI so that the FBI's area of investigation of the Watergate participants not be expanded into unrelated matters which could lead to disclosures of earlier national security or CIA activities.

Other steps were taken to "reduce adverse political and publicity fallout" arising from the many lawsuits and investigations related to the actual Watergate break-in. There was a third concern about "distortion or fabrication of facts in the heat of a political campaign that would unjustly condemn the innocent or prevent discovery of the guilty."

Haldeman insisted that underlying this "containment effort" and "counterat-tack" strategy was a "concurrent effort" to obtain facts about the Watergate and make that information public.

Haldeman told the committee that he did not recall authorizing Dean to have Herbert Kalmbach raise money for the Watergate defendants. (Like Kalmbach and Ehrlichman, Haldeman insisted that the money was intended for the defendants' legal fees and family support.) All his information about the fund came from Dean and John Mitchell, according to Haldeman.

Haldeman echoed a theme familiar in past Senate testimony about the payoff money: "The rest of us relied on Dean and all thought that what was being done was legal and proper." They remained convinced of that, Haldeman said, until March 1973 when Dean said the payoff money could prove to be a "political embarrassment."

Haldeman said Dean had not advised Nixon of a Watergate cover-up during the Sept. 15, 1972 meeting.

According to Haldeman's statement:

As was the case with all meetings in the Oval Office when the President was there, this meeting with Mr. Dean was recorded. At the President's request, I recently reviewed the recording of that meeting (at which I was present throughout) in order to report on its contents to the President. ...

There was, as Mr. Dean has indicated, quite a lengthy discussion of the Patman hearings and the various factors involved in that. There was some discussion of the reluctance of the IRS to follow up on complaints of possible violations against people who were supporting our opponents because there are so many Democrats in the IRS bureaucracy that they won't take any action.

Dean and Nixon held meetings between Feb. 27 and March 21 that were "primarily concerned with executive privilege," according to Haldeman, but Nixon was also "intensifying pressure on Dean to find out a way to get the full story out."

"Dean at this time point was clearly in charge of any matters relating to the Watergate. He was meeting frequently with the President and he still indicated that he was positive there was no White House involvement," Haldeman said.

Haldeman insisted that Dean's "erroneous conclusions" about Nixon's involvement in a cover-up were based partially on a confusion of dates. Several events which Dean testified took place on March

13 actually occured on March 21, according to Haldeman.

Haldeman's version of the March 21 meeting depicted a President thwarted in efforts to obtain information from Dean about the Watergate but continuing to press for the facts. His addendum stated:

I was present for the final 40 minutes of the President's meeting with John Dean on the morning of March 21. While I was not present for the first hour of the meeting, I did listen to the tape of the entire meeting. . . .

Dean reported some facts regarding the planning and the break-in of the DNC and said again there were no White House personnel involved. He felt Magruder was fully aware of the operation, but he was not sure about Mitchell. He said that Liddy had given him a full rundown right after Watergate and that no one in the White House was involved. He said that his only concerns regarding the White House were in relation to the Colson phone call to Magruder which might indicate White House pressure and the possibility that Haldeman got some of the fruits of the bugging via Strachan since he had been told the fruits had been supplied to Strachan. . . .

Regarding the post-June 17th situation, he indicated concern about two problems, money and clemency. He said that Colson had said something to Hunt about clemency. He did not report any other offers of clemency although he felt the defendants expected it. The President confirmed that he could not offer clemency and Dean agreed.

Regarding money, Dean said he and Haldeman were involved. There was a bad appearance which could be developed into a circumstantial chain of evidence regarding obstruction of justice. He said that Kalmbach had raised money for the defendants; that Haldeman had okayed the return of the $350,000 to the committee, and that Dean had handled the dealings between the parties in doing this. He said that the money was for lawyers' fees.

He also reported on a current Hunt blackmail threat. He said Hunt was demanding $120,000 or else he would tell about the seamy things he had done for Ehrlichman. The President pursued this in considerable detail, obviously trying to smoke out what was really going on. He led Dean on regarding the process and what he would recommend doing. He asked such things as—well, this is the thing you would recommend? We ought to do this? Is that right? And he asked where the money would come from? How it would be delivered? And so on.

He asked how much money would be involved over the years and Dean said probably a million dollars—but the problem is that it is hard to raise. The President said there is no problem in raising a million dollars, we can do that, but it would be wrong. I have the clear impression that he was trying to find out what it was Dean was saying and what Dean was recommending. . . .

There was no discussion while I was in the room, nor do I recall any discussion on the tape on the question of clemency in the context of the President saying that he had discussed this with Ehrlichman and with Colson. The only mention of clemency was Dean's report that Colson discussed clemency with Hunt and the President's statement that he could not offer clemency and Dean's agreement—plus a comment that Dean thought the others expected it.

Dean mentioned several times during this meeting his awareness that he was telling the President things the President had known nothing about. . . .

Now, to the question of impression. Mr. Dean drew the erroneous conclusion that the President was fully knowledgeable of a cover-up at the time of the March 13 meeting in the sense (1) of being aware that money had been paid for silence and that (2) the money demands could reach a million dollars and that the President said that was no problem. He drew his conclusion from a hypothetical discussion of questions since the President told me later that he had no intention to do anything whatever about money and had no knowledge of the so-called cover-up.

Haldeman acknowledged "having agreed to the suggestion" that the White House hire Donald Segretti and that Kalmbach arrange to pay his salary and expenses.

He said Segretti's role was to be that of a Republican "Dick Tuck, who has been widely praised by political writers as a political prankster, whose basic stock in trade is embarrassing Republican candidates by activities that have been regarded as clever and acceptable parts of our political tradition."

According to Haldeman, there was nothing "wrong with the Segretti activity as it was conceived." It was his "clear understanding" he said, "that [Segretti] was to engage in no illegal acts."

Haldeman said he had "no recollection" of seeing Gemstone material or other intelligence reports related to the Watergate break-in and had "no recollection" of ordering Gordon Strachan to destroy intelligence files.

Haldeman testified that to the best of his recollection, he had not talked about Watergate to Jeb Stuart Magruder after a June 18, 1972 phone conversation.

Haldeman testified July 31 that he did not know the identities of those who had transmitted secret cash to Gov. George C. Wallace's opponent in a 1970 gubernatorial race.

Regarding the $350,000 cash fund held in the White House at his request and transfered to the re-election committee with his approval, Haldeman admitted that the cash had never been used by his office for "polling purposes" as previously described. The eventual use of the money, identified in earlier testimony as payoff money for the Watergate defendants, remained unknown to him, Haldeman insisted.

Haldeman claimed that his authority over budget matters involving the re-election committee was very general, but he admitted authorizing an allocation of $90,000 for "black" campaign projects conducted by White House counsel Charles Colson's office. When asked what "black" projects referred to, Haldeman said he was "not sure," but added that he doubted the reference was to "black advance" projects described by previous witnesses.

Haldeman acknowledged Aug. 1 that as a counteroffensive against Administration opponents he had suggested Feb. 10 that a story be leaked blaming anti-Nixon demonstrations in 1972 on the Democratic presidential candidate Sen. George McGovern (S.D.) and Communist party financial support for the demonstrations.

The Aug. 1 session was also highlighted by disclosure of a March 30, 1972 memorandum to Haldeman from Charles W. Colson, then a White House counsel, which stated that documents still existed which could implicate Nixon and other Administration officials in the questionable events leading to the 1971 antitrust settlement favorable to the International Telephone and Telegraph Corp.

Colson specifically mentioned the "$400,000 arrangement" for the company's support for the Republican party's 1972 convention.

Helms & Cushman testify. The Senate committee took testimony from ex-CIA Director Richard Helms Aug. 2, 1973 in an effort to shed light on the role of the CIA in the Watergate break-in. The question that most concerned the committee was: had the White House attempted to use the CIA to block an FBI probe of the Mexican aspects of the Watergate burglary?

Testimony by Helms and the two succeeding witnesses—former Deputy CIA Director Robert E. Cushman and current Deputy CIA Director Vernon A. Walters—had previously been given privately before other Congressional committees investigating the CIA.

Former White House aides H. R. Haldeman and John D. Ehrlichman had contended in their own testimony before the Watergate committee that the White House had wanted the FBI to limit its investigation of the use of a Mexico City bank to "launder" money used by the Watergate burglars. Both had maintained they were fearful that the FBI might impinge on CIA operations in Mexico, a point that was confirmed, they said, in a June 23, 1972 meeting when Helms was unable to assure them that this would not happen.

Helms gave the committee his version of the June 23 meeting attended by Helms, his deputy Walters, Haldeman and Ehrlichman.

According to Helms, Haldeman, after making an "incoherent reference to an investigation in Mexico, or an FBI investigation running into the Bay of Pigs," turned to Walters and asked him to talk to Acting FBI Director L. Patrick Gray 3rd and indicate that the FBI probe might run into CIA operations in Mexico. Haldeman wanted the FBI to taper off its Mexican investigation.

Helms said Haldeman's references to Mexico were unclear but he acceded because the President often possessed information no one else had.

After the meeting, Helms said he advised Walters not to follow Haldeman's order but to confine himself to reminding Gray of a long-standing agreement between the FBI and the CIA that if either agency ran into operations of the other it would notify that agency immediately.

Helms said he learned later that funds used by the Watergate burglars had been channeled through a Mexico City bank.

Helms testified about meetings that Walters held June 26–28, 1972 with White House counsel John W. Dean 3rd. Helms said Dean put out "feelers" in the hope that he could get the CIA to offer support for the Watergate burglars. Helms stated that he told Walters, "to be absolutely certain that he permitted nothing to happen using the agency's name, facilities or anything else in connection with this business."

Cushman, current Marine Corps commandant and the next witness Aug. 2, had given Hunt technical assistance that was utilized in the 1971 burglary of Ellsberg's psychiatrist's office.

The committee's attention focused on whether Ehrlichman had asked Cushman to assist Hunt. In testimony before the Watergate committee and other Congressional panels, Ehrlichman consistently maintained that he could not recollect calling Cushman in July 1971 on the matter. The issue had been clouded when Cushman had first asserted that Ehrlichman had asked for assistance. Cushman then had said he could not remember who had asked for aid for Hunt. Cushman May 31 recanted and announced that after an intensive search, CIA documents had been found establishing that Ehrlichman had made the call to request CIA aid. Official minutes of a July 8, 1971 CIA staff meeting confirmed that Ehrlichman had made a request for CIA assistance the day before.

Cushman also produced for the Senate committee the transcript of the conversation he had with Hunt in his CIA office July 22, 1971. The conversation, tape recorded by Cushman, confirmed that Ehrlichman had made the call to Cushman.

Throughout their testimony, Cushman and Helms insisted they had not known that Hunt intended to use the CIA equipment to burglarize Ellsberg's psychiatrist's office. Both witnesses contended they had not learned of the break-in until it was made public during the Ellsberg trial April 27.

Walters' testimony. Deputy CIA Director Vernon A. Walters testified Aug. 3.

Offering a version of the June 23, 1972 meeting similar to that of Helms, Walters emphasized that Haldeman had directed him to see Gray even after Helms had repeatedly assured Haldeman that no CIA operations in Mexico would be compromised by an FBI investigation.

Walters' testimony differed with his former superior in one respect. At no time, Walters said, did Helms say that Haldeman's message was not to be delivered to Gray.

Gray's story. Before the committee recessed for the weekend Aug. 3, ex-

Acting FBI Director Gray read an opening statement. The statement was in two sections: the first dealt with CIA involvement in aspects of the Watergate burglary, the second with Gray's handling of E. Howard Hunt's White House files, which he later destroyed.

Gray told the committee of a meeting with White House counsel John Dean June 22, 1972. Dean told him that he [Dean] was to be the liaison between the White House and the FBI in the Watergate matter and, as the President's counsel, he would sit in on FBI interviews of White House staff members. During the meeting, Gray said, he indicated to Dean that the FBI had evidence linking the Watergate burglars to the Committee to Re-elect the President.

In a second meeting that day, Gray said he discussed with Dean some of the bureau's early theories about Watergate, one of which was that the burglary might somehow have been part of a CIA operation.

During the meeting, Gray said he probably informed Dean of a conversation he had with Helms, also that day, in which Helms had stated that the CIA was not involved in Watergate. When Dean raised the possibility that the FBI would uncover a CIA operation in Mexico if it pushed its investigation, Gray said he responded "that the FBI was going to pursue all leads aggressively unless we were told by the CIA that there was a CIA interest or involvement."

Gray next spoke of a meeting he had with Deputy CIA Director Walters June 23, 1972, in which Walters "informed me that we were likely to uncover some CIA assets or resources if we continued our investigation into the Mexican money chain." Gray's statement conflicted with Walters' testimony about the meeting. Gray insisted that Walters did not say that he had just come from the White House. Gray contended, "I understood him to be stating a CIA position, not a White House message." Walters had asserted in his testimony that he had told Gray he was on a White House-ordered mission.

After his meeting with Walters, Gray received a call from Dean who asked the FBI to hold up its investigation of Manuel

Ogarrio, who was a go-between in the Mexican money transactions. Four days later Dean called to ask the FBI not to interview Kenneth Dahlberg, another middle man in the Mexican money chain, because of alleged CIA interest in him. A call to Helms the next day revealed that the CIA had no interest in Ogarrio, Gray said.

Gray testified that he was ordered by John Ehrlichman to cancel a meeting he had scheduled with Helms and Walters for June 28, 1972. Gray had returned an earlier phone call from Ehrlichman. Ehrlichman's "first words, issued abruptly, were, 'cancel your meeting with Helms and Walters today; it isn't necessary.' I asked him for his reasons and he simply said that such a meeting is not necessary. I then asked him point blank who was going to make the decisions as to who was going to be interviewed. He responded, 'You do.'" Gray added that he canceled his meeting with Helms and Walters.

At a White House meeting with Ehrlichman and Dean June 28, 1972, Gray testified, Dean gave him two folders, which Dean said contained papers of a sensitive political nature that Hunt had been working on. Dean warned that the papers had national security implications and, while not related to Watergate, could not be allowed to confuse the Watergate issue, Gray said.

I asked whether these files should become a part of our FBI Watergate file. Mr. Dean said these should not become a part of our FBI Watergate file but that he wanted to be able to say if called upon later, that he had turned all of Howard Hunt's files over to the FBI.

I distinctly recall Mr. Dean saying that these files were "political dynamite," and clearly should not see the light of day.

It is true that neither Mr. Ehrlichman nor Mr. Dean expressly instructed me to destroy the files. But there was, and is, no doubt in my mind that destruction was intended. Neither Mr. Dean nor Mr. Ehrlichman said or implied that I was being given the documents personally merely to safeguard against leaks . . . The clear implication of the substance and tone of their remarks was that these two files were to be destroyed and I interpreted this to be an order from the counsel to the President of the United States issued in the presence of one of the two top assistants to the President of the United States.

Gray testified that he held the files until shortly after Christmas 1972, when he burned them at his home in Connecticut with trash that had been accumulated during the holiday. Before destroying the files, Gray opened one which contained what appeared to him to be a top-secret State Department cable.

I read the first cable. I do not recall the exact language but the text of the cable implicated officials of the Kennedy Administration in the assassination of President [Ngo Dinh] Diem of South Vietnam. I had no reason then to doubt the authenticity of the "cable" and was shaken at what I read. I thumbed through the other "cables" in this file. They appeared to be duplicates of the first "cable." I merely thumbed through the second of the two files and noted that it contained onionskin copies of correspondence.

Gray contested Ehrlichman's version of two phone calls that took place between them April 15. Gray said he did not remember ever telling Ehrlichman that he would deny having received the Hunt files from Dean.

At the time I accepted the two files from Dean and Ehrlichman, at the time I destroyed them, and on the several occasions, prior to my denial to [Watergate prosecution supervisor] Henry Petersen on April 16, in which I resisted disclosure of the fact that I had received and destroyed the documents, I believed that I was acting faithfully, loyally, properly and legally pursuant to instructions given me by top assistants to the President of the United States.

I have come to believe, however, what I should have realized then, that my acceptance of the documents in the first place, and my keeping them out of the normal FBI files, was a grievous misjudgment. My destroying them and resistance of disclosure only compounded the error.

That the documents were not in fact Watergate evidence, while legally significant, does not lessen my present belief that I permitted myself to be used to perform a mere political chore.

Kleindienst & Petersen testify. Ex-Attorney General Richard G. Kleindienst appeared before the committee Aug. 7. He testified that while he ordered a thorough investigation of Watergate immediately on learning of the break-in June 17, 1972, he did not have "credible evidence" implicating high Administration officials until April 15, 1973.

Early in the morning of April 15, he heard Watergate prosecutors Seymour Glanzer, Donald Campbell, and Earl J. Silbert summarize in detail testimony they had taken from John Dean and Jeb Stuart Magruder. Among those implicated in the cover-up were two of Kleindienst's closest friends, former Attorney General John Mitchell and Robert C. Mardian, an official of the Committee to Re-elect the President.

Hours later, Kleindienst said, he and Henry E. Petersen, assistant attorney general in charge of the Justice Department's

Criminal Division, met Nixon and laid before him what they had learned from the Watergate prosecutors. Kleindienst said Nixon was "dumbfounded" at the news. In the discussion that followed, Kleindienst agreed that he must remove himself from the Watergate investigation because of his links to those who were implicated.

Kleindienst recounted for the Senate committee that on the morning of June 17, 1972—three hours after Kleindienst had learned of the Watergate break-in—he was visited at the Burning Tree golf club outside Washington by Watergate conspirator G. Gordon Liddy and Powell Moore, a campaign aide to John Mitchell. Kleindienst said Liddy had come at the suggestion of Mitchell to talk about those arrested in the break-in. Kleindienst said he responded by immediately calling Henry E. Petersen. While Liddy and Moore listened, Kleindienst instructed Petersen not to treat the Watergate defendants any differently from anyone else. Kleindienst said he also asked the two men to leave.

Kleindienst told of a call he received from John Ehrlichman Aug. 8 or 9, 1972. Ehrlichman was agitated because Petersen had refused to follow his instructions, which were not to "harass" Maurice Stans, chairman of the Finance Committee to Re-elect the President. Kleindienst said he told Ehrlichman he was lucky that Petersen was someone who "does not blow off the handle." Kleindienst said he told Ehrlichman that Petersen could resign, call a press conference, repeat what Ehrlichman had said, and Ehrlichman would then be open to a charge of obstruction of justice.

Ehrlichman still was not placated, Kleindienst stated, and backed down only after Kleindienst himself threatened to resign if Ehrlichman did not stop interfering, Kleindienst testified.

The last witness before the committee recessed Aug. 7 was Petersen.

Petersen took credit for informing the President April 18 that the Watergate prosecution team had learned of the 1971 burglary of Daniel Ellsberg's psychiatrist's office. "The President said when I told him, 'I know about that. This is a national security matter. You stay out of that. Your mandate is to investigate Wa-

tergate.' Now he didn't say he knew about the burglary. He said he knew about it—about the [prosecutor's] report. I think that is a vital distinction to be made."

Petersen said he was dissatisfied with Nixon's instructions and conveyed his feelings to Kleindienst April 25. Kleindienst, Petersen said, agreed that the judge in the Pentagon Papers trial, William M. Byrne Jr., should be told. Prepared to resign, Petersen said, if Nixon did not agree with their suggested course of action, the two men met with Nixon. However, the President endorsed "without hesitation" their intention to pass information about the burglary to Byrne.

Petersen was asked by Sen. Gurney if at any time he had suspected there was a cover-up of Watergate taking place. Petersen responded that he had a "visceral reaction. The word I used to the prosecutors and Kleindienst, nobody acts innocent. You couldn't translate that. There was an overriding concern. There were no records. Things were destroyed. They didn't act like innocent people. Innocent people come in and say, 'Fine, what do you want to know?' It was not like that, it was a visceral reaction. Yes, that is the reason we were so insistent to get this thing, get them tied down to sentence and immunize them [the seven original Watergate defendants]."

Petersen's testimony—like that of Gray and Kleindienst—conflicted with part of Nixon's April 30 statement on Watergate. Petersen denied that the President directed him March 21 or any time before April 15 "to get all the facts" about Watergate.

Petersen, who accompanied Kleindienst April 15 to tell Nixon what the Watergate prosecutors had learned from Dean and Magruder, told the Senate panel that he advised the President to dismiss Haldeman and Ehrlichman.

Q. Now, did you make any recommendation with regard to Mr. Dean?

A. Yes, I did. The President said, "You know, Haldeman and Ehrlichman deny this and I have to go to find this out. Dean in effect has admitted it. Should I request his resignation?" And I said, "My goodness, no. Now, here is the first man who has come in to cooperate with us and certainly we don't want to give the impression that he is being subjected to reprisal because of his cooperation. So please don't ask for his resignation at this point."

Later that month, Petersen said he informed Nixon that the prosecutor's negotiations with Dean had reached an impasse and Dean should not be retained on the White House staff.

Nixon had another conversation with Petersen about Dean April 18. Dean had told Nixon that he had been given immunity from prosecution; Petersen said he told the President no such offer had been made. The President then responded that he had Dean's statement on tape. Petersen testified that he declined Nixon's offer to listen to the tape.

Nixon Urges End of 'Obsession'

Again accepts full responsibility. President Nixon told the nation in a nationally televised speech Aug. 15, 1973 to give up its "backward-looking obsession" with Watergate, turn the case over to the courts and start attending to "matters of far greater importance."

The speech, and an accompanying written statement, comprised the President's fifth major statement on the Watergate scandal.

In his speech, the President said it was clear that the Senate Watergate hearings and some of the commentary on them were directed toward implicating him personally in the illegalities that occurred. He accepted full responsibility for the abuses that occurred during his Administration and his re-election campaign and asserted it was his duty to defend the office of the presidency against false charges.

He declined to offer a point-by-point rebuttal of charges in the case and restated his previous denials of complicity.

Nixon explained his actions after the Watergate break-in. His explanation was largely a restatement of his previous assertion that he had pressed repeatedly for information and was repeatedly misled until mid-April of 1973.

At this point, he said, it was clear that the situation was "far more serious" than he had believed and that the investigation should be given to the Criminal Division of the Justice Department. At that time, Nixon said, he turned over all the in-

formation he had to that department with the instruction it should "pursue the matter thoroughly," and he ordered all members of his Administration "to testify fully before the grand jury." He pointed out that the case was now before a grand jury in the hands of a special prosecutor appointed with his concurrence.

"Far from trying to hide the facts," the President emphasized, "my effort throughout has been to discover the facts—and to lay those facts before the appropriate law-enforcement authorities so that justice could be done and the guilty dealt with."

Nixon dealt at length with his refusal to turn over to the special prosecutor or the Senate committee his recordings of conversations he held in his office or on his telephone. There was "a much more important principle" involved in this, he said, "than what the tapes might prove about Watergate." That principle was the confidentiality of presidential discussions. He related this confidentiality to that required in conversations between members of Congress and their aides, judges and their law clerks, a lawyer and a client or a priest and a penitent.

It was "even more important that the confidentiality of conversations between a President and his advisers be protected," he said. It was "absolutely essential to the conduct of the presidency, in this and in all future Administrations."

If he released the tapes, Nixon said, the confidentiality of the presidency "would always be suspect from now on."

He said he would continue to "oppose efforts which would set a precedent that would cripple all future Presidents by inhibiting conversations between them and those they look to for advice."

Turning to "the basic issues" raised by Watergate, Nixon said he recognized "that merely answering the charges that have been made against the President is not enough. The word 'Watergate' has come to represent a much broader set of concerns."

"To most of us," he said, Watergate had come to mean "a whole series of acts that either represent or appear to represent an abuse of trust. It has come to stand for excessive partisanship, for 'enemy lists,' for efforts to use the great institutions of government for partisan political purposes."

"No political campaign ever justifies obstructing justice, or harassing individuals, or compromising those great agencies of government that should and must be above politics," he said. "To the extent that these things were done in the 1972 campaign, they were serious abuses. And I deplore them. . . ."

Nixon linked the Watergate abuses to an attitude arising during the 1960s "as individuals and groups increasingly asserted the right to take the law into their own hands, insisting that their purposes represented a higher morality." He said their attitude "was praised in the press and even from some of our pulpits as evidence of a new idealism. Those of us who insisted on the old restraints, who warned of the overriding importance of operating within the law and by the rules, were accused of being reactionaries."

This new attitude, he said, "brought a rising spiral of violence and fear, of riots and arson and bombings," all in the name of peace and justice. Political discussion turned into "savage debate," he said. "Free speech was brutally suppressed, as hecklers shouted down or even physically assaulted those with whom they disagreed."

"The notion that the end justifies the means proved contagious," the President said, and it was not surprising that some persons adopted the same morality in 1972.

But, he said, "those acts cannot be defended. Those who were guilty of abuses must be punished."

The "extremes of violence and discord in the 1960s," he said, "contributed to the extremes of Watergate" and "both are wrong. Both should be condemned. No individual, no group and no political party has a corner on the market on morality in America."

"If we learn the important lessons of Watergate, if we do what is necessary to prevent such abuses in the future—on both sides—we can emerge from this experience a better and a stronger nation," he continued.

Speaking of the Senate hearings, Nixon said "we have reached a point at which a continued, backward-looking obsession with Watergate is causing this nation to neglect matters of far greater importance."

"We must not stay so mired in Watergate," he said, "that the nation failed to respond to its national and world challenges. "We cannot let an obsession with the past destroy our hopes for the future."

Nixon's written statement—The President's written statement, released just prior to his speech Aug. 15, covered much the same ground as the speech and contained sections of identical text.

The statement asserted it would be "neither fair nor appropriate" for the President" to assess the evidence or comment on specific witnesses or their credibility" since this was the function of the committee and the courts. It was not his intention to attempt "comprehensive and detailed response" to "the questions and contentions raised" during the hearings nor "attempt a definitive account of all that took place." He did not believe he "could enter upon an endless course of explaining and rebutting a complex of point-by-point claims and charges arising out of that conflicting testimony which may engage committees and courts for months or years to come, and still be able to carry out my duties as President."

The statement again repeated Nixon's denials of complicity in the break-in or cover-up, his assertions that he ordered vigorous pursuit of the federal investigation of the break-in and his repeated demands for reports on Watergate developments.

When the indictments were returned against only the seven original defendants, he stated, it seemed to confirm the reports he was getting that no one then employed at the White House was involved. "It was in that context," Nixon stated, that he met with his counsel John W. Dean 3rd Sept. 15, 1972, and Dean gave him "no reason at that meeting to believe any others were involved."

"Not only was I unaware of any cover-up," Nixon continued, "but at that time, and until March 21, I was unaware that there was anything to cover up."

Nixon cited the March 21 date on which he said he learned for the first time that the planning for the break-in "went beyond" those who had been tried and "that at least one, and possibly more, persons at the re-election committee were involved."

He also learned that funds had been raised for payment to the defendants, but "not that it had been paid to procure silence," only that it was for lawyers' fees and family support. He learned "that a member of my staff had talked to one of the defendants about clemency, but not that offers of clemency had been made." And he learned that one of the defendants (E. Howard Hunt Jr.) was trying "to blackmail the White House by demanding payment of $125,000 as the price of not talking about other activities, unrelated to Watergate, in which he had engaged." "These allegations were made in general terms," Nixon stated, as "being based in part on supposition."

The allegations were "troubling," Nixon stated, they gave "a new dimension" to the Watergate matter. They also reinforced his determination, he stated, to have the full facts made available to the grand jury or the Senate committee and to have any illegalities "dealt with appropriately according to the law." If there was White House involvement, or involvement by high campaign committee personnel, he said, "I wanted the White House to take the lead in making that known."

This was the time Nixon began new inquiries into the case, the statement asserted. By April 15, based on reports from his aide John D. Ehrlichman and from then-Attorney General Richard G. Kleindienst and Watergate prosecutor Henry Petersen, and based on "independent inquiries" of his own, Nixon said, he realized he "would not be able personally to find out all of the facts and make them public" and he decided "that the matter was best handled by the Justice Department and the grand jury."

In his statement, Nixon corrected an inaccurate date in his May 22 Watergate statement that it was not until the time of his own investigation, March 21, that he learned of the break-in at the office of Daniel Ellsberg's psychiatrist. He had since determined that he first learned of that break-in March 17, he stated.

Acting on Kleindienst's advice at a meeting April 25, Nixon said, he authorized reporting the break-in to the Ellsberg case judge, "despite the fact that since no evidence had been obtained [in the break-in], the law did not clearly require it."

Press conference. Nixon answered a number of questions about Watergate during a news conference at his home in San Clemente, Calif. Aug. 22.

He was asked about his March 21, 1972 meeting with John W. Dean 3rd on the subject of raising funds for the Watergate defendants. He replied:

Basically, what Mr. Dean was concerned about on March 21 was not so much the raising of money for the defendants but the raising of money for the defendants for the purpose of keeping them still. In other words so-called hush money.

The one would be legal, in other words raising the defense funds for any group, any individual, as you know is perfectly legal and is done all the time. But you raise funds for the purpose of keeping an individual from talking, that's obstruction of justice.

Mr. Dean said also, on March 21, that there was an attempt to, as he put it, to blackmail the White House, to blackmail the White House by one of the defendants; incidentally, that defendant has denied it, but at least this is what Mr. Dean had claimed and that unless certain amounts of money were paid, I think it was $120,000 for attorneys' fees and other support, that this particular defendant would make a statement, not with regard to Watergate but with regard to some national security matters in which Mr. Ehrlichman had particular responsibility.

My reaction very briefly was this: I said as you look at this, I said isn't it quite obvious, first, that if it is going to have any chance to succeed, that these individuals aren't going to sit there in jail for four years, they're going to have clemency. Isn't that correct?

He said yes.

I said we can't given clemency.

He agreed.

Then I went to another point. The second point is that isn't it also quite obvious, as far as this is concerned, that while we could raise the money, and he indicated in answer to my question that it would probably take a million dollars over four years to take care of this defendant and others on this kind of a basis, the problem was, how do you get the money to them? And also, how do you get around the problem of clemency because they're not going to stay in jail simply because their families are being taken care of.

And so that was why I concluded, as Mr. Haldeman recalls, perhaps, and did testify very effectively, when I said John, it's wrong, it won't work, we can't give clemency, and we've got to get this story out. . . .

Senate Hearings Resume

Hunt testifies. The Senate Watergate committee resumed its televised hearings Sept. 24, 1973 with convicted Watergate conspirator E. Howard Hunt Jr. in the witness chair.

Hunt, testifying under a grant of immunity from prosecution, gave his first public testimony on the case, although he had been questioned under oath by various judicial and Congressional panels behind closed doors on more than 25 occasions.

Hunt also related his personal plight in the aftermath of Watergate, that he had been physically attacked and robbed and had suffered a stroke in his six months in jail, that he was "isolated from my four motherless children," that he had an "enormous financial burden" from legal fees and that he was "crushed by the failure of my government to protect me and my family, as in the past it has always done for its clandestine agents." Hunt had been a CIA agent for 21 years before his retirement in 1970.

Hunt, visibly embittered by his Watergate involvement, pleaded abandonment by the Administration, whose high officials had encouraged his participation in Watergate for legitimate national security reasons. Hunt denied seeking executive clemency or influencing other defendants to plead guilty and said the large payments he had received after his arrest were not for his silence, but for his career of service.

When he became involved in the Watergate break-in, Hunt told the committee, "I considered my participation as a duty to my country." After a career as a spy, "following orders without question," he said, he had never thought to question the propriety or legality of the Watergate break-in.

He frequently cited his working relationship with Charles W. Colson, then a special counsel to the President.

Hunt said he had been offered his White House job as a consultant by Colson and had worked under Colson's direction. His original work involved probing the origins of the Vietnam war and leaks of classified information, specifically the Pentagon papers. He began collecting derogatory information about Ellsberg, Hunt said, and assumed it was to be made available by Colson to selected members of the media.

Hunt said he believed the Watergate break-ins May 27 and June 17, 1972 were "unwise" but "lawful" and undertaken to obtain information to back up a reported contribution of campaign funds to the Democratic party from the Cuban government.

He had advised Colson beforehand, Hunt said, that he was working with Liddy on an extensive political intelligence plan for the Nixon re-election committee. Colson's reaction was that he "indicated that he was aware of the overall intelligence plan."

Hunt disclosed to the committee that he had proposed to "junk" the June 17 Watergate break-in after discovering the tape put on the door locks had been removed, but Liddy and another convicted conspirator, James W. McCord Jr., overruled him.

After the burglars were caught that night, Hunt, who was not apprehended, said he went to the White House and deposited in his safe some of McCord's electronic equipment and removed $10,-000 of "contingency" funds that were used for bail bonds for those arrested.

The committee documented two subsequent contacts between Hunt and Colson. The first was an Aug. 9, 1972 letter from Hunt to Colson expressing regret at "your being dragged into the case through association with me, superficial and occasional though the association was."

The second was a Nov. 24, 1972 telephone conversation, taped by Colson, in which Colson repeatedly advised Hunt not to give him details of his involvement in Watergate, that his value to him would be tainted unless he remained "as unknowing as I am."

The thrust of Hunt's conversation was for financial assistance for the Watergate defendants. "We're protecting the guys who are really responsible," Hunt told Colson, "but now that's that—and of course that's a continuing requirement, but at the same time, this is a two-way street and as I said before, we think that now is the time when a move should be made and surely the cheapest commodity available is money."

"I'm reading you," Colson assured him. "You don't need to be more specific."

Hunt admitted receiving funds for his legal fees and family assistance after his indictment and conviction but denied he made threats in order to get the money. William O. Bittman, who withdrew as his attorney in August, received $156,000 in legal fees.

When the anonymous packets of money stopped coming, Hunt said, he called Colson about it but eventually went to the Nixon re-election committee to see Paul O'Brien. He told O'Brien he would like his family to have the equivalent of two years' subsistence before he was jailed. And he told him of his "other activities, which I believe I described as 'seamy activities,' for the White House." Hunt denied that this was a threat to extract the funds in return for his silence about the "seamy activities." Rather, he said, he was citing his long and loyal service as grounds for receiving the subsistence.

O'Brien advised him, he said, to contact Colson, who by now had left the White House to practice law. Hunt tried but was rebuffed.

After these events, Hunt related, he received a final payment of cash on March 20 or 21, totaling $75,000, but he said he put it in a safe deposit box and eventually paid Bittman $80,000 collected from his late wife's insurance.

Hunt testified Sept. 25 that he had never been offered and had not sought executive clemency.

Political sabotage probed. Following the two days of testimony by Hunt, the Senate Select Committee on Presidential Campaign Activities Sept. 26, 1973 opened the second phase of its probe, focusing on alleged political sabotage during the 1972 presidential campaign. The first witness was Nixon speechwriter Patrick J. Buchanan.

Questioning Buchanan, the committee's majority set out to show that the policy groundwork for the campaign sabotage in 1972 had been firmly laid in early political strategy memorandums. Memos were released revealing Buchanan's urgings during the 1972 primaries to Nixon supporters to act to knock out one Democratic contender— Sen. Edmund S. Muskie (Me.)— considered a strong challenger to Nixon, and to elevate another Democratic contender—Sen. George S. McGovern (S.D.)—considered a weak challenger to the President.

But Buchanan denied any illegal or unethical tactics. He asserted that he had neither suggested nor participated in such activity. He portrayed his memo recommendations as within the bounds of political precedent.

Segretti's 'dirty tricks.' The Senate Watergate committee took testimony Oct. 3 from Donald H. Segretti on the "dirty tricks" he had played on Democratic candidates seeking the presidential nomination in 1972.

Segretti appeared at the televised public hearing under a court grant of limited immunity from prosecution. Segretti, 32, had pleaded guilty Oct. 1 to three charges of conspiracy and illegal campaign activities.

Segretti, a lawyer, told the committee he had been recruited by and reported to a White House aide, Dwight L. Chapin, Nixon's former appointments secretary. He said he was told his work was secret and was not to be traced to the White House. He related his "dirty tricks"— fake letters, posters, pamphlets, press releases, all false, planting fake demonstrators and placards and questions in news conferences, even surveillance on a candidate.

His salary was arranged with Nixon's personal attorney, Herbert W. Kalmbach, Segretti said, and he was to receive $16,000 a year plus expenses. Kalmbach was unaware of the nature of his work, he testified. Eventually, he received a total of about $45,000 in salary and expenses for his activities during 1971 and 1972, Segretti said. From September until June of those years, he said, he traveled from state to state where important primaries were being conducted, devising ways to carry out his assignment "to foster a split between the various Democratic hopefuls." He said he had sent reports of his activities, and copies of the false campaign literature he was disseminating, to Chapin.

Segretti was especially penitent about a phony letter on Muskie's stationery he had distributed during the Florida primary election accusing two other Democratic contenders, Sens. Hubert H. Humphrey (Minn.) and Henry M. Jackson (Wash.), of sexual and drinking misconduct. "It was a scurrilous letter," he said, and he wished to "apologize publicly for this stupid act." He testified that Chapin's reaction to the letter, which cost about $20 to reproduce, was mixed. Chapin told him afterward, he said, "for your $20, you received $10,000 to $20,000 worth of free publicity, but be careful next time."

Segretti testified that he was not involved in the Watergate break-in in June 1972 and that he stopped his campaign disruption activity afterwards.

In October 1972 when press reports of his activity appeared, Segretti said, he was summoned to Washington by White House counsel John W. Dean 3rd to discuss his activity and prepare a response. It was indicated he should stay out of sight.

Martin Kelly, 24, and Robert M. Benz, 24, who said they had been hired by Segretti to work in the "dirty tricks" operation, testified Oct. 4.

Benz, who had received limited immunity from prosecution, had been named as an unindicted co-conspirator by the Florida grand jury that had indicted Segretti. Benz had recruited George Hearing to assist in the campaign of sabotage.

Benz said he committed the political sabotage and espionage to give the Democrats "a little bit of a dose of their own type of activities." He contended that the Democrats had performed similar activities against a Republican senatorial candidate in Florida whom Benz had unsuccessfully worked to elect in 1970. As for the fake letter sent by accomplice Hearing accusing two Democratic contenders of sexual misconduct, Benz said he knew it was an illegal act and he was not proud of it, but he said he "felt like I did what I should do." "If my actions in any way would have cleaned up politics," he said, "they would have contributed something."

Sen. Ervin, questioning Benz, indicated that this was the first time "in the history of this nation where money donated to advance the political fortunes of a President was used with the consent of the President's assistants in the White House to spread libels against the candidates of the opposition political party.

ACLU urges impeachment of Nixon. The American Civil Liberties Union called Oct. 4 for the impeachment of President Nixon.

In a resolution adopted "overwhelmingly" by its board of directors, the organization said "there is now substantial public evidence of President Nixon's participation in high crimes and misdemeanors, and these acts have violated the civil liberties of the people of the United States and the rule by law."

ACLU Chairman Edward J. Ennis said the impeachment was being sought on six grounds: "specific proved violations of the rights of political dissent; usurpation of Congressional war-making powers; establishment of a personal secret police which committed crimes; attempted interference in the trial of Daniel Ellsberg; distortion of the system of justice; and perversion of other federal agencies."

ACLU Executive Director Aryeh Neier said pursuit of the impeachment goal would be "a major purpose" of the organization, which would push a lobbying effort through its 250,000 members and three lobbyists in Washington.

Nixon Fires Prosecutor In Dispute Over Tapes

A dispute over President Nixon's refusal to turn over tapes of White House conversations to federal investigators resulted in the resignation of Attorney General Elliot L. Richardson and the dismissals of Deputy Attorney General William B. Ruckleshaus and special Watergate prosecutor Archibald Cox. Cox had rejected a compromise plan of Nixon's to end the dispute by providing a "summary" that would be verified by Sen. John Stennis (D, Miss.). The U.S. Circuit Court of Appeals for the District of Columbia had ordered Oct. 12, 1973 that the tapes be turned over to Federal Judge John J. Sirica.

Presidential immunity denied. In its Oct. 12 decision, the appeals court had denied that the President had any "special . . . immunities."

The appeals court ordered the President to turn over the complete tapes in question, specifying which parts should and should not be disclosed. The final decision to send any or all of the material to the grand jury would then be made by the district court. The judge would hold a closed hearing on the issue if either disputant desired. Then he could "order disclosure of all portions of the tapes relevant to matters within the proper scope of the grand jury's investigation," the appeals court held, unless it found in "particular" statements or information "that the public interest served by nondisclosure outweighed the grand jury's need for the information."

The majority opinion was rendered by David L. Bazelon, chief judge, J. Skelly Wright. Carl McGowan, Harold Leventhal and Spottswood W. Robinson 3rd. George E. MacKinnon and Malcolm R. Wilkey were in the minority.

As for the question of presidential immunity, the court said: "The Constitution makes no mention of special presidential immunities. Indeed, the executive branch generally is afforded none. This silence cannot be ascribed to oversight."

"Lacking textual support," it continued, the President's counsel "nonetheless would have us infer immunity from the President's political mandate, or from his vulnerability to impeachment, or from his discretionary powers. These are invitations to refashion the Constitution and we reject them.

"Though the President is elected by nationwide ballot, and is often said to represent all the people, he does not embody the nation's sovereignty. He is not above the law's commands. . . . Sovereignty remains at all times with the people and they do not forfeit through elections the right to have the law construed against and applied to every citizen.

"Nor does the impeachment clause imply immunity from routine court process. While the President argues that the clause means that impeachability precludes criminal prosecution of an incumbent, we see no need to explore this question except to note its irrelevance to the case before us. . . . By contemplating the possibility of post-impeachment trials for violations committed in office, the impeachment clause itself reveals that incumbency does not relieve the President of the routine legal applications that confine all citizens."

On the issue of executive privilege, the court said "the Constitution mentions no executive privilege, much less any absolute executive privilege." While there

had been "longstanding judicial recognition" of executive privilege, it noted, it was the longstanding corollary opinion of the courts that "the applicability of the privilege is in the end for them and not the executive to decide."

"Throughout our history," the court said, "there have frequently been conflicts between independent organs of the federal government, as well as between the state and federal governments. . . . Our constitutional system provides a means for resolving them—one Supreme Court. To leave the proper scope and application of executive privilege to the president's sole discretion would represent a mixing, rather than a separation, of executive and judicial functions."

As for the application of executive privilege to this case, the court said the presumption in favor of utilizing privilege "must fall in the face of the uniquely powerful showing made by the special prosecutor." The court referred to the President's decision not to assert a privilege for oral testimony by his aides, which diluted his claim of privilege for the tapes. It also referred to the prosecutor's showing from testimony by the aides that there was a "significant likelihood" of a broad criminal conspiracy, that important evidence about it was contained in conversations that were taped, and that there were "significant inconsistencies" relating to the taped conversations that raised a "distinct possibility" that perjury had been committed before a Congressional committee and perhaps a grand jury.

In conclusion, the court cautioned that its order "represents an unusual and limited requirement that the President produce material evidence. We think this required by law, and by the rule that even the chief executive is subject to the mandate of law when he has no valid claim of privilege."

In dissent, Judge MacKinnon expressed concern about the effect the majority's decision would have "upon the constitutional independence of our president for all time." Judge Wilkey stated that "the practical capacity of the three independent branches to adjust to each other their sensitivity to the approval or disapproval of the American people have been sufficient guides to responsible action, without imposing the authority of one co-equal branch over another."

Cox rejects Nixon plan. Nixon had announced his compromise Oct. 19, and it was rejected by Cox the same day.

The President said the compromise plan had been drawn up by Richardson and agreed to by Senate Watergate committee Chairman Sam J. Ervin Jr. (D, N.C.) and Vice Chairman Howard H. Baker Jr. (R, Tenn.). Nixon said Stennis had consented to his verification role.

The President expressed his opinion that the compromise tapes plan would resolve "any lingering thought that the President himself might have been in a Watergate cover-up."

Cox said the proposed summary would lack "the evidentiary value of the tapes themselves" and "no steps are being taken to turn over the important notes, memoranda and other documents that the court orders require." He expressed his judgment that "the President is refusing to comply with the court decrees."

Richardson, Ruckelshaus & Cox out. The White House announced at 8:24 p.m. Oct. 20 that President Nixon had discharged special prosecutor Cox and Deputy Attorney General Ruckelshaus for refusing to obey his orders on the handling of the Watergate tapes. Nixon also accepted the resignation of Attorney General Richardson.

White House Press Secretary Ronald L. Ziegler said Richardson had resigned rather than discharge Cox.

Ruckelshaus was then asked to carry out the President's order to discharge Cox. When he refused, according to Ziegler, Ruckelshaus was fired.

Cox's dismissal was finally carried out by Solicitor General Robert H. Bork, who was appointed acting attorney general.

The President also announced through Ziegler that he had abolished the special Watergate prosecutor's office as of 8 p.m. and transferred its duties back to the Justice Department where they would "be carried out with thoroughness and vigor."

Ziegler said Cox had been discharged

because he had "pressed for a confrontation at a time of serious world crisis." The press secretary said the President's tape plan would have provided the Watergate grand jury with "what it needs with the least possible intrusion into presidential privacy."

Acting Attorney General Bork announced Oct. 22 that he had placed Henry E. Petersen in direct charge of the Watergate case "and all related matters previously being directed by the special prosecutor." Petersen would use the evidence and staff already assembled, as well as other department personnel, Bork said, "to see that these cases are pressed to a conclusion and that justice is done." Bork, who said he would have "ultimate authority and responsibility in these matters," said he planned "to adhere exactly to President Nixon's directive" to pursue the cases "with full vigor."

At a news conference Oct. 24, Bork pledged to take any steps necessary to obtain evidence from the White House if it was vital to prosecution of the Watergate cases. "If the law entitles us to any item of evidence, I will go after it," he said. Bork said he was not going to be the person "who in any way compromised any investigation." He said the President had told him "I want you to carry out these investigations and prosecutions fully." On the basis of his talk with the President, Bork said, he believed he was free to conduct the Watergate probes "the way I think they ought to be done."

Nixon to provide tapes. President Nixon decided Oct. 23 to turn over the tapes to the court. The announcement was made before Judge Sirica.

Earlier Oct. 23, Sirica had summoned the two Watergate grand juries before him to assure the jurors their probes were still "operative and intact" and he himself would "safeguard" their rights and "preserve the integrity of your proceedings."

At a later hearing, Sirica asked the President's attorneys if they were prepared to file "the response of the President" to his Aug. 29 order as modified by the appeals court.

Charles Alan Wright, chief of the President's Watergate legal defense team, stepped forward and said "the President of the United States would comply in all respects" with Sirica's order as modified by the higher court.

New attorney general, prosecutor named.

In a brief appearance at the White House Nov. 1, President Nixon announced he would appoint Sen. William B. Saxbe (R, Ohio) to succeed Elliot L. Richardson as attorney general. Nixon then left the room without answering questions, and Acting Attorney General Robert H. Bork announced that with Nixon's approval he had appointed Houston lawyer Leon Jaworski, a Democrat, to succeed Archibald Cox as special Watergate prosecutor.

In announcing Jaworski's appointment, Bork said Jaworski would have the same charter as Cox, with the additional commitment that Nixon would not exercise "his constitutional powers" to fire him without the consent of a "substantial majority" of eight Congressional leaders from both parties.

Bork said Jaworski would have the "full cooperation of the executive branch" and, in the event of a disagreement with the Administration "with regard to the release of presidential documents, there will be no restrictions placed on his freedom of action."

Tape erasure disclosed.

The usefulness of presidential tape recordings as evidence in the Watergate case, as well as President Nixon's credibility, suffered further damage Nov. 21 when the White House revealed that a key segment of one of the subpoenaed tapes was blank. In subsequent testimony before U.S. District Court Judge John J. Sirica, Nixon's personal secretary Rose Mary Woods said she had made the "terrible mistake" of accidentally erasing a portion of a June 20, 1972 conversation between Nixon and H. R. Haldeman, then his chief of staff.

Special White House counsel J. Fred Buzhardt Jr. told Sirica Nov. 21 that an 18-minute portion of the tape contained an "audible tone" but no conversation. Buzhardt said he had learned of "the phenomenon" Nov. 14 in the process of preparing an analysis and index of the tapes for the court, and Nixon had been told "shortly thereafter."

Buzhardt said "a large number of technical tests" had been conducted with the problem tape Nov. 20 but had not provided an explanation for the unrecorded portion. "All other tapes are audible," Buzhardt added.

After Buzhardt's announcement, Sirica ordered the original tapes submitted to him for safekeeping, saying "this is just another instance that convinces the court that it has to take some steps, not because the court doesn't trust the White House or the President," but "in the interest of seeing that nothing else happens."

The White House Nov. 26 turned over to the court the subpoenaed tapes, along with a document analyzing the tapes and outlining claims of executive privilege for some of the material.

The document also contained the White House explanation for the blank space in the June 20, 1972 tape, which it said occurred approximately three minutes and 40 seconds after the beginning of Nixon's conversation with Haldeman. The erasure was caused, the document stated, "by the depression of a record button during the process of reviewing the tape, possibly while the recorder was in the proximity of an electric typewriter and a high intensity lamp."

Miss Woods gave her own account of the tape "accident" Nov. 26–28. She related that she had been in her White House office Oct. 1 transcribing the Ehrlichman meeting, with instructions to stop there, she said, because presidential chief of staff Alexander M. Haig Jr. had told her the Haldeman conversation which followed was not covered by the subpoena.

The Haldeman portion had just begun, she said, when her telephone rang. In reaching for the phone, "through some error on my part," she pressed the "record" button rather than the "stop" button. At the same time, Miss Woods continued, she must have pressed on the foot pedal of the machine, which could have erased a part of the tape.

After her phone conversation (which she described at various points in her testimony as lasting four, five or six minutes), she discovered the "record" button still depressed, replayed the tape and discovered the "gap." She immediately informed Nixon, who, she said, told her "don't worry about it." There was "no problem because that's not one of the subpoenaed tapes."

Miss Woods testified later that it was not until the White House was making copies of the tapes in preparation for complying with the subpoena that the full 18-minute length of the gap was discovered. She said she did not think she could have been responsible for the entire erasure.

Presidential counsel J. Fred Buzhardt Jr. revealed Nov. 28 that there were a "number" of spaces on the subpoenaed tapes without "identifiable sound." Buzhardt said the gaps were discovered in the process of copying the tapes Nov. 14.

Buzhardt and presidential lawyer Leonard Garment attempted to dismiss the new gaps as an inconsequential and "collateral" issue, the significance of which would have to be determined by technical experts. Assistant prosecutor Richard Ben-Veniste noted, however, that some of the spaces lasted "several minutes." Buzhardt said the gaps could have occurred when the "sound-actuated" taping system was set off by extraneous noises besides conversation.

(A White House spokesman said later Nov. 28 that the seven subpoenaed conversations were "intact," except for the disputed 18-minute gap in the Haldeman tape.)

White House legal team revamped. Boston lawyer James D. St. Clair was named special presidential counsel in charge of Watergate matters, replacing J. Fred Buzhardt Jr., the White House announced Jan. 4, 1974.

Buzhardt was named counsel to the President—technically a promotion, but widely seen as a reflection of presidential dissatisfaction with his handling of the tapes issue.

Krogh sentenced, denies Nixon role. Egil Krogh Jr., the former White House aide who once headed the special investigative unit known as the "plumbers," was sentenced to six months Jan. 24, 1974 in connection with the 1971 break-in at the office of the psychiatrist who had treated

Pentagon Papers defendant Daniel Ellsberg. Krogh had pleaded guilty Nov. 30, 1973 to a charge of conspiring to violate the civil rights of Dr. Lewis J. Fielding.

Although there had been widespread speculation that Krogh would implicate President Nixon in illegal activities by the plumbers, Krogh said in a statement released after the sentencing that he had "received no specific instruction or authority whatsoever regarding the break-in from the President, directly or indirectly."

In his appearance before U.S. District Court Judge Gerhard A. Gesell in Washington, Krogh said he accepted sole responsibility for "repulsive conduct" in the violation of individual rights in the guise of "national security."

Gesell sentenced Krogh to a term of 2–6 years, but suspended all but six months. Other charges had been dropped in return for the guilty plea.

In his statement, Krogh detailed how his role had begun on July 15 or 16, 1971, when John D. Ehrlichman, then Nixon's domestic affairs adviser, told him he was to "perform an urgent assignment in response to the unauthorized disclosure of the Pentagon Papers." The "entire resources of the executive branch" were to be used to determine responsibility for the leaks, and to assess Ellsberg's motives and "his potential for further disclosures."

The plumbers' mandate was expanded, Krogh continued, after his July 24, 1971 meeting with Nixon and Ehrlichman. The meeting followed the leak of the U.S. "fallback position" at the Strategic Arms Limitation Talks (SALT).

The unit's work on the SALT leak, the Ellsberg case and "some other unauthorized disclosures" was completely "fired up and overshadowed" by the "intensity of the national security concern expressed by the President."

It was in this context, Krogh said, that the "Fielding incident" took place. Krogh suggested that this "deep concern" explained why John W. Dean 3rd, Nixon's former counsel, had testified that Krogh had described the authority for the Fielding burglary as coming directly from "the oval office."

Krogh said he had "just listened" to the tape of the July 24, 1971 meeting, and

"Ellsberg's name did not appear to be mentioned." (The tape had been voluntarily turned over to the special prosecutor.)

That meeting, Krogh said, was the "only direct contact I had with the President on the work of the unit." As for the instructions to gather data on Ellsberg, they must have been "relayed to me by Ehrlichman."

Democrats' civil suit settled. Robert S. Strauss, chairman of the Democratic National Committee, announced Feb. 28, 1974 a final agreement to settle out of court for $775,000 its civil damage suit against the Committee to Re-elect the President. The Democrats had sued for $6.4 million over the break-in at the party's Watergate headquarters.

Co-defendants in the suit were former Nixon campaign officials and Cabinet members John N. Mitchell and Maurice H. Stans, convicted conspirators G. Gordon Liddy and E. Howard Hunt Jr., and former re-election committee treasurer Hugh W. Sloan Jr.

The settlement accord included commitments by the Republicans to drop countersuits against the Democrats.

The Democrats had charged that Stans and Sloan had delivered $114,000 to finance an "espionage squad" and had stated that the funds were accounted for in the committee's records although the records had been destroyed.

Nixon vs. break-in & cover-up. President Nixon was asked at a convention of the National Association of Broadcasters in Houston, Tex. March 19, 1974 whether the country would have been better served if the Watergate break-in had gone undetected.

"Certainly not," Nixon replied. It was "wrong" and "stupid" and "should never have happened" and "should not have been covered up and I have done the very best that I can over the past year to see that it is uncovered."

"When something happens like this, to say, cover it up, forget it, when it is wrong, this of course is completely against our American system of values and I would very, very seriously deplore it."

Nixon Aides Indicted

Grand juries in Washington March 1 and 7, 1974 indicted seven former key figures in the White House and President Nixon's re-election campaign.

Cover-up charges detailed. The historic indictment of seven former White House and campaign aides on charges of covering up the Watergate scandal was returned March 1 in a 15-minute session in the courtroom of Chief U.S. District Court Judge John J. Sirica.

The grand jury (the first of three dealing with the Watergate case) also delivered a sealed "report and recommendation" reportedly dealing with President Nixon's relation to the cover-up.

(The White House acknowledged June 6 that Nixon had been named in the indictment as an unindicted co-conspirator. Nixon's special counsel James D. St. Clair quoted Nixon as asserting that "They just don't have the evidence, and they are wrong.")

The defendants and the charges against them:

John D. Ehrlichman, Nixon's former domestic affairs adviser: one count each of conspiracy, obstruction of justice and making false statements to the Federal Bureau of Investigation (FBI), and two counts of false declarations before a grand jury or court.

H. R. Haldeman, former White House chief of staff: one count each of conspiracy and obstruction of justice and three counts of perjury (before the Senate Watergate Committee).

John N. Mitchell, former attorney general and director of Nixon's 1968 and 1972 campaigns: one count each of conspiracy, obstruction of justice, perjury, and false statements to the FBI, and two counts of false declarations to a grand jury or court.

Charles W. Colson, former presidential counsel: one count each of conspiracy and obstruction of justice.

Gordon C. Strachan, Haldeman's former assistant: one count each of conspiracy, obstruction of justice and false declarations.

Robert C. Mardian, former assistant attorney general and a 1972 Nixon campaign aide: one count of conspiracy.

Kenneth W. Parkinson, attorney for the Committee to Re-elect the President: one count each of conspiracy and obstruction of justice.

All seven pleaded not guilty March 9.

The charges: *conspiracy*—The overall conspiracy charge involving all seven defendants detailed the complex scenario in which the defendants—with other persons "known and unknown"—arranged "hush money" payoffs for those first charged in the Watergate burglary and wiretapping, offered executive clemency, destroyed documents and lied to various investigative bodies—all of which formed the basis for the other charges in the indictment.

A central figure in the grand jury's narrative was former presidential counsel John W. Dean 3rd, who had already pleaded guilty to one count of conspiracy and was cooperating with the prosecution.

According to the 45 "overt acts" of conspiracy cited by the grand jury, the cover-up began within hours after the break-in at Democratic Party headquarters June 17, 1972: Mitchell told Mardian to try to arrange for the intercession of Richard G. Kleindienst, then attorney general, in getting the arrested burglars out of jail.

Over the next few days, Strachan destroyed documents on Haldeman's orders, and Mitchell suggested to Jeb Stuart Magruder, deputy campaign director for the re-election committee, that other documents in Magruder's files be destroyed. Concern over G. Gordon Liddy and E. Howard Hunt Jr., the still-unarrested burglary conspirators, led Ehrlichman to direct Dean to tell them they "should leave the United States," and to tell Dean to "take possession" of the contents of Hunt's safe.

Liddy and Hunt did not leave, and after Liddy reminded Mardian and campaign aide Frederick C. LaRue of certain financial "commitments" to those involved in the break-in, the sequence of fund-raising and clandestine payoffs began.

On June 26 and June 28, 1972, Ehrlichman approved two suggestions re-lating to possible sources of funds. Dean's first approach was to the Central Intelligence Agency (CIA) for "covert funds to pay for bail and salaries." Having apparently failed, Dean went to Herbert W. Kalmbach, Nixon's personal attorney. The first payoff was delivered July 7—$25,000 in cash to William O. Bittman, Hunt's attorney.

A key "overt act" of obstruction occurred in mid-July: Mitchell, in the presence of Parkinson, told Dean to obtain FBI reports on its Watergate investigation; Mardian, meeting with Dean, examined the reports July 21.

Meanwhile, according to the indictment, the payoffs continued as demands escalated. By Oct. 13, 1972, an additional $182,500 had been delivered, mostly by Anthony T. Ulasewicz, a former New York City policeman who dealt with Kalmbach and Parkinson under "code names." Kalmbach remained the major fund-raiser, under instructions from Ehrlichman at a White House meeting that the fund-raising and payments should be kept secret.

Hunt was apparently not satisfied: in a telephone conversation with Colson in mid-November 1972, Hunt pressed the need for additional payments. Colson taped the conversation, and—through Dean—the demands were relayed to Haldeman, Ehrlichman and Mitchell. In early December 1972 and early January 1973 Haldeman gave Dean his approval for the use of a $350,000 cash fund then under Haldeman's control; shortly afterwards, Strachan delivered approximately $300,000 to LaRue.

As the trial of the break-in defendants approached in early January 1973, discussions among the cover-up conspirators began to focus on the possibility of executive clemency. One such meeting of Ehrlichman, Colson and Dean centered on "assurances" for Hunt, and during the same period Mitchell instructed Dean to relay a promise of clemency to James W. McCord Jr.

Payments to Hunt continued even after the first criminal trial ended Jan. 30, 1973 with the conviction of Liddy and McCord. (Hunt had pleaded guilty Jan. 11, 1973.)

Dean was told by Ehrlichman March 19, 1973 to inform Mitchell that Hunt had demanded another $120,000, and the demand was discussed further two days later at a White House meeting "attended by" Haldeman and Dean. After phone conversations involving Haldeman, Mitchell and LaRue, arrangements were made for a payment of $75,000 to Hunt's lawyer.

Perjury: Haldeman, Dean and Nixon meeting—The key perjury charge against Haldeman concerned his testimony before the Senate Watergate Committee about the March 21, 1973 meeting with Dean and President Nixon.

The first hour of the meeting had involved only Nixon and Dean; Haldeman was present for the following 40 minutes, he told the Senate panel, but had listened to a tape of the entire session.

Giving the "best of [his] recollection" of the meeting, Haldeman said Nixon, questioning Dean on Hunt's $120,000 "blackmail threat" over the "seamy things" Hunt had done for Ehrlichman, was trying to "smoke out what was really going on" and had "led Dean on." Dean said a million dollars might be needed over the years, "but the problem is that it is hard to raise." According to Haldeman, Nixon had said, "There is no problem" in raising the money, "but it would be wrong." Haldeman told the panel the tape of the meeting confirmed his recollection.

The grand jury charged that Haldeman's statements about Nixon's "it would be wrong," as Haldeman "then and there well knew, were false."

Nixon had backed up Haldeman's testimony as "accurate" in an Aug. 22, 1973 news conference, recalling that he had told Dean—concerning both clemency and payoffs—"John, it's wrong, it won't work, we can't give clemency, and we've got to get this story out."

Perjury: Haldeman and Mitchell; money and documents—Haldeman's Senate committee testimony on the $350,000 cash fund under his control, which according to the grand jury was used for "hush money" payments to the break-in defendants, resulted in a second perjury charge. Haldeman had said he was unaware of their use for "blackmail" until told by Dean in March 1973. This, the indictment charged, was false.

(Gordon Strachan's testimony before the grand jury on the handling of the money was the basis of the false declarations charge against him.)

Haldeman's third perjury count went back to the March 21, 1973 White House meeting, which—according to Dean's testimony before the Senate Committee—had included Dean's report on the preparation of a false story on the planning of the break-in to be used by Magruder. Haldeman later told the panel; "I don't believe there was any reference to Magruder committing perjury." This statement was false, the indictment charged.

Mitchell was charged with perjury in connection with his Watergate committee testimony on the so-called "Gemstone" file of wiretap information from Democratic Party headquarters. Asked about a meeting in his apartment June 19, 1972, Mitchell said he had not heard of the Gemstone file as of that date, nor to the "best of [his] recollection" had there been any destruction of documents. The statements were false, the grand jury charged.

False statements to probers—The indictment charged that Mitchell on two occasions testified falsely before the grand jury. On the first, Mitchell said he knew of no illegal, clandestine plans against the Democrats, "because, if there had been, I would have shut it off as being entirely nonproductive at that particular time of the campaign." Mitchell testified later that he could not recall being told by LaRue or Mardian that Liddy had confessed to a role in the break-in.

Ehrlichman was also charged with two counts of lying to the grand jury. According to the first charge, Ehrlichman testified falsely when he said he could not recall discussing Liddy's role in the break-in with Dean; nor could he recall when he first learned that Liddy was implicated. The grand jury also charged that Ehrlichman lied in testifying that he could not recall discussing with Kalmbach the purpose of Kalmbach's fund-raising or telling Kalmbach that the fund-raising should be kept secret.

Both Mitchell and Ehrlichman were accused of falsely telling the FBI that their knowledge of the break-in was limited to newspaper accounts. Mitchell's statement came less than three weeks after the break-in, but Ehrlichman was charged with saying as late as July 21, 1973 "that he had neither received nor was he in possession of any information relative to the break-in . . . other than what he had read in the way of newspaper accounts. . . ."

Ellsberg burglary indictment. A second Watergate grand jury March 7, 1974 indicted six men in connection with the September 1971 burglary of the office of Dr. Lewis J. Fielding, the Los Angeles psychiatrist who had treated Pentagon Papers defendant Daniel Ellsberg. The burglary had been carried out under the aegis of the special White House investigative unit known as the "plumbers."

The charge was conspiring to violate Fielding's civil rights by acting together to "oppress, threaten and intimidate" Fielding by entering his office "without legal process, probable cause, search warrant or other lawful authority" and by concealing "the involvement of officials and employes of the United States Government."

Those charged with conspiracy were:

John D. Ehrlichman.

Charles W. Colson.

G. Gordon Liddy, Bernard L. Barker and Eugenio R. Martinez, all of whom had been convicted in the Watergate break-in.

Felipe DeDiego, who had previously been named as an unindicted co-conspirator in a California state case relating to the Fielding burglary. (The charge against DeDiego was dismissed May 21 because he had been given immunity by the state prosecutors in return for his testimony.)

The indictment named as unindicted co-conspirators E. Howard Hunt Jr., Egil Krogh Jr. and David R. Young Jr.

Ehrlichman was also charged with three counts of false declarations to the grand jury and one count of lying to the Federal Bureau of Investigation (FBI).

The conspiracy—In a list of 19 "overt acts," the indictment related that the conspiracy began July 27, 1971 with a memorandum from Krogh and Young [the co-directors of the "plumbers"] to Ehrlichman dealing with a request for a

psychiatric study of Ellsberg. Ehrlichman was told three days later that the request had been directed to the Central Intelligence Agency.

Ehrlichman approved a "covert operation" Aug. 11, provided he was given the "assurance it is not traceable." By Aug. 30, Krogh and Young were able to give Ehrlichman the assurance he required.

Meanwhile, Colson, Young and Krogh began discussing raising covert funds to pay the actual burglars.

The money problem was solved around the first of September: Colson arranged to obtain $5,000 in cash, which was repaid by a transfer from the Trust for Agricultural Political Education (a dairy industry group). Krogh delivered the money to Liddy Sept. 1, and Liddy and Hunt went to Los Angeles to meet with Barker, DeDiego and Martinez. The latter three broke into Fielding's office Sept. 3.

The final act of conspiracy cited by the grand jury came March 27, 1973, when Ehrlichman "caused the removal of certain memoranda" on the burglary "from files maintained at the White House in which such memoranda would be kept in the ordinary course of business."

Ehrlichman's false statements—The one count charging Ehrlichman with lying to the FBI involved the agency's probe into whether the Fielding burglary might taint the prosecution of Ellsberg. Ehrlichman told the FBI May 1, 1973 that he had not seen material on the White House investigation of the Pentagon Papers affair in more than a year.

Ehrlichman appeared before a grand jury May 14, 1973 and maintained repeatedly that he knew of the burglary and the instructions to prepare a psychological profile of Ellsberg only "after the fact."

Chapin sentenced. Dwight L. Chapin, former appointments secretary to President Nixon, was sentenced to a term of 10 to 30 months May 15, 1974 for lying to a grand jury about his involvement in political sabotage operations during the 1972 presidential campaign.

Chapin had been convicted on two perjury counts April 5.

In passing sentence, U.S. District Court Judge Gerhard A. Gesell told Chapin he "apparently chose loyalty to your superiors above obligations as a citizen and a public servant." Chapin's "resort to the convenience of swearing falsely" could not be condoned, Gesell said.

Magruder sentenced. Jeb Stuart Magruder, former deputy director of the Committee to Re-elect the President, was sentenced to a prison term of 10 months to four years May 21, 1974 for helping to plot the Watergate break-in and cover-up. Magruder had pleaded guilty to a variety of charges, including perjury, conspiracy and obstruction of justice.

Colson pleads guilt to one count. Charles W. Colson, former special counsel to President Nixon, pleaded guilty in Washington federal court June 3, 1974 to a charge that he "unlawfully ... did ... endeavor to influence, obstruct and impede" the trial of Pentagon Papers defendant Daniel Ellsberg. In return for the plea, the Watergate special prosecutor's office agreed to drop all other charges pending against Colson.

As part of his understanding with the prosecutor's office, Colson consented to give it sworn testimony and provide relevant documents in his possession.

Colson pleaded guilty to a one-count criminal information accusing him of "devising and implementing a scheme to defame and destroy the public image and credibility of Daniel Ellsberg and those engaged in the legal defense of Daniel Ellsberg, with the intent to influence, obstruct and impede the conduct and outcome" of the 1973 Ellsberg trial.

In a statement issued after his plea had been entered, Colson maintained that he had been innocent of charges contained in the two indictments previously returned against him—the Watergate cover-up and the Ellsberg break-in.

Colson was sentenced to one to three years in prison and fined $5,000 by U.S. Judge Gerhard A. Gesell June 21.

Dairy & ITT Accusations

Two of the scandals that emerged during the 1972 campaign involved charges that Nixon administration officials had increased support prices for milk and settled anti-trust suits against the International Telephone & Telegraph Corp. in the expectation that the milk producers and the ITT would provide financial support for the Republican political cause.

THE DAIRY CASE

Milk price rise tied to politics. A consumer suit filed in U.S. court in Washington Jan. 24, 1972 charged that an increase in federal price supports for milk stemmed from "political considerations" and asked the court to rescind the increase. The suit was brought by consumer advocate Ralph Nader and three consumer groups.

The suit contended that the increase had been granted "illegally" in return for "promises and expectations of campaign contributions for the re-election campaign of the incumbent President [Nixon]."

The suit cited this sequence of events, all in 1971: a decision March 12 by then-Agriculture Secretary Clifford M. Hardin to deny as unjustified a rise in the milk price support level, a $10,000 contribution by milk producers to various GOP fund-raising committees March 22, a meeting of 16 dairy spokesmen with Hardin and President Nixon at the White House March 23 and Hardin's announcement March 25 reversing his decision 13 days earlier and granting an increase of 27¢ a hundredweight in federal price supports for milk.

Other charges in the suit: (1) a total of $322,500 had been donated by dairy producers to GOP committees by the end of 1971; (b) the price support increase, granted on "considerations extraneous" to those provided by law, would cost the government an additional $126.2 million during fiscal 1972; and (c) Hardin had "received no new information or evidence bearing upon dairy farmers' costs, including the costs of feed," after he denied the increase and up to the time he reversed himself.

Milk group sued in trust action—One of the main organizations named in the Nader lawsuit—Associated Milk Producers Inc. (AMPI)—was the target of a civil antitrust suit filed by the Justice Department Feb. 1 in San Antonio, Tex., where the milk marketing cooperative was headquartered. The suit charged the 40,000-member AMPI with violating the Sherman Antitrust Act by numerous anti-competitive practices since 1967 that spanned a 14-state area.

The Nader lawsuit Jan. 24 had alleged that the AMPI contributed $2.8 million to a "front" organization, the Trust for Agricultural Political Education (TAPE), for distribution to political candidates.

Milk price support suit reopened. A federal judge in Washington ruled Oct. 6, 1972 that Nader and three consumer organizations, Federation of Homemakers, D.C. Consumers Association and the Nader-sponsored Public Citizen, Inc., could begin to take sworn statements from dairy producers and Administration fund raisers.

The lawsuit had been dismissed in March on the grounds that the 1971 milk price support increase had terminated in March 1972, rendering the 1971 legal question moot.

But the appeals court reopened the case, declaring that any "improprieties" in the 1971 decision "were not negated simply by rendition of the 1972 decision," the Washington Post reported Sept. 12.

Correspondence uncovered in connection with another lawsuit and published in the Post Aug. 25, appeared to substantiate Nader's claim that the price support increase was politically motivated.

The letters, written by officials of Mid-America Dairymen, Inc, a dairy co-op, stated that the organization contributed $65,000 to the Republican party in 1971.

The money was funneled to GOP finance committees by Murray Chotiner, a longtime Nixon confidante, and by Marion E. Harrison, Chotiner's law firm partner.

In one letter, written March 29, 1971, Gary Hanman, chairman of Mid-Amer-

ica's political fund, ADEPT, wrote another official, saying, "I can assure you that the TAPE and ADEPT programs, as well as SPACE, played a major role in this administrative decision."

TAPE and SPACE were acronyms for political funds administered by two other dairy organizations, American Milk Producers, Inc. and Dairymen, Inc.

Another letter, written in 1971 and published by the Post Aug. 25, written by Mid-America President William A. Powell to a member stated:

"The facts of life are that the economic welfare of dairymen does depend a great deal on political action. If dairymen are to receive their fair share of the governmental financial pie that we all pay for, we must have friends in government. I have become increasingly aware that the sincere and soft voice of the dairy farmer is no match for the jingle of hard currencies put in the campaign funds of politicians by the vegetable fat interests, labor, oil, steel, airlines and others.

"We dairymen as a body can be a dominant group. On March 23, 1971, along with nine other dairy farmers, I sat in the Cabinet Room of the White House, across the table from the President of the United States, and heard him compliment the dairymen on their marvelous work in consolidating and unifying our industry and our involvement in politics. He said, 'You people are my friends and I appreciate it.'

"Two days later an order came from the U.S. Department of Agriculture increasing the support price of milk to 85% of parity, which added from 500 to 700 million dollars to dairy farmers' milk checks. We dairymen cannot afford to overlook this kind of economic benefit. Whether we like it or not, this is the way the system works."

The Administration had contended that the turnabout on the price support question resulted from new economic data which justified the increase, the New York Times reported Aug. 25.

Dairy donations examined. Sworn pretrial testimony filed Jan. 10, 1973 in consumer advocate Ralph Nader's suit seeking a rollback in the federal milk support price identified President Nixon's personal attorney, Herbert W. Kalmbach, as a campaign funds solicitor from a dairy group which had already made a large, controversial contribution.

The court papers also claimed that Kalmbach withdrew the request when the contributors insisted the gifts be made public.

George L. Mehren, an executive with Associated Milk Producers, Inc. (AMPI) of Texas and treasurer of its political group, TAPE (Trust for Agricultural Political Education), said he met with Kalmbach in Los Angeles in February 1972 when the Nixon spokesman asked "quite unequivocally" for campaign contributions. But Kalmbach ruled out any Administration quid pro quo for the dairymen, Mehren said.

At a later meeting in Washington, Kalmbach withdrew his request without giving specific reasons for the decision, Mehren testified.

Price increase-funds link denied. In a development related to the suit brought by Nader, former White House special counsel Murray Chotiner claimed there was no connection between his lobbying activities at the White House as a dairy industry advocate and the Administration's decision to raise the federal support price of milk.

Chotiner's deposition, made public Jan. 27, 1973, revealed that the law firm he had joined March 9, 1971 after leaving his White House post (Reeves & Harrison) represented several dairy cooperatives in addition to directing fund raising for the forthcoming Republican campaign.

Chotiner said he had "personally" spoken with Nixon's principal domestic aide, John D. Ehrlichman, and White House counsel Charles W. Colson, and he had told them that "what was good for the dairy farmers was good for the country, and what was good for the country was good for the dairy farmers."

The Washington Post reported Jan. 30 that Chotiner had been in touch with Administration aides March 9-25, 1971 on behalf of the dairy cooperatives; the Nixon Administration March 25 had reversed an Agriculture Department (USDA) ruling against the requested milk

price support increase; dairy farmers, in the company of Chotiner's law partner, Marion Harrison, met with the President March 23 and attended meetings March 24 to discuss political contributions with Chotiner. He later arranged to funnel their donations to various GOP finance committees, according to the deposition.

White House role & dairy funds. Harold S. Nelson, former general manager of AMPI, testified that he believed the White House and not government milk pricing experts made the decision to increase the price support of milk, the Washington Post reported May 21, 1973.

According to his pretrial deposition given in connection with Nader's suit, Nelson said, "No Cabinet officer is a free agent . . . he has to make decisions that are dictated by the White House."

Nelson also revealed that he and another dairy association leader had met with President Nixon before the March 23, 1971 meeting when more than a dozen dairy farmers' representatives held talks at the White House.

The Washington Post reported May 18 that three major dairy groups—AMPI, Mid-America Dairymen, Inc., and Dairy Men, Inc.—gave $422,500 to the Nixon re-election campaign during 1972.

Secret dairy farmers' contribution disclosed. The Lehigh Valley Cooperative Farmers, a Pennsylvania dairy group, made two $25,000 secret contributions (in $100 bills) to the Nixon re-election campaign during 1972, the Washington Post reported June 1, 1973.

The first secret donation was made April 20, 1972, when Agriculture Secretary Earl L. Butz addressed a stockholders meeting in Pennsylvania. (According to the Post, the association had pledged a $100,000 contribution if Vice President Spiro T. Agnew, who was scheduled to appear, addressed the group. When Butz substituted for Agnew, the offer was reduced.) A second Lehigh contribution was made in May 1972.

J. Curtis Herge, a former Nixon campaign aide, told the Post that the $50,000 from the Lehigh group was eventually turned over to former re-election committee aide Frederick C. LaRue in July 1972, "according to the absolute instructions" of former Attorney General John N. Mitchell and Jeb Stuart Magruder, former deputy campaign director. (LaRue had told the GAO that part of the secret money was used to finance the cover-up of Watergate defendants.)

Herge, currently a special assistant to Deputy Attorney General Joseph T. Sneed, said he and campaign scheduling director Herbert L. Porter delivered the $50,000 in cash to former committee treasurer Hugh W. Sloan Jr.

According to the GAO, Sloan, realizing that the anonymous funds had been donated in violation of the federal reporting law, refused to release the money until he could determine its source. When he resigned from the re-election committee in July 1972, the money was transferred to LaRue.

George E. Mehren, an official of one of the largest dairy cooperatives and trade associations, Associated Milk Producers, Inc. (AMPI), said July 24 that the Nixon campaign had sought additional contributions from the group two days after an antitrust suit was brought against them by the Justice Department.

Executive privilege claim. Federal district court in Washington July 27, 1973 ordered President Nixon to produce for court inspection 67 memos related to the Administration's 1971 decision to increase federal price supports for milk.

The order, involving Nixon's claims of executive privilege, was stayed Aug. 20 at the request of the Justice Department, which argued the case for the White House, and Archibald Cox, special Watergate prosecutor. They argued that the pending court test involving release of the White House tapes would better resolve the issue of executive privilege. According to the ruling, an appeals court in Washington would consider the milk suit at the same time that arguments concerning release of the White House tapes were being heard.

The interrelationship between Nixon's two assertions of executive privilege was compounded Sept. 18 when the White House acknowledged that tape recordings had been made of conversations held March 23, 1971 between the President and dairy industry representatives just prior to the Administration's announcement of milk price hikes; however, in the affidavit which revealed the tapes' existence, White House special counsel J. Fred Buzhardt also reiterated President Nixon's refusal to release the tapes.

An Aug. 12, 1970 memo between two unnamed presidential assistants and a Sept. 2, 1970 memo proposing 15 brief meetings for dairy industry representatives with the President also would be withheld from the court on grounds of executive privilege and separation of powers, Buzhardt said. The documents dealt with the "mechanics" and "advisability" of the presidential meetings and concerned "only the First Amendment protected activities of the President and his staff," he said.

Two other documents—a February 1972 memo dealing with "political contributions" and the milk fund lawsuit, and a list of pre-April 7, 1972 contributors to Nixon's re-election campaign—would be provided the court, according to Buzhardt.

Funds tied to quotas? Before his ouster, special Watergate prosecutor Archibald Cox had obtained a copy of a December 1970 letter to Nixon from a representative of Associated Milk Producers, Inc., it was reported Oct. 23, 1973. The letter suggested that if the Administration imposed import quotas on certain dairy products, Nixon could expect up to $2 million in campaign contributions from the group.

Fifteen days after the White House received the letter, dated Dec. 16, 1970, from Patrick J. Hillings, a California attorney, former GOP congressman, long time friend of Nixon and the Washington counsel, with Marion E. Harrison, for AMPI, Nixon ordered quotas set on four specific dairy products but at a level lower than desired by the dairy industry.

In his presidential proclamation of Dec. 31, 1970, Nixon sharply curtailed the import of cheese and its substitutes, chocolate containing butterfat, animal feeds containing milk or its derivatives and ice cream from 25%–90% for the different exporting nations. The dairy lobby had sought to ban all imports of those products.

Campaign contributions from AMPI and other major dairy cooperatives began to flow to the White House soon after another Administration decision, also sought by the industry, was announced in March 1971.

Hillings' letter complained that a favorable Tariff Commission ruling had been buried in the federal bureaucracy. "This problem is bogged down within the White House. We write you both as advocates and supporters. The time is ripe politically and economically to impose the recommended quotas," Hillings wrote.

"AMPI contributed about $135,000 to Republican candidates in the 1970 election," he continued. "We are ... working with Tom Evans and Herb Kalmbach in setting up appropriate channels for AMPI to contribute $2 million for your re-election. AMPI is also funding a special project."

Other information related to the dairy industry's ties to the Administration corroborated portions of the 1970 letter: one of the White House memos that had been sought by attorneys for Ralph Nader in connection with his court test of the Administration's increase of federal milk price supports was filed in the court record and published by the Washington Post Oct. 21.

The memo, written for then White House chief of staff H. R. Haldeman by his aide, Gordon Strachan, indicated that the dairy industry's original campaign "commitment" had been reduced to $1 million.

According to the Feb. 1, 1972 memo, "Kalmbach is very concerned about his involvement in the milk producers situation," a statement which prompted Strachan to recommend Kalmbach's dissociation with the milk project "because of the risk of disclosure."

Dairy funds linked to Ellsberg break-in. The Cox investigation had established a link between the White House plumbers' activities and secret contributions from dairy farmers, according to the Washington Post Oct. 11.

Joseph Baroody, a Washington businessman who had been a Nixon campaign fund raiser and organizer, said he had received a telephone call in the "last day or two" of August 1971 from White House special counsel Charles W. Colson. He sought an immediate loan of $5,000 from Baroody, who said he had not asked what the money would be used for.

Colson also called Marion Harrison, who was collecting dairy money for distribution to secret committees, and asked him to deliver $5,000 to one of those committees headed by another Washington attorney, George D. Webster. Colson had alerted him to receive the money, Webster said. (He added that in 1971 he had organized several of the paper committees for the purpose of receiving secret campaign donations at the request of Colson.)

Harrison obtained $5,000 from AMPI and turned it over to Webster Sept. 7, 1971. Colson telephoned again and instructed Webster to convert the money to cash and give it to a messenger whom Colson would send. Baroody retrieved the money shortly after Sept. 21, 1971.

Baroody, Harrison and Webster said lawyers from Cox's office had determined that the transaction had financed the break-in at the office of Dr. Lewis Fielding, a psychiatrist who had treated Pentagon Papers defendant Daniel Ellsberg.

Antitrust suits. Although the Justice Department had filed a civil antitrust suit in February 1972 against Associated Milk Producers (AMPI), the department acknowledged Dec. 26, 1973 that John Mitchell, then attorney general, had rejected two recommendations from the department's antitrust division that criminal proceedings be instituted against AMPI.

According to Richard McLaren, then head of the antitrust division, he authorized a civil suit against the dairy cooperative because of Mitchell's urging.

McLaren's testimony was filed as part of a government brief in the AMPI case, asking the court to reject a motion by the defense to obtain access to all government documents and tapes relating to a possible quid pro quo in the relationship between the price support increase and campaign contributions.

The defense contended that the

Administration had used extortion in extracting campaign donations from the industry and that the antitrust case had been initiated after AMPI refused a second request from Nixon fund raisers for a subsequent contribution.

According to McLaren, he had favored criminal proceedings be launched in recommendations made Sept. 9, 1971 and Oct. 29, 1971, whereas the decision to file a civil suit was made Jan. 22, 1972.

AMPI documents that could have shed light on the current investigations were destroyed in the spring of 1971 by employes in the Arkansas division office, according to the Chicago Tribune Nov. 28. David Parr of the Arkansas office had been instrumental in arranging meetings with President Nixon for dairy leaders, AMPI officials said.

THE ITT CASE

ITT trust decision tied to GOP funding. An alleged company memo disclosed Feb. 29, 1972 linked the settlement of a government antitrust action against the International Telephone and Telegraph Corp. (ITT) with a pledge to underwrite a large part of the funds needed to hold the Republican National Convention in San Diego.

The memorandum was made public by syndicated columnist Jack Anderson, who embroiled Attorney General-designee Richard G. Kleindienst in the matter March 1, accusing him of having lied about not being involved in the ITT negotiations in 1971. At a Senate Judiciary Committee hearing March 2, scheduled at his request, Kleindienst denied any improper role or knowledge, at the time, of the plans for the convention funding.

Denials of wrongdoing also were issued Feb. 29 by Attorney General John N. Mitchell and ITT. Mitchell denied he had been involved "in any way" in negotiations on the GOP convention site or in settlement of the ITT antitrust case. The company said "there was no deal of any kind to settle our antitrust cases."

The out-of-court settlement of ITT's three antitrust cases had been announced by the Justice Department July 31, 1971,

eight days prior to the announcement by the Republican National Committee of the selection of San Diego as the site of its party's 1972 presidential convention

The city's bid for the convention included a pledge by the Sheraton Corp. of America, an ITT subsidiary, to underwrite a major part of the $400,000 needed from private sources to obtain the convention. This did not become known until later.

The memorandum in question, which Anderson released to the press, was attributed to ITT lobbyist Mrs. Dita D. Beard as a "personal and confidential" message to W. R. Merriam, an ITT vice president, dated June 25, 1971 and concluding with a request that the memo be destroyed.

Mrs. Beard referred a number of times in the memo to the ITT "commitment," or "our participation in the convention," and connected it to the antitrust action. The memo referred to the commitment as composed of services or cash, or a combination of the two.

According to the memo: "Other than permitting [Attorney General] John Mitchell, [California Lt. Gov.] Ed Reinecke, [White House aide] Bob Haldeman and Nixon (besides [Rep. Bob] Wilson, of course), no one has known from whom that 400 thousand commitment had come"; ". . . because of several conversations with [former Kentucky Gov.] Louie [Nunn] re Mitchell, that our noble commitment has gone a long way toward our negotiations on the mergers eventually coming out as Hal [Harold Geneen, ITT president] wants them. Certainly the President has told Mitchell to see that things are worked out fairly. It is still only [Richard W.] McLaren's mickey mouse we are suffering" (McLaren, who headed the Justice Department's antitrust division, was then arguing staunchly for prosecution of the case against ITT); "if it [the commitment] gets too much publicity, you can believe our negotiations with Justice will wind up shot down. Mitchell is definitely helping us, but cannot let it be known."

Anderson reported Feb. 29 that Mrs. Beard, in an interview with his associate Brit Hume, had confirmed the authenticity of the memo. She said, according to Anderson, she had discussed the antitrust action with Mitchell for more than an hour during a Kentucky Derby party given by Nunn in 1971 and Mitchell had asked what she wanted and she told him the settlement ITT preferred, which conformed, she said, with the eventual settlement.

In his statement Feb. 29, Mitchell said he had not discussed the ITT antitrust action with anyone in the Justice Department or with ITT "with one exception." Mrs. Beard had approached him, he said, and he had advised her he was not familiar with the matter and "the appropriate people representing ITT should take the matter up with the appropriate people in the [Justice] Department."

Kleindienst role questioned—Kleindienst's name was brought into the case Feb. 29 by Democratic National Chairman Lawrence F. O'Brien, who said Kleindienst had assured him in December 1971, that Mitchell had not been involved in the ITT case. "It is now clear that these are not the facts, and Mr. Kleindienst knew it," O'Brien charged.

In his column March 1, Anderson ac-accused Kleindienst of having lied when, in his reply to O'Brien, he had denied involvement in the negotiations preceding the trust settlement and had said that (a) the settlement had been "handled and negotiated exclusively" by McLaren and (b) Kleindienst's only role was to concur in McLaren's recommendation for a settlement. Anderson quoted ITT director Felix G. Rohatyn as saying he had discussed the settlement in private with Kleindienst some half-dozen times prior to the settlement.

In his appearance before the Senate Judiciary Committee March 2, Kleindienst told of four private meetings with Rohatyn in 1971 and a meeting he arranged for Rohatyn and other ITT representatives—Kleindienst said he had attended but was silent—to explain the "drastic economic consequences" if the Justice Department pursued and won the antitrust cases against the company.

Kleindienst "categorically and specifically" denied exerting pressure for a settlement favoring ITT or knowing at the time of plans of an ITT subsidiary to secure the financing for the GOP convention site.

"I set in motion a series of events," Kleindienst said, "by which Mr. McLaren became persuaded that he ought to come off his position" against a settlement which would allow ITT to keep the Hartford Fire Insurance Co., a key goal of ITT in the negotiations.

His testimony was supported by McLaren, currently a federal judge, and Rohatyn, who also appeared before the committee March 2.

The antitrust decision—The questioning focused on McLaren's change of position to settle the ITT case out of court, since both the LTV and ITT cases had been considered precedents for a Supreme Court decision expanding the Clayton Antitrust Act to handle the conglomerate issue.

The committee had released March 7 a letter from ITT lawyer Walsh to Kleindienst in April 1971 conceding that "there is a high probability" that the government would succeed if it took its cases before the Supreme Court. McLaren had told the panel the chance of losing before the Supreme Court was another factor for settling the ITT cases without a court decision.

Solicitor General Erwin N. Griswold told the committee March 8 that while he was not an antitrust expert, he believed that the government would have lost all three of the ITT cases before the Supreme Court and that the settlement made was "a very substantial victory for the government."

Mitchell denies allegations—The Senate Judiciary Committee March 9 heard allegations that President Nixon had requested a settlement of the ITT trust case instead of an effort at a Supreme Court decision. The allegations were denied immediately by former Attorney General Mitchell.

Previously, columnist Jack Anderson March 3 had quoted Edgar Gillenwaters. an assistant to California Lt. Gov. Ed Reinecke, as saying the two had met with Mitchell in mid-May 1971 and told him of ITT's offer to underwrite the convention in San Diego by as much as

$400,000. Reinecke March 3 reported a similar story but said the meeting with Mitchell took place in September 1971. He said he had not mentioned ITT but only the Sheraton Hotel Corp. (a subsidiary). At a news conference March 2, Mitchell had said he had not known then "...and still don't know what arrangements the Republican party had with San Diego or anyone else."

An ITT statement March 3 said its subsidiary, Sheraton Corporation of America, contributed $100,000, with an additional $100,000 possible later on a matching basis, as a way to attract business to its new hotel in San Diego and that the contribution was "in no sense a political payment." (These were in actual funds. The commitment to underwrite the funding to a range, first of $300,000, later $400,000 reportedly was made by ITT President Harold Geneen.)

The Senate committee disclosed March 6 a statement from Solicitor General Erwin N. Griswold that Kleindienst, with McLaren present, had asked him to seek a delay from the Supreme Court in one of the antitrust cases after ITT lawyer Lawrence E. Walsh had requested the government to review its anti-merger policies in general. The delay was granted and the Justice Department never appealed the case, which involved the Grinnell Corp., a part of which ITT was allowed to retain in the eventual settlement.

Brit Hume, an associate of Anderson, testified before the committee March 9 on his Feb. 24 interview with Mrs. Beard to verify her controversial memo. He said she told him Mitchell had informed her during a conversation in 1971 that President Nixon had directed him to "lay off" ITT. After he questioned her specifically if she were referring to what the President had said, Hume testified, Mrs. Beard changed the alleged Nixon remark to a request for Mitchell to "make a reasonable settlement" with ITT rather than pursue the antitrust cases to the Supreme Court.

In a statement released later March 9, Mitchell called Hume's testimony about him involving the President "totally false." He said "the President has never, repeat never, made any request

to me directly or indirectly concerning the settlement of the ITT case and I took no part in that settlement."

Mitchell testified March 14 he had discussed the department's antitrust policies with Geneen privately in 1970 but that the subject of the department's three antitrust cases against ITT had been ruled out. Mitchell, who had disqualified himself from the ITT cases when attorney general because an ITT subsidiary was a client of his former law firm, disclaimed involvement in any way in the handling or settlement of the suits.

In his turn before the committee March 15, Geneen said "there was absolutely no connection" between ITT's pledge of up to $200,000 toward expenses of the GOP convention and the trust settlement with the government.

He corroborated Mitchell's testimony about their meeting, that he had agreed with Mitchell's condition ruling out discussion of the antitrust suits.

An ITT official reported to the committee March 16 that a day after publication of the Beard memo, ITT employes were ordered to destroy all unneeded or embarrassing papers in company files, that sacks of documents, some pertaining to the GOP convention and others to the antitrust settlement, were fed into a shredder, that a company representative had gone through Mrs. Beard's files with her to select the documents to be destroyed.

As for the ITT commitment to the GOP convention, Geneen said March 15 he personally had pledged the funds for an ITT subsidiary, the Sheraton Corporation of America, as a way to promote the opening of a new Sheraton hotel in San Diego. He said part of the arrangement was that President Nixon's headquarters at the convention would be in the new hotel.

Geneen said the pledge was not for $400,000 in cash and services, as reported, but for $100,000 in cash and another $100,000 on a matching basis if needed. He said smaller amounts had been spent to promote other Sheraton hotels.

Dr. Victor L. Liszka of Arlington, Va., who had been treating Mrs. Beard for a heart ailment, had testified March 6 that

Mrs. Beard had a "mental block" and could not remember writing the memo.

Liszka also volunteered testimony that Mrs. Beard had told him in Denver she never meant to imply in her memo there was any connection between the ITT trust settlement and the contribution to the GOP convention. He said she had telephoned him in 1971 and excitedly related: her meeting at a Kentucky Derby party with then-Attorney General John N. Mitchell; her attempt to argue the merits of the ITT trust case with Mitchell; Mitchell's rebuff to her—"a dressing down such as I never had in my life," as Liszka quoted her; and Mitchell's advice that "I should proceed in proper channels" and refusal to discuss the matter.

Former Kentucky Gov. Louie B. Nunn (R), who held the Derby party Mitchell and Mrs. Beard attended, told the Senate committee March 7: he was with Mitchell the entire time; Mitchell refused to discuss the ITT case with Mrs. Beard; he "heard no offer of no wrongdoing"; Mitchell told Mrs. Beard "he didn't like the approach she was making or the pressures that had been brought"; Mrs. Beard collapsed after the rebuff by Mitchell from exhaustion, her heart ailment and alcohol and "they laid her out on the floor" of the governor's mansion.

Hume and Anderson testify—During the committee's March 9 session, Hume, in addition to his testimony concerning Nixon, reported other Mrs. Beard statements to him that she had first discussed ITT's financial commitment to the GOP convention with Lt. Gov. Reinecke in January 1971 and that ITT President Geneen had promised to underwrite San Diego's bid to host the convention during a meeting with Rep. Bob Wilson (R, Calif.) May 12, 1971.

Anderson also testified March 9 and involved another White House aide, William Timmons, with the ITT contribution to the convention plus a former White House staff member, Jack Gleason, currently in the public-relations business with, Anderson said, ITT as a client.

Anderson said Gleason had informed him he had discussed, as an ITT public relations consultant, the convention with Timmons in June 1971 to clarify what assistance ITT would give the convention. Anderson said the alleged conversation between the two tended to "corroborate the circumstances mentioned in Mrs. Beard's memo."

SEC probe of ITT made public. The House Interstate and Foreign Commerce Committee's special subcommittee on investigations March 19, 1973 released a confidential document prepared by the Securities & Exchange Commission (SEC) as a summary of its two-year investigation of ITT. The paper revealed the extent and success of ITT's alleged attempt to pressure the Administration regarding a pending antitrust case.

At issue was ITT's acquisition of the Hartford Fire Insurance Co. A settlement reached in 1971 with the Justice Department permitted ITT to retain Hartford provided the corporation divested itself of several other companies.

Seven current and former administration officials were mentioned in the SEC report: Vice President Spiro Agnew, presidential assistant John D. Ehrlichman, former Attorney General John N. Mitchell, former special counsel Charles W. Colson, former presidential assistant and subsequently Secretary of Commerce Peter Peterson, former Secretary of Commerce and then chief fund raiser for Nixon's Presidential campaign Maurice Stans and former Treasury Secretary John B. Connally Jr.

According to the SEC summary, ITT senior vice president Edward J. Gerrity wrote Agnew Aug. 7, 1970 to thank him for an unspecified action and suggest that Mitchell could make ITT's argument for the antitrust settlement known to Richard W. McLaren, head of the Justice Department's antitrust division and ITT's principal antagonist in the case.

Gerrity's letter implied that Agnew had already held conversations on the subject with McLaren.

An SEC memo attached to Gerrity's letter disclosed details of a meeting between Mitchell and ITT President and Chairman Harold S. Geneen. "It indicates that Mitchell told Geneen that

Nixon was not opposed to the [ITT] merger," the SEC report concluded.

An April 27, 1971 letter from William Merriam, chief of ITT's Washington office, to Connally said that Connally and Peterson had been "instrumental in the delay" of a government appeal to the Supreme Court in one of three cases against ITT related to the antitrust charges. That case was eventually settled out of court as part of a package arrangement with the Justice Department.

Colson memo. The Senate Watergate Committee Aug. 1, 1973 made public an internal White House memo written March 30, 1972 by then special counsel Charles Colson. It warned that hearings on Richard G. Kleindienst's confirmation as attorney general could directly link President Nixon and other high officials to a controversial ITT antitrust ruling.

It was Colson's concern that this incriminating evidence would provide the Democrats with additional ammunition against the President. Nixon, Colson contended, was the Senate's real target in the confirmation fight.

The Colson memo appeared to provide new evidence to support charges that political considerations had influenced prosecution of a major antitrust case, as well as allegations that perjury had been committed during the Senate's investigation of the case.

Kleindienst had testified before the Judiciary Committee that the ITT case had been handled "exclusively" by Assistant Attorney General Richard McLaren, chief of the Justice Department's Antitrust Division, and the White House had made repeated claims that the Justice Department's decision not to pursue antitrust charges against ITT was unrelated to ITT's financial backing of the 1972 GOP convention.

Colson's memo, addressed to Haldeman, included a summary of those additional documents posing a political risk to the Administration if they were made public during the confirmation hearings:

■ Colson mentioned ITT files "which were not shredded" and had been turned over to the SEC. One referred to Nixon's "instructions" to the Justice Department. One of the internal ITT memos linked Agnew and Kleindienst to the pressure on McLaren.

■ An unknown number of copies existed of a June 30, 1971 memo describing ITT's $400,000 offer to defray costs of the Republican convention.

■ Another memo, which would contradict Mitchell's testimony and directly involve the President, Colson said, was unaccounted for.

Contacted by reporters Aug. 1, Colson verified the memo and said Mitchell would have committed perjury at the Senate hearings "if he had read his mail." But in a subsequent interview, Colson contended he had written the memo as a "good staff guy" in the "devil's advocate role" of presenting facts and problems of appearance "in their worst context."

The memo did not substantiate charges of a "quid pro quo" arrangement with ITT, Colson contended.

Kleindienst reveals Nixon role. Richard Kleindienst, who had resigned as attorney general, told Watergate special prosecutor Archibald Cox two weeks before Cox was fired by President Nixon that the President had personally intervened in the Justice Department's antitrust case against ITT. Nixon had ordered him not to appeal a lawsuit against ITT to the Supreme Court, Kleindienst said.

The New York Times broke the story Oct. 29, 1973, and Kleindienst issued a statement confirming the report Oct. 31.

The political aspects of the case originated with the Justice Department's challenge of three acquisitions made by the ITT conglomerate in the late 1960s: Canteen Corp., a large food vending firm; Grinnell Corp., a plumbing and fire equipment maker, and Hartford Fire Insurance Co.

Lower courts had ruled against the government on the Grinnell and Canteen cases, but an appeal to the Supreme Court was expected in 1971 because the high court had not ruled against the Justice Department on a major merger case during the 1960s.

Solicitor General Erwin N. Griswold and Richard W. McLaren, chief of the Justice Department's antitrust division, had testified before Congress in March 1972 that they had urged Kleindienst, then deputy attorney general, to appeal the Grinnell case.

In his statement Oct. 31, Kleindienst said:

"On Monday afternoon, April 19th, 1971 [presidential domestic affairs advisor John] Ehrlichman abruptly called and stated that the President directed me not to file the appeal in the Grinnell case. That was the last day in whch that appeal could be taken. I informed him that we had determined to take that appeal, and that he should so inform the President. Minutes later the President called me and, without any discussion, ordered me to drop the appeal."

"Immediately" after receiving Nixon's phone call, Kleindienst said, "I sent word to the President that if he persisted in this direction I would be compelled to submit my resignation. Because that was the last day in which the appeal could be perfected, I obtained an extension of time from the Supreme Court to enable the President to consider my position.

"The President changed his mind and the appeal was filed 30 days later in the exact form it would have been filed one month earlier."

The issue of an appeal to the Supreme Court became moot when the Justice Department announced July 31, 1971 that an out of court settlement had been reached with ITT. The government agreed to drop its three lawsuits against the corporation, and ITT was allowed to retain Hartford Fire if, among other provisions, it began divestiture proceedings for Canteen, a division of Grinnell and four other firms.

The Times report Oct. 29 said that negotiations leading to the settlement began immediately after Kleindienst ordered the appeal delayed. Kleindienst met with Felix Rohatyn, an ITT director, and Peter M. Flanigan, a White House aide, to discuss the terms of the agreement.

On April 16, 1971, ITT officials and lawyers sought appointments with Kleindienst and other Administration officials to seek a delay. On April 19, Kleindienst was reported to have said that a delay was impossible because of McLaren's op-position. The presidential phone call to Kleindienst was made that afternoon.

The Senate Judiciary Committee, which then was considering Kleindienst's nomination to succeed Mitchell as attorney general, held hearings on the ITT question and examined Kleindienst's role in the controversy.

In his statement Oct. 31, Kleindienst denied that he had committed perjury before the Senate committee:

"At the time of my testimony before the Senate Judiciary Committee, I was not asked whether I had had any contacts with the White House at the time of this decision, and I did not deny any such contacts.

"The focus of the hearings dealing with the I.T.T. affair was the negotiations in May, June and July of 1971 leading to settlement of the pending cases on July 31. I was questioned at length concerning these negotiations and particularly with reference to any conversations or meetings I might have had with Mr. Peter Flanigan of the White House staff. It was in the context of those questions that I made the statement quoted on C.B.S. news last evening, as follows:

" 'In the discharge of my responsibilities as the acting attorney general in these cases, I was not interfered with by anybody at the White House. I was not importuned; I was not pressured; I was not directed.' "

Kleindienst pleads guilty. Kleindienst pleaded guilty May 16, 1974 to a misdemeanor charge—refusal to testify "accurately and fully" before a Congressional committee investigating the Administration's handling of the controversial ITT antitrust settlement.

The minor criminal offense related to Kleindienst's testimony in March and April 1972 before the Senate Judiciary Committee, which was considering his nomination to succeed John Mitchell as attorney general.

Kleindienst was the first person who had served as the nation's top law enforcement officer to be convicted of criminal misconduct.

Kleindienst pleaded guilty to concealing from the committee his communication about ITT with President Nixon and John Mitchell and circumstances surrounding the Justice Department's decision to appeal one of the antitrust cases against ITT to the Supreme Court.

Kleindienst received a suspended sentence June 7. Chief U.S. District Court Judge George L. Hart Jr. imposed the minimum sentence under law—a $100 fine and one month jail term—and suspended both penalties.

Nixon's Milk & ITT Statements

President explains involvement. President Nixon Jan. 8, 1974 released two white papers detailing his involvement in the controversial decisions made in 1971 to increase the federal price support for milk and to settle an antitrust suit against the International Telephone & Telegraph Corp. (ITT).

The President called "utterly false" charges that presidential actions were offered in the matters as a quid pro quo "either in return for political contributions or the promise of such contributions."

Nixon had promised Nov. 17, 1973 to "put out all the facts" on the milk fund and ITT cases but no tapes or documents were issued with the statement. However, according to the White House release, supporting material had been provided the Watergate special prosecutor. It "should be clear that the accounts published today are consistent with the basic facts contained in these documents and tapes," the Nixon statement added.

The milk fund—In a 17-page statement, Nixon defended as "totally proper" his decision to reverse an Agriculture Department ruling and allow an increase in the federal price support of milk, although he admitted for the first time that before he ordered the increase he was aware that the dairy industry had pledged at least $2 million to his re-election campaign.

However, the statement continued, "he at no time discussed the contributions with the dairy industry and the subject was not mentioned in his meeting of March 23, 1971" with dairy representatives. The statement added, "It is also

worth noting that the ultimate contributions by the dairy industry to the President's re-election effort (1) were far less than the industry leaders had hoped to raise; (2) were far less than the dairy industry gave to other candidates for the House and Senate, including many prominent Democrats; and (3) represented less than 1% of the total contributions to President Nixon's re-election campaign."

Nixon said his decision to raise the price support was based on three factors:

■ "Intensive Congressional pressure"

■ "The economic merits of the case itself, as presented by the industry leaders in the meeting with the President, and as weighed by the President's advisers [in a meeting later that day]"

■ "Traditional political considerations relating to needs of the farm states."

According to Nixon, dairy lobbyists had mobilized 29 senators and more than 100 congressmen in an effort to raise price supports to levels that were 85%–90% of parity. To bring this about, legislation had been introduced that appeared certain of passage, according to Nixon, and any presidential veto also appeared certain to be overridden.

"Moreover," the statement continued, "if the President were to try to force his will in this matter (i.e., to push parity down to 80%) it could be politically disastrous in some of the Midwestern states, and, in the light of known Congressional intentions, would be both foolish and futile."

During the conference with advisers March 23, 1971, "the political power of the dairy industry lobby was also brought to the President's attention," according to the statement. Treasury "Secretary [John B.] Connally [Jr.] said that their votes would be important in several Midwestern states and he noted that the industry had political funds which would be distributed among House and Senate candidates in the coming election year—although neither the secretary nor anyone else discussed possible contributions to the President's campaign," the statement continued.

"The fundamental themes running through this March 23 meeting were two:

(1) the unique and very heavy pressures being placed upon the President by the Democratic majority leadership in the Congress and (2) the political advantages and disadvantages of making a decision regarding a vital political constituency.

"The President himself concluded that the final decision came down to the fact that the Congress was going to pass the higher support legislation, and he could not veto it without alienating the farmers—an essential part of his political constituency."

The paper acknowledged: that Charles W. Colson, then a White House special counsel, had sent a memo to the President in September 1970 informing him of Associated Milk Producers Inc.'s (AMPI) pledge of $2 million for the re-election campaign; that a letter had been sent in December 1970 to Nixon confirming the pledge, but the President claimed not to have seen it; that AMPI's first Nixon contribution had been given to Herbert Kalmbach in August 1969 (Nixon said he knew nothing of this money although it was deposited by Kalmbach in a trustee bank account used for money left over from the 1968 presidential campaign); that $232,500 in dairy funds had been recorded on a list of secret campaign contributions kept by Rose Mary Woods, Nixon's personal secretary, as "House Account" money.

(At his press conference Oct. 26, 1973, Nixon had declared that throughout his public life he had refused to personally accept campaign contributions, that he had "refused to have any discussion of contributions" and that prior to the 1972 presidential campaign, he had issued orders "that he did not want to have any information from anybody with regard to campaign contributions.")

The ITT case—Nixon claimed that his order to Deputy Attorney General Richard Kleindienst to drop a pending appeal with the Supreme Court on one of the government's antitrust suits against ITT was based entirely on Nixon's personal philosophy that corporations should not be challenged on grounds of "bigness per se." Further, Nixon said in his eight-page statement, he was unaware of ITT's campaign pledge to fund the Republican National Convention when he personally intervened in the case in April 1971.

Nixon limited his role in the case to the phone call to Kleindienst April 19, 1971 and a subsequent call April 21, 1971 reversing his earlier instruction. The order to halt a court appeal of one of three suits pending against ITT was withdrawn, Nixon said, because he feared that Solicitor General Erwin Griswold would resign if the Supreme Court were prevented from considering the case. This warning came from Attorney General John Mitchell, who said Nixon's decision to halt court proceedings was "inadvisable," the President said. (In earlier testimony, Kleindienst claimed that it was his threat to resign which prompted Nixon's turnaround.) Nixon also claimed that Mitchell feared unspecified "legislative repercussions" if the case were dropped.

According to the statement, Nixon's intercession resulted from his "irritation" with Richard McLaren, head of the Justice Department's antitrust division, who refused to follow Administration policy on the case as it was set down by John Ehrlichman, Nixon's domestic policy adviser.

The ITT case eventually was filed for appeal with the high court but a settlement was reached before arguments were heard. Nixon said he did not "direct the settlement or participate in the settlement negotiations directly or indirectly."

ITT President Harold Geneen tried to discuss the case with Nixon during the summer of 1969, Nixon disclosed, but the meeting was never held because Administration aides considered it "inappropriate." However, other White House aides did discuss the case with ITT representatives, the statement added without further detail.

According to the statement, ITT did not make its offer to underwrite the Republican National Convention in San Diego until June 1971. "Apparently," its pledge totaled $200,000, of which $100,000 was returned when the site was moved from San Diego to Miami Beach. In any case, the site-selection process was "separate and unrelated" to considerations in the federal antitrust case against ITT, Nixon stated.

Nixon contradicted. Apparent discrepancies in Nixon's dairy and ITT statements were pointed out by various sources:

Lawyers for Ralph Nader introduced into evidence Jan. 11 an extract from a tape recording of Nixon's meeting March 23, 1971 with dairy industry leaders. According to the brief, Nixon's remarks contradicted his assertions in the white paper that campaign contributions were not mentioned.

According to the tape, Nixon told the group:

"I first want to say that I am very grateful for the support that we have had [inaudible word] from this group. I know that in American agriculture you're widely recognized; that it cuts across all the farmer organizations, is represented in all the states.

"I know, too, that you are a group that are politically very conscious, not in any party sense, but you realize that what happens in Washington not only affects your business success but affects the economy; our foreign policy [inaudible word] affects you.

"And you are willing to do something about it. And I must say a lot of businessmen and others I get around this table, they yammer and talk a lot but they don't do anything about it. But you do and I appreciate that. I don't need to spell it out. Friends talk and others keep me posted as to what you do."

Nader's lawyers also contended that a memo prepared for the President by his staff prior to the March 1971 meeting reminded Nixon of the campaign pledge. The memo "briefly noted that the dairy lobby—like organized labor—had decided to spend political money," according to the testimony of a Nixon aide, David Wilson.

Former Solicitor General Erwin Griswold said Jan. 9 that he disagreed with part of Nixon's statement claiming that on April 19, 1971, he had "authorized the Justice Department to proceed with the [ITT] case in accordance with its own determination." Griswold claimed that he had not received authorization from the White House to file for appeal with the Supreme Court until "about May 15, 16, or 17, 1971."

In another major contradiction with previous sworn testimony, Nixon's asser-

tion that he had discussed the case with John Mitchell, then attorney general, and Kleindienst, then deputy attorney general, conflicted with their statements at Senate hearings considering Kleindienst's nomination as attorney general.

Dairy Fund Charges Mount

Fresh milk price-Nixon fund link. According to documents filed in the AMPI antitrust case, the firm's lobbyist, Robert Lilly, claimed that AMPI had made a "commitment" of campaign funds to President Nixon's re-election race "in conjunction with the 1971 price support" increase authorized by Nixon. Lilly's statement, reported in the press May 2, 1974, was made to Edward L. Wright. Wright's notes of the interview with Lilly had been subpoenaed for the antitrust trial.

Lilly said he was told of the arrangement April 4, 1972 during a meeting with AMPI's general manager, George L. Mehren, and Mehren's predecessor, Harold S. Nelson. "The commitment [of a campaign contribution] was made in March of 1971 by Nelson, [David] Parr, Marion Harrison, and [Jake] Jacobsen," Lilly told Wright.

"There was a big argument over how much money had been committed," Lilly said. "The figures ranged from $500,000 to $1 million. Jacobsen contacted Connally in March of 1971 about the contribution. Connally said there had to be new money or additional money."

When he and other industry officials met with Nixon March 23, 1971, Mehren said, they were not hopeful about their chances to win White House support for a price increase. But the Nixon campaign received a check for $25,000 from the political arm of Dairymen Inc. the next day, and on March 25, 1971, the Agriculture Department announced that it had reversed a previous ruling and would allow an increase in the support price of milk.

According to press reports May 4, Lilly also told Wright that Mehren had offered $150,000 to Nixon's campaign in an effort to secure Administration efforts that would "slow down the antitrust action" against AMPI and then "reduce it to just a wrist slap."

Lilly claimed that 30 checks for $5,000 each, with the payee unspecified, were drawn up and signed by Mehren April 4–5, 1972, but were later voided. Mehren was reported to have told Senate investigators that he "had no recollection" of the checks, according to the Washington Post May 4.

Lilly said the decision to make the contribution grew out of a Washington meeting held March 16, 1972 between Treasury Secretary John B. Connally Jr. and AMPI officials. According to Mehren, "Connally called Attorney General [John] Mitchell and said rather harshly, 'Get off your [expletive deleted]. You're losing votes in the Midwest.' " Connally then suggested that AMPI delay making any more contributions "until near the end of the election,' " Mehren told Senate investigators.

The deal to quash the antitrust suit was never carried out, according to Mehren, because Herbert Kalmbach, one of President Nixon's chief fund raisers, called off the request for more AMPI contributions at another Washington meeting April 24, 1972. No reason was given, Mehren said.

Kalmbach also discussed the dairy industry's pledge of funds, it was reported May 6.

Kalmbach told the Senate Watergate Committee staff that a secret midnight meeting was held March 24, 1971 in his Washington hotel room for the purpose of asking dairymen to reconfirm their offer (made in 1970) to contribute $2 million to Nixon's campaign. Murray Chotiner, a Nixon confidant who had left the Administration three weeks earlier and set up private law practice, conveyed the message to Harold Nelson. (Chotiner had also just been retained by AMPI as its Washington counsel.) Nelson reaffirmed the pledge, Kalmbach testified.

The information was passed on to the House Judiciary Committee, according to the Washington Post, and formed the basis of the committee's request for White House tapes and other documents relating to the milk fund controversy. Sources close to the Senate Watergate Committee said testimony from Kalmbach and others caused the committee to conclude that the efforts to seek re-

confirmation of the $2 million pledge were launched with Nixon's approval by John Ehrlichman, his top domestic affairs aide. Ehrlichman telephoned White House Special Counsel Charles Colson, who then met with Chotiner, investigators said. The arrangements were concluded March 23, 1971, immediately after Nixon had met with Ehrlichman and other aides and decided to authorize the milk price increase. (Nixon had met earlier that day with the dairy representatives.) Later that night, the dairymen agreed to make an immediate donation of $25,000—Dairymen Inc. met the deadline with its contribution March 24, 1971, according to Congressional investigators. Public announcement of the price increase was not made until March 25, 1971 when the White House was certain it would receive additional campaign funds, investigators charged.

Senate staff sees fund-price tie. Reporting on the inquiry into links between the Administration price decision and dairy industry campaign contributions, the staff of the Senate Watergate committee concluded that campaign pledges made by major dairy cooperatives (totaling $2 million) "apparently [were] directly linked to a favorable milk price support decision by the President worth hundreds of millions of dollars to the industry—and costing the same amount to the government and consumers."

The staff's draft report, published May 31, 1974, had been submitted for consideration to members of the Senate panel chaired by Sen. Sam Ervin (D, N.C.).

In analyzing the President's decision to overturn an Agriculture Department ruling and authorize the support rise, the report said Nixon "ignored the opinion of every agriculture expert in his Administration and the criteria of the government statute."

The committee staff also accused Nixon of misrepresenting the significance of the co-ops' campaign pledges in his re-election race. Nixon had admitted he was aware that major dairy co-ops had pledged $2 million but said this information had not influenced his decision. The White Paper had also emphasized that the dairymen eventually contributed an estimated

$427,500, or "less than 1% of the total" received by the Nixon campaign.

In rebuttal, the staff report charged that Nixon and his fund raisers had no reason "not to expect the full amount of the pledge," which, "even by the standards of the 1972 presidential campaign" was "enormous." It "represented one of the three largest pledges of his campaign and a full 1/20th of this entire projected campaign budget of $40 million," the report stated.

The dairy donations were important for other reasons, according to the staff paper: the money, which was pledged in 1970, "represented the 'early money' which is critical to every campaign;" the commitments also represented a "potential loss of $2 million" to the Democratic campaign which had benefitted from dairy industry donations in the past. Hence, the pledge could have been worth $4 million to Nixon, the report concluded.

In March 1971, the polls showed Sen. Edmund S. Muskie (D, Me.), a leading contender for the Democratic nomination, to be running a close race with Nixon, the report continued. "The pledge thereby took on even greater significance," the staff paper declared.

Financing Nixon's Homes

During 1973 President Nixon was accused of shady practices involving Federal money and election campaign funds, in the buying and improving of his California home in San Clemente.

San Clemente financing. The White House issued a statement May 25 on the financing of President Nixon's home in San Clemente, Calif. According to the statement, the bulk of the estate was controlled by an investment company formed by millionaire industrialist Robert H. Abplanalp, a personal friend of the President.

The statement was issued after a California newspaper, the Santa Ana Register, published a report May 13 from unidentified investigators for the Senate Watergate committee that some $1 million in unreported 1968 Nixon campaign funds may have been used in purchasing the estate. Committee sources disavowed the report, and White House Press Secretary Ronald L. Ziegler denied it May 14 as "a total fabrication."

According to the May 25 statement, the San Clemente home was financed by proceeds from the sale of Nixon's New York apartment, a mortgage and two loans from Abplanalp. The latter, totaling $625,000 at one point (promissory notes bearing interest at 8%), were canceled, "with the exception of accrued interest," according to the statement, in December 1970 when Abplanalp purchased through the investment company all but 5.9 acres of a much larger tract originally purchased by Nixon.

The original seller insisted on selling the larger tract—26 acres—as a single unit, and "it was the Nixons' intention to seek a compatible buyer" for all but a 5.9 acre homesite area, the statement said. No such buyer was found prior to the closing of the sale in July 1969, and the Nixons took a loan from Abplanalp to acquire the larger site.

A title insurance company was then named trustee to buy and hold title to the property, which enabled sale of the extra land the Nixons did not intend to keep without renegotiation of the mortgage. The trustee bought the site for $1.4 million, $400,000 of which was in cash, the remainder mortgage. Two months later, in September 1969, the trustee acquired for the Nixons an additional 2.9 adjoining acres for $100,000, $20,000 of which was in cash, $80,000 in mortgage.

Since then, the statement said, the Nixons had spent $123,514 for improvements on their 5.9 acre site.

$10 million spent on Nixon homes. The Nixon Administration disclosed Aug. 6 that about $10 million of federal funds was spent for security at President Nixon's homes at San Clemente, Calif. and Key Biscayne, Fla., at Grand Cay, an island resort in the Bahamas frequented by the President and owned by Abplanalp, and at places where the Nixon daughters lived.

When the sale to the Abplanalp investment company was made in December 1970, the price was $1,249,000. In addition to canceling the Nixon loans, the funds covered the assumption of Nixon's mortgages from both land purchases, or $624,000.

The statement put the net investment by the President for the 5.9-acre home site at $374,514.

In a subsequent statement May 26, the White House said government-financed improvements to the San Clemente estate totaled $39,525. The improvements were said to be security measures.

The May 25 White House statement also listed the ownership of Nixon's Key Biscayne property in Florida. It said two of the five houses in the compound were owned by the Nixons, one by C. G. Rebozo, another personal friend of Nixon, one by Mr. and Mrs. Abplanalp and one by a trustee of an Indiana bank which was trustee for the former owner. The latter two units were leased to the General Services Administration for office space and security and communications for the President.

The Associated Press reported May 30 that Abplanalp was a principal stock-holder—$125,000 worth—in a Yonkers, N.Y. bank, the Hudson Valley National Bank, chartered by the federal government after the purchase by Abplanalp of the San Clemente land. It also said Abplanalp's attorney, William E. Griffin Jr., one of the bank's founders, bought two Key Biscayne lots from Nixon in late 1972—one originally purchased in 1967 for $30,000, another bought in 1971 for $23,100—for $150,000.

Special Watergate prosecutor Archibald Cox said Oct. 18 that he had found "no evidence of improper conduct" in the Justice Department's 1971 decision not to file antitrust charges against Abplanalp, owner of the nation's largest manufacturer of aerosol valves, Precision Valve Corp., which was accused of pricing violations.

Rep. Bertram L. Podell (D, N.Y.) had asked Cox to investigate the circumstances of the government's action when it was revealed that Abplanalp had financed Nixon's home.

Previous estimates of federal money spent on security at the Nixon homes were much lower.

Arthur F. Sampson, administrator of the General Services Administration, said the earlier estimates were announced in line with a "basic decision" taken in 1969 by White House staff members, GSA

officials and members of the Secret Service to "minimize" the figures in order not to jeopardize the President's security. The latest accounting, he said, was made at the direction of the President because of "the atmosphere that exists today." Sampson said about $100,000 had been spent by the government to "satisfy press inquiries" on the matter.

The majority of the federal funding—$6 million—was spent for military facilities, mostly communications installations, at the homes in San Clemente and Key Biscayne and at Grand Cay.

Total GSA spending on presidential homes and adjacent offices was put at $3.7 million.

The Secret Service said Aug. 6 it had spent about $300,000 since 1969 for detection devices for the homes of the President and his two daughters.

Military expenditures at San Clemente totaled $3.7 million, including $1 million for communications systems and annual recurring costs of $677,000. At Key Biscayne, the one-time military cost totaled $730,000, including $418,000 for a helicopter pad, $14,000 for a shark net and about $300,000 for communications equipment. The annual recurrent cost of communications was put at about $330,000 for each of four years.

Military spending at Grand Cay and a nearby cay for installing communications equipment totaled $160,000.

The largest item in the GSA spending was $1.7 million for an office complex at San Clemente, about two-thirds of which covered maintenance and operation over a four-year period. GSA expenditures for security installations and improvements on the grounds at San Clemente (walls, lighting, alarm systems) totaled $635,000. GSA spending on the main house at San Clemente was $68,148. Some of this, $13,500, was to replace a gas furnace the Secret Service considered inherently unsafe. Electric heating was installed.

Spending by Agency

Location	GSA	Military
San Clemente	$2,444,447	$3,700,000
Key Biscayne	1,180,522	2,050,000
Grand Cay	16,000	160,000
Nixon Daughters	50,000	....
Totals*	$3,690,969	$5,910,000

*The Secret Service also spent a total of $300,000, which was not broken down by location.

GSA spent $137,482 at Key Biscayne on Nixon's two homes, $130,000 of that on bulletproof windows and doors. Another $152,000 went for security lights and alarms at Key Biscayne, $131,000 for a command post and $75,000 for walls, fences and screening.

The GSA spent $16,000 at Grand Cay, most of it for a bunkhouse and a trailer outpost for security agents and for exterior lighting.

About $50,000 was expended by the GSA at five privately-owned residences occupied at various times by Nixon's daughters, much of it for communications systems and security command centers.

All of the installations at San Clemente and Key Biscayne were to be removed eventually, Sampson said, "provided that the cost of removal is not prohibitive." However, a major cost at San Clemente was for landscaping necessitated by installing power lines and cables underground and subsequent restoration of the property.

A GSA report June 21 had said less than $1.9 million in federal funds had been spent on the Key Biscayne and San Clemente homes.

The total included $1,180,522.64 for improvements and maintenance at Key Biscayne—$579,907.24 for improvements, $554,321 for operation and maintenance and $46,294.40 for equipment.

At San Clemente, the figures were $698,552.70 for improvements and $4,834.60 for equipment.

The $703,367.20 San Clemente total was an upward revision of a $460,312 estimate released by the GSA and White House aides June 14 as the amount spent on security at the California estate. The figure also contrasted sharply with the $39,525 figure listed by the White House May 26 as the amount for the same purpose.

A breakdown of the costs released by the GSA June 22 showed, among other items, expenditures at San Clemente of $184,174 for electrical work, $13,850 for landscaping, $12,315 for roof tile and repairing walls and a gazebo, $13,500 for a heating system, $2,800 for a swimming pool heater, $11,561 for a redwood fence, $3,800 for a sewer line, $4,834 for furniture in the President's den, $1,853 for installation of a flagpole and $476 for painting the flagpole.

Among the items at Key Biscayne were $122,708 for bullet-resistant glass doors and windows, $122,714 for constructing a Secret Service command post, $995 for a septic tank and lid, $587 for a flagpole, $3,030 for golf carts for Secret Service patrol, $6,321 for an ice maker for Secret Service men and $475 for swimming pool cleaner.

Funds were also spent to clean the beach at San Clemente and to correct beach erosion at Key Biscayne.

At a hearing by a House Appropriations Committee subcommittee, headed by Rep. Tom Steed (D, Okla.), Secret Service Director James J. Rowley said June 27 most of the public funds spent on the two Nixon homes had been requested by his agency for security reasons. Among the items not requested were the expenditures for a swimming pool cleaner, the flagpoles, the den furniture and the ice maker. Other items not requested by the Secret Service but paid by federal expense were surveys of the San Clemente property, one made prior to Nixon's purchase.

GSA Administrator Arthur F. Sampson also testified and said all of the funds were expended in relation to presidential business or to save additional federal expense.

Both men were of the opinion that the word "improvements" as applied to the costs was misleading in that the items were really "installations" installed for security reasons.

Both officials also told the subcommittee the spending was done by the GSA at the request of the Secret Service and not on orders of the President. Sampson said the GSA had consulted with the White House staff, particularly then Nixon chief of staff H. R. Haldeman, in preparing for the work.

Steed defended the federal expenditures as "not excessive." He said his panel, which approved the overall budget for the projects, had urged that decisions on presidential security "always be made on the side of too much rather than too little."

Nixon reveals personal financial data. Nixon disclosed data on his personal finances Dec. 8 to "remove doubts" that had arisen and "correct misinformation" about "what I have earned and what I own." The data included his income tax returns for 1969–72 and an audit of his private financial affairs since Jan. 1, 1969 conducted by the New York accounting firm of Coopers & Lybrand.

According to the data, Nixon had become a millionaire during his presidency, his net worth having more than tripled (from $307,141 to $988,522). It also revealed that he had paid unusually low federal income tax payments for one with his income and no state income tax, although he maintained a residence and voted in California.

It was also disclosed that a wealthy friend, head of a pharmaceutical firm, had set up a trust fund for Nixon's daughter, Tricia, in 1958 at the time a drug-price probe was being undertaken.

The President acknowledged the controversial nature of two major tax decisions which substantially reduced his federal income tax obligations. One involved his gift to the U.S. of his vice presidential papers, which enabled him to list huge continuing deductions. The other involved the sale of some California property in 1970 for which no capital gain was reported and no capital gain tax paid.

The President offered to submit both matters for re-evaluation to a Congressional tax committee and to abide by its decision. This could amount to an additional claim of nearly $300,000 in taxes. The committee selected, which consented to Nixon's request, was the Congressional Joint Committee on Internal Revenue Taxation, composed of the five senior members of the House Ways and Means Committee and the five senior members of the Senate Finance Committee.

In his statement on his financial affairs, Nixon declared his intention to make a gift to the American people of his home at San Clemente, Calif. at the time of his death or the death of Mrs. Nixon, whichever was later. He had requested the legal action to accomplish this, he said, "so that future Administrations and future generations can take advantage of this beautiful Western setting to help maintain a truly national perspective for the presidency."

Nixon's statement—In his statement, Nixon said he was making "a full disclosure" of his financial affairs as President and that "no previous President, to my knowledge, has ever made so comprehensive and exhaustive a disclosure" of assets and liabilities, expenses and income during his tenure of office.

"To the open-minded," he said, the data "will lay to rest such false rumors as that campaign contributions were converted to my personal use, that campaign funds were used in the purchase of my home in San Clemente, that I have hidden away a secret $1 million investment portfolio, that I sheltered the income on which my daughter, Tricia, should have paid taxes, and that $10 million in federal funds was spent on my homes in Key Biscayne and San Clemente."

His private affairs had been conducted "in a manner I thought both prudent and in the best interests of my family," Nixon stated, and even though both law and tradition protected the privacy of such matters, he was releasing the data "because the confidentiality of my private finances is far less important to me than the confidence of the American people in the integrity of the President."

Nixon was aware that "questions and controversies may continue as a consequence of these disclosures." Even his financial advisers and those who prepared his financial records, he said, "have disagreements of professional opinion among themselves." But the tax lawyers and accountants who assisted him in preparing his federal income tax returns, Nixon said, advised him that the two controversial tax items—the California land sale and gift of vice presidential papers— "were correctly reported" to the Internal Revenue Service (IRS). "My tax attorneys today are giving me similar advice," he said, and the IRS advised him that the items were correctly reported when it conducted an examination of his tax returns for 1971 and 1972.

The President also raised "another concern" of his—"the degree of public misunderstanding about government expenditures at my home in San Clemente."

"The perception is now widespread," he said, "that the government spent anywhere from $6 million to $10 million on improvements at my home. One myth breeds another, so many observers also believe that the government improvements have vastly enriched me personally. Those views are grossly inaccurate."

The facts, the President stated, were that the General Services Administration (GSA) spent $68,000 on his San Clemente home and $635,000 on the grounds surrounding the home, all for protection, security and safety reasons. By comparison, he said, almost $6 million was spent by the military services on the Western White House office complex on government property adjacent to San Clemente. "Unfortunately," Nixon contended, "the American people have been misled into believing that the funds for the office complex were spent on my home. The fact that the total spent on my home was $68,000 has been ignored; the fact that my wife and I spent ourselves three times as much as that, $187,977 out of our own funds, for real improvements to our homes, has been lost altogether."

Data on income—According to the data released by the President, he and Mrs. Nixon had a total adjusted gross income of $1,122,264 for the four years 1969–72, or an average of $280,556 a year. The total federal income tax paid on that income was $78,650, an annual average of $19,662, which was the level paid by a family with an income of $67,000.

In the years 1970–72, the Nixons paid an income tax for each respective year at the level of families' with incomes of $7,500, $8,500 and $25,000; the average for the three years was at the level of a family with $15,000 income a year. For 1970, the Nixons listed no taxable income, but paid a $793 tax because of the "minimum tax" clause of the 1969 tax act.

The year-by-year breakdown:

	Income	Tax
1969	$328,161	$72,682
1970	262,942	793
1971	262,384	878
1972	268,777	4,298

Of the $200,000 Nixon received in expense allowances—$50,000 a year—he used about $108,000, which was deducted from his income tax; $92,000 went into his bank accounts and was taxable.

The President's paycheck was sent monthly to California to his personal attorney, Herbert W. Kalmbach, who deposited it in the Nixon account at a Key Biscayne, Fla. bank headed by Nixon's friend C. G. Rebozo.

Nixon's net worth when he entered the presidency was $307,141. This rose to $988,522 as of May 31.

Major deductions—The President's deductions for his federal income tax returns for 1969–72 totaled $988,964. The breakdown by year: 1969—$178,535; 1970—$307,182; 1971—$255,677; and 1972—$247,570.

The four-year total included deductions of $482,019 for the donation of the vice presidential papers to the government. It also included total deductions of $257,376 over the four-year period for interest payments on his properties, $81,255 for property taxes, $142,700 for the miscellaneous category. The latter included unreimbursed official expenses ($56,956) for use of his properties at San Clemente and Key Biscayne. A deduction was claimed for $1.24 in interest payments to a Washington department store, another for $3,332 in "depreciation of personally owned White House furniture."

The President's taxes were so low—in 1970 his deductions actually exceeded his income and the minimum tax provision of the tax code was applied—that his returns in 1971 and 1972 were automatically targeted by the IRS for closer inspection.

Tricia's trust fund—According to the data released by the White House, a Nixon friend, Elmer H. Bobst, established a trust fund of more than $25,000 for Nixon's older daughter Tricia in 1958 when he was chairman of the Warner-Lambert Pharmaceutical Co. The fund consisted primarily of Warner-Lambert stock. After Tricia received the proceeds from the fund when she reached 21 in 1967, Nixon borrowed $20,000 from her for a $38,080 purchase of two undeveloped lots in Key Biscayne. Under an "oral agreement," Tricia was to get 40% of any profit from the real estate. The lots were sold for $150,000 in December 1972. The data showed that Tricia paid $11,617 in capital gains in 1972.

The vice presidential papers—Nixon donated his vice presidential papers to the national archives after they were appraised by rare books expert Ralph

Newman of Chicago at $576,000. The Nixons deducted $482,019 from their income taxes for the years 1969–72 because of the donation, which would leave them $93,981 more for deduction on their 1973 tax return. The law permitting such deductions was repealed by Congress with a July 25, 1969 cutoff date. Nixon attorneys said the gift was made on March 27, 1969.

But questions had been raised about the procedures for the deductions: whether Nixon himself should have signed the deed for transferring the papers to the government; whether Edward L. Morgan, the White House lawyer who signed it, had the legal authority to do so; whether the notarization of the date of the deed was valid since the corroborating record required by California law had not been located; whether the transfer was made before the deadline since the deed was not transmitted to the GSA until April 1970.

Response to disclosures—Nixon's financial disclosures, according to newly sworn Vice President Gerald Ford Dec. 9, should satisfy "any reasonable member of Congress" and the American people. Appearing on the ABC "Issues and Answers" broadcast, Ford said Nixon had "followed the law" as far as his tax payments were concerned and, in any event, the promise to donate the San Clemente home to the nation would "wipe out" any alleged impropriety.

Ford had strongly supported Nixon after meeting with the President Dec. 7. "I can assure you that the President has no intention whatever of resigning," Ford told reporters. "It was reiterated to me this morning."

He added: "There is no evidence that would justify impeachment" and "I don't think the President is a political liability to any candidate [and] in his five years he has done a super job in foreign policy. He has many more pluses in the political scene than minuses."

Senate Democratic Leader Mike Mansfield (Mont.) suggested Dec. 10 that the President's financial activity was legal but "it still raises questions of appearances."

Sen. Lowell P. Weicker Jr. (R, Conn.), a member of the Senate Watergate committee, questioned the tax deduction for the vice presidential papers. "There was no gift" of the papers before the cutoff date, Weicker said Dec. 11.

Campaign to Oust Nixon

Impeachment Drive Starts

*Nixon's dismissal of Watergate prose-
cutor Archibald Cox Oct. 12, 1973 provoked a strengthened effort to drive the
President out of office.*

House gets impeachment resolutions.
Eight impeachment resolutions, co-spon-
sored by a total of 31 Democrats, were
introduced in the House of Representatives Oct. 23, 1973.

Also introduced were 13 resolutions,
with a total of 76 co-sponsors, proposing
inquiries into possible impeachment or
studies of possible presidential misconduct.

One of the impeachment resolutions
was from Rep. Thomas L. Ashley (D,
Ohio), who told the House the original
resolution for impeachment of President
Andrew Johnson had been introduced by
his great-grandfather.

Rep. Dan Kuykendall (R, Tenn.),
urging the House Oct. 23 "to go slow and
don't be part of a legislative lynch mob,"
was hissed from the aisle and the gallery
when he held up a noose as "a symbol of
your action."

House Democratic leaders agreed
unanimously Oct. 23 to have the Judiciary
Committee begin an inquiry into possible
impeachment. House Republican leaders,
facing the Democratic move, endorsed the
inquiry.

The Washington Post reported Oct. 24
that House Republican leaders had
warned Nixon, through his counselor
Bryce N. Harlow, that they would not "go
to the wall" with him in blocking impeachment proceedings unless he made
the Watergate tapes available to the
courts. The warning was said to have been
delivered prior to the President's decision
to turn the tapes over to the court.

Strong statements against Nixon continued. The Congressional Black Caucus
Oct. 24 urged a Congressional probe of
what it called a "cascade" of "executive
crimes." Rep. Robert L. Leggett (D,
Calif.) accused Nixon Oct. 25 of violating
at least seven criminal laws in the Watergate case and other matters. "Just at a
glance," he said, "I can see a prima facie
case of commission of sufficient felonies
in Mr. Nixon's record to imprison him for
173 years."

Vice President-designate Gerald Ford
said Oct. 25 he thought the investigation
"should carry on." He also said he would
support an independent Watergate investigation, outside the Justice Department, if that was the will of a majority of
the Congress.

The House Judiciary Committee met
Oct. 30 to consider impeachment proceedings against Nixon.

The committee approved a grant of
broad subpoena power to its chairman,
Rep. Peter W. Rodino Jr. (D, N.J.), after
rejecting two Republican proposals to

permit the panel's Republican minority to share in the subpoena authority or exercise its own separate subpoena authority. All three votes were on straight party lines, 21 D. vs. 17 R.

The impeachment inquiry was launched on a partisan note despite Rodino's assurances that he would not engage in any "wholesale issuing of subpoenas," that he would consult with the committee's ranking Republican, Rep. Edward Hutchinson (Mich.), on each subpoena and that he would "respect" Republican requests for subpoenas.

In an interview Oct. 29, Rodino had said "this cannot be a partisan effort" but "has to be something that all of our members understand—an attempt to clear the air. If we find there are impeachable offenses, then we've got to move ahead. If not, fine."

The panel's Republicans, however, considered the committee action Oct. 30 as test votes on whether the inquiry would be bipartisan or not.

The Democratic National Committee, meeting in Louisville, Ky. Oct. 26, had called on Congress to "take all necessary action, including impeachment . . . if warranted" against the President. "The political process has been sullied and the high calling of public service has been subjected to cynical manipulation and criminal behavior which has reached into the highest office of the land," the resolution stated.

Helen Wise, president of the National Education Association representing 2.2 million teachers, wrote Nixon Oct. 21 saying teachers shared the "groundswell of public outrage" at the Administration's handling of Watergate. Teachers were asking, she told him, "how they can fulfill their responsibilities in teaching young people the moral, ethical and spiritual values required in a free society while the President . . . disregards the nation's traditionally high standards of morality."

Some 350 law students and lawyers met Oct. 30 to lobby for appointment of an independent Watergate prosecutor and continuation of the probe of charges against the President that could lead to impeachment.

"He must leave office for the common good," Sen. John V. Tunney (D, Calif.)

said Oct. 30. "The people do not believe him and he has shamed them."

Congressional mail was heavy with support of impeachment: Tunney reported Oct. 30 a 16-1 ratio for impeachment in his office mail, Sen. Alan Cranston (D, Calif.) a 22-1 ratio, Sen. Jacob Javits (R, N.Y.) a 40-1 ratio. Sen. James Buckley (Conservative-Republican, N.Y.) said 95% of his telegrams backed impeachment.

More than 200 political scientists, led by Professors James MacGregor Burns and Robert Dahl, announced formation Oct. 31 of "Political Scientists for Impeachment."

AFL-CIO urges Nixon to quit. Delegates to the 10th biennial convention of the American Federation of Labor and Congress of Industrial Organizations (AFL-CIO), meeting in Bal Harbour, Fla. Oct. 18–23, passed a resolution by acclamation Oct. 22 calling on President Nixon to resign and the House to impeach him "forthwith" if he did not.

"Clearly a President who has placed himself on the brink of impeachment," the resolution added with reference to Nixon's nomination of Rep. Gerald Ford (R, Mich.) to succeed Spiro Agnew as vice president, "should not be allowed to name his successor until charges against him have been disposed of satisfactorily."

The resolution, which was a statement drafted by and presented to the delegates by the AFL-CIO executive council, blamed Nixon for precipitating a "constitutional crisis" by trying to "prevent judicial examination" of the Watergate tapes "no matter what the cost to our constitutional system."

AFL-CIO President George Meany, 79, opened the convention Oct. 18 with a condemnation on the Nixon Administration, whose policies, he charged, were geared to "making a fast buck" for big corporations, the banks and other "fat cats" at the expense of the working man. "In the final analysis, let us keep in mind that Watergate and the cover-up itself were paid for by the great corporations of America—members of the National Association for Manufacturers and the [U.S.] Chamber of Commerce," Meany said.

In a break with AFL-CIO tradition, neither President Nixon nor Secretary of Labor Peter J. Brennan was invited to address the convention.

Among the speakers addressing the convention were Sens. Henry M. Jackson (D, Wash.), Edward M. Kennedy (D, Mass.), Daniel Inouye (D, Hawaii) and Hubert H. Humphrey (D, Minn.).

The Nixon Administration "makes the Harding Administration look like boy scouts and the Hoover Administration look like economic geniuses," Jackson said Oct. 19. Inouye, a member of the Senate Watergate committee, called on the President to resign Oct. 22.

A nationwide campaign for Nixon's impeachment was launched Nov. 8 by the AFL-CIO, which was distributing 500,000 copies of a statement listing 19 charges against Nixon, including that he used his office "for personal enrichment" and had "consistently lied to the American people."

The International Executive Board of the AFL-CIO Newspaper Guild adopted a resolution Nov. 15 calling for initiation of impeachment proceedings against Nixon "without further delay." Wire service groups dissociated themselves from the resolution, and there was some dissent within the guild that the action would compromise editorial objectivity. The resolution itself passed by a 15–1 vote.

Congressional 'discussion.' "A lot of discussion" of resignation was heard in the cloakrooms of Congress, according to Rep. Robert H. Michel (Ill.) Nov. 3. Michel was chairman of the GOP Congressional Campaign Committee. Rep. John H. Rousselot (R, Calif.) said "discussion of how effective he can be as a President is very much evident."

Sen. Edward W. Brooke (Mass.) became the first Republican senator to publicly call for Nixon's resignation. On the ABC "Issues and Answers" broadcast Nov. 4, Brooke said "there is no question that President Nixon has lost his effectiveness as the leader of this country, primarily because he has lost the confidence of the people of the country, and I think, therefore, that in the interests of this nation that he loves that he should step down, should tender his resignation."

Nixon could remain in office to "sort of limp along," Brooke said, but he had "reluctantly" come to the conclusion he should resign. "The lack of confidence is so deep," he said, he did not know "of anything that the President could do now to turn it around."

Sen. Henry M. Jackson (D, Wash.), said on NBC's "Meet the Press" program Nov. 4 that "the real issue is whether or not there is enough confidence left for the President to govern this nation." He urged Nixon to appear before the Senate Watergate committee to "lay his cards on the table." If Nixon did not do this, Jackson felt he would face "an unchallengable demand on impeachment or the possibility of a direct request for resignation, and I think the push will come from the Republican leadership, not just from Democrats."

Sen. Peter H. Dominick (R, Colo.), normally an Administration supporter, said in Denver Nov. 5 he was "reluctant to talk about impeachment" but "the genie was already out of the bottle and it cannot be put back in. The confidence of the American people cannot be restored until the impeachment question is disposed of and this must be done as quickly as possible." Dominick urged Nixon to divulge everything he knew about Watergate and permit complete access to the data requested by the Senate and federal probers. "There can be no more deals and no more technical arguments about evidence," he said. Dominick said the Republican party "would be well advised to follow a more independent course" from the Administration.

Sen George D. Aiken (Vt.), 81, dean of Congressional Republicans, told the Senate Nov. 7 Congress should move to impeach Nixon or "get off his back." He said it was the President's duty "not to resign" and Congress' duty to make a decision on the impeachment question. He said the House should set a deadline for a charge of impeachment or not, and, if the latter, make public an explanation. The White House had shown "relentless incompetence" in dealing with its domestic troubles and had been "astonishingly inept" in its Watergate explanations, he said, but these were not sufficient grounds for impeachment.

Sen. Barry Goldwater (R, Ariz.) opposed Nixon's resignation. He told reporters Nov. 5 the only way out for Nixon now "would be to show up some morning at the Ervin committee . . . and say, 'Here I am, Sam. What do you want to know?'" Senate GOP Leader Hugh Scott (Pa.) supported Goldwater, expressing hope Nov. 5 "a forum" could be found, possibly through the Ervin committee or by the White House, for "all relevant information" about the tapes to be made public. (Ervin said Nov. 6 there was a "general consensus" among committee members at a meeting that morning that the panel should explore with the White House the possibility of some kind of meeting with Nixon.)

Scott opposed resignation, as did House Speaker Carl Albert (D, Okla.), who was next in line at the moment to succeed the President. "Based on anything I know at this time," Albert said Nov. 5, "I would not join the group that thinks the President should resign."

Rep. George E. Danielson (D, Calif.) predicted Nov. 7 Nixon would resign within four months. Democratic Reps. Clarence D. Long (Md.) and Charles B. Rangel (N.Y.) introduced separate resolutions Nov. 7 calling on Nixon to submit his resignation. "I am calling upon the House," Rangel said, "to offer the President its honorable means of averting a total collapse of national leadership."

Sen. Philip A. Hart (D, Mich.) said Nov. 14 "if the President should resign with grace it might be the best way to bring us out of the situation."

Another senator, William D. Hathaway (D, Me.), presented legislation Nov. 9 for a new national election if both the presidency and vice presidency became vacant. The bill, based on a precedent in the Succession Act of 1792, would designate the senior House member from the president's party to serve as acting president until the election was held. Hathaway told the Senate there was "something troubling about a President who is under threat of impeachment or forced resignation having the power to name his successor."

Vice President-designate Gerald R. Ford urged Nixon supporters Nov. 13 to "speak up and speak now" to offset the impeachment and resignation demands.

Editorials urge resignation. The Detroit News, which supported Nixon for re-election in 1972, called for his resignation in an editorial Nov. 4. Another newspaper which also supported Nixon's re-election, the Denver Post, also called upon the President to resign.

Editorials calling for Nixon's resignation appeared in the New York Times Nov. 4 and the Nov. 12 issue of Time magazine (published Nov. 4), the first editorial in Time's 50-year history.

Resignation also was advocated Nov. 2 by syndicated columnist Joseph Alsop, long a Nixon supporter on defense and Vietnam policies, and the same week by ABC-TV anchor man Howard K. Smith. Conservative spokesman William F. Buckley Jr. told a Kansas State University audience Nov. 2 he believed Nixon would resign upon the urging of Republicans and friends.

An editorial in the Long Island, N.Y. newspaper Newsday Nov. 9 called for Nixon's impeachment "as soon as possible."

Nixon says he won't resign. Demands for President Nixon's resignation increased in the first week of November but White House spokesmen repeatedly insisted that the President intended to remain on the job. Nixon himself, in a national address Nov. 7, 1973 on energy, said he did not intend to quit.

He put aside his prepared text to conclude the 25-minute energy message "on a personal note."

"I would be less than candid if I were not to admit that this has not been an easy year . . . as all of you are quite aware.

"As a result of the deplorable Watergate matter, great numbers of Americans have had doubts raised as to the integrity of the President of the United States. I've even noted that some publications have called on me to resign the office of President of the United States.

"Tonight I would like to give my answer to those who have suggested that I resign.

"I have no intention whatever of walking away from the job I was elected to do.

"As long as I am physically able, I am going to continue to work 16 to 18 hours a day for the cause of a real peace abroad, and for the cause of prosperity, without inflation and without war, at home."

"And in the months ahead, I shall do everything that I can to see that any doubts as to the integrity of the man who occupies the highest office in this land—to remove those doubts where they exist," Nixon said.

"And I am confident that in those months ahead, the American people will come to realize that I have not violated the trust that they placed in me when they elected me as President of the United States in the past.

"And I pledge to you tonight that I shall always do everything that I can to be worthy of that trust in the future."

Nixon fights for post. Fighting to keep his job, Nixon undertook meetings with Republican members of Congress Nov. 9–15 to counteract the serious decline in public confidence in his leadership in the wake of the Watergate scandal. In his only public appearance (his first in public in nearly three months), before a friendly convention in Washington Nov. 15, Nixon again vowed he would not resign.

In his speech before the National Association of Realtors, Nixon spoke in general terms about his foreign and economic policies and then about Watergate and mistakes made in his 1972 presidential campaign by some "overzealous people," "mistakes I wouldn't have approved of, mistakes I wouldn't have tolerated, but mistakes for which I must accept responsibility." "As far as the President of the United States is concerned," Nixon continued, "he hasn't violated his trust and he isn't going to violate his trust now." The statement evoked a 45-second standing ovation from the real estate executives, who also cheered his entrance and exit. They also applauded when he said "I was elected to do a job" and "I'm not going to walk away until I get that job done." Earlier he had told his audience that "all I own in the world is real estate. I think it's a good investment. I believe in America and I believe in America's real estate."

In his closed meetings with the legislators, which included some friendly Democrats, Nixon sought their approval with assurances of his innocence of

wrongdoing and his intentions to prove it by disclosure of Watergate documents in his possession, to the courts first and public next.

By the end of the week, a partisan dispute broke out in the House. Democratic Leader Thomas P. O'Neill Jr. (Mass.) accused Nixon Nov. 15 of trying to "curry favor with his prospective grand jurors" by his White House sessions. O'Neill said the meetings represented an "unbecoming, if not improper" attempt to influence the outcome of the impeachment investigation. His remarks drew hisses from Republicans, who retorted with charges that the impeachment effort was being run by the House Democratic leadership.

The dispute erupted in debate over a resolution authorizing the House Judiciary Committee to spend $1 million on its inquiry into possible impeachment of the President. The resolution was adopted 367–51. Rep. David Dennis (R, Ind.) considered the action "improvident" and "premature." O'Neill cautioned the House to "preserve a cool impartiality" because "ultimately the entire House may be called upon to sit as a grand jury on charges against the President."

The key vote during the session was on a Republican move to recommit the resolution for revision to give the GOP minority one-third of the committee staffing funds and stipulate that none of the inquiry funds be spent until the nature and scope of the probe were defined. It was rejected by an almost straight party line vote of 227–190.

The White House meetings—Nixon's meetings with members of Congress began Nov. 9 when he summoned seven Republican leaders of the Senate and House to the White House for a two-hour discussion. Afterwards, Rep. John B. Anderson (Ill.), chairman of the House Republican Conference, told reporters that he felt "very much encouraged," that White House advisers had communicated a "full understanding" of the President's credibility problem and a determination "to take steps to restore confidence." The President "was very open, he seemed to be accessible," Anderson reported, and "it was not a presidential monologue." Nixon "indicated," Anderson said, "he is going to be totally cooperative with [Watergate Judge John J.] Sirica, the court and the special prosecutor and that he will devote a good deal of time to assuring the American people he was not involved in the Watergate burglary or coverup."

Meets with committee—A Republican Coordinating Committee assembled at the White House Nov. 12 and heard a 40-minute speech from Nixon promising full cooperation and several specific pieces of evidence to the Watergate probers. The committee, consisting of party leaders from Congress, governors, the national committee and regional officers, had been created in the party's crisis after the 1964 presidential landslide defeat. GOP National Chairman George Bush said Nov. 9 he had been authorized to reconvene the group at a Sept. 10 meeting of the national committee.

After meeting with Nixon Nov. 12, the 28-member committee issued a resolution welcoming Nixon's pledges of "full disclosure" and asserting its own intention to "develop positions" on national policy matters, cater to the interests of local party workers, study election reforms and "actively involve itself in assessing and developing issues of major importance in future campaigns."

Comments of some of the participants were restrained about the President's attempt to regain credibility. Anderson, one of the participants, reported he had stressed at the meeting that "time is not on [Mr. Nixon's] side" and that the new offensive would be a "futile gesture" if it was only an exercise in public relations. Asked about the future of impeachment proceedings, he said, "This is a time when mere words will not suffice. But this will give him an opportunity to make his case before we rush headlong into action."

Another member of the GOP committee, Gov. Francis W. Sargent (Mass.), said the President was starting "a campaign to attempt to reveal everything that's occurred" but "it will be awfully difficult to restore the trust of the people of this country in his Administration." "The vast majority of people in my state," he said, "don't know whether to believe [Mr. Nixon] or not." Asked if he believed the President's statement that day, Sargent said, "I'm trying very hard to."

Gov. Robert Ray (Iowa) indicated the attempt at disclosure might be too late. "This is something we hoped he might have done a long long time ago," he said.

Meeting with Democrats—Later Nov. 12, Nixon held a Watergate session in his family quarters in the White House with six southern Democratic senators and Sen. Harry F. Byrd Jr. (Va.), an independent. The others were James O. Eastland and John C. Stennis of Mississippi, John J. Sparkman and James B. Allen of Alabama, Russell B. Long of Louisiana and John L. McClellan of Arkansas.

Key GOP senators hear comments—The President held a 2 hour 20 minute meeting at the White House Nov. 13 with 15 Republican senators. "Everyone in the room—everyone—agreed on the need for full disclosure," Senate Republican leader Hugh Scott (Pa.) said afterwards.

"It was more comments than questions," observed Sen. William E. Brock (Tenn.). "The emphasis was primarily on the more fundamental question of how do we get this information to the courts, the Congress and especially the American people."

Sen. Edward W. Brooke (Mass.) said he had reiterated to Nixon his view that the President should resign. He said Nixon replied that resignation "would be the easy way out and he was not going to take it."

He said Nixon also rejected another suggestion from another senator to voluntarily submit to an impeachment inquiry to clear the air.

Early impeachment vote urged. Melvin R. Laird, who announced Dec. 19 his resignation as presidential counselor, effective Feb. 1, 1974, said he believed a vote on impeaching President Nixon "would be a healthy thing" in resolving the issue. He thought the House should take the vote by March 15, 1974 because of the Congressional elections later in the year.

Vice President Gerald R. Ford told reporters Dec. 12 if the impeachment question were not voted by the end of April 1974, "then you can say it's partisan."

House Judiciary Committee Chairman Peter Rodino (D, N.J.), after meeting with a bipartisan leadership group of his committee, announced Dec. 19 that the panel had agreed on an April target date for reporting to the House on its impeachment inquiry.

Polls find credibility loss. Nixon's loss of credibility extended to almost three-quarters of the American public, according to a Louis Harris survey published Dec. 24. By 73%–21%, it found, the public agreed that Nixon "has lost so much credibility that it will be hard for him to be accepted as President again."

However, the survey query that "he has reached the point where he can no longer be an effective President and should resign for the good of the country," was rejected 45%–44% (11% undecided).

A Gallup sampling Nov. 30–Dec. 3 (results published Dec. 16) found the public 54% against (35% for) compelling Nixon to leave office. The 35% in favor included 5%, or an estimated seven million persons, who had taken action in support of their opinion, such as a petition or message to Congress. The finding a month earlier was 54%–37%.

Louis Harris pollsters asked this question of a cross section of households Nov. 13–16: "Would you respect President Nixon more or less if he resigned from the office of President to allow Gerald Ford to take over as President in an act of national unity?" The results, published Dec. 17: more respect 45%; less respect 31%; not sure 24%.

Resignation discussed. Rep. Wilbur D. Mills (D, Ark.) said Jan. 18, 1974 that his advice to President Nixon would be to "resign in the near future." He told reporters during an informal news conference: "Under existing circumstances, we would be better off with [Vice President] Jerry Ford as president."

Mills expressed doubt that there was enough proof on the public record of Nixon's participation in the "high crimes and misdemeanors" set by the Constitution as grounds for impeachment. But he said if the House Judiciary Committee recommended impeachment, then "it would be much better for the President to consider resigning rather than put the country into the greatest schism since the Civil War."

"If it takes legislation granting him immunity from criminal prosecution after leaving office for him to resign," Mills said, "I would be willing to sponsor it."

As Congress reconvened Jan. 21, a recommendation that Nixon resign came from House Democratic Leader Thomas P. O'Neill Jr. (Mass.) Nixon had "lost the credibility of the nation," he said, resignation "would be in the best interest of the nation economically" and "we'd be better off" with Ford in the White House.

Several other Democrats also called for Nixon's resignation—Reps. B. F. Sisk (Calif.), Wayne Hays (Ohio) and Jack Brooks (Tex.).

But House Speaker Carl Albert (D, Okla.) said he would "have to think a long time before I'd recommend to the President that he resign." Several other House leaders—Democratic Whip John J. McFall (Calif.) and Republican Leader John J. Rhodes (Ariz.)—considered resignation suggestions "premature."

Rep. John B. Anderson (Ill.), chairman of the House Republican Conference, said some were "wistfully" talking of resignation, which he opposed. The Constitutional course for removal or exculpation was impeachment, he noted. And "it's a Republican problem and we can't turn aside from it."

The National Committee for an Effective Congress predicted Jan. 19 that Nixon would be impeached because of developing legal and political problems. While many members of Congress "seek to make themselves innocuous and indispensable parts of the political architecture, a function performed previously by the hat racks," it said in a statement, by spring, "for most congressmen it will take more courage to vote against impeachment than for impeachment." According to the statement, Republicans could more easily explain impeachment to Nixon loyalists as a chance for exoneration before the Senate than justify a vote against impeachment to Nixon critics. Both Democrats and Republicans, it said, faced the risk that a vote against impeachment could be construed by challengers as "trying to suppress the facts."

Former Attorney General Elliot L.

Richardson also believed a House vote for impeachment would be "easier" to cast than a vote against it. Meeting with reporters Jan. 22, Richardson said, "A congressman can say, 'All I did was say there are grounds to justify a charge—that the whole thing should be aired.' "

Richardson opposed resignation as a resolution, favoring the impeachment process for "a Congressional and public verdict."

Nixon Defended

Ford scores Nixon's critics. Vice President Gerald R. Ford asserted Jan. 15, 1974 that President Nixon's critics were waging "an all-out attack" in an attempt to "crush" him and his policies.

Addressing members of the American Farm Bureau Federation in Atlantic City, N.J., Ford identified the President's antagonists as "a few extreme partisans" and as a "relatively small group of political activists." He specifically cited the American Federation of Labor and Congress of Industrial Organizations (AFL-CIO) and Americans for Democratic Action. These and other "powerful pressure organizations," he said, were waging the "massive propaganda campaign against the President of the United States."

"Their aim," Ford said, "is total victory for themselves and the total defeat not only of President Nixon but of the policies for which he stands. If they can crush the President and his philosophy, they are convinced that they can then dominate the Congress and, through it, the nation."

If they were successful, the vice president said, "with the super-welfare staters in control of the Congress, and the White House neutralized as a balancing force, we can expect an avalanche of fresh government intervention in our economy, massive new government spending, higher taxes and a more rampant inflation."

Ford said "the majority of responsible, thinking Americans must not let it happen, and I don't believe they will."

Ford said there were no valid grounds for impeaching Nixon. He said he thought that most members of the House commit-

tee inquiring into the issue would reach the same conclusion. "But whatever their feelings," he added, "they owe it to all of us to do their job promptly and responsibly. They have no right to leave America hanging, when so much that is important remains to be done."

(A text of Ford's speech was released by the White House but presidential spokesman Gerald L. Warren assured reporters, while he had "no quarrel" with the speech, President Nixon had not ordered it. A Ford aide similarly assured Ford's independence. "This is the vice president's speech; he meant every word of it." But Warren and Ford both acknowledged Jan. 16 that the speech had been drafted by White House speech writers. Ford said he had provided the ideas.)

Later Jan. 15, the Americans for Democratic Action issued a statement by its national director, Leon Shull, saying, "No amount of rhetoric by Vice President Ford can obscure the fact that ADA's call for the impeachment of President Nixon is based on solid evidence."

Ford said Jan. 22 that the White House had information that could clear Nixon of wrongdoing in the Wagergate affair.

Ford asserted to reporters that the information "will exonerate the President" and "will totally undercut" testimony of former presidential counsel John W. Dean 3rd that Nixon had knowledge of the cover-up prior to March 21, 1973, when Nixon said he learned of it.

"I spent time talking to the President about Watergate yesterday," Ford asserted, "and I know from our conversation that the President had no prior knowledge of the Watergate break-in or had any part of the cover-up."

"I haven't had time to read the information," Ford said, but said the President had volunteered to show it to him. "There's some question in my mind whether I should see it," he said later. "It's an open question with me."

Asked why the data had not been made public, Ford said he understood the material had been turned over to the special Watergate prosecutor and "it would be improper for the White House to release it now."

Ford assured the reporters Nixon had had nothing to do with an 18½-minute erasure of the key Watergate tape. "I know that the President was not involved," he said.

Ford said he believed it would be "very unwise" for Nixon to resign and assured reporters that Nixon "is not going to resign."

Scott considers Nixon innocent. Senate Republican leader Hugh Scott (Pa.) also said he had reason to believe Nixon innocent.

Scott, interviewed by CBS Jan. 20, was asked if he had information "which gives you the feeling that the President can establish his complete innocence" on Watergate. Scott's reply: "I have the feeling, and information available to me—and I wouldn't want you to misinterpret how complete that is—which would indicate that on specific items the President would be exculpated entirely, yes."

Scott added later he had "some information which is not yet public—which is enormously frustrating to me, because it seems to me to exculpate the President—but I cannot break through the shell down there of all of his advisers, who feel differently about it, who feel that the President no longer needs to make some of these replies. I think it would help if he did. I have found nothing that indicates any guilt on the part of the President of a nature that would be impeachable, but I think they'd help themselves if they told the public some of the things that I know."

Scott said he had advised Nixon "to let it all hang out" and release the information.

McGovern: 'Mysterious contentions'—Sen. George McGovern (S.D.), the 1972 Democratic candidate for president, commented Jan. 20 on "these mysterious contentions" from Scott and others that "if the President would just tell us what he has told them we might be less inclined to indict him." McGovern said, "Well, all of that could presumably come out, whatever it is, . . . but an impeachment trial is a fair system."

McGovern thought there were "ample grounds" to vote a bill of impeachment in the House. "I'd like to see that supported by a good many Republicans," he added,

pointing out that this did not mean conviction but merely a trial in the Senate.

Goldwater blames liberal Democrats. Sen. Barry Goldwater (R, Ariz.) Jan. 15 assailed what he called an "impeachment lobby" to remove President Nixon from office. "This matter has dragged on and on for an insufferable period of time," he said, "for what appears to be no better reasons than to gain political advantage for the liberal Democrats or to make unbearable the life of the President."

Goldwater said he did not think Nixon "will ever resign as President and I don't believe the liberal Democrats have what it takes, either in evidence or guts, to push through an impeachment in the House and a subsequent trial in the Senate."

Goldwater made the remarks in a speech at a Baltimore Republican fund-raising dinner.

Interviewed Jan. 13, on NBC's "Meet the Press," Goldwater was asked about the possibility, which had been subject to speculation, that he might be called upon to be the bearer of the Republican Party's message to Nixon to resign.

"I don't think I would because I don't think it's the prerogative of one man to put himself above 46 or 47 million Americans who voted for Mr. Nixon or the 23 or 24 per cent of the American people who still believe he should be the President."

In his estimation, Nixon had "started a recovery" of his leadership status and was "better off now" than two months ago when he, Goldwater, had considered Nixon's credibility at an "all-time low."

"We have much greater problems in this country and in this world than Watergate," Goldwater said, "and I think the American people are taking that attitude—let's get these other things solved. And unless there's something more unusual about the President in Watergate than what's come out, let's get off his back."

Nixon to 'fight like hell.' Nixon was quoted Jan. 23 as having told a group of Republican congressmen he would "fight like hell" against impeachment. Nixon told them, according to Rep. Peter H. B.

Frelinghuysen (R, N.J.): "There is a time to be timid. There is a time to be conciliatory. There is a time, even, to fly and there is a time to fight. And I'm going to fight like hell."

Nixon met with the 18 House members Jan. 22. Frelinghuysen, who had taken notes, said Nixon had authorized release of the quotes.

The President's decision to serve out his term and not be "consumed another year by the Watergate matter" was relayed to reporters Jan. 22 by his press secretary, Ronald L. Ziegler. The President, he said, "is not entertaining at all the subject of resignation. He feels there are a number of programs and a number of initiatives that remain to be done in the next three years in both the foreign and domestic areas, and that is his attitude. That is how he feels, and that is what he is doing."

Ziegler said Nixon had been "under massive attacks" and been "substantially maligned" over the past year but he [Nixon] knew he had "not been involved in any wrongdoing." Ziegler said the President believed that "we have had almost a year of extensive investigation of Watergate . . . and that it's time to wrap this matter up and conclude it."

Nixon delivered his State-of-the-Union Message in person before a joint session of Congress Jan. 30.

At the conclusion of his address, Nixon added "a personal word" on "the so-called Watergate affair." He said all of the probes should be concluded and the guilty prosecuted and innocent cleared. "One year of Watergate is enough," he said. It was time to get on with the "great issues" outlined in his address. He would cooperate with the House impeachment inquiry consistent with the responsibilities of his office and with "only one limitation"—he would not do anything "that weakens the office of the President" or "impairs the ability of the President of the future to make the great decisions" vital to the nation and the world. He affirmed his intention not to walk away from the job to which he was elected.

Ford: House should get jury report. Vice President Gerald R. Ford said March 2 the sealed report of the Watergate grand jury should be turned over to the Judiciary Committee because the committee was the "proper place" to consider President Nixon's involvement or non-involvement in the cover-up.

Ford made the comment at a news conference in Phoenix, Ariz., a stop during his extensive travels around the country.

In Boston March 11, Ford said "I don't happen to believe on the basis of the evidence I am familiar with—and I think I'm familiar with most of it—that the President was involved in Watergate per se or involved in the cover-up, but time will tell."

Appearing before the Harvard College Republican Club, Ford said he would not join those asking Nixon to resign for the good of the country or the party. "That would be asking a person to admit guilt when he believes he is innocent."

"You don't have a president and vice president going off in two directions," he said. "Policywise, this Administration has done a good job and I have no hesitancy to approve its policies."

Grounds for Impeachment

Question of Nixon responsibility. The view that President Nixon should be held responsible for actions of his aides that would be impeachable offenses if committed by the President was expressed on a Chicago TV program Jan. 13, 1974 by Albert E. Jenner Jr., chief Republican counsel for the House Judiciary Committee's impeachment probe. "Certainly within some areas," he said, "the President should be responsible for the actions of aides even if he didn't know, for example, that an aide was doing something that would be regarded as an impeachable offense if the President himself did it." The President, he said, "can only act through his aides . . . He appoints them and has to be responsible for them."

Judiciary Committee member Charles E. Wiggins (R, Calif.) objected to the remark Jan. 14. He said a staff member should not be "making pronouncements" on the impeachment inquiry.

Impeachable offenses cited—A public interest law firm had said Nov. 24, 1973 that there was "ample" evidence that President Nixon could be held accountable for 28 "indictable common crimes." In releasing a study of the criminal law involved in the allegations of wrongdoing against the White House, William A. Dobrovir, head of the law firm, specified: "What we're saying is that the President could properly be indicted and made to stand trial on all these charges—on the basis of probable cause"; "we're also saying that the House of Representatives could, today, impeach Richard Nixon for these same offenses."

The "indictable common crimes" listed in the study involved conspiracy, illegal wiretapping, burglary, obstruction of justice, perjury, conspiracy to defraud the U.S., bribery, fraud, embezzlement and tax evasion. The activities cited included the Watergate scandal, campaign financing, violation of civil liberties and use of federal funds for personal enrichment.

Chesterfield Smith, president of the American Bar Association, giving his personal position, spoke out Nov. 27 against "continuation of this political never-never land" of public doubt and suspicion against the President. Nixon's "continued right to the Presidency" he said, should be decided in a Congressional impeachment investigation. Smith opposed a forced resignation because it could be construed as "nothing more than a political assassination."

New York City bar report. A broad definition of an impeachable offense was supported in a report filed with the House committee Jan. 26 by the Association of the Bar of the City of New York. Investigating the general question of impeachment, the report concluded that Congress had the sole power to impeach and remove a president for a "gross breach of public trust or serious abuse of power" whether or not the conduct was also a crime. Without mentioning Nixon, the report stated that the impeachment process was not subject to court review and was significantly different from conventional criminal litigation. It cited the fact that the process encompassed only removal from office, that the power contained no other penalty, such as fine or imprisonment, and was no barrier to subsequent criminal prosecution.

In assessing the constitutional basis for impeachment, the phrase "treason, bribery or other high crimes and misdemeanors," the report concluded that the phrase referred to "acts which, like treason and bribery, undermine the integrity of government." The term "high misdemeanor," it said, deriving from English impeachment law, was "a catch-all term covering serious political abuses."

The report provided several warnings: Congress should exercise its own "firm sense of constitutional restraint" in any impeachment proceeding; Congress should not impeach a particular president "except for conduct for which it would be prepared to impeach and remove any president;" and "impeachment was not intended as a method by which a president could be turned out of office because Congress dislikes his policies." Differences on "purely political" grounds, it noted, could be resolved by periodic elections.

The report rejected two recent pragmatic views of impeachment—Gerald R. Ford's in 1970 that an impeachable offense "is whatever a majority of the House of Representatives considers it to be" and two-thirds of the Senate agreed; Richard G. Kleindienst's in 1973 (then attorney general) that to impeach a president "you don't need facts, you don't need evidence . . . all you need is votes."

"These statements," the New York bar report said, "bear no resemblance to the considered judgments of the Founding Fathers," who were committed "to a government of constitutional principle."

In support of its position, the report cited some views of the framers of the Constitution: Benjamin Franklin said "that impeachment was necessary to prevent the drastic remedy of assassination where a president 'has rendered himself obnoxious' "; James Madison said a president was subject to impeachment for failure to prevent the excesses of subordinates as well as for personal misconduct; Alexander Hamilton said impeachment dealt with "the misconduct of public men, or, in other words, from the abuse or violation of some public trust," that impeachments were "of a nature which may with peculiar propriety be denominated political, as they relate chiefly to injuries done immediately to the society itself."

Aides say House need not allege crime. In a study on the nature of presidential impeachment, counsel for the House Judiciary Committee concluded that violation of criminal law need not be a requisite for impeachment. The study, released by the committee Feb. 21, 1974, was prepared by committee special counsel John M. Doar and Republican counsel Albert E. Jenner Jr. and their staffs.

Committee Chairman Peter W. Rodino Jr. (D, N.J.) affirmed his agreement with the study's conclusion that grounds for impeachment "don't necessarily have to arise out of criminal conduct."

The committee's ranking Republican, Rep. Edward Hutchinson (Mich.), disagreed. "There should be criminality involved," he said. Hutchinson emphasized that the study was a staff report and that "it speaks to the committee, not for the committee." The second-ranking GOP member, Rep. Robert McClory (Ill.), said he and Hutchinson were "very close together" on the issue but in his own view "it may be that certain offenses that don't fit any definition of a crime might be regarded as impeachable."

The staff report stressed that impeachable offenses "cannot be defined in detail in advance of full investigation of the facts." It said "no fixed standards for determining whether grounds for impeachment exist" were being offered in the report, and, in fact, the framers "did not write a fixed standard" into the Constitution but had adopted from English history "a standard sufficiently general and flexible to meet future circumstances."

The study found that this standard for presidential impeachment could include commission of "constitutional wrongs that subvert the structure of government, or undermine the integrity of office and even the Constitution itself." It found that a president's "entire course of conduct in office" could be considered in as much as, "in particular situations, it may be a course of conduct more than individual acts that has a tendency to subvert consti-

tutional government." It found that, flowing from the Constitutional requirement that a president faithfully execute the laws, he was responsible "for the overall conduct of the executive branch."

The study concluded that impeachment was "a constitutional remedy addressed to serious offenses against the system of government," that in the American experience of 13 impeachments criminality may or may not have been charged, and that "the emphasis has been on the significant effects of the conduct—undermining the integrity of office, disregard of constitutional duties and oath of office, abrogation of power, abuse of the governmental process, adverse impact on the system of government."

It noted the three major presidential duties explicitly stated in the Constitution—to "take care that the laws be faithfully executed," to faithfully execute the office and to preserve, protect and defend the Constitution. It also noted that these embraced an affirmative duty involving "the responsibility of a president for the overall conduct of the executive branch" and an affirmative duty "not to abuse his powers or transgress their limits—not to violate the rights of citizens . . . and not to act in derogation of powers vested elsewhere by the Constitution."

The study stressed one further requirement for impeachment, a finding of "substantiality," that "the facts must be considered as a whole in the context of the office, not in terms of separate or isolated events." Impeachment was "a grave step," it cautioned, and "it is to be predicated only upon conduct seriously incompatible with either the constitutional form and principles of our government or the proper performance of constitutional duties of the presidential office."

In its arguments that legal criminality was not a requisite for impeachment, the counsel report said impeachment and the criminal law "serve fundamentally different purposes," that the former was remedial—for removal from office and possible disqualification from future office—and its purpose not personal punishment but "primarily to maintain constitutional government." It pointed out that the Constitution itself provided that impeachment was no substitute for criminal law since it did not immunize the officer from criminal liability later.

"To confine impeachable conduct to indictable offenses," the report said, "may well be to set a standard so restrictive as not to reach conduct that might adversely affect the system of government. Some of the most grievous offenses against our constitutional form of government may not entail violations of the criminal law."

Nixon calls criminal offense an impeachment requirement. Nixon said at a televised news conference Feb. 25 that the Constitution permitted the impeachment of a president only for a criminal offense.

He said the Constitution was "very precise" in defining an impeachable offense and it was "the opinion of White House counsel and a number of other constitutional lawyers . . . that a criminal offense on the part of the President is the requirement for impeachment."

The President was asked if it would not be in his best interest and that of the country "to have this matter finally resolved in a proper judicial form, that is, a full impeachment trial in the Senate?"

Nixon replied that a full impeachment trial in the Senate "comes only when the House determines that there is an impeachable offense. It is my belief that the House, after it conducts its inquiry, will not reach that determination. I do not expect to be impeached."

(The President also disclosed that he had declined, "on constitutional grounds," a request from the special prosecutor to testify before the federal grand jury investigating Watergate.)

White House says crime finding vital. The White House presented its legal position on the nature of presidential impeachment Feb. 28. According to its 61-page analysis, "a president may only be impeached for indictable crimes" and those crimes must be of "a very serious nature" and "committed in one's governmental capacity."

Nixon's attorneys, under the direction of James D. St. Clair, submitted the analysis of constitutional standards for impeachment to the House Judiciary Committee.

The White House analysis said the words of the Constitution "inherently require a criminal offense" for justification of impeachment and that such offense be serious and committed in an official capacity. It said "the use of a predetermined criminal standard for the impeachment of a president is also supported by history, logic, legal precedent and a sound and sensible public policy which demands stability in our form of government."

Among its other arguments:

■ The impeachment clause was drafted in the context of the English precedents, which hewed to two distinct types of impeachment—a criminal process "for reaching great offenses committed against the government by men of high station," and a criminal process for "the political purpose of achieving the absolute political supremacy of Parliament over the executive." The framers of the U.S. Constitution rejected the political impeachments.

■ The enabling phrase, "high crimes and misdemeanors," meant to the framers "such criminal conduct as justified the removal of an officeholder from office." And, "in light of English and American history and usage," there was "no evidence to attribute anything but a criminal meaning" to the phrase.

■ The framers had "emphatically rejected 'maladministration' as a standard for impeachment" and their debates "clearly indicate a purely criminal meaning for 'other high crimes and misdemeanors.'"

These words, along with "treason" and "bribery," the other part of the enabling phrase, then and now "mean what they clearly connote—criminal offenses."

■ A study of American impeachment precedents revealed that the House "has supported different standards for the impeachment of judges and a president since 1804." A president was subject to elections, a judge was not, therefore the Constitution had a "good behavior" clause applying to judges that "must be construed together" with the impeachment clause. "Thus, consistent with House precedent, a judge who holds office for a life tenure may be impeached for less than an indictable offense. Even here, however, Senatorial precedents have demonstrated a reluctance to convict a judge in the absence of criminal conduct."

■ A review of the one American precedent of presidential impeachment (President Andrew Johnson in 1868) "indicates that the predicate for such action was a bitter political struggle between the executive and legislative branches of government." The first attempt to impeach then "failed because 'no specific crime was alleged to have been committed.'" The acquittal by the Senate "strongly indicates that the Senate has refused to adopt a broad view of 'other high crimes and misdemeanors' as a basis for impeaching a president. This conclusion is further substantiated by the virtual lack of factual issues in the proceeding. The most salient lesson to be learned from the widely criticized Johnson trial is that impeachment of a president should be resorted to only for cases of the gravest kind—the commission of a crime named in the Constitution or a criminal offense against the laws of the United States."

■ ". . . The Constitutional proscription against ex post facto laws, the requirement of due process, and the separation of powers . . . preclude the use of any standard other than 'criminal' for the removal of a president by impeachment."

Justice Department study—A Justice Department study of the nature of impeachment indicated the viability of both interpretations concerning the necessity of a finding of criminality in a presidential impeachment. The study was released in two phases Feb. 22 and 27. In issuing the first, Assistant Attorney General Robert G. Dixon stressed that the study was an "overview" that did not "reach conclusions or propose solutions" or address itself to any current charges.

The study issued Feb. 22 said "one can make a strong argument, based on the text of the Constitution alone, that impeachment can only be predicated on a 'high' criminal offense." The words, it said, "suggest the need for a criminal offense, although, of course, they do not expressly forbid an additional noncriminal penumbra."

But, the study continued, "as soon as one turns to the background of the impeachment clause and the precedents set under it, the matter becomes far more complicated. There are historical precedents and writing showing a broad definition" of the impeachable ingredient. The study cited the first American impeachment in 1798 involving a senator, stating that it was a political process "not so much designed to punish an offender as to secure the State." "Under this hypothesis," it continued, "one can conceive of serious abuses of power which have not been made crimes" as grounds for impeachment.

The study put forward the view it ascribed to "many citizens and many members of Congress" that "impeachment of a president is, if anything, more serious than an ordinary criminal trial . . . and that strict standards should be applied."

According to the section of the study issued Feb. 27, the framers of the Constitution intended the phrase "high crimes and misdemeanors" to have a "rather limited technical meaning." There was "no clear intent to adopt wholesale English practice and precedent on impeachment," which, it said, imparted a broader definition that extended to abuse of office.

But it also appraised the Federalist papers and the record of state ratification conventions as "lend[ing] support to the view that impeachment may be based upon certain types of non-criminal conduct."

The report supported the view that the impeachment process was not within the purview of court review. This in turn, it pointed out, favored the position that impeachment may be based on political, instead of criminal acts, but it also pointed out that the broader basing "rests upon the view that the underlying purpose of the impeachment process is not to punish the individual but to protect the public against gross abuse of power."

The Justice Department analysis said there was no precedent for a president to withhold information in the impeachment process under a claim of executive privilege. If such a situation persisted, it warned, "a constitutional confrontation of the highest magnitude would ensue."

Mills believes Nixon should resign. Rep. Wilbur D. Mills (D, Ark.) said March 8 he expected the pressure for President Nixon's resignation to intensify when the Congressional Joint Committee on Internal Revenue Taxation investigating Nixon's income tax returns reported its findings. Mills was a member of the committee.

Asked if he believed the report would provide more pressure for resignation than the Watergate scandal, Mills replied, "Yes, I do." He said he had talked to "some key Republican members of Congress who say that if he is still in office by the month of June, they will ask him to resign."

Mills had reportedly told colleagues he believed the public would be outraged by the forthcoming report because of the picture of narrow legality or morality in so many areas. "What I said," Mills explained in Washington March 12, "was that the tax issue could hurt the President more than Watergate, simply because people understand taxes. If the figures that have been talked about—$250,000 to $300,000 owed—are correct, people certainly will be asking questions."

Mills was reported as indicating to colleagues that the tax owed by Nixon could go as high as $500,000. The $500,-000 figure could be reached in back taxes and interest if all the big controversial items on Nixon's returns were assessed against him, even without a finding of fraud, which carried a further penalty of 50% of all delinquent taxes owed during any tax year. Mills denied March 12 he was accusing the President of tax fraud.

Sen. Russell B. Long (D, La.), chairman of the joint committee studying the Nixon returns, had expressed doubt Feb. 8 that Nixon was guilty of fraud on the back tax issue but indicated the likelihood of a finding that back taxes would be owed. Long repeated his views March 8. "I have said that evidence thus far indicates the President will owe more taxes but that we do not have proof of fraud," he said. "That statement still stands."

Presidential power assailed. A panel of experts in public administration reported to the Senate Watergate Committee March 20 that many of the abuses associated with the Watergate scandals could be traced to a "centralization of power in the presidency," under which "the prevailing view is that the whole government should be run from the White House."

The report, by a 12-member panel from the National Academy of Public Administration, had been commissioned by the Senate committee in preparation for the final report on its investigations.

While noting that many of the problems in the federal government had begun in earlier administrations, the report stated that Watergate was an "aberration" and culmination of "converging trends" which had seriously damaged the image of the public service.

Much of the report dealt with the White House staff system under which presidential assistants had become "assistant presidents," interposed—possibly illegally—between the President and departmental and agency heads. The panel concluded that the apparent policy of the Nixon Administration was that agency officials "must obey orders from the White House staff even in those areas where statutory powers" were vested in the agency official. Suggestions from presidential assistants were "to be construed as orders coming directly from the oval office."

The report criticized the "increasing and disturbing" politization of the White House staff and the civil service, and a tendency to appoint "political executives" to administer "duly legislated programs," sometimes with a "clear mandate from above in the hierarchy to 'gut' these programs."

A public manifestation of these trends, the report said, came in the hearings before the Senate committee, during which "almost none" of the top witnesses "mentioned any special considerations of public service for the public interest apart from the President's interest."

The report said the Nixon Administration had shown a tendency to run the government "like a corporation" with power concentrated at the top and exercised by White House staff members and "loyal followers" in executive agencies.

The report said the "most alarming" of the Watergate disclosures had been the misuse of law enforcement and intelligence agencies against supposed "enemies" and the increasingly "partisan climate" in the Justice Department.

Regarding impeachment, the report acknowledged that there was a misunderstanding over constitutional language on impeachable offenses. The panel said, however, that the phrase "high crimes and misdemeanors" needed to be understood in its historical context, which would include "crimes against the state or society as well as indictable crimes." The report also suggested that the impeachment process be extended—perhaps by constitutional amendment—to cover "serious misconduct in the political campaign prior to assumption of office."

Nixon Takes Case to Public

President Nixon took his case to the public with televised appearances at the Executives Club in Chicago March 15, 1974, the Grand Ole Opry in Nashville March 16 and the National Association of Broadcasters in Houston March 19. He stressed his determination not to resign.

Nixon's Chicago appearance. In a Chicago appearance March 15, President Nixon stressed his determination not to resign and to resist the demand of the House impeachment committee for more White House documents and tapes. The televised appearance, at a luncheon of the Executives' Club of Chicago, was attended by about 2,000 persons. The format was an hour-long question and answer period.

The questions were diverse and largely general, and the President's answers were well-received. More than 1,000 demonstrators, pro- and anti-Nixon, gathered outside the meeting site.

Most of the questions covered domestic issues, and most of these involved Watergate and impeachment or resignation issues. The energy shortage drew three queries, inflation one. The only other topics raised were about politics as a profession—should youth enter it—and the presidency—should the U.S. adopt a

procedure for a vote of confidence in the presidency between elections? Nixon opposed the latter, saying the founders of the U.S. had rejected the principle because of "a need for stability in the chief executive." "If a president is always watching the polls to see what he should or should not do," Nixon said, "he will be a weak president." He did not think "that a vote of confidence coming up, with the people or the Congress for that matter, being able to throw a president out because he happens to be unpopular, would be in the national interest, apart from the president's interest."

He amplified this position in response to a query whether it would not be better, because of the adverse effect of Watergate on the nation, if he were to resign and "allow yourself the public forum as a private citizen to answer all accusations on all parts."

Nixon replied that "the nation and the world needs a strong president" and, from a personal standpoint, "resignation is an easy copout; resignation, of course, might satisfy some of my good friendly partisans who would rather not have the problem of Watergate bothering them.

"On the other hand, apart from the personal standpoint, resignation of this President on charges of which he is not guilty, resignation simply because he happened to be low in the polls, would forever change our form of government. It would lead to weak and unstable presidencies in the future and I will not be a party to the destruction of the presidency of the United States of America."

If a president resigned when he was not guilty of charges, Nixon said, "then every president in the future could be forced out of office by simply leveling some charges and getting the media to carry them and getting a few congressmen and senators who were on the other side to exploit them."

He conceded that Watergate "has had a disturbing effect" on people and it was "wrong and very stupid to begin with." But he believed it had been "over-publicized and a lot of charges have been made that frankly have proved to be false." He said charges against him were "totally false."

He was sure many had heard of such

charges: "That the President helped to plan the Watergate thing before and had knowledge of it; that the President was informed of the cover-up on Sept. 15 of 1972; that the President was informed that payments were being made on March 13, [1973] and that a blackmail attempt was being made on the White House on March 13, rather than on March the 21st when I said was the first time those matters were brought to my attention. That the President had authorized the issuance of clemency or a promise of clemency to some of the defendants, and that the President had ordered the burglarizing—again, a very stupid act, apart from the fact that it's wrong and illegal—of Dr. Ellsberg's psychiatrist's office in California. Now all of those charges have been made. Many Americans—perhaps a majority—believe them. They are all totally false and the investigation will prove it, whatever the Congress does—the tapes, etc.—when they all come out, will establish that they are false."

Cooperation with House inquiry—Nixon said "we have cooperated" with the House impeachment inquiry, and had turned over to it the material furnished the special prosecutor plus "several caseloads of documents" from five different executive departments and two agencies. It seemed "reasonable" to him that the committee should first examine that material because the special prosecutor "said that he had what he considered to be the full story of Watergate—and we want the full story out."

Nixon again opposed giving the committee "a fishing license or a complete right to go in and go through all the Presidential files in order to find out whether or not there is a possibility that some action had been taken which might be and might result in an impeachable offense."

"It isn't the question that the President has something to hide," he said. It was necessary to protect the confidentiality of presidential conversations "and if that confidentiality principle is completely destroyed, future presidents will not have the benefit of the kind of advice that an executive needs to make the right decision. He will be surrounded by a group

of eunuchs insofar as their advice is concerned . . . In order to make the right decision you have to have opinion expressed very freely, discussed very freely from a completely wide range."

"But when you come to the point of simply saying to a committee of Congress," Nixon continued, "without regard to relevancy, before they determine what they say is an impeachable offense, just come in and paw through the documents, it would lead" to delay of resolution of the matter and erode the principle of confidentiality.

Personal taxes—Nixon said Sen. Russell B. Long (D, La.), chairman of the Congressional panel investigating his tax returns, and the panel's ranking Republican, Sen. Wallace Bennett (Utah), were correct in indicating "there's been no evidence of fraud on the part of the President. There may be evidence that he may owe more taxes, due primarily, apparently, to the debatable technical point as to whether a gift of three-quarters of a million dollars worth of Presidential papers, which was delivered three months before the deadline, whether the paperwork on it was completed in time to qualify for the deduction.

"If it was completed in time, as I understand it, I get the deduction. If it was not completed in time, I don't get the deduction. I pay the tax and the government gets to keep the papers.

"Well, under the circumstances that's hard for me to realize, but the President, when the I.R.S. is concerned, I assure you, is just another citizen and even more so. And that's perfectly proper."

Nixon's Houston news conference. President Nixon followed his Chicago appearance with a similar session in Houston March 19 before a convention of the National Association of Broadcasters (NAB).

The same topics dominated the hourlong question and answer appearance— the Watergate scandal, his resignation and cooperation with the impeachment inquiry.

Nixon reiterated that he had cooperated with the House impeachment committee and would cooperate because he wanted to get the story out. "We want them to have all the facts they need to conduct a thorough inquiry," he said. "Dragging out Watergate drags down America, and I want to bring it to a conclusion as quickly as we can."

But, he said, "the committee has enough information to conduct its investigation" and he was "following the precedent that every President, Democrat and Republican, since the time of Washington has followed, and that is defending the confidentiality of presidential conversations and communications."

Presidential advisers must have the assurance, Nixon said, "that anything they say, even though it's very unpopular at the moment," was not going to be made public later or the president would find only "a bunch of yes men around him, or ones that are going to play it so safe that he isn't going to get the variety of views he needs to make the right kind of decision."

The House, like the President, Nixon said, was bound by the Constitution and it specifically stated "that a president shall be impeached for treason, bribery or other high crimes or misdemeanors. It is the Constitution that defines what the House should have access to and the limits of its investigation. And I am suggesting that the House follow the Constitution. If they do, I will."

He was trying to meet the demands of Congress, Nixon said, and "trying to be as forthcoming as possible," but he also had "another responsibility. I must think not of myself, but I must think also of future presidents of this country, and I am not going to do anything, and I am not going to give up to any demand I believe would weaken the presidency."

Pressure on Nixon

Buckley urges resignation. Sen. James L. Buckley (Conservative-Republican, N.Y.) urged President Nixon March 19 to resign because he had lost his 1972 election mandate to carry out his proclaimed goals.

In a public statement, Buckley proposed "an extraordinary act of states-manship," the act of "Richard Nixon's own voluntary resignation." The "trauma" of Watergate had stripped Nixon of the ability to fulfill his mandate, Buckley said, and there was a "spreading cynicism" about the policital process and "a perception of corruption that has effectively destroyed the President's ability to speak from a position of moral leadership." There was also a "widespread conviction," he said, "that Watergate and all that it has brought in its wake has done unique and perhaps irrevocable damage to our entire system of government."

Referring to Nixon's defense that his resignation would weaken the office of the presidency, Buckley said "precisely the opposite is the case." The office had been "irrevocably weakened by a long slow agonizing inch-by-inch process of attrition," and was "in danger of succumbing to the death of a thousand cuts," he said. "The only way to save it is for the current President to resign, leaving the office free to defend itself with a new incumbent."

Buckley agreed with Nixon's argument that loss of office from low poll standings would destroy the presidency, but he said it did not apply in current circumstances since Nixon's popularity loss reflected "a cumulative loss of faith that has eroded his credibility and moral authority . . . beyond repair."

"We need the balance wheel that alone can be provided by a president able to exercise the full authority of his office," Buckley said, "or we run the risk of a runaway Congress that could commit us to new and dangerous programs from which we may never be able to extricate ourselves."

"There is little point in protecting the office of the president if at the same time irreparable damage is done to the republic as we have known it."

Resignation was the only way to resolve the crisis, Buckley said, impeachment could not. A Senate trial would be "a Roman circus" and either verdict—to convict or not to convict—would leave an "embittered" segment of the electorate. One would think "that the media had hounded" Nixon out of office, the other that "Congress had placed political expediency above its duty."

Nixon said at his news conference later Match 19 that Buckley's plea "does not cause me to reassess my position." While it might be an act of courage "to run away from a job that you were elected to do," he said, "it also takes courage to stand and fight for what you believe is right, and that's what I intend to do." To resign because of false charges and a popularity decline, Nixon said, "might be good politics but it would be bad statesmanship.... It would mean that our system of government would be changed for all presidents ... [and it would mean] a very unstable government."

Buckley's statement was described as "devastating" by Sen. Bill Brock (R, Tenn.) March 19. Sen. Charles H. Percy (R, Ill.) said Buckley's stand made the situation "more perilous" for the President.

Sen. Barry Goldwater (R, Ariz.) said Nixon's resignation at this time would involve questions of fair play and of precedent, "whereby any man in the White House who was philosophically unacceptable to certain politicians and segments of the media might be forced to resign." But, he said, "if any evidence of criminal act on the part of the President is proven, I shall change my position and support the Buckley proposal."

Sen. Jesse A. Helms (R, N.C.) agreed that Nixon should resign only if he was guilty.

Rep. Dan Kuykendall (R, Tenn.) objected to Buckley's call as "most dangerous." "His willingness to see a man forced out of office without proof of impeachable conduct," he said, "shows a lack of understanding as to how this republic was formed and how it operates."

William A. Barnstead of Massachusetts became the first Republican state chairman to call for Nixon's resignation. A long-time Nixon supporter, Barnstead said in Boston April 17, "I believe he is guilty, at least of covering up the facts on Watergate."

Sirica directs report to House panel. U.S. District Court Judge John J. Sirica ruled March 18 that a secret grand jury report and compilation of evidence dealing with President Nixon's role in the Watergate case should be released to the House Judiciary Committee for its impeachment investigation. The grand jury had submitted the material to Sirica March 1 with its indictment of seven former White House and campaign aides in connection with the Watergate cover-up.

The U.S. Court of Appeals upheld the decision March 21.

Noting that "the person on whom the report focuses, the President," had not objected to its release to the committee, Sirica emphasized the "compelling need" for an "unswervingly fair" impeachment inquiry "based on all the pertinent information." He added that it was the committee's "responsibility to determine the significance of the evidence," and that he was offering no opinion as to relevance.

Sirica said Nixon was referred to in the report "in his public capacity, and, on balance with the public interest, any prejudice to his legal rights caused by disclosure to the committee would be minimal." The report was not an indictment, Sirica noted, "and the President would not be left without a forum in which to adjudicate any charges against him that might employ report materials."

All of these considerations, Sirica said, "might well justify even a public disclosure of the report, but are certainly ample basis for disclosure to a body that in this setting acts simply as another grand jury."

Sirica emphasized that the report drew no "accusatory conclusions" and was "not a substitute for indictments." It contained no recommendations, advice or statements that might "infringe on the prerogatives of other branches of government"; in fact, Sirica added, the grand jury's only recommendation was to the court and therefore sustained separation of powers principles rather than "injuring" them. The report rendered "no moral or social judgments," and according to Sirica, was "a simple and straightforward compilation of information gathered by the grand jury, and no more."

Data dispute brings impeachment warning. White House refusal to release further data requested by House impeachment probers resulted in a warning from Senate Republican leader Hugh Scott (Pa.) that this position could lead to impeachment.

The warning from Scott was delivered to Nixon's counsel James D. St. Clair during a meeting, sought by St. Clair, in Scott's office March 19. Also present were Nixon counselor Dean Burch, Senate Republican whip Robert P. Griffin (Mich.); Sen. Wallace F. Bennett (Utah), secretary of the Senate Republican Conference; and Sen. Bill Brock (Tenn.), chairman of the Senate Republican Campaign Committee.

Reports quoting Scott did not appear until March 24. According to the New York Times account, Scott said he had warned St. Clair that Nixon "would be impeached" if the confrontation on the tapes continued. "I gave a clear message," Scott said, and he also reported cautioning St. Clair that defiance of the House committee would "imperil" Nixon's position in the Senate, if the House voted to send it a bill of impeachment.

Ziegler criticized the House committee again March 25. He suggested that its staff "should perhaps work late into the evening" to complete assessment of the White House material on hand. "We feel that they should move within a matter of weeks" to finish that job, he said, whereupon the White House attorneys would "stand ready to hold cooperative discussions" about access to further material.

The White House position was not outright rejection, Ziegler said, which "would be a difficult matter to deal with." "We stand ready to cooperate," he said.

Mansfield: vote to impeach 'there'—Senate Democratic Leader Mike Mansfield (Mont.) told reporters March 28 "the votes are there" for the House to impeach President Nixon. He attributed the situation in part to the White House's "dilatory tactics" on the materials requested by the House committee.

Mansfield said that if the House voted impeachment, the Senate's trial should begin within two weeks, regardless of any possible conflict with the fall elections. "The election will be secondary," he said.

He favored telecasting of any Senate impeachment trial because of its "extraordinary importance" and the "salutary exposure of democracy in action."

Mansfield stated his opposition to proposals to grant the President immunity from subsequent criminal procecution as an inducement for his resignation.

Nixon yields on subpoena. President Nixon avoided a showdown with the Watergate prosecution March 29 by surrendering materials subpoenaed two weeks previously.

White House Press Secretary Ronald L. Ziegler said he had been told by St. Clair that "all the materials requested by subpoena" would be delivered, and a spokesman for Jaworski said St. Clair had given no indication that any material might be missing. According to both spokesmen, the subpoena did not involve tape recordings.

Midwest Republicans air issue. Vice President Gerald R. Ford drew cheers from a group of Midwest Republican Party leaders March 30 with a denunciation of President Nixon's 1972 re-election committee, the Committee for the Re-election of the President.

"The political lesson of Watergate is this," Ford told the group in Chicago, "never again must America allow an arrogant, elite guard of political adolescents like CREEP [an acronym for the committee] to bypass the regular party organization and dictate the terms of a national election."

Ford told reporters later his remarks should not be interpreted as criticism of President Nixon personally. "I'm not blaming the President for CREEP," he said. "He picked people he thought would do a good job. Unfortunately, they made mistakes."

The 13-state GOP conference drew more than 1,000 party workers and major party figures.

Most of the speakers spoke of the party's accomplishments, rather than the Nixon Administration's, and attacked the Democratic record in Congress. Ford's attack on the re-election committee struck the most enthusiastic response. But former Gov. Nelson A. Rockefeller (R, N.Y.) was applauded when he said: "Let's face it: Watergate is a tragedy, but everyone is entitled to a fair trial and that applies to the President of the United States. Those who would push him out of office or force his resignation would be circumventing the constitutional process."

Gov. Ronald Reagan (R, Calif.), another participant, said, "I have always thought the President is innocent. I've taken his word for it, but this is in the legal process to be determined."

Sen. Charles Percy (R, Ill.) flatly predicted that the House would impeach Nixon. Percy charged that the White House was responsible for the move toward impeachment because Nixon publicly pushed for quick resolution of the issue while his counsel was doing "everything conceivable" to delay the resolution. "That contradiction has not escaped the Congress," he said. "It has not escaped the American people."

At a reception he gave for participants March 29, Percy said it was important "that we deal with the real world, with the political facts of life, if we are to avoid political disaster." "Our immediate problem, of course, is that the leader of our party, the President of the United States, is in danger of being forced from office," he said.

Tax probers report. A White House announcement April 3 said President Nixon would pay $432,787.13 in back taxes plus interest on the basis of a report from the Internal Revenue Service (IRS) that he owed that amount. With interest, the total amount was about $465,000.

The announcement followed by about four hours release of a staff report of the Congressional Joint Committee on Internal Revenue Taxation that found Nixon's income tax delinquency totaled $476,431 during his first term.

The IRS specified it would not seek a civil fraud penalty against the President for the years involved because it "did not believe any such assertion was warranted."

The committee, by a 9–1 vote, with Sen. Carl Curtis (R, Neb.) in dissent, approved a statement endorsing the staff report and commending Nixon for his "prompt decision" to pay the tax deficiencies and interest. Announcing the decision to conclude its inquiry, the statement said the committee members "agree with the substance of most of the recommendations made by the staff."

The White House statement—Details of the IRS report, which the President said he received April 2, were not released, although the White House statement said it "rebuts any suggestions of fraud on the part of the President." The Nixon statement also said the Congressional report "offers no facts which would support" any charge of fraud. It added that "any errors which have been made in the preparation of the President's returns were made by those to whom he delegated the responsibility for preparing his returns and were made without his knowledge and without his approval."

The statement said Nixon's counsel believed the largest item involved in the claimed tax delinquency—charitable deductions of $482,018 from 1969–1972 for a gift of papers to the government—could be "sharply and properly contested in court proceedings such as are open to an ordinary taxpayer to review the decisions" of the IRS. It said the President also believed his counsel could make "a very strong case against the major conclusions" of the Congressional staff report.

Since Nixon had requested the committee to examine his tax returns and stated he would abide by its judgment, he was directing that the back taxes be paid. Noting that the Congressional staff report indicated that the proper amount to be paid must be determined by the IRS, he was using the IRS-calculated amount, the statement said.

The Congressional staff report—Release of the Congressional staff report was decided by a 9–1 committee vote, with only Sen. Curtis in dissent. Its release prior to formal assessment by the committee was decided upon to prevent news leaks about it.

The staff report itself stressed that it was "a report only" and "not a demand for payment of taxes," which was a matter between the taxpayer and the IRS. It also stressed that no attempt had been made "to draw any conclusions whether there was, or was not, fraud or negligence involved" on the part of the President or his representatives. This aspect was shunned to avoid prejudgment, it said, by committee members in light of the current impeachment investigation.

The staff report made other observations. One was that the committee inquiry was not confined to the two items mentioned by Nixon in his request to the panel for the probe—the gift of the papers and the sale of some property at San Clemente, Calif. A broader examination was necessary, it said, because of the possible interrelationship of items on a tax return and because in this case, "so many questions have been raised" and "the general public can only be satisfied by a thorough examination." It cited the necessity of public "confidence in the basic fairness of the collection system."

The report also noted that "because of the office held by the taxpayer, it has not been possible to call upon him for the usual substantiation," although counsel to Nixon—Kenneth W. Gemmill and H. Chapman Rose—had "been helpful in the staff examination" of the returns and "supplied most of the information requested." "As is true in any examination of a tax return," the report said, it was "not possible to give assurance that all items of income have been included." The staff report, it continued, "contains recommendations on two categories of income which it believes should have been included but were not; namely, improvements made by the government to the San Clemente and Key Biscayne properties which the staff believes primarily represent personal economic benefits to the President, and economic benefits obtained by family and friends from the use of government aircraft for personal purposes."

One final comment in the report was that the staff limited its recommendations to income tax matters "although in this examination it found instances where the employment taxes were not paid and gift tax returns not filed."

The staff report figures—The committee staff found a total tax deficiency in Nixon's returns for 1969–1972 of $444,-022. With interest due as of April 3 of $32,409, the deficiency would total $476,-431.* The breakdown by year:

	Proposed Deficiency	Interest	Deficiency Plus Interest
1969	$171,055		$171,055
1970	93,410	$16,638	110,048
1971	89,667	10,547	100,214
1972	89,890	5,224	95,114
Total	$444,022	$32,409	$476,431

No interest payment was included for 1969 because the general statute of limitations had expired for that year's return. The report noted that any payment by the President for that year would be voluntary. If interest were to be included, it said, the amount would be $40,732.

The report also cited deductions the President would be entitled to if certain reimbursements were made to the government as a result of the report's findings. These involved $106,262 for General Services Administration improvements "which the staff believes were primarily personal in nature"; $27,015 the staff found represented the cost for personal trips of family and friends; and $4,816.84 for a Cabinet table purchased by Nixon but which the staff believed the government should have bought.

A summary of the report's 10 parts:

1. The staff disallowed the $482,018 deductions for Nixon's gift to the government of his vice presidential papers "because the gift was made after July 25, 1969," the effective date of the Tax Reform Act eliminating such deductions. The deed of the gift, dated March 27, 1969, "which purportedly was signed on April 21, 1969, was not signed (at least by all parties) until April 10, 1970 and was not delivered until after that date." It was signed by Edward Morgan rather than the President "and the staff found no evidence that he was authorized to sign for the President."

Furthermore, the staff found the gift was "so restricted" it was "a gift of a future interest in tangible personal property, which is not deductible cur-

*President Nixon paid $78,651 in federal income taxes in 1969–1972 on income of $1,122,266. The payments were $72,682.09 in 1969, $792.81 in 1970, $878.03 in 1971 and $4,298.17 in 1972 on listed income in those years. They were: 1969-$328,161.52; 1970-$262,-942.56; 1971-$262,384.75; and 1972-$268,777.54.

rently under law, even if the gift was valid in all other respects."

Nixon's 1968 gift of papers, it found, "contains the same restrictions as the second gift so that in the staff's opinion, it, too, is a non-deductible gift of a future interest. As a result, the staff believes that the amount of the 1968 gift in excess of what was deducted in 1968 is not available to be carried over into 1969."

2. In 1970, "no capital gain was reported on the sale of the President's excess San Clemente acreage. The staff believes that there was an erroneous allocation of basis between the property retained and the property sold and that a capital gain of $117,835 should have been reported."

3. A capital gain of $151,848 should have been declared, the report said, on the 1969 sale of Nixon's New York City apartment because the staff "does not view the San Clemente residence in which he reinvested the proceeds of the sale (within one year) as his principal residence." The capital gain figure was larger than the $142,912 reported on Nixon's 1969 tax return "because the President's cost basis should be reduced by the depreciation and amortization allowable on the New York apartment resulting from its use in a trade or business by Mr. Nixon."

4. The report found "that depreciation on the San Clemente house and on certain furniture purchased by the President, business expense deductions taken on the San Clemente property, as well as certain expenditures from the White House 'guest fund' are not proper business expenses and are not allowable deductions. These deductions totaled $91,452."

Among the items disallowed was $5,-391.43 for a "masqued ball" given by Nixon's daughter Tricia in 1969 and $22.50 for cleaning Mrs. Nixon's bathroom rug.

5. Nixon reported 60% of a capital gain on the 1972 sale of Cape Florida development lots, his daughter, Patricia, reported 40%. The report said "the entire amount should be reported as income to the President," and that he should report $11,617, the amount allocated to his daughter, as a capital gain in 1972 and the remainder of the gain in 1973. His daughter should file an amended return for 1972 and the President could deduct as interest part of the payment he made in 1973 to his daughter on the money she loaned him and she should report the interest as income in 1973.

6. The President should declare as income, the report said, the value of flights in government planes taken by his family and friends "when there was no business purpose for the furnishing of the transportation." "The staff was given no information about family and friends on flights where the President was a passenger," it noted, "but "for other flights the first-class fare costs of his family and friends are estimated to be $27,015." The reported noted that Nixon had paid for most of such travel expense himself from April 1971 through March 1972 and again after Nov. 7, 1972.

7. Nixon should declare as income $92,-298 in improvements made to his Key Biscayne and San Clemente estates, the report said, since the improvements were "undertaken primarily for the President's personal benefit."

The total amount of the federal spending at the two estates, not counting the cost of the federal offices supporting presidential use of the estates, was said to be $1.4 million.

The staff cited the expenditures it believed should have been declared as income. They included public funding for such items as landscaping and landscape maintenance, boundary surveys, sewer and paving, a cabana and repair to a gazebo.

At San Clemente, in a den of the house, four bullet-proof picture windows were installed facing the ocean, at a cost of $1,-600. They had not been requested by the Secret Service. The report concluded that their purpose was aesthetic rather than useful and that Nixon should have paid their entire cost. On an $18,494 heating system in the house, installed at Secret Service request, the staff decided that Nixon should pay $12,988 of the amount since some system, although possibly not the type insisted upon by the Secret Service, would have had to be installed anyway and Nixon intended to install it on his own.

At Key Biscayne, a security fence was installed at a cost of $71,000, but it had been remodeled since Nixon desired it to look like the fence around the White House. The report said $12,679 of the cost should be considered taxable income because of the "additional cost resulting from the President's personal tastes." A $400 concrete shuffleboard court ruined in construction of security facilities was replaced by a $2,000 terrazzo tile court; the report held the $1,600 difference was taxable income.

8. The staff found that Nixon "should be allowed an additional $1,000 in sales tax deductions."

9. On state gasoline tax deductions, the staff found that $148 should not be allowed for 1969 through 1971 but an additional $10 was allowable for 1972. The deductions were taken for a pickup truck used at San Clemente and based on more than 10,000 miles use a year, which the staff considered excessive.

10. The staff found that several other income items should be reported but they were entirely offset by deductions and did not increase taxable income.

Addenda—The staff reported it had submitted a series of questions for consideration by the President, questions relating "to issues still not fully answered."

Information also was requested, it said, "with respect to a so-called 'special projects fund,'" because "the staff was made aware that certain expenditures out of this fund possibly had been made for personal items of the President relating to his San Clemente residence." It reported an answer from Nixon's counsel indicating only one possible instance, a $6.30 expenditure for light bulbs at San Clemente.

Impeachment Committee Acts

House probers subpoena data. The House Judiciary Committee April 11, 1974 voted, 33–3, to issue a subpoena ordering Nixon to give it by April 25 all tape recordings and other materials related to 42 presidential conversations the committee deemed relevant to its impeachment inquiry. The subpoena was served on special presidential counsel James St. Clair that same day.

In effect, the committee's vote was a rejection of a compromise offered by St. Clair in an April 9 letter to John Doar, chief counsel to the Judiciary Committee. St. Clair's letter said President Nixon had ordered a review of the material in question and would furnish by April 22 "additional materials" that would "permit the committee to complete its inquiry promptly." St. Clair's letter did not indicate which tapes or material would be turned over to the committee.

The 42 presidential conversations cited in the subpoena took place from Feb. 20, 1973 to April 18, 1973. The subpoena demanded records—"all tapes, dictabelts or other electronic recordings, transcripts, memoranda, notes or other writings or things"—of meetings the President had with former White House aides H. R. Haldeman, John D. Ehrlichman and John W. Dean 3rd; former Attorney General Richard G. Kleindienst; and Henry E. Petersen, assistant attorney general in charge of the criminal division of the Justice Department.

St. Clair made a last effort to head off a subpoena 45 minutes before the committee met the morning of April 11. He called Doar and offered to turn over "within a day or two" records of conversations involving the President, Haldeman, Ehrlichman and Dean between Feb. 20 and March 30, 1973. The offer did not include conversations Nixon had with Haldeman, Ehrlichman, Kleindienst and Petersen between April 15 and April 18, 1973.

President releases tape transcripts— Nixon, in a televised address April 29, said he would turn over to the House Judiciary Committee the next day, and also make public, 1,200 pages of edited transcripts of his conversations with key aides concerning Watergate. Nixon said the transcripts included "all the relevant portions of all of the subpoenaed conversations that were recorded and related to Watergate or the cover-up. The transcripts also covered other conversations, he said, which were not subpoenaed by the committee "but which have a significant bearing on the question of Presidential action with regard to Watergate."

The President pointed repeatedly to a double stack of binders nearby containing the transcripts, which, he said, together with material already made available, "will tell it all" as far as what he personally knew and did with regard to Watergate and the cover-up.

Nixon offered a verification procedure. He invited the committee's chairman and ranking Republican member "to come to the White House and listen to the actual full tapes of these conversations so that they can determine for themselves beyond question that the transcripts are accurate and that everything on the tapes relevant to my knowledge and my actions on Watergate is included. If there should be any disagreement over whether omitted material is relevant, I shall meet with them personally in an effort to settle the matter."

Nixon reasserted his duty to defend the principle of executive privilege, but said he believed it was vital now "to restore the principle itself by clearing the air of the central questions" involved and to provide the evidence "which will allow this matter to be brought to a prompt conclusion." He said he felt that the public was entitled to the facts because of "the current impeachment climate." "I want there to be no question remaining about the fact that the President has nothing to hide in this matter," Nixon said.

The President cited the "wrenching ordeal" for the nation of an impeachment proceeding and "the impact of such an ordeal" throughout the world. Therefore, he was making the transcripts public and would also make public transcripts of all the parts of the tapes already turned over to the special prosecutor and the committee that related to his actions or knowledge of Watergate.

During the past year, Nixon said, "the wildest accusations have been given banner headlines and ready credence as well," leaving "a vague, general impression of massive wrongdoing, implicating everybody, gaining credibility by its endless repetition."

"The basic question at issue today," he continued, "is whether the President personally acted improperly in the Watergate matter. Month after month of rumor, insinuation and charges by just one Watergate witness, John Dean [former counsel to the President], suggested that the President did act improperly. This sparked the demand for an impeachment inquiry."

Returning to the principle of confidentiality, he believed a reading of the raw transcripts made it "more readily apparent why that principle is essential and must be maintained in the future." "The same kind of uninhibited discussion," he said, the "same brutal candor is necessary in discussing how to bring warring factions to the peace table or how to move necessary legislation through the Congress."

The transcripts, Nixon said, would demonstrate his concern during the period covered. "The first and obvious one," he said, "was to find out just exactly what had happened and who was involved." He also was concerned, he said, for the people involved and, "quite frankly," about the political implications. "This represented potentially a devastating blow to the Administration and to its programs."

"I wanted to do what was right," he stressed. "But I wanted to do it in a way that would cause the least unnecessary damage in a highly charged political atmosphere to the Administration."

His other concerns were not to prejudice the rights of potential defendants and "to sort out a complex tangle" not only of facts but also of legal and moral responsibility. "I wanted, above all, to be fair," Nixon said.

Nixon specifically cited several conversations with Dean. The transcripts "show clearly," he said, that, contrary to Dean's charge he was fully aware of the cover-up in September 1972, "I first learned of it" from Dean on March 21, 1973 some six months later. He learned in that conversation, Nixon said, that Watergate defendant Howard Hunt was "threatening blackmail" unless $120,000 was extended to legal fees and family support, and that the blackmail involved exposure not on Watergate but on "extremely sensitive, highly secret national security matters [such as, presumably the Ellsberg case break-in]."

Later, Nixon said, he learned "how much there was that he [Dean] did not tell me then; for example, that he himself had authorized promises of clemency, that he had personally handled money for the Watergate defendants, and that he had suborned perjury of a witness."

In his March 21 talk, he said, he kept returning to the blackmail threat, "which to me was not a Watergate problem but one which I regarded, rightly or wrongly, as a potential national security problem of very serious proportions." "I considered long and hard," Nixon said, "whether it might in fact be better to let the payment go forward, at least temporarily." In the course of this consideration "and of just thinking out loud," he suggested several times that meeting Hunt's demands "might be necessary."

But then, he said, he also "traced through where that would lead."

"The money could be raised," he continued. "But money demands would lead inescapably to clemency demands, and clemency could not be granted, I said, and I quote directly from the tape—It is wrong, that's for sure."

Nixon tracked his subsequent actions— assigning Dean to write a report and, when it was not forthcoming, giving the task to his aide John D. Ehrlichman; having another aide H. R. Haldeman pursue other independent lines of inquiry; having Ehrlichman inform the attorney general of his findings; and agreeing to have Assistant Attorney General Henry Petersen put in charge of the investigation and his follow-up and cooperation with Petersen.

"I made clear there was to be no cover-up," Nixon stressed. He quoted his own remarks against extending clemency and for doing "the right thing," his advice "to prick the boil and take the heat" and for Dean to "tell the truth. That is the thing I have told everybody around here."

In essence, the transcripts would show, Nixon said, "that what I have stated from the beginning to be the truth has been the truth, that I personally had no knowledge of the break-in before it occurred, that I had no knowledge of the cover-up" until March 21, 1973 that he never offered clemency and that, after March 21, "my actions were directed toward finding the facts and seeing that justice was done."

Never before in the history of the presidency, Nixon said, "have records that are so private been made so public. In giving you these records—blemishes and all—I am placing my trust in the basic fairness of the American people."

11 conversations missing—The transcripts, which were released April 30, did not cover 11 of the 42 conversations sub-poenaed by the committee. Four of them, according to White House counsel J. Fred Buzhardt, occurred on April 15, 1973 and were not recorded because the machine ran out of tape; five were on phones not connected to recorders, and tapes of two others were not found.

The transcripts themselves were found to be liberally sprinkled with deletions marked "unintelligible," "expletive deleted" or "inaudible." Many passages actually were unintelligible because of the markings. One entire comment attributed to Nixon, whose conversation was dotted with "expletives," was: "P. [expletive removed]! [unintelligible]"

A brief attached as an introduction to the volume of transcripts said the expletives had been removed, except where necessary to maintain relevancy, in the interest of good taste. Other deletions, allowable on the relevancy test, it said, were made to eliminate characterization of third persons and material not relating to the President's conduct.

The House Judiciary Committee received a 1,308-page volume measuring 2¼ inches thick; reporters obtained an eight-by-10-inch book, the pages typewritten and double-spaced, about the size of a big-city phone directory.

Copies of the transcripts, at $12.25 each, were available from the Government Printing Office. Its Washington bookstore sold 800 copies in three hours May 1.

Vice President Gerald R. Ford added his voice in support of the President's action. In a statement April 29, he said the Judiciary Committee should be "satisfied," that Nixon was being "more than cooperative" and supplying it with "more than enough" data to carry out its investigation.

Brief claims innocence—A White House legal brief accompanying the transcripts April 30 asserted President Nixon's innocence in the Watergate matter. Released several hours before the transcripts, it maintained that "the raw material of these recorded confidential conversations establishes that the President had no prior knowledge of the break-in and that he had no knowledge of any cover-up to March 21, 1973."

Written by Nixon's special counsel James D. St. Clair, the brief said: "In all of the thousands of words spoken, even though they are unclear and ambiguous, not once does it appear that the President of the United States was engaged in a criminal plot to obstruct justice."

The brief, as the President did in his speech, attacked in particular John Dean's credibility. It indicated Dean had repeatedly perjured himself in sworn testimony and accused him of trying to blackmail the President in an effort to gain immunity from prosecution.

It said Assistant Attorney General Henry E. Petersen had reported to Nixon on April 27, 1973 that Dean's lawyer was threatening to "bring the President in— not in this case [the cover-up] but in other things" if Dean did not get immunity. Nixon's reply, according to the brief, was: "All right. We have the immunity problem resolved. Do it [grant immunity] to Dean if you need to, but I am telling you—there ain't going to be any black-mail." (Dean was not extended full immunity. He pleaded guilty to one count of conspiracy to obstruct justice and was awaiting sentencing. Dean's attorney, Robert C. McCandless, denied ever making such a threat April 30.)

The brief's interpretation of the controversial Sept. 15, 1972 conversation between Dean and the President was that the transcript did "not in any way" support Dean's testimony that the President was fully aware of the cover-up. It referred to Nixon's compliment then to Dean that he had handled things skillfully by "putting your fingers in the leaks that have sprung here and sprung there." This was "said in the context not of a criminal plot," St. Clair contended, but "in the context of the politics of the matter, such as civil suits, counter-suits, Democratic efforts to exploit Watergate as a political issue and the like. The reference to 'putting your fingers in the leaks' was clearly related to the handling of the political and public relations aspect of the matter."

Committee denies compliance—The House Judiciary Committee voted 20–18 May 1 to inform President Nixon by letter than he had "failed to comply with the committee's subpoena" requesting the White House tapes and documents.

The vote was almost along party lines. Two of the panel's 21 Democrats—Reps. John Conyers Jr. (Mich.) and Jerome R. Waldie (Calif.)—voted against the motion because they considered it too weak; they favored holding the President in contempt of the House. One of the committee's 17 Republicans, Rep. William S. Cohen (Me.). voted for the Democratic motion to send the letter and became the deciding vote.

Conyers' motion to recommend contempt action against the President was rejected 32–5.

The committee decision came during a long evening session. In addition to the absence of 11 of the 42 subpoenaed conversations, because they had not been recorded or could not be found. Nixon's response to the subpoena did not cover notes or memos or Dictabelts requested under the subpoena.

The committee's special counsel John M. Doar also informed the panel the White House transcripts were "not accurate." After comparison with some overlapping material obtained peviously, some of it from the special prosecutor, the staff's own tape experts, Doar said, had been able to "pick up parts of conversations" that were marked "unintelligible" in some of the White House transcripts.

Doar also said there were sections of the White House transcripts where words had been omitted without any notation that the deletion had been made. Doar stressed that he was not suggesting there had been any "intentional distortion" in the White House version, only that the committee staff could detect, if the actual tapes were available, many of the parts marked "unintelligible" by the White House.

Doar advised the committee it would not be "prudent" for the two senior committee members, as the President offered, to attempt to verify the accuracy of the transcripts without professional help. Chairman Peter W. Rodino Jr. (D, N.J.), who would be one of the verifiers along with Rep. Edward Hutchinson (R, Mich.), agreed.

Nixon bars release of more tapes—Special presidential counsel James D. St. Clair announced May 7 that President Nixon would "respectfully" decline "to produce any more Watergate tapes" for use in the House Judiciary Committee's impeachment inquiry, and that Nixon had instructed him to "press forward" with the effort to quash special prosecutor Leon Jaworski's subpoena for tapes of 64 White House conversations.

The surprise announcement came only a few hours after presidential counselor Dean Burch had said St. Clair was attempting to negotiate a settlement with Jaworski, and one day after U.S. District Court Judge John J. Sirica had delayed to May 13 a hearing on the White House motion to quash the prosecution subpoena.

In his news conference, St. Clair said discussions with Jaworski had broken off, and that Nixon had definitely decided that there would be no "accommodation" with Jaworski or any "further adjustments" in the White House stance against compliance.

Regarding the impeachment panel's request for additional evidence, St. Clair said Nixon would release material on "non-Watergate" matters such as the International Telephone & Telegraph Corp. antitrust controversy and the dairy industry campaign fund issue. But on the Watergate issue, St. Clair said, if the committee issued a subpoena "we are going to have a confrontation, because the President is firm in his resolve that he has done more than is necessary."

Republican criticism & calls for Nixon's departure mount. Senate Republican Leader Hugh Scott (Pa.) severely criticized and renounced support May 7 for the "immoral" activities delineated in the transcripts of White House conversations on Watergate. Scott asserted that the transcripts revealed "deplorable, disgusting, shabby, immoral performances" by all participants in the conversations.

House Republican Leader John J. Rhodes (Ariz.) said May 7 he "wouldn't quarrel" with Scott's description of the transcript performances. Rhodes said May 9 "the content of the transcripts was devastating" and resignation a "possible option." He did not see "much choice" between resignation and impeachment, since both were "traumatic." Rhodes said as a lawyer he preferred the impeachment process as the best way to reach the truth, but he was unsure if it were worth the agony or could "settle the dust."

Rhodes thought Nixon could continue to operate effectively as President at the

moment, but he said "we might have to reconsider it" if "the erosion" of the President's position continued. He said Nixon's departure and the accession of Vice President Gerald Ford would be "beneficial" to the Republican Party.

Rep. John B. Anderson (Ill.), chairman of the House Republican Conference, predicted May 9 Nixon would be impeached if he did not resign.

Sen. Marlow W. Cook (R, Ky.) suggested May 9 that Nixon seriously consider resigning because of the "moral turpitude" revealed in the transcripts.

Vice President Gerald R. Ford mixed his reaction to the transcript material, which he deplored, with renewed support for the President. He was "a little disappointed" by the transcripts, he said in Myrtle Beach, S.C. May 3. In reply to a reporter's question, "Is this the President you have known for 25 years?" he said "the answer is no." In Ann Arbor, Mich. May 4, in a commencement address at his alma mater, the University of Michigan, Ford said the transcripts "do not exactly confer sainthood on anyone concerned." In a New York speech May 6, he added: "But when you add it all up, I haven't lost my faith in the capability of the President to do a great job."

Sen. Richard S. Schweiker (Pa.) May 10 joined those calling for the President's resignation. He was the third Republican senator to do so. "I cannot remain silent in the face of the now obvious moral corrosion destroying and debasing the presidency," Schweiker said.

Sen. Milton R. Young (R, N.D.) said May 10 "it would be a whole lot easier for members of Congress and myself" if Nixon "used the 25th Amendment and stepped aside until this thing is cleared up." The amendment permitted the vice president to assume executive authority if he and the Cabinet persuaded Congress the President was unable to discharge the powers and duties of office. Nixon was "getting in deeper trouble all the time," Young said, and "it's a question of whether he can continue as President." "I doubt if there is anyone in the Senate who'd urge him to stay," Young said. "There wouldn't be over five who you'd call hard-core supporters."

Chairman John Anderson (Ill.) of the House Republican Conference declared

May 11 that "the most propitious time to convince him to resign would be now," that "once the impeachment resolution is voted on, the lines may have hardened again and the President may have been persuaded that he can last a little longer." Anderson said "he should spare the nation one last agony. . . . If he is capable of a last act of nobility, he should resign."

Democratic leaders vs. resignation— Senate Democratic leaders and prominent Senate conservatives voiced opposition to resignation May 13.

Senate Democratic Leader Mike Mansfield (Mont.) said "resignation is not the answer." He said it was "time to keep cool, the evidence must be forthcoming."

Senate Democratic whip Robert Byrd (W. Va.) said if the President resigned under current conditions a significant number of citizens would feel he had been driven from office by his political enemies. "The question of guilt or innocence would never be fully resolved," he said, "the country would remain polarized" and "confidence in government would remain unrestored."

Sen. William E. Brock 3rd (R, Tenn.), who said the transcripts had caused "deep concern and depression" among conservatives, said "the President has a right to decide what he wants to do and to have a trial if he wants it, which he seems to."

Other statements May 13 against resignation were made by Sen. Carl T. Curtis (R, Neb.), who warned against "mob rule," Sen. Strom Thurmond (R, S.C.), who said Nixon was "the only President we have," and Sen. Henry L. Bellmon (R, Okla.), who said a resignation "would create a disastrous precedent for future presidents."

The stand by the Democratic leaders was endorsed May 14 by the party's national chairman, Robert S. Strauss, who met in Washington with the House and Senate Democratic leaders along with Gov. Wendell Ford (Ky.), chairman of the Democratic Governors Conference. House Speaker Carl Albert (D, Okla.), a participant, said he did not believe Nixon should or would resign.

Senate Republican Leader Hugh Scott (Pa.) also agreed with the Democrats May 14 "to allow the system to function." "I think our nation is strong enough to withstand the functioning of its own Constitution," Scott said.

*Key editorial support lost—*William Randolph Hearst Jr., editor of the Hearst newspapers and a firm Nixon supporter, said in his Sunday column May 5 (published May 3) the transcript conversations "add up to as damning a document as it is possible to imagine short of an actual indictment." The conversations, he said, revealed Nixon as a man "with a moral blind spot" and made his impeachment inevitable. "The gang talking on the tapes, even the censored version, comes through in just that way—a gang of racketeers talking over strategy in a jam-up situation," Hearst said.

The Chicago Tribune, an influential Republican newspaper, in an editorial in its May 9 edition (published May 8), called for Nixon to leave office for the sake of "the presidency, the country and the free world." Speaking of the transcripts, it said "We have seen the private man and we are appalled." "The key word is immoral," it said of Nixon. "Two roads are open. One is resignation. The other is impeachment. Both are legitimate and would satisfy the need to observe due process."

The Omaha World-Herald called May 7 for Nixon's resignation. Although it had endorsed Nixon's presidential candidacy three times, the paper said his accomplishments were "overshadowed now by the appallingly low level of political morality in the White House."

Editorials urging impeachment of the President were published May 10 by the Los Angeles Times and the Cleveland Plain Dealer.

Nixon Renews Struggle

Nixon to 'fight' for office. The White House acted May 10, 1974 to squelch rumors flooding Washington that President Nixon would resign.

In the evening, Press Secretary Ronald L. Ziegler telephoned the New York Times with this message: "The city of Washington is full of rumors. All that have been presented to me today are false, and the one that heads the list is the one that says President Nixon intends to resign. His attitude is one of determination that he will not be driven out of office by rumor, speculation, excessive charges or hypocrisy. He is up to the battle, he intends to fight it and he feels he has a personal and constitutional responsibility to do so."

Earlier May 10, White House chief of staff Alexander M. Haig Jr., in an interview with the Associated Press, said: "I think the only thing that would tempt resignation on the part of the President would be if he thought that served the best interests of the American people. At this juncture, I don't see anything on the horizon which would meet that criterion. Admittedly, that's a subjective view on my part, and I think it is one the President shares very strenuously."

(Haig later emphasized that this was not a softening of Nixon's position against resignation but rather an assertion that the public interest was paramount over Nixon's personal interest.)

The rumors of resignation had intensified May 10 with Vice President Gerald Ford's hasty return to Washington from a speaking tour to meet privately with the President.

Questioned about the meeting later in the day, Ford said the subject of resignation had not come up, "but I could infer that he had no intention of resigning."

In a commencement address at Texas A. & M. University May 11, Ford said he had told Nixon that he was not among those "trying to jump off" Nixon's "ship of state." Ford added that his message to all graduates in his series of commencement appearances was that "the government in Washington wasn't about to sink." Ford told a Republican fundraising dinner in Dallas that evening that he "very strongly" disagreed with GOP leaders calling for Nixon's resignation.

Ford added in Pensacola, Fla. May 13 that he had "diligently read" the White House Watergate tapes. The "overwhelming weight" of the evidence "proves" the President innocent of any of the charges, Ford declared.

Nixon's daughter Julie (Mrs. David Eisenhower) had reported May 11 on a family gathering the night before aboard the presidential yacht on the Potomac. At a press conference with her husband at the White House, Julie, speaking of her father "He said he would take this constitu-

tionally down to the wire. He said he would go to the Senate and he said if there were one senator that believes in him, that that is the way it would be."

"I feel that as a daughter it is my obligation to come out here and say, no he is not going to resign," she said, even though "I know that he doesn't want me out here. He doesn't want anyone to construe that I'm trying to answer questions for him."

As for the transcripts, they portrayed "a human being reacting in a difficult situation," she said.

Nixon said May 16 that he was determined to stay in office, even if impeached by the House and tried by the Senate. The statement was made to syndicated columnist James J. Kilpatrick during an interview requested by Nixon.

"I would have to rule out resignation. And I would have to rule out the rather fatuous suggestion that I take the 25th Amendment and just step out and have Vice President Ford step in for a while," Nixon told Kilpatrick. Nixon asserted that the office of the Presidency would be fatally weakened if he resigned.

If impeached, Nixon said, he would defend himself before the Senate, while continuing to perform his presidential duties.

Nixon rejects subpoenas. President Nixon informed the House Judiciary Committee May 22 that he would not comply with two subpoenas for Watergate-related tapes and documents the panel had issued a week before for its impeachment inquiry. Nixon also said that any future subpoenas "allegedly dealing with Watergate" would be rejected.

Earlier in the day, presidential counsel James D. St. Clair informed the committee that its requests for additional material on the International Telephone and Telegraph Corp. (ITT) antitrust controversy and campaign contributions by the dairy industry would not be met, with the possible exception of an edited transcript of one conversation on the ITT case.

In a letter to Judiciary Committee Chairman Peter W. Rodino Jr. (D, N.J.), Nixon reiterated the basic White House argument that production of additional material "would merely prolong the inquiry without yielding significant additional evidence." "More fundamentally,"

Nixon continued, compliance "with an endless series of demands would fatally weaken this office" in his own Administration and for future presidents.

Nixon contended that the subpoenaed White House diaries were obviously "intended to be used to identify even more presidential conversations, as a basis for even more subpoenas."

Nixon said the House panel had "the full story of Watergate, in so far as it relates to presidential knowledge and presidential actions." Nixon added, however, that he was prepared to answer, under oath, "pertinent written interrogatories, and to be interviewed, under oath," by Rodino and ranking Republican Edward Hutchinson (Mich.).

Panel warns Nixon of impeachment—The House Judiciary Committee formally notified President Nixon May 30 that his refusal to comply with its subpoenas "might constitute a ground for impeachment" that the committee could take before the House. The committee also approved May 30 issuance of another subpoena for White House tapes and documents.

The committee's actions had strong bipartisan backing. Rep. Robert McClory (Ill.), the panel's second-ranking Republican, said: "We are reviewing allegations that the President obstructed the [Watergate] inquiry of the Department of Justice, the Senate [Watergate] committee and the special prosecutor. His current conduct does not make it easier for this member to conclude that such allegations are without merit."

The warning to the President, a letter from committee chairman Rodino, also cautioned Nixon that the committee members would "be free to consider whether your refusals warrant the drawing of adverse inferences concerning the substance of the materials," or inferences, that is, that the materials withheld were incriminating.

Such inferences could not properly be drawn, according to James D. St. Clair, Nixon's chief defense lawyer later May 30, because the President's stand was based on his constitutional duty to protect the presidency.

The letter was sent following a 28–10 vote by the panel favoring the action.

All but one of the committee's 21 Democrats—Rep. John Conyers Jr. (Mich.)—voted to send the letter. They were joined by eight of the 17 Republicans. The eight: Reps. William S. Cohen (Me.), Henry P. Smith 3rd (N.Y.), Hamilton Fish Jr. (N.Y.), Charles W. Sandman (N.J.), Lawrence J. Hogan (Md.), M. Caldwell Butler (Va.), Robert McClory (Ill.) and Tom Railsback (Ill.).

Conyers wanted stronger action by the committee on the issue. He proposed seeking an immediate House vote to impeach the President for "contempt for and obstruction of the constitutional process" of impeachment, but the committee rejected this by a 29-9 vote. The committee also rejected, by a 27–11 vote, a proposal by Rep. Jerome R. Waldie (D, Calif.) to seek a House decision to cite the President for contempt of Congress.

The committee also rejected two alternative proposals, by votes of 32–6, suggested by Republicans. One of these, from Railsback, called for seeking legislation to give the federal courts jurisdiction to decide whether the President had a constitutional right to refuse impeachment evidence. The other, from Rep. David W. Dennis (Ind.), would have the committee enter, as an amicus curiae (friend of the court) the Supreme Court suit brought by the special Watergate prosecutor in his pursuit of White House tapes for criminal trials.

Both court procedures were opposed by chief Republican counsel Albert E. Jenner Jr. because of the "serious legal and constitutional problems" raised by submission to the judiciary of the impeachment issue on which Congress had sole constitutional authority.

Ford differs with Nixon on tapes. Vice President Gerald Ford acknowledged May 26 he disagreed with President Nixon on the issue of providing relevant information to the House impeachment panel. Ford said the difference "was laid out quite candidly" during a meeting with Nixon May 23. The meeting came after Ford had called several times for White House cooperation with the House probe.

At a news conference in New York May 22, Ford said he planned to "talk to the White House about the content" of further taped Watergate conversations being sought by the House Judiciary Committee. "I hope," he said, "that when the committee gets through the present vast amount of evidence, if it needs any additional evidence relating to impeachment, the White House would cooperate."

A few hours after his meeting with Nixon May 23, about which little immediate detail was available, Ford told ABC correspondent Bill Zimmerman, in an interview broadcast May 24, "a stonewall attitude" in refusing to provide the committee with relevant information "isn't necessarily the wisest policy." It "could be" the issue that could bring about House impeachment, he thought, and he wanted the House "to make its judgment on the facts, not on some emotional, institutional issue."

At a news conference in Danbury, Conn. May 26, Ford related some details of his May 23 meeting with Nixon. He was asked about reports of differences between him and Nixon on the issue of White House release of information to the House Judiciary Committee. "This difference existed before the meeting," he replied. "It was laid out quite candidly during the meeting, and I haven't backed off from it since." Ford said he "wants the facts out in the open so that the House committee can act on the facts," that he felt there "should be as much disclosure as possible." "Obviously, he [Nixon] has a somewhat different opinion and I respect it," he said. He said he told the President a refusal to provide relevant information "could lead to an emotional institutional confrontation."

Easing his stand on the issue, Ford told reporters in Birmingham, Ala. May 29 he thought Nixon's position was "proper" at the current time. "I will keep pressing the committee to open up their hearings, I will keep pressing them to call these witnesses," he said. "Until they have done that, I think the President's attitude is proper."

48% favor ouster. A Gallup Poll issued May 26 showed that a plurality of those interviewed, by a 48%–37% margin, believed that President Nixon's actions were serious enough to warrant his removal from the presidency. In mid-April,

the finding was 46% 42% in favor of removal from office. The latest survey was taken May 10 13.

Louis Harris pollsters found a 49% 41% call for Nixon's impeachment and removal from office. Results of the survey were published May 11. The previous finding on the question in April was 42% 42%.

The Harris interviewers also asked if there was any belief that Nixon "will be found to have violated the law." The replies: 51% yes, 30% no (previous month's survey, 40% yes, 34% no).

Gallup reported very little change in a year in the public belief about Nixon's involvement in the Watergate scandal. In the May 10 13 survey, interviewers found that 73% believed Nixon was involved to some extent, similar to the 71% finding in February and 67% finding in June 1973.

Both major polling groups found that release of the White House transcripts had little or no effect on the President's popularity rating. Gallup put the rating at 25%, a drop of one point from April; Harris at 32%, a one point increase over March and April. Results of both surveys were issued May 22. The Gallup polling period was May 10–13, Harris's May 7–8.

Senate Democratic Whip Robert C. Byrd (W.Va.) said May 26 the situation had somewhat "hardened" in the Senate against Nixon, partly because of "the stonewalling that the President and his lawyer have been exhibiting all the way down the line." Byrd said he could not repeat his March 3 estimate doubting that two-thirds of the Senate was ready to vote to convict Nixon on impeachment.

Archibald Cox, who was ousted as special Watergate prosecutor during the 1973 tapes dispute with Nixon, said May 30 "if the President pursues his refusal to give the committee all evidence it deems relevant, that would be grounds for impeachment on which I would say he ought to be convicted." Cox had said May 27 failure by the President to submit evidence ordered by the courts, either to the committee or the special Watergate prosecutor, constituted "the most serious of impeachable offenses."

Evangelist Billy Graham, in a statement May 28, reaffirmed that President Nixon remained "my friend and I have no intention of forsaking him now," but he said reading the Nixon transcripts had been "a profoundly disturbing and disappointing experience." "What comes through in these tapes is not the man I have known for many years," Graham said, and indicated that as a nation "we have lost our moral compass." He added, however, that "it would be nothing less than hypocrisy to call for a moral housecleaning at the White House unless we are willing to do the same at your house and my house."

According to a survey of more than 100 leading newspapers in 45 states, conducted by Editorials on File. (results released May 31), 47 had called for President Nixon's resignation (32) or impeachment (15), and nine continued to support the President without significant reservations. Some 50 other newspapers surveyed were generally critical of Nixon's refusal to turn over all evidence to the House Judiciary Committee but did not specifically conclude whether or not he should give up his office.

Charges of partisanship. As the House Judiciary Committee entered the phase of taking testimony from witnesses in its impeachment inquiry, there were attacks on Chairman Peter W. Rodino Jr. (D, N.J.) and charges that the inquiry was "a partisan lynch mob." The discord between the committee's Democrats and Republicans had erupted June 26 over the list of witnesses.

The committee's decision to schedule testimony from five witnesses, including only two of six requested by President Nixon's attorney, James D. St. Clair, was assailed by White House spokesmen June 27. Committee Chairman Rodino was denounced, and defended himself in a floor speech June 28, after a report was published attributing to him a statement that all 21 Democrats on the committee were prepared to vote to recommend impeachment of the President. Rodino announced his readiness July 1 to allow all six witnesses sought by Nixon's lawyer to testify, but the partisan breach was not healed.

The failure to schedule all six witnesses requested by St. Clair came under strong attack from the White House June 27. Dean Burch, special counselor to the President, characterized the committee's

impeachment inquiry as a "partisan lynch mob." "The Constitution indicates," he said, "that the defendant, in any kind of proceeding that has a smack of fairness, is entitled to have witnesses." To curb that right, he said, was "patently unfair" and the President was being deprived of basic 6th Amendment rights he would have if he had "stolen a loaf of bread." Burch said he believed the committee was rushing to bring the issue to a vote, "at the expense of the rudiments of due process," in response to "pressure within the Democratic hierarchy." He attributed the "remarkable step-up in the tempo" of the committee's inquiry to "blatant partisanship."

At the Overseas Press Club, the Rev. John McLaughlin, a deputy special assistant to the President, attacked Rodino June 27 on the witness issue for trying to "railroad" the President's impeachment and "denying Mr. Nixon his day in court."

The attack by Nixon's supporters on Rodino intensified after a report in the Los Angeles Times June 28 by Jack Nelson quoted Rodino as saying that all 21 Democrats on the panel were prepared to vote to recommend Nixon's impeachment. Nelson had met with Rodino June 27. Another reporter at the meeting, ABC correspondent Sam Donaldson, corroborated Nelson's account but said Rodino was giving only his personal assessment of the mood of the way committee members were reacting to the evidence, "that he believed all 21 Democrats would most likely reach that conclusion."

At the urging of House Speaker Carl Albert (D, Okla.), Rodino went to the floor of the House June 28 to deny the newspaper report and affirm his intention to conduct the inquiry fairly. "I want to state unequivocally and categorically that this statement is not true," he said of the newspaper report. He had never asked any of the committee members "how he or she will vote" on the issue, Rodino said, and had insisted throughout the inquiry that "only when there is a complete presentation of evidence should members draw a conclusion."

House Republican whip Leslie C. Arends (Ill.) said June 28 the newspaper article about Rodino was "one of the most disturbing things I've seen since this thing started." Rep. Lawrence J. Hogan, a Rodino committee member who announced June 27 his candidacy for the Republican nomination for governor of Maryland, told the House June 28 he thought the impeachment inquiry "has been biased and it has been unfair."

But other Republicans on the committee supported Rodino June 28. Ranking GOP member Edward Hutchinson (Mich.) said he was "satisfied" that Rodino had not acted improperly. Rep. Robert McClory (Ill.), speaking after Rodino, told the House "I know the chairman has tenaciously avoided statements that would prejudge the case." Rep. Wiley Mayne (Iowa) said "most members of the committee discounted the story as soon as they saw it. I know I did."

Talk of censure, not impeachment— There were reports June 29–30 of an effort by conservative Republicans to turn the case against Nixon into a vote of censure, rather than impeachment. But House Republican Leader John J. Rhodes (Ariz.) opposed it strongly June 29 as "exactly the wrong thing to do." "What we are trying to do," he said, "is to strengthen the presidency one way or another, not weaken it. To censure the President and leave him in office would be doing the country a grave disservice. It would completely cripple the man and would be giving him the worst of two worlds."

Increasing Pressure on Nixon

Nixon an 'unindicted co-conspirator.' The White House acknowledged June 6 that a Watergate grand jury had voted in February to name President Nixon as an unindicted co-conspirator with his former aides, who were indicted for the cover-up of the Watergate break-in.

The grand jury's vote, reported to be unanimous, had been kept secret under an order by U.S. District Court Judge John J. Sirica. But after a report of the jury's action appeared in the June 6 editions of the Los Angeles Times, special presidential counsel James D. St. Clair said he had been informed of the vote three or four weeks earlier by special Watergate prosecutor Leon Jaworski.

St. Clair related that when he had told

Nixon, the President responded: " 'They just don't have the evidence and they are wrong.' " St. Clair said Nixon "regretted" the jury's action and considered it "inappropriate."

For his own part St. Clair contended that Nixon was "not a co-conspirator only because a grand jury says he is." "It won't be the first time a grand jury was wrong. Grand jury allegations are far from proof and have no legal effect."

According to news reports, the grand jury had at first been inclined to indict Nixon, but had been dissuaded by Jaworski's contention that such action could not be taken against a President in office.

Ford: Evidence clears Nixon. Vice President Gerald R. Ford expressed confidence after meeting with President Nixon July 13 that the House would not vote to impeach the President. There was a "possibility" that the House Judiciary Committee would vote a bill of impeachment, he said, but he felt "strongly" that the House would reject it because the "preponderance of the evidence favors the President."

At a news conference in Albuquerque, N.M. July 12, Ford said that the "new evidence as well as the old evidence" exonerated Nixon of any impeachable offense.

Ford said at a news conference July 18 that because he was concerned about discrepancies between White House and House Judiciary Committee transcripts of presidential tapes, he had requested and received permission to listen to portions of two tapes.

Although he had said earlier that it would be improper for him to hear the White House recordings, Ford said he had concluded that it was now in his "interest" to "find out the quality."

Ford said he now understood how there "could be a different interpretation of the words that were spoken." Asked which version was more accurate, he replied, "I think you could read it either way."

Nixon aide convicted in 'plumbers' case. John D. Ehrlichman, former domestic affairs adviser to President Nixon, was found guilty July 12 by a federal jury in

Washington of conspiring to violate the civil rights of Dr. Lewis J. Fielding, the psychiatrist of Pentagon Papers defendant Daniel Ellsberg. Three other defendants in the trial—G. Gordon Liddy, Bernard L. Barker and Eugenio Martinez—were convicted of the same charge. Ehrlichman was also found guilty of three of four counts of making false statements.

Instructing the jury on the conspiracy charge July 12, U.S. District Court Judge Gerhard A. Gesell said that it need not find Ehrlichman had known in advance of plans for a "covert entry" into Fielding's office files to obtain Ellsberg's psychiatric records. Moreover, Gesell told the jurors, an illegal search need not entail "physical break-in," which only tended to emphasize "lack of permission." The law had been broken if the government attempted to acquire private information without a search warrant, he said. "When a government agency invades an area in which there is a legitimate expectation of privacy to look through such papers without permission, that is a search," the judge stated.

Gesell's instructions struck at the heart of Ehrlichman's defense that he had not authorized an illegal break-in but merely a legal "covert operation." Ehrlichman's attorneys objected that the judge had failed to charge the jury with Ehrlichman's theory of the case. Gesell replied, out of the hearing of the jury, that Ehrlichman's "defense has been one of guarding and dodging around various issues of the case. . . ."

In his other instructions, Gesell said, "An individual cannot escape criminal liability simply because he sincerely but incorrectly believes that his acts are justified in the name of patriotism, of national security or the need to create an unfavorable press image or that his superiors had the authority to suspend without a warrant the protections of the Fourth Amendment." (The 4th Amendment guaranteed against unreasonable searches.)

Ehrlichman was acquitted on a charge of false testimony to a grand jury May 14, 1973. At that time, Ehrlichman stated that he did not know who, other than Egil Krogh Jr., co-director of the White House "plumbers" unit, had files on the unit's investigation of Ellsberg. However, the jury concluded that Ehrlichman had twice made false statements to the grand jury when he said he had not been aware before the break-in of the plan to obtain Ellsberg's psychiatric files. In addition, the jury convicted Ehrlichman of the charge of falsely stating to the Federal Bureau of Investigation May 1, 1973 that he had not seen any material relating to the White House investigation of the Pentagon Papers affair for more than a year.

Interview with Rabbi Korff. President Nixon told Rabbi Baruch Korff, leader of a pro-Nixon group, that Watergate would be remembered as "the broadest but the thinnest scandal in American history." The interview, held on May 13, was released by the President's press office in San Clemente, Calif. July 16, when Nixon met again with Korff, president of the National Citizens Committee for Fairness to the Presidency.

After their July 16 meeting, Korff told reporters that Nixon had agreed with him that the recent conviction of former Nixon aide John Ehrlichman for conspiracy and lying was "a blot on justice."

In the May 13 interview, Nixon said the Watergate figures had been "tried and convicted in the press and on television" and it would be "extremely difficult" for them to get "a fair trial" in Washington.

Watergate "caught the imagination of the press," Nixon said, because "I am not the press' favorite pin-up boy. If it hadn't been Watergate, there would probably have been something else. So now they have this. But I will survive it and I just hope they will survive it with . . . as much serenity as I have."

As for impeachment, Nixon said "when a Congressman and Senator gets right down to the tough call, he is going to think a long time before he wants to impeach a President, unless he finds wrongdoing." He thought his own impeachment would have "devastating consequences" on foreign policy, would "jeopardize" world peace and would have a "very detrimental effect on our political system for years to come."

Senate Watergate panel report. In its last official action, the Senate Select Committee on Presidential Campaign Activities, known as "the Watergate Committee" or "the Ervin Committee," released the final report July 13 on its investigation of the Watergate and other scandals related to the 1972 presidential campaign.

The committee, whose televised hearings in 1973 had focused public attention on the scandals, said in an introduction to the 2,250-page report that its investigation had not been conducted, nor its report prepared, "to determine the legal guilt or innocence of any person or whether the President should be impeached."

The panel said, however, that "to be true to its mandate from the Senate and its constitutional responsibilities," it "must present its view of the facts" of the Watergate affair and related matters in addition to recommending remedial legislation to "safeguard the electoral process."

Announcing the report's release at a news conference in the committee's hearing room July 12, Chairman Sam J. Ervin Jr. (D, N.C.) contended that the report was not weaker because it did not make specific accusations. Ervin said, "There are two ways to indicate a horse. One is to draw a picture that is a great likeness. And the other is to draw a picture that is a great likeness and write under it, 'This is a horse.' We just drew the picture."

The report said the picture presented by its compilation of evidence demonstrated that "campaign practices must be effectively supervised and enforcement of the criminal laws vigorously pursued against all offenders—even those of high estate—if our free institutions are to survive."

Sen. Ervin appended to the report a "statement of individual views" studded with historical references and verbal equivalents of the arched eyebrows that had marked his appearance during the televised hearings. Ervin condemned the "illegal and unethical activities" by campaign officials and White House aides, which he said corrupted both the electoral process and the workings of government.

Answering his own question, "Why was Watergate?" Ervin said presidential aides' "lust for political power blinded them to ethical considerations and legal requirements. . . . They had forgotten, if they ever knew, that the Constitution is designed to be a law for rulers and people alike at all times and under all circumstances; and that no doctrine involving more pernicious

consequences to the commonwealth has ever been invented by the wit of man than the notion that any of its provisions can be suspended by the President for any reason whatsoever."

Doar says evidence merits impeachment. John M. Doar, special counsel to the House Judiciary Committee, urged committee members July 19 to recommend the impeachment of President Nixon on one or more charges. Doar was seconded by Albert E. Jenner Jr., special Republican counsel to the committee.

Abandoning the neutrality that had characterized his staff's 10-week presentation of evidence, Doar presented to the panel five sets of proposed articles of impeachment and a 306-page summary of evidence, which he said buttressed his arguments.

The proposed articles of impeachment, 29 in all, were composed by both the members and staff of the committee. Essentially, the articles centered on four allegations against the President:

He obstructed justice by participating in the cover-up that followed the Watergate break-in.

He abused the powers of the presidency by invading the civil rights and privacy of U.S. citizens and by misusing or attempting to misuse agencies of the U.S. government.

His refusal to honor subpoenas by the Judiciary Committee was contemptuous of Congress.

He committed fraud in connection with his income taxes and expenditure of public funds on his personal property.

The summary of evidence presented by Doar was intended to draw together the mountain of impeachment data into a cohesive argument that, in the view of the committee staff, "demonstrates various abuses of Presidential power."

"Circumstances strongly suggest," the summary said, "that President Nixon decided, shortly after learning of the Watergate break-in, on a plan to cover up the identities of high officials of the White House and the Committee for the Reelection of the President directly involved in the illegal operation." Until after the 1972 election, the summary added, "President Nixon's policy of con-

tainment—of 'cutting the loss'—worked
... because two of the President's assistants, John Dean, counsel to the President, and Herbert Kalmbach, personal attorney to the President, assigned to carry out the President's policy, did their jobs well—with the full support of the power and authority of the office of President of the United States."

Contrary to Nixon's statement that on Sept. 15, 1972 he knew nothing of the case, the summary contended he had already done the following things: met with H.R. Haldeman, his chief of staff, and John N. Mitchell, his campaign manager, both of whom were "fully apprised of" White House connections to Watergate; arranged a misleading explanation for Mitchell's resignation; received from L. Patrick Gray 3rd, then acting director of the FBI, a warning about White House interference in the FBI's Watergate inquiry; "prevented" a personal appearance before the Watergate grand jury by Maurice H. Stans, his chief campaign fund raiser and former commerce secretary; and "made an untrue public statement about Dean's 'complete investigation' of the Watergate matter," when in fact Dean "acted to narrow and frustrate the FBI investigation" and "conducted no independent investigation of his own."

The summary also reviewed Nixon's March 21, 1973 meeting with Dean, during which Dean detailed the payment of "hush money" to the convicted Watergate conspirators: "The President did not condemn the payments or the involvement of his closest aides. He did not direct that the activity be stopped. The President did not express any surprise or shock. He did not report it to the proper investigatory authorities." Subsequently, the summary added, the President repeatedly modified his accounts of the meeting.

"The 'report' that the President ... requested Dean to make in March 1973 was one that was designed to mislead investigators and insulate the President from charges of concealment," the summary asserted.

When his associates lied or "stonewalled" to sustain the cover-up, the summary said, "the President condoned this conduct, approved it, directed it, rewarded it and, in some cases, advised witnesses on how to impede the investigators." Moreover, when the cover-up began to unravel in late March 1973, "there is clear and convincing evidence that the President took over in late March the active management of the cover-up," the Doar summary stated.

Other areas touched by the summary: wiretapping and other "illegal and improper" intelligence gathering activities; the burglary of Daniel Ellsberg's psychiatrist's office and the concealment of those activities; use of the Internal Revenue Service (IRS) in improper ways; the International Telephone & Telegraph (ITT) case; the milk-fund case; and expenditures on Nixon's personal properties in Florida and California.

GOP counsel cautions vs impeachment. Samuel A. Garrison, the newly designated special Republican counsel, cautioned the Judiciary committee July 22 against impeaching the President unless it appeared probable he would be convicted and removed from office by the Senate. (Garrison, who was deputy minority counsel, was given the title of chief minority counsel July 21, replacing Jenner, who the panel's Republican leadership thought had been too pro-impeachment. Jenner remained as an associate counsel.)

Even if Nixon were shown to have committed an impeachable offense, it might not be in "the best interests of the country" to impeach and remove him from office, Garrison said. The primary purpose of impeachment was not to punish the President, Garrison stated, but "to protect the country's system of government, and thereby protect the people."

Other arguments advanced by Garrison were that Nixon should not be impeached for "abuse of power" unless he had done things other presidents hadn't. While not passing on Nixon's guilt or innocence of tax fraud, Garrison questioned if the framers of the Constitution had intended such an offense to be impeachable. The President should not be impeached for refusing to comply with committee subpoenas, he said, unless Nixon's refusal was not "justifiable or excusable." Garrison also suggested to the committee that Nixon's reliance on executive privilege to withhold evidence was analogous to invocation of the 5th Amendment against self-incrimination. In that context, he said, committee members should not draw adverse inferences from Nixon's refusal to honor the subpoenas.

Hogan would vote to impeach. Rep. Lawrence J. Hogan (R, Md.) July 23 became the first Republican member of the House Judiciary Committee to announce that he would vote for President Nixon's impeachment. In a surprise announcement, Hogan said, "Nixon has, beyond a reasonable doubt, committed impeachable offenses, which, in my judgment, are of sufficient magnitude that he should be removed from office."

Hogan, a moderate conservative who had been a staunch defender of the President in the past, charged that Nixon had "lied repeatedly, deceiving public officials and the American people. He has withheld information necessary for our system of justice to work. Instead of cooperating with prosecutors and investigators, as he said publicly, he concealed and covered up evidence, and coached witnesses so that their testimony would show things that really were not true. He tried to use the CIA to impede and thwart the investigation of Watergate by the FBI. He approved the payment of what he knew to be blackmail to buy the silence of an important Watergate witness."

Nixon "praised and rewarded those whom he knew had committed perjury," Hogan continued. "He personally helped to orchestrate a scenario of events, facts and testimony to cover up wrongdoing in the Watergate scandal and to throw investigators and prosecutors off the track. He actively participated in an extended and extensive conspiracy to obstruct justice. To my mind," Hogan concluded, "he is guilty beyond a reasonable doubt of having committed these impeachable offenses."

High Court orders tapes yielded. The Supreme Court ruled 8–0 July 24 that President Nixon must provide "forthwith" the tapes and documents relating to 64 White House conversations subpoenaed by special Watergate prosecutor Leon Jaworski for the pending Watergate cover-up trial of six former presidential aides.

The decision did not mention presidential impeachment or the current impeachment inquiry in the House, and it defined the limits on presidential privilege on the relatively narrow grounds of the evidentiary needs imposed by Watergate criminal cases.

In an opinion written by Chief Justice Warren E. Burger, a Nixon appointee, the court said that a generalized claim of executive privilege, while not explicitly provided by the Constitution, was "constitutionally based." But in the current case, Burger continued, such an assertion of privilege "must yield to the demonstrated, specific need for evidence in a pending criminal trial."

In a statement issued late the same day from San Clemente, Calif., Nixon said he had instructed special counsel James D. St. Clair, who had argued for the President before the court, to "take whatever measures are necessary" to comply with the decision "in all respects."

Addressing a secondary issue in a footnote to the opinion, the court left standing a grand jury citation of Nixon as an unindicted co-conspirator in the cover-up case. Calling this issue "unnecessary" to resolution of the privilege question, Burger said the court had "improvidently" granted a White House petition for review of District Court Judge John J. Sirica's refusal to expunge the citation.

The court also denied a White House request that the court examine the grand jury's evidence to determine if the citation was justified.

Before dealing with the primary issue of confidentiality of presidential conversations, Burger rejected White House contentions that the tape dispute was an internal issue within the executive branch and should not be considered by the court. A "mere assertion of a claim of 'intra-branch' dispute," Burger wrote, was insufficient. The court noted that regulations establishing the independence of Jaworski's office had the force of law and had not been revoked by the attorney general. Under such conditions, the court said, Jaworski had the standing to pursue specific requests for applicable evidence through the courts, if necessary.

Burger also ruled that Jaworski had made sufficient preliminary showing that the potential evidence in the tapes and documents was both relevant and necessary to a criminal proceeding. And, because of the co-conspirator citations of Nixon and others, their statements could be preliminarily deemed admissible at trial.

Turning to the White House argument that the separation of powers doctrine should preclude judicial review of a claim of presidential privilege, Burger wrote that while one branch's interpretation of its powers "is due great respect from the others," the court must currently reaffirm a principle enunciated by an earlier court (in Marbury vs. Madison, 1803): "it is emphatically the province and duty of the Judicial department to say what the law is."

Burger said the powers constitutionally vested in the courts "can no more be shared with the executive branch than the chief executive, for example, can share with the judiciary the veto power, or the Congress share with the judiciary the power to override a presidential veto. Any other conclusion would be contrary to the basic concept of separation of powers and the checks and balances that flow from the scheme of a tripartite government."

Burger conceded that a President's need for candor and objectivity from advisers deserved "great deference from the courts." But a claim of privilege based solely on the "broad, undifferentiated claim of public interest in the confidentiality of such conversations," Burger continued, causes a confrontation with "other values."

Without a claim of need to protect "military, diplomatic or sensitive national security secrets," the court said, the confidentiality of presidential communications would not be "diminished" by submission of the material to Judge Sirica for private inspection under strict security precautions.

On the other hand, the court said, the impediment imposed upon the administration of justice by such a claim of absolute privilege would "upset the constitutional balance" of government and "gravely impair the role of the courts."

Burger also discounted the possibility that presidential advisers would be "moved to temper the candor of their remarks" because such conversations might "be called for in the context of a criminal prosecution."

Affirming Sirica's order that the material be submitted to him for inspection and determination of relevance and admissibility, the court emphasized Sirica's "very heavy responsibility" to accord irrelevant and sensitive portions the confidentiality and "high degree of respect due the President." Under the procedures set by Sirica, particular claims of privilege by the White House would be considered before the material was sent to Jaworski.

Nixon pledges compliance—President Nixon's reaction to the Supreme Court order that he surrender subpoenaed tapes and documents was read to reporters later July 24 by special counsel James D. St. Clair near the "western white house" in San Clemente, Calif.:

"My challenge in the courts to the subpoena of the special prosecutor was based on the belief that it was unconstitutionally issued, and on my strong desire to protect the principle of presidential confidentiality in a system of separation of powers.

While I am, of course, disappointed in the result, I respect and accept the court's decision, and I have instructed Mr. St. Clair to take whatever measures are necessary to comply with that decision in all respects. For the future it will be essential that the special circumstances of this case not be permitted to cloud the right of Presidents to maintain the basic confidentiality without which this office cannot function. I was gratified, therefore, to note that the court reaffirmed both the validity and the importance of the principle of executive privilege, the principle I had sought to maintain. By complying fully with the court's ruling in this case, I hope and trust that I will contribute to strengthening rather than weakening this principle for the future, so that this will prove to be not the precedent that destroyed the principle but the action that preserved it."

St. Clair added that the President "has always been a firm believer in the rule of law, and he intends his decision to comply fully with the court's ruling as an action in furtherance of that belief."

Committee Votes to Impeach

3 articles of impeachment approved. The House Judiciary Committee approved three articles of impeachment charging President Nixon with obstruction of justice in connection with the Watergate scandal, abuse of presidential powers and attempting to impede the impeachment process by defying committee subpoenas for evidence. The committee rejected two other proposed articles, one charging that Nixon had usurped the powers of Congress by ordering the secret bombing of Cambodia in 1969, the other concerning income tax fraud and the unconstitutional use of government funds to make improvements on his properties in California and Florida.

The committee's final deliberations, which were nationally televised, began July 24 with a motion by Rep. Harold D. Donohue (Mass.), second ranking Democrat on the panel: "I move that the committee report to the House a resolution, together with articles, impeaching the President of the United States, Richard M. Nixon."

In so moving, Donohue asked the committee to adopt two broad articles of impeachment. The first accused the President of obstructing justice by engaging in a cover-up of the Watergate affair. The second charged Nixon with abuses of presidential power, including defiance of committee subpoenas.

Opening statements by committee chairman Peter W. Rodino Jr. (D, N.J.) and ranking Republican Edward Hutchinson (Mich.) preceded Donohue's motion. In his remarks, Hutchinson noted the Supreme Court's ruling earlier that day that Nixon must surrender tape recordings of 64 Watergate-related conversations to U.S. District Court Judge John J. Sirica for determination of relevancy to the Watergate cover-up trial. He suggested that the committee postpone consideration of the articles until it considered the contents of the tapes. Rodino rejected the suggestion and was sustained by 27–11 committee vote July 26.

Following Donohue's motion, Rodino opened 10 hours of general debate, after which the committee concerned itself with amending and voting on each proposed article.

Whether the impeachment articles would have bipartisan support had not been certain before the general debate. Pro-impeachment forces feared that White House charges of partisanship would be substantiated if no more than one or two Republicans supported impeachment. Proponents also felt that failure by the committee's Southern Democrats to back impeachment would have an adverse affect on other Southern Democrats when the full House considered the committee's recommendations.

Thus, the opening debate allowed some members of the committee to explain the "agony" they felt over impeaching a President. It provided an opportunity for others to explain to a constituency that had voted overwhelmingly for the President in 1972 why in their opinions it was necessary to impeach the President:

Rep. Walter Flowers (D, Ala.)—"The alternatives are clear: to vote to impeach ... or to vote against impeachment.... We do not have a choice that, to me, represents anything desirable. I wake up nights ... wondering if this could not be some sordid dream.... The people I represent ... really want to support the President. Surely we want to support the Constitution and the best interests of the country.... What if we fail to impeach? Do we ingrain forever in ... our Constitution a standard of conduct in our highest office that in the least is deplorable and at worst is impeachable? This is indeed a terrible choice we have to make."

Rep. M. Caldwell Butler (R, Va.)—"It ... has [been] argued that we should not impeach because of comparable conduct in previous administrations. There are frightening implications for the future of our country.... If we fail to impeach, we have condoned and left unpunished a course of conduct totally inconsistent with the reasonable expectations of the American people.... In short, a power appears to have corrupted. It is a sad chapter in American history, but I cannot condone what I have heard, I cannot excuse it and I cannot and will not stand for it."

Article I: obstruction of justice—The first article, a substitute for the Donohue proposal by Paul Sarbanes (D, Md.), was adopted July 27 by a 27–11 vote. Six Republicans joined the panel's 21 Democrats in voting for impeachment. The Sarbanes substitute specifically charged Nixon with failure "to take care that the laws be faithfully executed" by engaging "personally and through his subordinates and agents in a course of conduct or plan designed to delay, impede and obstruct" the investigation into the June 17, 1972 break-in at the headquarters of the Democratic National Committee at the Watergate complex in Washington. The article also accused Nixon of covering up for, concealing and protecting those responsible, as well as concealing "the existence and scope of other unlawful covert activities."

The Sarbanes substitute listed nine methods by which Nixon was alleged to have carried out the obstruction. The methods included allegations that Nixon had made "false and misleading statements" to investigators, had withheld evidence of criminal wrongdoing, had counseled associates to commit perjury, had interfered in lawful investigations of Watergate, had condoned payment of hush money, had "endeavored to misuse the Central Intelligency Agency," had passed on to prospective defendants secret grand jury information, had made "false and misleading" statements that a complete investigation had cleared White House and campaign personnel of involvement in Watergate, and had caused prospective defendants to expect "favored treatment" in return for their "silence or false testimony."

The final vote on the Sarbanes substitute came after two days of debate, during which the anti-impeachment bloc of Republicans attacked the article for its lack of specificity. The President, they asserted, was entitled, like any other defendant, to know the exact details of any offense he had allegedly committed. They said the general nature of the Sarbanes substitute showed that its proponents lacked specific evidence directly tying Nixon to any wrongdoing and were relying on "inferences upon inferences."

Pro-impeachment committee members responded that general charges were preferable because they allowed later introduction of evidence currently not on hand and were easier to prove. As for lack of evidence tying Nixon to the cover-up, the proponents insisted that the evidence, while circumstantial in nature, was overwhelming. The article's backers also contended that the President's attorney, James D. St. Clair, had been present at the time of presentation of evidence to the committee and fully knew the allegations against which he would have to defend the President.

The first formal vote on the Sarbanes amendment was taken July 26 on a motion by Rep. Charles W. Sandman Jr. (R, N.J.), who sought to delete the first of the nine elements listed in the obstruction charge. The amendment was defeated 27–11.

In answer to Republican charges that the Sarbanes substitute was not specific enough, John M. Doar, special counsel to committee, also drew up and presented to the committee July 27 a list of 50 incidents to defend the charge that President Nixon made a decision to participate in the Watergate cover-up. "This decision by the President," the preamble to the list said, "is the only one that could explain a pattern of undisputed incidents that otherwise cannot be explained."

Article II: abuse of power—The second article, a substitute set of charges offered by Rep. William L. Hungate (D, Mo.), was approved July 29 by a 28-10 vote. Rep. Robert McClory (Ill.), second ranking Republican on the committee who opposed Article I, joined six Republican colleagues and 21 Democrats in recommending Nixon's impeachment for abuse of power.

This omnibus charge against Nixon, which McClory called the "crux" of the matter, specifically focused on the following allegations:

Personally and through his subordinates and agents, Nixon attempted to use the Internal Revenue Service to initiate tax audits or obtain confidential tax data for political purposes. He initiated a series of secret wiretaps under the guise of "national security" and misused the results of the taps. He authorized and permitted to be maintained in the White House a secret, privately financed investigative unit which engaged in "covert and unlawful activities," including the 1971 burglary of the office of the psychiatrist of Pentagon Papers trial defendant Daniel Ellsberg. He failed to act on the knowledge that "close subordinates" endeavored to impede the Watergate investigation and related matters. He "knowingly misused the executive power by interfering" with the lawful activities of the Federal Bureau of Investigation, the Central Intelligence Agency, the Justice Department, and the Watergate special prosecutor's office.

Rep. Charles E. Wiggins (R), whose district in California approximated the one from which Nixon was first elected to Congress in 1946, charged that the Hungate article represented a "step toward a parliamentary system of government" by trying to make Nixon accountable, after the fact, for subjective "notions of morality and propriety."

Another charge by Wiggins that the article was out of order was answered by Rep. George E. Danielson (D, Calif.), who said, "The offenses charged against the President ... are uniquely presidential offenses. No one else can commit them. ... You or I ... can violate any of the statutes in our criminal code, but only the President can violate the oath of office of the President. Only the President can abuse the powers of the office of the President."

Defenders of the President challenged elements of the Hungate substitute dealing with the wiretaps and the use of a special investigations unit against Ellsberg. They said the President would have been derelict in his duty had he not acted against leaks of classified information.

However, proponents of the articles countered that while Nixon's intentions might have been well meant at the outset, his wiretaps were in contravention of existing wiretap laws and degenerated into political surveillance in the 1972 presidential campaign. Regarding the special investigation unit, the "plumbers," Rep. Joshua Eilberg (D, Pa.) remarked, "The Nixon White House made secret police a reality in America."

Article III: defiance of subpoenas—The third article in the bill of impeachment, approved July 30, charged that the President had sought to impede the impeachment process by refusing to comply with eight committee subpoenas for 147 recorded White House conversations and other evidence. Although the article was introduced by McClory, it failed to gain broad bipartisan backing and passed by the narrow margin of 21-17.

Opponents of Article III warned their colleagues that it was "political overkill" and predicted a bitter debate on the House floor. Other opponents, noting the Supreme Court's ruling against Nixon with regard to the tapes demanded by the Watergate special prosecutor, contended that the committee should have gone to the court for a definitive ruling, or, failing that, declared Nixon in contempt of Congress.

In contrast, backers of Article III insisted that failure to hold Nixon responsible for his defiance would, as Rep. Don Edwards (D, Calif.) put it, "destroy the only safety valve in the Constitution to protect ourselves against a President who so misbehaves that he poses a threat to the country." In defense of his own article, McClory added that the committee could not conduct a "thorough and complete and fair investigation" if the President were the "sole arbiter" on questions of relevant evidence.

Rep. Ray Thornton (D, Ark.) offered an amendment, adopted 24-14, designed to make clear that Presidential defiance of a Congressional subpoena was an impeachable offense only in an impeachment inquiry and not in response to a committee drafting legislation.

Article IV: Cambodia issue rejected— The fourth article, proposed by Rep. John J. Conyers Jr. (D, Mich.), charged that Nixon had usurped Congress' power to declare war by approving and then concealing from Congress the secret bombing of Cambodia in 1969. After limited debate July 30, the committee rejected the article 26-12. Nine Democrats joined the committee's 17 Republicans in opposing it.

Opponents of this article asserted that Congress should bear much of the blame. While Nixon's decision to bomb constituted a usurpation of Congress' power, Rep. William S. Cohen (R, Me.) said, this seizure of prerogative came about "not through the bold power of the President but rather through the sloth and default on the part of Congress." Rep. Flowers said that if Nixon were impeached for Cambodia, then President Johnson should be impeached posthumously for Laos and Vietnam, President Kennedy for "Santo Domingo and the Bay of Pigs," President Eisenhower for the U-2 incident, and President Truman for the Korean conflict.

Article V: personal finances issue rejected—The last article to be considered by the impeachment panel concerned the President's personal finances. This article, sponsored by Rep. Edward Mezvinsky (D, Iowa), failed by a vote of 26-12 July 30. Nine Democrats and 17 Republicans voted to oppose.

According to Mezvinsky's charge, the President abused his office by "knowingly" underpaying his federal income taxes and by accepting government-paid-for improvements to his personal property in San Clemente, Calif. and Key Biscayne, Fla.

By and large, committee debate on this motion did not center on the substance of the charges but on their appropriateness as an article of impeachment. Reps. Jerome Waldie (D, Calif.), Wayne Owens (D, Utah) and Cohen agreed that Nixon's activities in these areas bordered on criminality, but each felt that an impeachable offense should be of greater magnitude. "Impeachment . . . is . . . designed to redefine Presidential powers in cases . . . [of] enormous abuse . . . and to limit the power as a concluding result of the impeachment process. . . . I do not find a Presidential power [in this instance] that has been so grossly abused that it deserves redefinition and limiting."

Proponents of the fraud charge insisted that the President, like every other U.S. taxpayer, had to be held accountable under the tax laws. Moreover, Rep. Jack Brooks (D, Tex.) said, with reference to the matter of direct evidence of Nixon's guilt of criminal violations, the committee possessed "specific proof of the execution of fraudulent deeds, the filing of false returns, the failure to report income, [and] the enrichment of one's personal estate at public expense." No President was any less accountable for his personal misdeeds than he was for his public misdeeds, Brooks said.

Committee members call inquiry fair— A bipartisan group of members of the Judiciary Committee said on the ABC television program, "Issues and Answers," July 21 that the impeachment inquiry against the President had been conducted fairly.

Rep. Charles E. Wiggins (R, Calif.), who emerged in subsequent committee debate as one of the President's chief defenders, said that "by and large it has been fair." "I have no great quarrel" with the investigation, he remarked, adding that it had been essentially nonpartisan "up until the last few days."

Others, who appeared on the program and basically agreed with Wiggins' characterization, were Reps. Don Edwards (D, Calif.), Walter Flowers (D, Ala.) and Robert McClory (R, Ill.).

Ford backs Nixon—Vice President Gerald R. Ford criticized Democrats on the House Judiciary Committee July 27 for failing to give specific details in the first article of impeachment. Ford said if the full House considered impeachment "on the facts," Nixon would be found innocent. Ford said he was convinced that Nixon was innocent of any impeachable offense.

Referring to the committee's vote on the obstruction of justice article, Ford said the fact that all 21 Democrats approved the article "tends to make it a partisan issue." Asked about the six Republicans who voted for the article, Ford said he was "disappointed."

Campaigning for Rep. David W. Dennis (R, Ind.), one of Nixon's strongest supporters on the Judiciary Committee, Ford had said in Muncie July 25 that Nixon was the victim of "Democratic partisan politics." If Nixon were impeached, Ford said, "the impact on the country would be very, very bad."

Ford said in a speech at a fund-raising dinner: "I can say from the bottom of my heart, the President of the United States is innocent and he is right."

Nixon Resigns, Ford Becomes President

Ford Succeeds Nixon

The Watergate scandal finally put an end to the Nixon Administration Aug. 9, 1974, and Gerald R. Ford became the first U.S. President who had been elected neither President nor Vice President. Richard M. Nixon, who resigned as the House of Representatives appeared to be preparing to impeach him, was the first U.S. President to give up the office.

Smooth transition of power. Richard Milhous Nixon, 61, resigned as president of the United States Aug. 9 after a week of dramatic developments. Vice President Gerald Rudolph Ford, 61, was sworn in as his successor. It was the first time in the history of the nation that its president had resigned.

The resignation, a dramatic conclusion to the effects of the Watergate scandal on the Nixon presidency, was announced Aug. 8, three days after Nixon released a statement and transcript of tape recordings admitting "a serious act of omission" in his previous accounts of the Watergate cover-up.

According to Nixon's statement, six days after the break-in at the Democratic Party's national headquarters in the Watergate building in Washington, D.C. June 17, 1972, he had ordered the Federal Bureau of Investigation's probe of the break-in halted. Furthermore, Nixon stated, he had kept this part of the record secret from investigating bodies, his own counsel and the public.

The admission destroyed what remained of Nixon's support in Congress against a tide of impeachment that was already swelling. The President's support had been eroding dangerously since the House Judiciary Committee had debated and drawn, with substantial bipartisan backing, three articles of impeachment to be considered on the House floor. Within 48 hours of his statement of complicity, which he said did not in his opinion justify "the extreme step of impeachment," the 10 committee members who had voted against impeachment reversed themselves, on the basis of the new evidence, and announced that they would vote to impeach Nixon. This, in effect, made the committee vote for impeachment unanimous.

The development was accompanied by serious defections in the Republican Congressional leadership and acknowledgment from all sides that the vote for impeachment in the House was a foregone conclusion and conviction by the Senate certain.

This assessment was delivered to the President by the senior Republican leaders of the Congress. Shortly afterwards, Nixon made his final decision to resign. He announced his decision the evening of Aug. 8, to a television audience estimated at 110–130 million persons. In his 16-minute address, Nixon conceded he had made "some" wrong judgments. He said he was resigning because he no longer had "a strong enough political base in Congress" to carry out his duties of office. He also reviewed what he hoped would be his legacy of accomplishment in office.

In a discussion with reporters after the Nixon resignation announcement Aug. 8, Ford said, "This is one of the most difficult and very saddest periods, and one of the very saddest incidents I've ever witnessed." In addition to affirming continuity of foreign policy, he said he expected to "start out working with Democrats and with Republicans in the House as well as in the Senate to work on the problems—serious ones—which we have at home." He said he had "a good many adversaries in the political arena in the Congress, but I don't think I have a single enemy in the Congress."

He praised Nixon for having made "one of the greatest personal sacrifices for the country and one of the finest personal decisions on behalf of all of us as Americans by his decision to resign."

Nixon bade farewell to his staff Aug. 9 and departed the White House, with Vice President Ford waving farewell. At 11:35 a.m., the resignation—a single sentence, "Dear Mr. Secretary: I hereby resign the office of President of the United States. Sincerely, Richard Nixon"—was handed to Secretary of State Henry A. Kissinger, and the duties of that office devolved upon Vice President Ford.

Ford was administered the oath of office by Chief Justice Warren E. Burger, who had hastily returned to Washington from a vacation in Europe, at 12:03 p.m. in the East Room of the White House. In brief remarks, Ford stressed his awareness that he had not been elected to the office and pledged "openness and candor" in his administration. He told the nation "our long national nightmare" of Watergate was over and the nation remained "a government of laws and not of men." He urged prayer for himself, "to confirm" him in his new role, and, his voice breaking, for his predecessor so that the man "who brought peace to millions" would "find it for himself."

At the time, Ford's predecessor was aloft near Jefferson City, Mo. aboard the presidential aircraft, Spirit of '76, en route to his home at San Clemente, Calif.

The changeover took place in the second term of the Nixon presidency, after 5½ years (2,026 days) in office for the 37th president. Ford assumed the post as the 38th president to serve the remaining 2½ years of the second Nixon term. He would be eligible for only one full term in office.

Ford moved immediately to assure stability of government. He retained Kissinger as secretary of state, affirmed the Nixon Administration's foreign policy, met with foreign envoys, Congressional leaders, the Cabinet, economic advisers and the National Security Council. He solicited recommendations for a vice presidential choice. Ford appointed a four-man team to ease the transition, and he named a press secretary, pledging an "open" and "candid" Administration.

A resolution expressing support for Ford as a "good and faithful friend" was adopted unanimously by both houses of Congress Aug. 9. It stated Congress's "sincere best wishes, its assurances of firm cooperation and its fervent hopes for success in office."

Nixon's resignation speech—President Nixon's 16-minute speech of resignation was delivered from the White House Oval Office at 9 p.m. EDT and was seen by a national television audience estimated at 110-130 million people.

"Throughout the long and difficult period of Watergate, I have felt it was my duty to persevere; to make every possible effort to complete the term of office to which you elected me," Nixon said.

But, the President continued, it had become "evident" in the last few days that he no longer had a "strong enough political base in the Congress to justify continuing that effort." As long as that base existed, he felt it necessary, Nixon said, to see the "constitutional process" through to its conclusion, for to do otherwise would be "unfaithful to the spirit of that difficult process, and a dangerous destabilizing precedent for the future."

"But with the disappearance of that base, I now believe that the constitutional purpose has been served, and there is no longer a need for the process to be prolonged," he said. Nixon conceded he lacked the support of Congress required for him to carry out the duties of his office.

The President said he had never been a "quitter." Nonetheless, he was resigning to spare the country a fight for his personal vindication that would absorb the attention of Congress and the President in the months ahead, when both branches needed to place their "entire focus" on the problems of world peace and domestic inflation.

Nixon said he was leaving his office in the "good hands" of Vice President Ford, who could begin the "essential" task of healing the "wounds of the nation."

Nixon said he "deeply regretted" any injuries that came in the course of the events that led to his decision to resign. "I would only say that if some of my judgments were wrong—and some were wrong—they were made in what I believed at the time to be the best interests of the nation." He thanked those who had supported him and said he held "no bitterness" toward those who had not.

Nixon then cited his efforts to achieve peace throughout the world. This, he said, "more than anything, is what I hope will be my legacy to you, to our country, as I leave the presidency."

Text of Nixon's Aug. 8 address to the nation:

Good evening.

This is the 37th time I have spoken to you from this office in which so many decisions have been made that shape the history of this nation.

Each time I have done so to discuss with you some matters that I believe affected the national interest. And all the decisions I have made in my public life I have always tried to do what was best for the nation.

Throughout the long and difficult period of Watergate, I have felt it was my duty to persevere; to make every possible effort to complete the term of office to which you elected me.

In the past few days, however, it has become evident to me that I no longer have a strong enough political base in the Congress to justify continuing that effort.

As long as there was such a base, I felt strongly that it was necessary to see the constitutional process through to its conclusion; that to do otherwise would be unfaithful to the spirit of that deliberately difficult process, and a dangerously destabilizing precedent for the future. But with the disappearance of that base, I now believe that the constitutional purpose has been served. And there is no longer a need for the process to be prolonged.

I would have preferred to carry through to the finish whatever the personal agony it would have involved, and my family unanimously urged me to do so.

But the interests of the nation must always come before any personal considerations. From the dis-

cussions I have had with Congressional and other leaders I have concluded that because of the Watergate matter I might not have the support of the Congress that I would consider necessary to back the very difficult decisions and carry out the duties of this office in the way the interests of the nation will require.

I have never been a quitter. To leave office before my term is completed is opposed to every instinct in my body. But as president I must put the interests of America first.

America needs a full-time president and a full-time Congress, particularly at this time with problems we face at home and abroad.

To continue to fight through the months ahead for my personal vindication would almost totally absorb the time and attention of both the president and the Congress in a period when our entire focus should be on the great issues of peace abroad and prosperity without inflation at home.

Therefore, I shall resign the presidency effective at noon tomorrow. Vice President Ford will be sworn in as president at that hour in this office.

As I recall the high hopes for America with which we began this second term, I feel a great sadness that I will not be here in this office working on your behalf to achieve those hopes in the next two and a half years.

But in turning over direction of the government to Vice President Ford I know, as I told the nation when I nominated him for that office 10 months ago, that the leadership of America will be in good hands.

In passing this office to the vice president I also do so with the profound sense of the weight of responsibility that will fall on his shoulders tomorrow, and therefore of the understanding, the patience, the cooperation he will need from all Americans. As he assumes that responsibility he will deserve the help and the support of all of us. As we look to the future, the first essential is to begin healing the wounds of this nation. To put the bitterness and divisions of the recent past behind us and to rediscover those shared ideals that lie at the heart of our strength and unity as a great and as a free people.

By taking this action, I hope that I will have hastened the start of that process of healing which is so desperately needed in America.

I regret deeply any injuries that may have been done in the course of the events that led to this decision. I would say only that if some of my judgments were wrong—and some were wrong—they were made in what I believed at the time to be the best interests of the nation.

To those who have stood with me during these past difficult months, to my family, my friends, the many others who've joined in supporting my cause because they believed it was right, I will be eternally grateful for your support.

And to those who have not felt able to give me your support, let me say I leave with no bitterness toward those who have opposed me, because all of us in the final analysis have been concerned with the good of the country however our judgments might differ.

So let us all now join together in affirming that common commitment and in helping our new president succeed for the benefit of all Americans.

I shall leave this office with regret at not completing my term but with gratitude for the privilege of serving as your president for the past five and a half years. These years have been a momentous time in the history of our nation and the world. There has been a time of achievement in which we can all be proud—achievements that represent the shared efforts of the Administration, the Congress and the people. But the challenges ahead are equally great.

And they, too, will require the support and the efforts of a Congress and the people, working in cooperation with the new Administration.

We have ended America's longest war. But in the work of securing a lasting peace in the world, the goals ahead are even more far-reaching and more difficult. We must complete a structure of peace, so that it will be said of this generation—our generation of Americans—by the people of all nations, not only that we ended one war but that we prevented future wars.

We have unlocked the doors that for a quarter of a century stood between the United States and the People's Republic of China. We must now insure that the one-quarter of the world's people who live in the People's Republic of China will be and remain, not our enemies, but our friends.

In the Middle East, 100 million people in the Arab countries, many of whom have considered us their enemies for nearly 20 years, now look on us as their friends. We must continue to build on that friendship so that peace can settle at last over the Middle East and so that the cradle of civilization will not become its grave.

Together with the Soviet Union we have made the crucial breakthroughs that have begun the process of limiting nuclear arms. But, we must set as our goal, not just limiting, but reducing and finally destroying these terrible weapons so that they cannot destroy civilization. And so that the threat of nuclear war will no longer hang over the world and the people, we have opened a new relation with the Soviet Union. We must continue to develop and expand that new relationship so that the two strongest nations of the world will live together in cooperation rather than confrontation.

Around the world—in Asia, in Africa, in Latin America, in the Middle East—there are millions of people who live in terrible poverty, even starvation. We must keep as our goal turning away from production for war and expanding production for peace so that people everywhere on this earth can at last look forward, in their children's time if not in our time, to having the necessities for a decent life.

Here in America we are fortunate that most of our people have not only the blessings of liberty but also the means to live full and good, and by the world's standards even abundant, lives. We must press on, however, toward a goal not only of more and better jobs but of full opportunity for every man, and of what we are striving so hard right now to achieve—prosperity without inflation.

For more than a quarter of a century in public life, I have shared in the turbulent history of this evening. I have fought for what I believe in. I have tried, to the best of my ability, to discharge those duties and meet those responsibilities that were entrusted to me.

Sometimes I have succeeded. And sometimes I have failed. But always I have taken heart from what Theodore Roosevelt said about the man in the arena whose face is marred by dust and sweat and blood, who strives valiantly, who errs and comes short again and again because there is no effort without error and shortcoming, but who does actually strive to do the deed, who knows the great enthusiasm, the great devotion, who spends himself in a worthy cause, who at the best knows in the end of triumphs of high achievements and with the worst if he fails, at least fails while daring greatly.

I pledge to you tonight that as long as I have a breath of life in my body I shall continue in that spirit. I shall continue to work for the great causes to which I have been dedicated throughout my years as a congressman, a senator, vice president and president,

the cause of peace—not just for America but among all nations—prosperity, justice and opportunity for all of our people.

There is one cause above all to which I have been devoted and to which I shall always be devoted for as long as I live. When I first took the oath of office as president five and a half years ago, I made this sacred commitment: to consecrate my office, my energies and all the wisdom I can summon to the cause of peace among nations. I've done my very best in all the days since to be true to that pledge.

As a result of these efforts, I am confident that the world is a safer place today, not only for the people of America but for the people of all nations, and that all of our children have a better chance than before of living in peace rather than dying in war.

This, more than anything, is what I hoped to achieve when I sought the presidency. This, more than anything, is what I hope will be my legacy to you, to our country, as I leave the presidency.

To have served in this office is to have felt a very personal sense of kinship with each and every American. In leaving it, I do so with this prayer: May God's grace be with you in all the days ahead.

Ford asks for nation's 'prayers.' After his swearing-in, Ford made a brief address to those gathered in the East Room of the White House and to a national television audience. "I am acutely aware," the new President said, "that you have not elected me as your president by your ballots. So I ask you to confirm me as your president with your prayers. And I hope that such prayers will also be the first of many."

He added: "If you have not chosen me by secret ballot, neither have I gained office by any secret promises. I have not campaigned either for the presidency or the vice presidency. I have not subscribed to any partisan platform, I am indebted to no man and only to one woman—my dear wife—as I begin the most difficult job in the world."

Ford promised not to shirk the responsibilities he had not sought and pledged to be President of all the people. "We must go forward, now, together," he said.

Noting that "truth is the glue" holding together "not only our government, but civilization itself," Ford vowed "openness and candor" in all his public and private acts as President.

The "long national nightmare" of Watergate was over, Ford said, and he asked that its "wounds" be bound up. "Before closing," Ford said, "I again ask your prayers for Richard Nixon and his family.

May our former President, who brought peace to millions, find it for himself."

Text of Ford's Aug. 9 address:

Mr. chief justice, my dear friends, my fellow Americans. The oath that I have taken is the same oath that was taken by George Washington and by every president under the Constitution.

But I assume the presidency under extraordinary circumstances never before experienced by Americans. This is an hour of history that troubles our minds and hurts our hearts.

Therefore, I feel it is my first duty to make an unprecedented compact with my countrymen. Not an inaugural address, not a fireside chat, not a campaign speech, just a little straight talk among friends. And I intend it to be the first of many.

I am acutely aware that you have not elected me as your president by your ballots. So I ask you to confirm me as your president with your prayers. And I hope that such prayers will also be the first of many.

If you have not chosen me by secret ballot, neither have I gained office by any secret promises. I have not campaigned either for the presidency or the vice presidency. I have not subscribed to any partisan platform. I am indebted to no man and only to one woman, my dear wife.

As I begin this very difficult job, I have not sought this enormous responsibility, but I will not shirk it. Those who nominated and confirmed me as vice president were my friends and are my friends. They were of both parties, elected by all the people and acting under the Constitution in their name. It is only fitting then that I should pledge to them and to you that I will be the president of all the people.

Thomas Jefferson said the people are the only sure reliance for the preservation of our liberty. And down the years, Abraham Lincoln renewed this American article of faith asking is there any better way for equal hopes in the world.

I intend on Monday next to request of the speaker of the House of Representatives and the president pro tempore of the Senate the privilege of appearing before the Congress to share with my former colleagues and with you, the American people, my views on the priority business of the nation and to solicit your views and their views. And may I say to the speaker and the others, if I could meet with you right after this—these remarks I would appreciate it.

Even though this is late in an election year, there is no way we can go forward except together and no way anybody can win except by serving the people's urgent needs. We cannot stand still or slip backward. We must go forward now together.

To the peoples and the governments of all friendly nations, I hope that could encompass the whole world, I pledge an uninterrupted and sincere search for peace. America will remain strong and united. But its strength will remain dedicated to the safety and sanity of the entire family of man as well as to our own precious freedom.

I believe that truth is the glue that holds governments together, not only our government but civilization itself. That bond, though strained, is unbroken at home and abroad.

In all my public and private acts as your president, I expect to follow my instincts of openness and candor with full confidence that honesty is always the best policy in the end.

My fellow Americans, our long national nightmare is over. Our Constitution works. Our great republic is a government of laws and not of men. Here, the people rule.

But there is a higher power, by whatever name we honor him, who ordains not only righteousness but love, not only justice but mercy. As we bind up the internal wounds of Watergate, more painful and more poisonous than those of foreign wars, let us restore the Golden Rule to our political process. And let brotherly love purge our hearts of suspicion and of hate.

In the beginning, I asked you to pray for me. Before closing, I ask again your prayers for Richard Nixon and for his family. May our former president, who brought peace to millions find it for himself. May God bless and comfort his wonderful wife and daughters whose love and loyalty will forever be a shining legacy to all who bear the lonely burdens of the White House.

I can only guess at those burdens although I witnessed at close hand the tragedies that befell three presidents and the lesser trials of others.

With all the strength and all the good sense I have gained from life, with all the confidence of my family, my friends and dedicated staff impart to me and with the goodwill of countless Americans I have encountered in recent visits to 40 states, I now solemnly reaffirm my promise I made to you last Dec. 6 to uphold the Constitution, to do what is right as God gives me to see the right and to do the very best I can for America. God helping me, I will not let you down. Thank you.

Ford picks up reins. Before the Nixon resignation, but after the announcement of it, Ford assured reporters at his home near Alexandria, Va. Aug. 8 that he would retain Henry Kissinger as secretary of state and continue the foreign policy of the Nixon Administration. On Aug. 9, Ford and Kissinger met at the White House with nearly 60 ambassadors or chiefs of mission, in groups and individually, to assure continued friendly relations. A personal message from Ford was sent to Soviet Communist Party leader Leonid I. Brezhnev. The diplomatic sessions were continued at the State Department Aug. 10.

After his swearing-in Aug. 9, Ford met with a bipartisan group of Congressional leaders and the Nixon Administration's top economic advisers.

Ford also met Aug. 9 with the senior members of the Nixon White House staff, still intact except for Press Secretary Ronald L. Ziegler, who resigned and accompanied Nixon to California. Ford asked the staff to remain through the transition and appealed for their "help and cooperation." Gen. Alexander M. Haig Jr., chief of staff, pledged the same loyalty to Ford "in our hour of common cause."

Ford Aug. 9 named a four-member committee of his own to oversee the transition: former Gov. William W. Scranton

(R, Pa.); Donald M. Rumsfeld, ambassador to the North Atlantic Treaty Organization; Interior Secretary Rogers C. B. Morton; and former Rep. John O. Marsh (D, Va.), a member of Ford's vice presidential staff.

In his first full day as President Aug. 10, Ford met with the Nixon Cabinet and asked its members, as well as all federal agency chiefs, to remain in their posts in the name of "continuity and stability." He also met with the National Security Council and announced he was seeking suggestions from Republicans and Democrats for the choice of a vice president.

Nixon's Admissions Made Resignation Inevitable

Blocking of investigation admitted. The presidential statement and tape transcripts that triggered the intense pressure leading to Nixon's resignation August 9 had been released August 5. They effectively constituted a confession to obstruction of justice—the charge contained in the first article of impeachment voted by the House Judiciary Committee.

The transcripts he released covered three meetings with H. R. Haldeman, then White House chief of staff, on June 23, 1972, six days after the Watergate break-in. Informed that the Federal Bureau of Investigation's (FBI) probe of the break-in was pointing to officials in his reelection campaign, Nixon instructed Haldeman to tell the FBI, "Don't go any further into this case period!"

While Nixon's earlier statements on the Watergate case attributed his concern over the FBI's investigations to national security problems and possible conflicts with the Central Intelligence Agency (CIA), the latest transcripts—and Nixon's own statement about them—finally indicated that political considerations had played a major role.

According to the transcripts, Nixon told Haldeman to base the curtailment of FBI activities on possible reopening of questions about the CIA's role in the abortive 1961 "Bay of Pigs" invastion of Cuba (some of the Watergate

burglary conspirators had been involved in the CIA operation). Haldeman assured Nixon that the CIA ploy would give L. Patrick Gray, then acting FBI director, sufficient justification to drop the investigation of the "laundering" (through a Mexican lawyer and bank) of the campaign funds used to finance the Watergate operation.

Nixon then told Haldeman that Gray should be instructed—through CIA Director Richard Helms and Deputy Director Vernon A. Walters—to curtail the investigation.

In the written statement announcing release of the transcripts, Nixon referred to other transcripts released earlier (April 29–30), which he said then would "tell it all" concerning his role in Watergate and the cover-up.

But in early May, he continued, he had begun a "preliminary review" of some of the 64 conversations subpoenaed by Watergate special prosecutor Leon Jaworski, including two from June 23, 1972. Nixon said he recognized that the tapes "presented potential problems," but he "did not inform my staff or my counsel of it, or those arguing my case, nor did I amend my submission to the Judiciary Committee. . . ." As a result, those arguing and judging his case were proceeding with "information that was incomplete and in some respects erroneous. This was a serious act of omission for which I take full responsibility and which I deeply regret."

Nixon stated that since the July 24 Supreme Court order that the tapes be surrendered for the Watergate prosecution, he and his counsel had reviewed many of the tapes, and this "made it clear that portions of the tapes of these June 23 conversations are at variance with certain of my previous statements."

These included, Nixon said, the statement of May 22, 1973, in which he recalled that he had been concerned that the FBI's investigation of Watergate might expose "unrelated covert activities" of the CIA or "sensitive national security matters" involving the special White House unit known as the "plumbers." He therefore ordered that the FBI "coordinate" its investigation with the CIA. The May 22 statement, he said, was based on his "recollection at the time"—some 11 months after the break in—"plus documentary materials and relevant public testimony of those involved."

In his latest statement, however, Nixon acknowledged that the June 23 tapes showed he had discussed the "political aspects of the situation" at the time he gave the instructions, and that he was "aware of the advantages this course of action would have with respect to limiting possible public exposure of involvement by persons connected with the re-election committee."

Nixon said his review of additional tapes had not revealed other "major inconsistencies with what I have previously submitted," and that he had no reason to believe that there would be others.

Acknowledging that a House vote of impeachment was "virtually a foregone conclusion," Nixon addressed two points of caution to the potential Senate trial: first, as to "what actually happened" as a result of his instructions concerning the FBI, Nixon said Walters had informed Gray that the CIA would not be "compromised" by the FBI's probe. When Gray had expressed concern about "improper attempts to limit his investigation, as the record shows, I told him to press ahead vigorously with his investigation—which he did."

Nixon also urged that "the evidence be looked at in its entirety, and the events be looked at in perspective." Whatever his mistakes in handling Watergate, Nixon continued, "the basic truth remains that when all the facts were brought to my attention I insisted on a full investigation and prosecution of those guilty." Nixon concluded that the full record "does not justify the extreme step of impeachment and removal of a President."

The courts, the tapes and St. Clair—

Nixon's Aug. 5 statement said the three key transcripts had been made public partly as a result of the process of compliance with the July 24 Supreme Court decision. This reflected the central role played by that order in the events leading to his resignation.

In setting procedures for compliance with the order, U.S. District Court Judge John J. Sirica, who was to screen the tapes before transmitting them to the Watergate prosecution, had suggested that special presidential counsel James D. St.

Clair personally review the tapes, along with Nixon. (St. Clair had told the Supreme Court that he had not listened to any of the tapes.)

According to news reports Aug. 5-6, St. Clair had first become aware of the incriminating material involving Nixon and the cover-up during this review and—threatening resignation—had insisted that the transcripts be made public and that Nixon let it be known that he had withheld evidence from his counsel.

White House Deputy Press Secretary Gerald L. Warren denied Aug. 6 that Nixon's decision to release the transcripts had been based on "any sort of ultimatum or anything like that" from St. Clair.

According to news reports Aug. 7-10, key roles in the prelude to resignation were played by White House chief of staff Alexander M. Haig Jr. and Rep. Charles E. Wiggins (R, Calif.), a spokesman for the Nixon defense in the House.

After learning the content of the tapes, Haig—along with St. Clair—reportedly sensed the inevitability of Nixon's fall. To get a reading on Congressional reaction to the evidence, Haig and St. Clair summoned Wiggins to the White House Aug. 2. Wiggins said later that he was stunned by the transcripts and the direct evidence that Nixon had ordered the cover-up. Wiggins told the Nixon aides that impeachment and conviction would no longer be in question and that Nixon should consider resigning. Haig and St. Clair reportedly agreed, setting the stage for convincing Nixon that further struggle against leaving office would be futile.

August 5 statement—Text of Nixon's August 5 statement:

I have today instructed my attorneys to make available to the House Judiciary Committee, and I am making public, the transcripts of three conversations with H. R. Haldeman on June 23, 1972. I have also turned over the tapes of these conversations to Judge Sirica, as part of the process of my compliance with the Supreme Court ruling.

On April 29, in announcing my decision to make public the original set of White House transcripts, I stated, "as far as what the President personally knew and did with regard to Watergate and the cover-up is concerned, these materials—together with those already made available—will tell it all."

Shortly after that, in May, I made a preliminary review of some of the 64 taped conversations subpoenaed by the special prosecutor.

Among the conversations I listened to at that time were two of those of June 23. Although I recognized that these presented potential problems, I did not inform my staff or my counsel of it, or those arguing my case, nor did I amend my submission to the Judiciary Committee in order to include and reflect it. At the time, I did not realize the extent of the implications which these conversations might now appear to have. As a result, those arguing my case, as well as those passing judgment on the case, did so with information that was incomplete and in some respects erroneous. This was a serious act of omission for which I take full responsibility and which I deeply regret.

Since the Supreme Court's decision 12 days ago, I have ordered my counsel to analyze the 64 tapes, and I have listened to a number of them myself. This process has made it clear that portions of the tapes of these June 23 conversations are at variance with certain of my previous statements. Therefore, I have ordered the transcripts made available immediately to the Judiciary Committee so that they can be reflected in the committee's report, and included in the record to be considered by the House and Senate.

In a formal written statement on May 22 of last year, I said that shortly after the Watergate break-in I became concerned about the possibility that the FBI investigation might lead to the exposure either of unrelated covert activities of the CIA or of sensitive national security matters that the so-called "plumbers" unit at the White House had been working on because of the CIA and plumbers connections of some of those involved. I said that I therefore gave instructions that the FBI should be alerted to coordinate with the CIA and to ensure that the investigation not expose these sensitive national security matters.

That statement was based on my recollection at the time—some 11 months later—plus documentary materials and relevant public testimony of those involved.

The June 23 tapes clearly show, however, that at the time I gave those instructions I also discussed the political aspects of the situation, and that I was aware of the advantages this course of action would have with respect to limiting possible public exposure of involvement by persons connected with the re-election committee.

My review of the additional tapes has, so far, shown no other major inconsistencies with what I have previously submitted. While I have no way at this stage of being certain that there will not be others, I have no reason to believe that there will be. In any case, the tapes in their entirety are now in the process of being furnished to Judge Sirica. He has begun what may be a rather lengthy process of reviewing the tapes, passing on specific claims of executive privilege on portions of them, and forwarding to the special prosecutor those tapes or those portions that are relevant to the Watergate investigation.

It is highly unlikely that this review will be completed in time for the House debate. It appears at this stage, however, that a House vote of impeachment is, as a practical matter, virtually a foregone conclusion, and that the issue will therefore go to trial in the Senate. In order to ensure that no other significant relevant materials are withheld, I shall voluntarily furnish to the Senate everything from these tapes that Judge Sirica rules should go to the special prosecutor.

I recognize that this additional material I am now furnishing may further damage my case, especially because attention will be drawn separately to it rather than to the evidence in its entirety. In considering its implications, therefore, I urge that two points be borne in mind.

The first of these points is to remember what actually happened as a result of the instructions I gave on June 23. Acting Director Gray of the FBI did coordinate with Director Helms and Deputy Director Walters of the CIA. The CIA did undertake an extensive check to see whether any of its covert activities could be compromised by a full FBI investigation of Watergate. Deputy Director Walters then reported back to Mr. Gray, that they would not be compromised. On July 6, when I called Mr. Gray and when he expressed concern about improper attempts to limit his investigation, as the record shows, I told him to press ahead vigorously with his investigation—which he did.

The second point I would urge is that the evidence be looked at in its entirety, and the events be looked at in perspective. Whatever mistakes I made in the handling of Watergate, the basic truth remains that when all the facts were brought to my attention I insisted on a full investigation and prosecution of those guilty. I am firmly convinced that the record, in its entirety, does not justify the extreme step of impeachment and removal of a President. I trust that as the constitutional process goes forward, this perspective will prevail.

Impact in Congress devastating. President Nixon's statement and release of new tapes Aug. 5 had a devastating effect upon his support in Congress. That support had been perceptibly slipping away since the House Judiciary Committee's televised hearings and decision to bring impeachment articles to the House. The trend in the House toward a vote for impeachment had been conceded even by Vice President Ford Aug. 3.

In the Senate, where a two-thirds vote was necessary for conviction, the prediction was less certain although there was a definite trend against the President. Even prior to release of Nixon's statement Aug. 5, Sen. Robert P. Griffin (Mich.), assistant Senate Republican leader, appeared before television cameras to call for Nixon's resignation. "I think we've arrived at a point where both the national interest and his own interest will best be served by resigning," he said. "It's not just his enemies who feel that way. Many of his friends, and I count myself one of them, believe now that this would be the most appropriate course. Needless to say, this would be an awesome and very difficult decision for him to reach but I believe he will see it that way too." Later in the day, Griffin expressed disappointment that Nixon seemed determined to remain in office.

Following release of the President's statement, with its concession of knowledge of the Watergate cover-up, coupled with acknowledgement that impeachment by the house was "virtually a foregone conclusion," Republican defections became epidemic.

Rep. Charles E. Wiggins (R, Calif.), Nixon's strongest defender during the Judiciary Committee hearings, asserted, while struggling to retain composure, that he had reached the "painful conclusion" that it was in the "national interest" for Nixon to resign. "The facts then known to me have now changed," he said in reference to his committee stance that there was no direct link to the President of a criminal offense. Wiggins said it was established now "beyond a reasonable doubt" that the President had agreed to a "plan of action" to obstruct the Watergate investigation. "These facts standing alone," Wiggins said, "are legally sufficient in my opinion to sustain at least one count against the President of conspiracy to obstruct justice." If Nixon did not resign, Wiggins said, "I am prepared to conclude that the magnificent career of public service of Richard Nixon must be terminated involuntarily and shall support those portions of Article I of the bill of impeachment adopted by the Judiciary Committee which are sustained by the evidence."

The President's loss of support spread Aug. 5 to the House Republican leadership. House GOP Policy Committee Chairman Barber B. Conable Jr. (N.Y.), who supported Nixon on more House votes in 1973 than any Republican, said he was prepared to vote for impeachment and predicted it would have "overwhelming support in the House." "I guess we have found the smoking gun, haven't we?" Conable observed in reference to the Republican argument that impeachment should not be voted without solid evidence of direct presidential involvement in a criminal offense.

House Republican Conference Chairman John B. Anderson (Ill.) said Aug. 5 the Nixon statement "goes to the very heart of the first article of impeachment. The President's own words seem to convict him of that article."

House Republican Leader John J. Rhodes (Ariz.) issued a statement that "the apparent attempt to use the CIA to cover up the depth of the Watergate conspiracy is shocking. The fact that the President's veracity is put in question by this disclosure is a tragedy."

A cry that "I'm still a Nixon man" was raised by Rep. Earl Landgrebe (R, Ind.), who added that the situation looked like "a mutiny on a ship—a kind of madness has broken out."

House Democratic Whip John McFall (Calif.) observed that the situation had changed for the President's supporters in the House, that they were now "off the hook." "Anyone can now vote for impeachment without any fear of criticism," he said, "because the President virtually concedes and invites it."

Defection almost total—By Aug. 6, the collapse of Nixon support appeared almost total. Only two of the 435 House members took public stands against impeachment—Rep. Otto E. Passman (D, La.) joined Landgrebe.

GOP Leader Rhodes announced for impeachment. "Cover-up of criminal activity and misuse of federal agencies can neither be condoned nor tolerated," he said.

The remaining 10 members of the Judiciary Committee who opposed the impeachment articles in that panel's hearings, reversed their stands Aug. 6. "I feel that I have been deceived," one of them, ranking GOP member Rep. Edward Hutchinson (Mich.), commented.

Public defenders of the President in the Senate Aug. 6 had dropped to one—Carl Curtis (R, Neb.), who accused the U.S. of emulating a "banana republic." He pointed out the anomaly that if Vice President Ford succeeded Nixon and appointed his vice president, neither incumbent would have been elected to the office.

The consensus of the Senate Republican Policy Committee, which met at noon Aug. 6, was that the gravity of his situation, had worsened, that there had been "great erosion of support," should be relayed to the President. Sen. Tower, reporting the consensus, said a majority at the meeting felt that resignation would be "in the national interest."

Sen. Robert Dole (Kan.), former GOP national chairman, estimated Aug. 6 that if Nixon could count on 40 votes against conviction in the Senate a week ago, he had no more than 20 that day.

It dropped to 15 by Aug. 7. Sen. Barry Goldwater (R, Ariz.) said he and Scott had given Nixon that estimate when they, with Rhodes, met with the President at the White House that day.

It was estimated that in the House there were perhaps only 10 votes against impeachment.

Impeachment preparations continued— Even as President Nixon's resignation appeared more certain each day, Congressional leaders continued preparing for House consideration of the proposed impeachment articles and the Senate trial that might follow House action.

The House leadership indicated agreement on the rules for consideration of the proposed articles.

Meanwhile, House members Aug. 5 began five days of hearing the tapes of presidential conversations already heard by Judiciary Committee members. Four specially equipped rooms in two House office buildings contained headsets for 204 representatives to listen at one time.

House majority whip John J. McFall (D, Calif.) announced Aug. 5 that special security measures had been planned for the period of the impeachment debate.

The full House voted 385–25 Aug. 7 to allow gavel to gavel television coverage of the impeachment proceedings. The previous day, the Senate Rules Committee had agreed to permit some type of television coverage of a Senate trial.

While House preparations were under way, the Senate Rules Committee began the first of a series of closed meetings July 31 on revision of rules for the trial. According to published reports, the committee focused on the role of the chief justice, who would preside in the trial, the standard of proof necessary for conviction and the limits on admissibility of evidence.

Ford drops 'not-guilty' stand. Gerald Ford removed himself from the impeachment debate Aug. 5 after release of the presidential statement admitting Nixon's knowledge of the Watergate cover-up. Returning to Washington from a weekend swing through Mississippi and Louisiana, Ford issued a statement that he had "come to the conclusion that the public interest is no longer served by repetition of my previously expressed belief that, on the basis of all the evidence known to me and to the American people,

the President is not guilty of an impeachable offense under the constitutional definition of 'treason, bribery or other high crimes and misdemeanors.' Inasmuch as additional evidence is about to be forthcoming from the President, which he says may be damaging, I intend to respectfully decline to discuss impeachment matters in public or in response to questions until the facts are more fully available."

A vice president, Ford said, "is a party of interest as the constitutional successor if a president is removed from office" and "there are many urgent matters on America's agenda in which I hope to continue to serve this great country as a communicator and conciliator. The business of government must go on and the genuine needs of the people must be served. I believe I can make a better contribution to this end by not involving myself daily in the impeachment debate, in which I have no constitutional role."

The next day Ford attended a luncheon meeting of Republican senators, briefing them on the Cabinet meeting he attended with Nixon that day. He left the luncheon, according to reports, when the conversation turned to impeachment and calls for Nixon's resignation.

Early on the morning of Aug. 7, Ford met for an hour in his office with Nixon's chief of staff, Gen. Alexander M. Haig Jr. The meeting was at Haig's request.

In an interview with the New York Times that day, Ford did not respond to questions on sensitive issues. He did answer questions about whether he felt prepared to assume the presidency. "No question about that," he said. He had "worked real hard" and visited every executive department for top-level conferences and had confidential military briefings during his recent travels around the country. He had regular meetings with Secretary of State Henry Kissinger. "I think I know as much, if not more," Ford said, "about the government than any vice president" and "I think I'm well prepared for any contingency."

Aftermath

House accepts impeachment report. The House Judiciary Committee's report on its impeachment inquiry of President Nixon was accepted by the House Aug. 20 by a vote of 412–3. The report was submitted to the House by Committee Chairman Peter W. Rodino Jr. (D, N.J.). House Democratic Leader Thomas P. O'Neill Jr. (Mass.) offered a resolution stating that the House "accepts the report," commending the committee for its "conscientious and capable" effort and calling the inquiry "full and complete."

House Republican Leader John J. Rhodes (Ariz.) took the necessary parliamentary step of demanding a second and the resolution was voted without debate. The three votes against it were cast by Reps. Earl F. Landgrebe (R, Ind.), G. V. Montgomery (D, Miss.) and Otto E. Passman (D, La.).

The report thus became part of the official House record. It was published Aug. 22 as House Report 93-1305 and as Part II of the Congressional Record.

The majority and minority opinions were expressed on each article after the listing of evidence.

On Article I, a finding that Nixon participated in a criminal conspiracy to cover up the Watergate burglary, there was a unanimous recommendation of impeachment. The committee had approved the article July 27 during its inquiry by 27–11 vote. But after Nixon had released additional evidence Aug. 5, the 11 Republicans who had voted against the article reversed their stands.

This new evidence was cited by the 11 in their "minority views" of the committee's report. "We know," they said, "that it has been said, and perhaps some will continue to say, that Richard Nixon was 'hounded from office' by his political opponents and media critics. We feel constrained to point out, however, that it was Richard Nixon who impeded the FBI's investigation of the Watergate affair by wrongfully attempting to implicate the Central Intelligence Agency; it was Richard Nixon who created and preserved the evidence of that transgression and who, knowing that it had been subpoenaed by this committee and the special prosecutor, concealed its terrible import, even from his own counsel, until he could do so no longer. And it was a unanimous Supreme Court of the United States,

which in an opinion authorized by the Chief Justice whom he appointed, ordered Richard Nixon to surrender that evidence to the special prosecutor, to further the ends of justice. The tragedy that finally engulfed Richard Nixon had many facets. One was the very self-inflicted nature of the harm. It is striking that such an able, experienced and perceptive man, whose ability to grasp the global implications of events little noticed by others may well have been unsurpassed by any of his predecessors, should fail to comprehend the damage that accrued daily to himself, his Administration and to the nation, as day after day, month after month, he imprisoned the truth about his role in the Watergate coverup so long and so tightly within the solitude of his Oval Office that it could not be unleashed without destroying his Presidency."

The majority's report on Article I cited 36 specific items against the President that it said formed "a pattern of undisputed acts" that "cannot otherwise be rationally explained" except as part of a conspiracy to obstruct justice.

"President Nixon's action," the majority said, "resulted in manifest injury to the confidence of the nation and great prejudice to the cause of law and justice, and was subversive of constitutional government. His actions were contrary to his trust as President and unmindful of the solemn duties of his high office. It was this serious violation of Richard M. Nixon's constitutional obligations as President, and not the fact that violations of federal criminal statutes occurred, that lies at the heart of Article I."

All in all, President Nixon's conduct, the majority concluded, "posed a threat to our democratic republic."

On Article II, concerning abuse of presidential power and violation of the oath of office to execute the nation's laws, the report reaffirmed the committee's 28–10 vote for adoption July 29. The 10 Republicans who formed the minority said they did "deplore in strongest terms the aspects of presidential wrongdoing to which the article is addressed." But they found the article vague and a "catch-all repository for miscellaneous and unrelated Presidential offenses." "It is a far-reaching and dangerous proposition," they said, "that conduct which is in violation of no known law but which is considered by a temporary majority of Congress to be 'improper' because undertaken for 'political' purposes can constitute grounds for impeachment."

The majority view on Article II cited allegations against Nixon of attempted misuse of the Internal Revenue Service, the Federal Bureau of Investigation and other agencies. It concluded that Nixon had "repeatedly used his authority as President to violate the Constitution and the law of the land. In so doing, he violated the obligation that every citizen has to live under the law. But he did more, for it is the duty of the President not merely to live by the law but to see that law faithfully applied. Richard M. Nixon repeatedly and willfully failed to perform that duty. He failed to perform it by authorizing and directing actions that violated the rights of citizens and that interfered with the functioning of executive agencies. And he failed to perform it by condoning and ratifying, rather than acting to stop, actions by his subordinates interfering with the enforcement of the laws."

In an individual statement, Rep. Wiley Mayne (R, Iowa), who had voted in committee against Article II, reversed himself because of Nixon's Aug. 5 admission of complicity in the Watergate cover-up. Mayne said on the basis of that he would have voted for impeachment on Article II on the ground of misuse of agencies.

The minority held to its view of Article III, which had been adopted by the committee July 30 by a 21–17 vote and dealt with Nixon's refusal to comply with the committee's subpoenas for tape recordings and for production of other data. The minority held that such refusal in itself was not sufficient ground for impeachment and there was an "element of unfairness" in removing a president from office "for failure to cooperate in his own impeachment."

The majority held that "unless the defiance of the committee's subpoenas is considered grounds for impeachment, it is difficult to conceive of any president acknowledging that he is obligated to supply the relevant evidence necessary for Congress to exercise its constitutional

responsibility in an impeachment proceeding. If this were to occur, the impeachment power would be drained of its vitality."

Immunity agreement denied. There was widespread speculation both before and after Nixon's resignation as to what legal action, if any, might be taken against him as a private citizen.

Watergate special prosecutor Leon Jaworski said after the resignation announcement that bargaining regarding possible immunity from prosecution had not played a part in Nixon's decision to leave office. "There has been no agreement or understanding of any sort between the President and his representatives and the special prosecutor relating in any way to the President's resignation," the statement said.

Jaworski said his office "was not asked for any such agreement or understanding and offered none." He added that he had been informed of Nixon's decision to resign during the afternoon.

Another legal possibility concerning Nixon's future—pardon by President Ford either before or after an indictment—was indirectly dismissed by Ford's press secretary Aug. 9. Asked about such prospects at a news briefing, J. F. terHorst said he had not spoken to Ford about the issue directly, but cited Ford's statements during his 1973 vice presidential confirmation hearings. (Ford had been asked: if a President resigned would his successor have the power to prevent further investigation or prosecution? Ford replied: "I do not think the public would stand for it.... The attorney general, in my opinion, with the help and support of the American people, would be the controlling factor.") News reports Aug. 9–10 cited doubts expressed by members of Congress and other analysts that Ford would grant such a pardon.

Ford pardons Nixon for all crimes. President Ford granted ex-President Nixon Sept. 8, 1974 a full pardon for all federal crimes he had "committed or may have committed or taken part in" during his 5½ years as President.

Nixon issued a statement accepting the pardon and expressing regret that he had been "wrong in not acting more decisively and more forthrightly in dealing with Watergate."

The White House also announced Sept. 8 that the Ford Administration had concluded an agreement with Nixon giving him title to his presidential papers and tape recordings but guaranteeing they would be kept intact and available for court use for at least three years.

The pardon for Nixon was unexpected. Ford made his announcement from the Oval Office on Sunday morning after attending church. After reading a brief statement on his decision before a small pool of reporters and photographers—the event was filmed for broadcast later—Ford signed a proclamation granting Nixon the pardon.

Nixon had not been formally charged with any federal crime and the granting of a pardon in advance was a reversal of Ford's position on the issue, expressed as recently as his Aug. 28 news conference.

The announcement drew wide protest and some support. Generally, it was split along partisan lines and the Democratic protest was more heated than the Republican support for the Nixon pardon. One protester was White House Press Secretary J. F. terHorst, the first appointee of the Ford Administration, who resigned Sept. 8 as a matter of "conscience."

The controversy broadened Sept. 10 when a White House spokesman, in response to a question, said Ford was considering pardons for all Watergate defendants. Following further adverse criticism, the White House shifted its stance Sept. 11 and announced that individual requests for pardons would be considered.

In his statement, Ford said Nixon and "his loved ones have suffered enough, and will continue to suffer no matter what I do." "Theirs is an American tragedy in which we all have played a part," he said. "It can go on and on, or someone must write 'The End' to it. I have concluded that only I can do that. And if I can, I must."

There were no historic or legal precedents on the matter, Ford said, "but it is

Ford Pardon Proclamation

Richard Nixon became the thirty-seventh president of the United States on January 20, 1969, and was re-elected in 1972 for a second term by the electors of forty-nine of the fifty states. His term in office continued until his resignation on August 9, 1974.

Pursuant to resolutions of the House of Representatives, its Committee on the Judiciary conducted an inquiry and investigation on the impeachment of the President extending over more than eight months. The hearings of the committee and its deliberations, which received wide national publicity over television, radio, and in printed media, resulted in votes adverse to Richard Nixon on recommended Articles of Impeachment.

As a result of certain acts or omissions occurring before his resignation from the office of president, Richard Nixon has become liable to possible indictment and trial for offenses against the United States. Whether or not he shall be so prosecuted depends on findings of the appropriate grand jury and on the discretion of the authorized prosecutor. Should an indictment ensue, the accused shall then be entitled to a fair trial by an impartial jury, as guaranteed to every individual by the Constitution.

It is believed that a trial of Richard Nixon, if it became necessary, could not fairly begin until a year or more has elapsed. In the meantime, the tranquility to which this nation has been restored by the events of recent weeks could be irreparably lost by the prospects of bringing to trial a former president of the United States. The prospects of such trial will cause prolonged and divisive debate over the propriety of exposing to further punishment and degradation a man who has already paid the unprecedented penalty of relinquishing the highest office in the United States.

NOW, THEREFORE, I, Gerald R. Ford, president of the United States, pursuant to the pardon power conferred upon me by Article II, Section 2, of the Constitution, have granted and by these presents do grant a full, free, and absolute pardon unto Richard Nixon for all offenses against the United States which he, Richard Nixon, has committed or may have committed or taken part in during the period from January 20, 1969, through August 9, 1974.

IN WITNESS WHEREOF, I have hereunto set my hand this 8th day of September in the year of our Lord nineteen hundred seventy-four, and of the independence of the United States of America the 199th.

common knowledge that serious allegations and accusations hang like a sword over our former president's head and threaten his health as he tries to reshape his life."

He cited the "years of bitter controversy and divisive national debate" and the prospect of "many months and perhaps more years" before Nixon "could hope to obtain a fair trial by jury in any jurisdiction" of the country. He "deeply believe[d] in equal justice for all Americans, whatever their station or former station," Ford said, but "the facts as I see them are" that a former president, "instead of enjoying equal treatment with any other citizen accused of violating the law, would be cruelly and excessively penalized either in preserving the presumption of his innocence or in obtaining a speedy determination of his guilt in order to repay a legal debt to society."

Ford continued: "During this long period of delay and potential litigation, ugly passions would again be aroused, our people would again be polarized in their opinions, and the credibility of our free institutions of government would again be challenged at home and abroad. In the end, the courts might well hold that Richard Nixon had been denied due process and the verdict of history would be even more inconclusive with respect to those charges arising out of the period of his presidency of which I am presently aware."

His conscience told him, Ford said, "that I cannot prolong the bad dreams that continue to reopen a chapter that is closed" and that "only I, as President, have the constitutional power to firmly shut and seal this book." "My conscience says," he continued, "it is my duty, not merely to proclaim domestic tranquility, but to use every means I have to ensure it. . . . I cannot rely upon public opinion polls to tell me what is right. I do believe that right makes might. . . ."

The proclamation granting Nixon "a full, free, and absolute pardon" referred to the articles of impeachment recommended by the House Judiciary Committee. "As a result of certain acts or omissions" occurring during his presidency, it stated, Nixon had become liable to possible indictment and trial for offenses against the U.S. "It is believed," the proclamation continued, that a trial, if it became necessary, could not "fairly" begin for a year or more and "in the meantime, the tranquility to which this nation has been restored by the events of recent weeks could be irreparably lost by the prospects of bringing to trial a former president of the United States. The prospects of such trial will cause prolonged and divisive debate over the propriety of exposing to further punishment and degradation a man who has already paid the unprecedented penalty of relinquishing the highest elective office in the United States."

Nixon's statement—In accepting the pardon Sept. 8, Nixon said he hoped that this "compassionate act will contribute to lifting the burden of Watergate from our country." His "perspective on Watergate" had changed, he said, and "one thing I can see clearly now is that I was wrong in not acting more decisively and more forthrightly in dealing with Watergate, particularly when it reached the stage of judicial proceedings and grew from a political scandal into a national tragedy."

He spoke of "the depths of my regret and pain at the anguish my mistakes over Watergate have caused the nation and the presidency." He knew, he said, "that many fair-minded people believe that my motivation and actions in the Watergate affair were intentionally self-serving and illegal. I now understand how my own mistakes and misjudgments have contributed to that belief and seemed to support it. This burden is the heaviest one of all to bear. That the way I tried to deal with Watergate was the wrong way is a burden I shall bear for every day of the life that is left to me."

Buchen: no conditions imposed—White House counsel Philip W. Buchen said Sept. 8 that the pardon for Nixon had been granted without any demands being made upon Nixon, that no effort had been made to obtain acknowledgment of wrongdoing. He also said the advice of the Watergate special prosecutor, Leon Jaworski, had not been sought.

Buchen described the pardon as an "act of mercy" and Nixon's statement as a "statement of contrition." The decision was predicated, he said, on the belief that "it was very likely" Nixon would have been indicted and ordered to stand trial.

Ford had asked him to make a study of the issue about a week before, Buchen said, and he had first consulted Jaworski on the probable timing of a Nixon trial in the event of an indictment. Jaworski responded that a trial could not be held for at least nine months to a year or more, that it would take that time to settle the legal problem of possible prejudicial pretrial publicity.

Buchen said he was assured by Jaworski

that there were no new "time bombs" in the Nixon investigation.

Buchen said he had asked a friend, Washington lawyer Benton L. Becker, who also was a friend of Ford, to broach the issue with Nixon and his counsel, and said Becker had gone to San Clemente the previous week and advised Nixon that a pardon was probable. Nixon was said to have responded with his intention in that event to issue a statement.

Buchen said Sept. 10 that Ford "did not make a deal" with Nixon on the pardon before Nixon left office. He made the point, in another press briefing, that the granting of a pardon "can imply guilt— there is no other reason for granting a pardon." The fact that someone accepted a pardon, he said, "means that it was necessary for him to have the pardon."

Ford denies 'deal' for pardon. President Ford, in an historic appearance before a House subcommittee Oct. 17, defended his pardon of former President Nixon.

Ford was not put under oath for his testimony, in which he reiterated he had made "no deal" with Nixon on the pardon but had acted "out of my concern to serve the best interests of my country."

The hearing which was televised, was before the House Criminal Justice Subcommittee of the Judiciary Committee. Its members were allotted five minutes each to question the President after his 5,-000-word opening statement. The toughest questioning was by Rep. Elizabeth Holtzman (D, N.Y.), but, protesting the time limit, she did not wait for answers except to one query, whether Ford would be willing to turn over to the panel all tape recordings of his conversations with Nixon. Ford responded that the Nixon tapes were safe, "in our control," and being held for the Watergate special prosecutor. They "will not be delivered to anybody until a satisfactory agreement is reached with the special prosecutor's office," Ford said.

Holtzman said there were "dark suspicions" in the public mind about the pardon. Why was no crime cited, no guilt confessed? she asked. Other Holtzman questions: Why was the action done in haste and secrecy, and without consultation with the attorney general or the special prosecutor? Why did the pardon accompany a tapes agreement that was contrary to the public's right to know and prosecutor's access to the materials?

Ford stressed "there was no deal, period" between himself and Nixon. He said his main purpose in granting the pardon was to turn national attention "from the pursuit of a fallen president to the pursuit of the urgent needs" of the country. No conditions were placed on the pardon, and no confession sought, Ford said, although acceptance of the pardon in his mind implied admission of guilt. The tapes arrangement, while "related in time to the pardon discussions," was "not a basis" for the decision to grant the pardon. Ford said he acted at the time he did out of concern that continuation of the legal processes against Nixon and thus the preoccupation of the nation with the controversy would have consumed at least a year and probably longer.

Rep Don Edwards (D, Calif.) asked Ford to put himself in the position of a high school teacher. " . . . how would you explain to the young people the American concept of equal justice under the law?"

Ford's response: "Mr. Nixon was the 37th president of the United States. He had been preceded by 36 others. He is the only president in the history of this country who has resigned under shame and disgrace. I think that in and of itself can be understood, can be explained to students or to others. That was a major, major step and a matter of, I'm sure, grave, grave deliberations by the former president and it certainly, as I've said several times, constituted shame and disgrace."

Ford broke little new ground, except to reveal that Nixon Administration officials just prior to Nixon's resignation were considering such options as Nixon pardoning himself, or pardoning various Watergate defendants, then himself, before resigning. A third option, Ford said, was "a pardon to the President should he resign," granted by Ford, who would be his successor. Ford said the options were broached to him by Nixon aide Alexander M. Haig Jr. at an Aug. 1 meeting when Haig advised him of the critical evidence on tape against Nixon which would probably lead to Ford's accession to the office.

Ford said he told Haig he wanted "time to think" about the pardon option, then informed him the next day that "I had no intention of recommending what President Nixon should do about resigning or not resigning and that nothing we had talked about the previous afternoon should be given any consideration in whatever decision the President might make."

Ford also admitted that he made misleading public statements after that time—that he did not believe Nixon was guilty of an impeachable offense—because "any change from my stated views, or even refusal to comment further, I feared, would lead in the press to conclusions that I now wanted to see the President resign to avoid an impeachment vote in the House and probably conviction vote in the Senate."

Nixon pardon inquiry dropped. A House Judiciary subcommittee voted 6–3 Nov. 22 against further pursuit of resolutions of inquiry on President Ford's pardon of former President Nixon. The resolutions were filed by Reps. Bella Abzug (D, N.Y.) and John Conyers Jr. (D, Mich.).

Subcommittee Chairman William L. Hungate (D, Mo.) voted with the four Republican members and Rep. James R. Mann (D, S.C.) to end the probe. Abzug urged continuation of the inquiry "in view of President Ford's incomplete and often contradictory testimony" before the panel Oct. 17.

Nixon provided $200,000. The Senate passed an appropriations bill Nov. 20 containing $200,000 for former President Nixon for pension and transition expenses. The funds were in an $8.3 billion fiscal 1975 supplemental appropriations bill approved by a 65–18 vote.

The $200,000 level for Nixon, the same approved by the House earlier, had been recommended by the Senate Appropriations Committee in reporting the bill Oct. 9.

An appropriations subcommittee headed by Sen. Joseph M. Montoya (D, N.M.) had reported Oct. 8 that government spending on personnel and support services for Nixon was at the rate of nearly $2 million a year. Montoya, releasing data provided by the White House, said 64 government employes were assigned to Nixon's San Clemente, Calif. estate. Secret Service protection there was costing $622,000 a year and federal costs for personnel at Nixon's Key Biscayne, Fla. home were costing more than $500,000 a year.

Jaworski announces resignation. Leon Jaworski announced Oct. 12 his resignation as Watergate special prosecutor. The resignation, to be effective Oct. 25, was submitted to Attorney General William B. Saxbe.

In an interim report to Saxbe, Jaworski said that "the bulk of the work" entrusted to him had been "discharged."

A large part of the interim report was devoted to the question of the "the validity" of the pardon granted Nixon by Ford. The legal right to grant the pardon, and the legality of one granted prior to filing of charges, were "so clear, in my opinion, as not to admit of doubt," Jaworski said. He had also concluded that there was nothing in the charter and guidelines of his office "that impairs or curtails the President's free exercise of the constitutional right of pardon."

For him to challenge the pardon for a court test of its legality, he said, would be "intellectually dishonest," "a spurious proceeding in which I had no faith; in fact, it would be tantamount to unprofessional conduct and violative of my responsibility as prosecutor and officer of the court." Jaworski explicitly denied there was any connection between his resignation and the pardon or the suggestions that Nixon be indicted to test the pardon.

Says Nixon guilt evident—In an interview published by the Wall Street Journal Oct. 16, Jaworski conceded that the pardon of Nixon had prevented an indictment and trial but he said the pardon itself, and evidence that was or would become public would show Nixon guilty of obstruction of justice. "The evidence will show he's guilty, just as much as a guilty plea," Jaworski said. He said a pardon "isn't just a beautiful document to frame and hang on the wall. You are offered a pardon only because it is believed you can be charged and convicted. You accept it only if you want to be cleared."

Jaworski said he had not spoken out until a jury had been chosen for the Watergate conspiracy trial of Nixon aides and until he had announced his resignation. He denied the resignation had resulted from the pardon and said it was a mistake to think more evidence against Nixon would have become public if the case had gone to trial. "If he had gone to trial," Jaworski said, "he could have invoked his Fifth Amendment guarantees against self-incrimination, pleaded nolo contendere, or even pleaded guilty, and we wouldn't have learned any new details." As it was, he said, the evidence forthcoming at the current Watergate trial would further involve Nixon in the cover-up. "We can paint a very ·full picture of Mr. Nixon's role in obstructing justice," Jaworski said.

Rockefeller Becomes Vice President

Ford Chooses Rockefeller

The difficult task of choosing the nation's second unelected Vice President was completed by President Ford Aug. 20, 1974. But it took four months of deliberation before Congress approved the selection and the new Vice President could take office.

Rockefeller nomination announced. President Ford announced Aug. 20 that Nelson A. Rockefeller, 66, former governor of New York for 15 years, was his choice to be the 41st vice president of the U.S. The nomination was sent to Congress that day for confirmation which required a simple majority vote of each house.

The announcement was made in a brief ceremony in the Oval Office at the White House attended by Congressional leaders of both parties and the Cabinet, who were informed of Ford's choice just prior to the announcement.

The President introduced Rockefeller as "a good partner for me" and "for our country and the world." Rockefeller was "known across the land as a person dedicated to the free enterprise system," he said, "a person who is recognized abroad for his talent, for his dedication to making this a peaceful world." "It was a tough call for a tough job," Ford said, adding he

had considered a number of men and women "of great quality" for the post.

Rockefeller accepted the challenge as a "great honor" to serve the President and through him all of the people of the country. "These are very serious times," he said, that required "the closest cooperation" between Congress and the executive branch and "the dedication of every American to a common national interest."

"You, Mr. President," he continued, "through your dedication and your openness, have already reawakened faith and hope. And under your leadership, we, as a people, and we, as a nation, have the will, the determination and the capability to overcome the hard realities of our time. I'm optimistic about the long-term future."

Following the ceremony, which was broadcast on national radio and television networks, Ford presented Rockefeller at a news conference as "a great teammate." Rockefeller, in turn, said he was "fully cognizant" of the fact that the responsibilities of the vice president were to preside over the Senate "and otherwise simply carry out any assignment" received from the President. "I will look forward to that opportunity of serving him in any way that can be useful to him," Rockefeller said.

Rockefeller reaffirmed that point in the question-and-answer period that followed. The role of a vice president, he said, "totally depends on the President. If the President wants to use him, wonderful. If he doesn't, fine."

The majority of questions dealt with politics and the way Rockefeller, a millionnaire, would meet the personal financial requirements of the vice presidency. Rockefeller said he would conform "totally" to whatever the law required, would answer any questions from members of Congress during the confirmation proceedings and would "be prepared to do whatever I am asked" by Congress regarding full disclosure. He assumed, he said, that conformity to the law would entail putting his assets into trust.

Later in the day, Rockefeller, twice a contender for the Republican presidential nomination, told reporters he believed Ford had "every intention" of seeking a four-year term in the presidency in 1976 "and I wholeheartedly support his candidacy."

Praise from both parties—The choice of Rockefeller for vice president was applauded by Republicans and Democrats in Congress Aug. 20. Leaders in both houses of both parties expressed pleasure and predicted confirmation.

The favorable reaction extended to conservatives and liberals. One of the former, Sen. Carl Curtis (R, Neb.), said "I shall vote for his confirmation." On the other side of the aisle and spectrum, Sen. Edward M. Kennedy (D, Mass.) said the President had selected "an outstanding American with a record of long and dedicated public service to New York and the nation."

Dissent came from Sen. Barry Goldwater (R, Ariz.), who said Rockefeller was "not the one to put the party together." Goldwater said he had "ducked out on at least two presidential races," an apparent reference to the 1964 race when Goldwater was the unsuccessful nominee and to Richard M. Nixon's successful campaign in 1968. Goldwater said he could support the nomination but doubted that the nominee would be acceptable to "rank-and-file Republicans" in 1976.

Another former Republican contender for the presidential nomination, against Nixon in 1972, Rep. John M. Ashbrook (Ohio), also dissented. Rockefeller, he

said, "has continually been rejected nationwide by the majority of the Republican Party."

Presidential Counselor Robert T. Hartmann told reporters Aug. 20 "the overwhelming criterion" in Ford's decision on choosing a vice president was whether the person could handle the presidency if circumstances required it. The President, he said, "was not looking for survival of the Republican Party but survival of the republic."

President Ford informed former President Nixon of his choice just prior to the announcement Aug. 20, according to White House Press Secretary J. F. terHorst. A telephone call was placed to Nixon's San Clemente, Calif. home, with Rockefeller listening in, terHorst said, and Nixon's reaction was that the President had made "a good choice" by picking "a big man for a big job."

Attempted smear of Rockefeller—While the President was winnowing the list, there was a brief flurry of reports that Rockefeller funds might have helped fund a project to disrupt the 1972 Democratic National Convention with hired thugs.

The White House said Aug. 17 the allegation was unfounded, but it had gained some currency from the White House itself, by a report from that source that the Watergate special prosecutor's office was investigating to see if the Rockefeller link existed. White House spokesman terHorst said Aug. 17 he had promulgated the report after syndicated columnist Jack Anderson had raised the issue, noting it was only hearsay. Anderson mentioned the conjecture that the secret files of Watergate conspirator E. Howard Hunt Jr., which were thought to have been destroyed, could contain evidence of the link between Rockefeller and the "dirty tricks." The White House had been tipped off about the link and an investigation by the special prosecutor was ordered. Several lockboxes in undisclosed cities reportedly were opened but found to be empty; the special prosecutor concluded that the allegation against Rockefeller was baseless.

TerHorst said Aug. 17 the investigation was closed and attributed the original tip to "extremists who wished for reasons of their own to discredit" Rockefeller.

Other names on final list—Another person notified just prior to the announcement was Republican National Chairman George Bush. Bush, 50, was widely reported to have been on the final list from which Ford made his selection for vice president. Others included Sen. Howard H. Baker (R, Tenn.), 48; Gov. Daniel J. Evans (R, Wash.), 48; Elliot L. Richardson, 54, who held several Cabinet posts in the Nixon Administration before resigning in a dispute over the Watergate case; Donald Rumsfeld, 42, ambassador to NATO; Melvin R. Laird, 51, former Congressman and Nixon's first defense secretary.

Congress Investigates Nominee

Family wealth probed. Nelson A. Rockefeller's vast family fortune was the principal topic as the Senate Rules Committee held public hearings Sept. 23-26 on his nomination. Rockefeller expressed hope that the "myth" about the family financial empire would be "dissipated" by the hearings.

Sen. Robert C. Byrd (D, W.Va.) led the challenge on the issue—whether the Rockefeller money posed a problem of undue power for a vice president. Byrd also aggressively interrogated Rockefeller on the pardon President Ford extended to former President Nixon, on the agreement concluded by the Administration at the same time with Nixon on disposition of his presidential papers and tapes and on the doctrine of executive privilege.

Byrd told Rockefeller Sept. 24, "With all due respect, I am a great admirer of yours, you're about the hardest man to pin down I've ever seen." Rockefeller told Byrd, "You've got an ability to put someone on the spot beyond what I've ever seen."

However, Byrd said after the Sept. 24 session that he agreed with the committee chairman, Sen. Howard W. Cannon (D, Nev.), that there was nothing in sight that would endanger confirmation.

Cannon had stated that view Sept. 11 in announcing the committee's vote to ask Rockefeller to make a full public disclosure of his worth in lieu of a requirement

for divestiture of holdings or establishment of a blind trust. Public disclosure, he said, would permit the public and the press to be a "watchdog against conflict of interest." Arriving in Washington Sept. 22 for the hearings, Rockefeller pledged to do whatever Congress required to resolve the conflict-of-interest issue, including the method of a blind trust.

A preliminary figure of $33 million was disclosed Sept. 12 as the estimate of Rockefeller's immediate personal worth. The total was upped Sept. 19 to $182.5 million—$62.5 million as the net worth of himself and his wife plus the income from two trusts worth $120 million. Rockefeller, in releasing the figures to counter "incomplete and therefore misleading data" leaked to the press, said the $33 million total did not include the value of art ($12.5 million) and real estate ($8 million) he had pledged to the public. Another $9 million difference largely came, he said, from updated appraisals of the art and real estate.

Rockefeller Sept. 23 read parts of a 72-page autobiographical statement submitted to the committee. It included summaries of his tax returns for the past 10 years. He stressed his family's tradition of philanthropy deriving from the "ethic" of social responsibility from wealth. His own contribution to various philanthropic and charitable institutions totaled $33 million, he said, not counting the $20.5 million pledged in art and real estate.

To correct a possible public misconception about the family influence in the oil industry, he said he owned no more than .2% of the outstanding share in any oil company and the family did not hold more than 2.06% of the stock of any oil company. He said he did not own any shares in the Chase Manhattan Bank, which was headed by his brother, David, although one of the trusts of which he was a beneficiary did own 325,000 shares worth $25.4 million.

"I hope that the myth or misconception about the extent of the family's control over the economy of this country will be totally brought out and exposed and dissipated," Rockefeller said.

Among the personal financial data he disclosed: his total holdings amounted to $218 million, mostly in trusts; he was the life beneficiary of trusts totaling $116.5

million; his wife was the beneficiary of securities and trusts totaling $3.8 million and his six children held assets totaling $35.6 million; he had paid $69 million in taxes during his lifetime; his income over the past decade totaled $46.8 million, of which about $1 million a year in tax-free securities held by two trusts, was not subject to taxation.

Byrd spoke of the Rockefeller family's "economic power" as a "stranglehold" on segments of the economy. Rockefeller, rejecting the idea of "empire," said the family had "interests" but not "controlling interests."

Byrd sought a commitment from Rockefeller on the Nixon pardon issue, which had been the opening line of inquiry used by Cannon, the committee chairman. Cannon had asked, in light of Ford's statement at his vice presidential hearings that the country "wouldn't stand for" a prior pardon of a president, "What assurances do we have that your responses will be anything more than empty phrases given at the moment?" Rockefeller affirmed a "total inclination" against granting such a pardon, adding that at the same time he "would not amend the Constitution—and renounce the power that the Constitution gives to a president." Byrd, however, insisted on a firm commitment from Rockefeller. He asked him, "Do you, yes or no, consider the questions today to be hypothetical" and the answers "can be lightly put aside at some future date?" "The answer is 'no,'" Rockefeller replied.

Rockefeller was asked by Sen. James B. Allen (D, Ala.) whether he had "moved philosophically to the right" in recent years, hoping "that this is so." Rockefeller said he considered himself "progressive or liberal in terms of meeting human needs, more conservative in terms of fiscal affairs."

Sen. Mark O. Hatfield (R, Ore.) asked his stand on U.S. interference in foreign countries, "such as in Chile" by the Central Intelligence Agency (CIA). Rockefeller said "a gray world" did exist among nations, "sad and tragic" as that was, and in the case of Chile the CIA activities had the approval of "top administrators in our government" and he assumed "they were done in the national interest."

Rockefeller Sept. 24 was again questioned on the family wealth and Nixon pardon issues. He told Cannon that Nixon "accepted a pardon, which in my opinion was tantamount to admitting guilt."

Byrd questioned whether Rockefeller would be able to "perceive the national interest against the background of your own wealth." Can't we agree, he asked, that "the influence is tremendous—tremendous, colossal influence?" "Can't I add the word, 'potential'?" Rockefeller rebutted. "Very well," said Byrd.

The two also dueled on the Nixon papers agreement, Byrd wanting a yes or no answer on whether Rockefeller approved it. "You're asking me to differ with the President on a matter about which I don't have all the facts," Rockefeller insisted. Rockefeller eventually said he agreed "in principle" with Byrd's view that the tapes agreement could block disclosure of the truth about Watergate.

Questioned about the Attica, N.Y. prison revolt in 1971, Rockefeller called it "a great tragedy" and stated his position against "negotiating with people who are holding hostages on threat of death."

On another issue, he indicated support for use of highway trust funds for mass transit and for the use of federal funds for operating subsidies to hold down mass transit fares.

Byrd Sept. 25 challenged Rockefeller for a commitment that he would not invoke executive privilege to keep any member of the executive branch from testifying to Congress on non-security matters. Rockefeller said he could think "of no cause at the present time in which I would invoke the doctrine" but said it would be "irresponsible to make a flat commitment."

Rockefeller also disclosed that he had received and rebuffed appeals for financial aid from former Nixon aide John D. Ehrlichman and former Vice President Spiro T. Agnew after they had left office.

Rockefeller money gifts questioned. Senate Rules Committee Chairman Howard W. Cannon (D, Nev.) said Oct. 9 he would make public the response of Vice President-designate Nelson A. Rockefeller to the panel's request for full details of financial gifts Rockefeller had made over the years to various associates. Recent disclosure of substantial gifts to such persons as Secretary of State Henry A. Kissinger, former New York State Republican Chairman L. Judson Morhouse and William J. Ronan, chairman of the Port Authority of New York and New Jersey, put the nomination of Rockefeller as vice president into immediate controversy.

The gift to Kissinger—$50,000 in early 1969 after Kissinger left the Rockefeller staff and before he joined the Nixon Administration—was disclosed by the Gannett newspaper chain. A Kissinger spokesman confirmed the report Oct. 4, saying Rockefeller had told Kissinger at the time he wanted to make him a gift "at the close of their some 15 years of association."

Reports of the Morhouse gift surfaced at the same time. Morhouse, a former member of the New York State Thruway Authority, had been sentenced to two-three years imprisonment in 1966 on bribery and unlawful-fee charges stemming from a state liquor authority scandal in New York. The conviction was upheld by state higher courts, but Rockefeller commuted the sentence in 1970.

The conviction was upheld by higher state courts but Rockefeller commuted his sentence in 1970.

Rockefeller's press secretary, Hugh Morrow, confirmed Oct. 5 the Kissinger and Morhouse gifts and said Ronan also received a gift but did not specify the sum. Rockefeller had made "many gifts to institutions and individuals" over the years, Morrow said, and had paid the appropriate gift taxes. Any impropriety was denied. The Kissinger gift had been made out of gratitude for long-time service, Morrow said. The Morhouse gift—$86,000—was made to ease "overwhelming financial problems," he said, and in Ronan's case, it was "friendship and the governor's desire to help keep a good man in government."

According to Morrow, Rockefeller loaned Morhouse $100,000 in 1969, when Morhouse was GOP state chairman, then an unsalaried post. Because of Morhouse's illness and financial problems, Rockefeller canceled the outstanding balance of the loan—$86,000—in 1973

and paid federal and state gift taxes of about $48,000.

The gift to Ronan was also in the form of a debt cancellation, Morrow said, and was made after Ronan resigned in April 1973 as chairman of the (New York State) Metropolitan Transportation Authority, carrying a $75,000 a year salary, and before he became chairman of the Port Authority, an unsalaried post. The size of the gift to Ronan was disclosed Oct. 7—$550,000. Ronan, who currently was a paid adviser to the Rockefeller family and a trustee of the New York State Power Authority ($12,500 annual salary), had borrowed that amount in a series of loans over the years, Morrow explained Oct. 8, and Rockefeller canceled the entire debt in the spring of 1973 as a gift that "could be related," Morrow said, "to the year-end bonus given to executives of large corporations." The gift tax paid by Rockefeller in this instance totaled $330,000.

Morrow said Rockefeller had received a "personal and confidential" letter from Cannon requesting information "on certain facts the committee has had for several weeks," a reference to gift-tax returns filed with the panel. Morrow told reporters Oct. 7 Rockefeller had also made "nominal contributions" to a number of Senate and House campaigns.

Senate Republican Leader Hugh Scott (Pa.) said Oct. 8 he had "seen nothing which has impaired the integrity of Gov. Rockefeller in any way," but Sen. Jesse A. Helms (R, N.C.), a critic of Rockefeller, called Oct. 8 for a reopening of the Senate hearings. Rep. Jerome R. Waldie (D, Calif.), a member of the House Judiciary Committee, which was expected to hold hearings on the nomination after the fall elections, said Oct. 8 the Rockefeller largesse "raises big qualms in my mind." "If the reason is to further your political career," he said, "that's important to know."

Rockefeller asks immediate hearing. Rockefeller Oct. 15 requested "immediate" Congressional hearings on his nomination because the issue was "being tried in the press . . . without my having the opportunity to present all the facts." Rockefeller was referring to continued reports concerning his substantial gifts of money to former aides and public officials. Rockefeller also was linked Oct. 10 to a derogatory biography of Arthur J. Goldberg published during Rockefeller's campaign against Goldberg for governor of New York in 1970.

The request for hearings was made to the chairmen of the Senate Rules Committee, Howard W. Cannon (D, Nev.), and the House Judiciary Committee, Peter W. Rodino Jr. (D, N.J.).

In response to reports that the Congressional probers were looking into the book affair, Rockefeller issued a statement Oct. 10 saying that he was unaware of it at the time but his brother Laurance had invested $60,000 in the book as a business venture. The book, "Arthur J. Goldberg, the Old and the New," by Victor Lasky, was expected to "sell well," the statement said, but "was a total flop" and Laurance sustained a net loss of about $52,000 but did not take a tax deduction on the business loss. "Had he only told me about it at the time," Rockefeller said, "I would have been totally opposed to it and would have strongly advised against his participation in any form."

He said he learned about Laurance's investment through the Federal Bureau of Investigation (FBI) during a background check because of the vice presidential nomination. Rockefeller said he told the FBI he had heard of the book at the time "but knew nothing about its preparation or financing." An aide had told him early in the 1970 campaign, Rockefeller said, that Lasky was working on a Goldberg biography but he "really didn't pay any attention because I never felt that such books coming out during campaigns cut much ice one way or another. I never heard any more about it until the book was out and someone showed me a copy, which I never even opened."

The Rockefeller campaign organization in 1970, however, reportedly received 100,000 copies of the book.

Later Oct. 10, Goldberg expressed shock that the Rockefellers "would participate in such a dirty campaign trick" and said they owed him an apology "for financing a scandalous and libelous book."

Rockefeller apologized to Goldberg by phone Oct. 12. The apology's text was released to the press. Citing the "derogatory" book, it said: "It is quite clear that when the project was brought to my attention, I should have immediately taken steps to see to it that it was stopped as utterly alien to and incompatible with the standards I have always tried to observe in my political life. I take full responsibility for the whole regrettable episode."

On the money gifts, Rockefeller made public Oct. 11 a list of 20 current and former public officials and staff aides to whom he had given about $2 million over the past 17 years. The list, prepared for the Congressional inquiries, was released because of leaks to the press, which Rockefeller deplored as "very unfair in terms of the privacy of individuals and also unfair in the sense of giving an atmosphere of uncertainty and suspicion."

Among those on the list were William J. Ronan, chairman of the Port Authority of New York and New Jersey, who was listed as recipient of $625,000, or $75,000 more than the total that was previously reported; Alton G. Marshall, president of Rockefeller Center, Inc. and a former secretary to Rockefeller during his governorship, who was listed as having received $306,867; Emmet J. Hughes, a former Rockefeller speechwriter and political adviser, $155,000; Edward J. Logue, chairman of the New York State Urban Development Corporation, $131,389, of which $100,000 was an outstanding debt from a loan of $145,000; James W. Gaynor, former New York state commissioner of housing and community renewal, $107,000; Henry L. Diamond, former New York state commissioner of environmental conservation, $100,000; and Victor Borella, former labor aide to Rockefeller as governor, $100,000.

Goldwater retracts support—During an appearance at Arizona State University in Tucson Oct. 23, Sen. Barry Goldwater (R, Ariz.) disclosed that "I've had to tell President Ford I'm not hidebound in my statement I could support Rockefeller because of things coming out in the hearings." He told a United Press International reporter afterwards that what concerned him was "not whether he has millions of dollars" but "whether or not he's used these millions of dollars to buy power. I think that's wrong."

Rockefeller owes back taxes.
Rockefeller made public Oct. 18 the results of a delayed audit by the Internal Revenue Service (IRS) of his income tax returns for a five-year period ending in 1973. According to the results, which were also submitted to the House and Senate committees handling his nomination hearings, Rockefeller had underpaid his federal taxes in that period by 21%, or $903,718. The IRS disallowed $824,598 in claimed deductions for office and investment expenses on the returns and $420,649 in deductions for charitable contributions, resulting in a recomputation that $820,718 in additional income taxes were due plus $83,000 in gift taxes.

Revised summaries of the totals on his joint tax returns with his wife also were released. Total income for the years 1964 through 1973 was reported at $47,053,-817, federal income tax payments totaled $12,165,378.

Rockefeller disclosed Oct. 19 that he had given about $24.7 million in charitable donations to 193 organizations during the past 17 years. The gifts, which ranged from $10 to a private school to nearly $6.6 million to the Museum of Primitive Art in New York City, included $6,500 to the U.S. government and a total of $656,393 to New York State.

Testimony on Goldberg book changed.
The Senate Rules Committee Nov. 13 opened the second phase of its hearings into Rockefeller's nomination. At the televised hearings, the primary focus was on the financing of the Goldberg book and on Rockefeller's gifts.

Rockefeller was apologetic Nov. 13 about the book, which he called a "hasty, ill-considered decision in the middle of a hectic campaign." "Let's face it, I made a mistake," he said in revising his earlier story of the financing of the book. Rockefeller admitted that he, rather than his brother Laurance, initiated the financing venture. The project had been broached to him, Rockefeller testified, by his political aide Jack Wells, who said he was seeking investors for the book, which he felt would be profitable. Wells described the book as "a high-level, analytical" biography of Goldberg, Rockefeller said.

Rockefeller said he "sent a message" to his brother asking if he could help find investors, but Laurance "didn't have time to find other investors and simply authorized his people to underwrite" the book. That was Laurance's "only connection" with the project, Rockefeller said, admitting that he was "embarrassed" and "humiliated" by his role because "I did an injustice to my brother." He stressed that his previous "incorrect" version of the financing came from faulty recollection and that he was "delinquent in not clearing this up sooner."

When Sen. Robert Byrd (D, W.Va.) suggested the belated disclosure of the true financing was "a throwback to what we have had over the past two years," reminiscent "of the dirty tricks of the Nixon era," Rockefeller protested, "No sir. I must bitterly object to that."

Rockefeller also was questioned Nov. 13 about his substantial money gifts. Chairman Howard Cannon (D, Nev.) questioned whether they "placed the recipients into what we might call psychological servitude."

The money was not "designed to corrupt," Rockefeller said, nor did it "corrupt either the receiver or the giver." "I'd not do this for someone in government who was not working for me and was not a close personal friend," he said.

Pressed by Sen. Claiborne Pell (D, R.I.) about whether he would continue the practice if he became vice president, Rockefeller said he was "hesitant" to renounce it solely on "humanitarian" grounds. "I would have to think that under certain circumstances I would want to help," he said. "There might be a case where I would feel in humanity that I ought to do something."

There were several further financial disclosures Nov. 13: Rockefeller's net worth was estimated by the Congressional Joint Committee on Internal Revenue Taxation at $73 million, higher than Rockefeller's own latest estimate of $62 million; a total of $3,265,374 in political contributions was made by Rockefeller over the past 18 years, $1,031,637 of it to his own presidential campaigns. The Rockefeller family's political contributions exceeded $20 million.

Rockefeller had made public Oct. 28, and made available to the committee, a list of loans totaling $507,656 made over the past 17 years to friends, associates and family members. The largest—$84,000—was to Robert B. Anderson, former Navy secretary and Treasury secretary. The form of the loan was in stock purchases in the International Basic Economy Corp., a Rockefeller-controlled corporation with extensive holdings in Latin America, which Anderson paid for with a 10-year installment note at a 3% interest rate, but sold in a short time back to Rockefeller for the price paid for the shares. The loan was made in 1957, before Anderson was named to the Treasury post and repaid shortly after his appointment.

Rockefeller was questioned primarily Nov. 14 about his money gifts. He conceded that his generosity could be "misinterpreted" and offered to "cut it out." He volunteered to pledge in writing to forego gifts or loans to federal employes if confirmed except for "nominal" gifts, such as for birthdays or weddings, or "in the event of medical hardships of a compelling human character." After some partisan squabbling over whether to keep the latter restriction or require public disclosure of such gifts, the commitment as testified to was let stand.

Sen. Byrd brought out in questioning that several of Rockefeller's loans or gifts of money had been made while the recipients held public office in New York.

Testimony Nov. 15 and 18 was on the Goldberg book and Rockefeller's large gifts of money over the years to friends and aides. The principal witness Nov. 15 was Laurance S. Rockefeller, who told of his investment in the Goldberg book as a business venture after a five-minute conversation. He regretted it, he said, "least of all because of the loss involved, but most importantly because it has proved to be an embarrassment to my brother Nelson and Mr. Justice Goldberg, who happens to be someone I personally admire."

The principal witness Nov. 18 was William J. Ronan, chairman of the Port Authority of New York and New Jersey and a $100,000-a-year Rockefeller adviser. There was no "sinister purpose" in Rockefeller's loans and gifts to him of $625,000, he told the committee. They were "motivated solely by friendship and a lifelong practice of sharing."

Ford urges action. In a letter to Senate Republican Leader Hugh Scott (Pa.) Nov. 11, President Ford urged Congress to "give the highest priority" to completing the confirmation process for Rockefeller, whom he considered "eminently qualified" for the position.

The President met Nov. 12 with House Speaker Carl Albert (D, Okla.), who said they agreed that the nomination was the most important business of the expiring Congress and it was important "to try to get the confirmation . . . out of the way" in the lame-duck session.

In Phoenix, Ariz. Nov. 14, appearing at the convention of the Society of Professional Journalists, Sigma Delta Chi, Ford said Congress should "fish or cut bait" on the Rockefeller nomination. He asserted "there aren't any conditions I can imagine" that would lead him to withdraw it.

Ford said he planned to ask Congress to revise the constitutional procedure on selection of a vice president so there would be "a specific deadline both for the president to nominate and Congress to confirm."

Senate committee approves. The Senate Rules Committee Nov. 22 unanimously approved Rockefeller's confirmation.

The committee, by unanimous vote, also refused to impose any formal requirement on Rockefeller to put his holdings in a blind trust or to refrain from making any further personal gifts of money to public officials.

House committee hearings. The House Judiciary Committee began hearings on the Rockefeller nomination Nov. 21.

Rockefeller promised the House panel, if he were confirmed, to put all securities he owned outright in "blind" trusts and to instruct the trustees of his existing trusts to act as though they were handling blind trusts, or those over which he would neither have control nor knowledge of its operation. In opening the hearing, Chairman Peter W. Rodino (D, N.J.) said "we must attempt to measure the network of Rockefeller family wealth and place it into the perspective of both the American economy and the American political system." Rep. Don Edwards (D, Calif.) indicated the Rockefeller family holdings could constitute a "conflict of interest" if he became vice president. Rockefeller responded with this comparison: in a single week, he said, the three largest U.S. insurance companies invested $156 million, the nation's pension funds invested $200 million and the Arab oil states took in $1 billion. "These figures dwarf to the point of absurdity the funds my family owns," he said. "The Arabs in a week accumulate more money than my family in three generations of work."

Rockefeller reiterated earlier testimony he had given before the Senate committee. He regretted the loss of life in the 1971 Attica (N.Y.) prison riot, but upheld his refusal to negotiate with those holding hostages. He said he regretted his role in the Goldberg book's financing, and he disputed a suggestion that public officials who received gifts from him would "never forget" their benefactor. "You lose more friends than you gain by giving money," Rockefeller said. "It's a strain on a relationship."

During Rockefeller's second day of testimony before the panel Nov. 22, Democratic members expressed concern about the issue of a person of Rockefeller's great wealth being placed in such high political office. "I'm not sure you are fully sensitive to the depth of this feeling" among the public, Rep. Wayne Owens (D, Utah) said. Rockefeller replied that the hearings had been "tremendously instructive to me. I have gotten an insight into the reaction around the country. I'm grateful. I am sympathetic to what you say. I am weighing everything."

Rockefeller promised another member, Rep. Edward Mezvinsky (D, Iowa), to discuss with his family Mezvinsky's request for disclosure to the committee of the financial holdings of the entire family. "There is a suspicion that the family acts as a unit," Mezvinsky said. However, other members said the committee would be content to obtain such information in closed session from family advisers.

Closely questioned Nov. 22 by Rep. Charles Rangel (D, N.Y.) on the Attica prison riot, Rockefeller admitted for the first time making a "serious mistake" in his handling of the situation by not

ordering officials to retake the prison in the early part of the crisis before the pressure intensified further. He continued to defend his decision not to personally negotiate with the prisoners. Just before the move to retake the prison, Rockefeller said, he was asked to go to Attica by aides who felt unsure of what he could accomplish but hoped for a miracle. "Well, I'm no messiah," Rockefeller said. "I didn't see there was anything I could do. So there on national television would be Nelson Rockefeller and he would be the man who failed. That's the way I read it."

Confirmation of Rockefeller was opposed Nov. 25 by spokesmen for the Liberty Lobby, National Right to Life Committee, National Lawyers Guild and American Conservative Union. A variety of reasons was cited, including his wealth, Attica and his veto of a New York bill to repeal the state's pro-abortion law. Arthur O. Eve, a New York assemblyman who was chairman of the observer team at Attica in 1971, accused Rockefeller of "engineering the massacre."

"We've had it from the left and the right, and none of it's worth anything," commented Rep. David W. Dennis (R, Ind.) near the end of the hearing. "There are reasons to be against Rockefeller," he said, "but we're not hearing them."

The only testimonial support for Rockefeller Nov. 25 was presented by a spokesman for the Council of 100, a national organization of 100 black Republicans.

Spokesmen for Americans for Democratic Action (ADA) and the United States Labor Party testified against Rockefeller Nov. 26, and testimony was taken for and against him on the Attica issue. Committee chairman Peter W. Rodino Jr. (D, N.J.) was concerned about the question of whether Rockefeller "should be precluded from this opportunity to serve" because of his wealth alone, aside from other considerations. When ADA spokesman Joseph L. Rauh Jr. responded in the affirmative, Rodino said the conclusion "doesn't sit too well with me."

A letter of caution about Rockefeller on the abortion issue was sent to the committee, and to the Senate Rules Committee, by eight Roman Catholic bishops Nov. 22, including John Cardinal Cody of

Chicago. It urged the panels to assure that the nominee "will not use the office of vice president to promote a personal viewpoint on permissive abortion."

Testimony in support of the Rockefeller nomination was given Nov. 27 by House Republican Leader John J. Rhodes (Ariz.), House Republican Conference Chairman John B. Anderson (Ill.), Howard W. Robison (R, N.Y.) and Shirley Chisholm (D, N.Y., who sent a statement to the committee). Testimony against the nomination was given by Rep. Bella Abzug (D, N.Y.).

University of California Professors G. William Domhoff and Charles L. Schwartz testified Dec. 2 that financial advisers of the Rockefeller family were "actively involved" in directing a dozen major U.S. corporations and sat on the boards of directors of nearly 100 corporations over a number of years, the combined assets of the corporations currently amounting to some $70 billion. The Rockefeller family and the institutions established by the family "have been extremely influential," the professors reported, "in shaping this country's foreign policy, conservation and population policies, many aspects of the arts and sciences and perhaps still more."

J. Richardson Dilworth, head of an investment team for 84 members of the Rockefeller family, testified Dec. 3 that the family owned securities or received lifetime income from trusts owning securities worth a total of $1,033,988,000. In addition, charitable institutions created by the Rockefellers but not benefitting them nor under their control, were valued at an additional $1 billion. "The family members are totally uninterested in controlling anything," Dilworth reported. They were "simply investors."

The nominee's brother, Laurence S. Rockefeller, testified Dec. 4. The principal topic was a $30,000 loan Laurance made, at Nelson's initiative, to then Republican National Chairman William E. Miller. Laurance said the loan was made at 5% interest repayable in three years and that Miller repaid all of the loan with interest but $1,934.50, which was forgiven.

The House committee then concluded nine days of hearings on the nomination Dec. 5 with a third day of testimony from Rockefeller. He was asked by Rep. Bar-

bara Jordan (D, Tex.) what he considered the top national priorities. "Freedom and human dignity and equality of opportunity," Rockefeller replied.

House committee approves. The House Judiciary Committee recommended confirmation of Rockefeller as vice president by a 26–12 vote Dec. 12. The opposition votes were cast by 12 Democrats; nine Democrats joined all 17 committee Republicans on the affirmative side. The opposition included six of the eight Democrats who voted in 1973 against the nomination of Gerald Ford. They were Reps. Robert W. Kastenmeier (Wis.), Don Edwards (Calif.), John Conyers Jr. (Mich.), Jerome R. Waldie (Calif.), Robert F. Drinan (Mass.) and Elizabeth Holtzman (N.Y.).

The other votes against Rockefeller were cast by Reps. Joshua Eilberg (Pa.), John F. Seiberling (Ohio), Paul S. Sarbanes (Md.), George E. Danielson (Calif.), Wayne Owens (Utah) and Edward Mezvinsky (Iowa).

Rockefeller Confirmed

Nelson A. Rockefeller became vice president Dec. 19, 1974 after his appointment was approved by both houses of Congress.

Congress accepts Rockefeller. The Senate approved the nomination of Nelson Rockefeller to be vice president by a 90–7 vote Dec. 10. The votes against confirmation were cast by Republicans Barry Goldwater (Ariz.), Jesse Helms (N.C.) and William Scott (Va.) and Democrats James Abourezk (S.D.), Birch Bayh (Ind.), Howard Metzenbaum (Ohio) and Gaylord Nelson (Wis.).

The House vote Dec. 19 to approve the nomination was 287–128 (153 R & 134 D vs. 99 D & 29 R). The vote in the House was taken after a six-hour debate featuring an unusual opposition coalition of liberal Democrats and conservative Republicans. The Democrats expressed concern over the merging of great economic power—Rockefeller's wealth—with great political power in the nation's second-highest public office. The conservatives considered Rockefeller a liberal and "big-spender."

Rockefeller sworn in. Nelson A. Rockefeller, 66, was sworn in as the 41st vice president of the U.S. Dec. 19. It was the first time in history that both a president and vice president who occupied those offices had not been elected to them. The oath of office was administered by Chief Justice Warren E. Burger in a ceremony in the Senate chamber following the House's vote to confirm Rockefeller to the post. President Ford attended the ceremony, which was televised, the first time an event had been televised in the Senate chamber. In a brief speech, Rockefeller expressed "a great sense of gratitude for the privilege of serving the country I love" and asserted that "there is nothing wrong with America that Americans cannot right." He pledged to cooperate with the President and Congress in coping with "the grave new problems we confront as a nation and as a people."

Rockefeller assured reporters Dec. 20 "I'm not going to pose a problem for anybody." He said he wanted to be "helpful and only do that which is appropriate and useful to the President and to the people of this country." The question of a possible dominant role for him had been raised in the House debate.

Rockefeller's role in the Ford Administration was the topic of a meeting with Ford at the White House Dec. 21. White House Press Secretary Ron Nessen said afterward Rockefeller would serve as vice chairman of the Domestic Council, of which Ford was ex officio chairman. Rockefeller would have a major role in "explaining" the President's domestic and foreign programs "throughout the country," Nessen said.

Rockefeller, at his own request, would have a "special interest in handling the Domestic Council role in coordinating activities with governors and mayors," Nessen said.

Rockefeller also would be vice chairman of the National Security Council and a member of a special commission overseeing foreign policy for implementation and improvement.

Other assignments were to help plan for the nation's bicentennial in 1976 and to help recruit "top people" for the Administration. Rockefeller was to make a special study for Ford of the White House mode of obtaining scientific advice.

Index

219